COMMERCIAL LEASES

LAW AND PRACTICE

Editors

Robert Merkin, LLB, LLM
Professor of Law, University of Cardiff

Robert Lee, LLB
Professor of Law, University of Cardiff

Loyita Worley
Head of Library, Richards Butler, London

LAW AND PRACTICE

COMMERCIAL LEASES

Peter Luxton
LLB LLM PhD Solicitor
Senior Lecturer in Law
Institute for Commercial Law Studies
University of Sheffield

and

Margaret Wilkie
LLB, LLM Solicitor
Visiting Lecturer in Law
University of Surrey

CLT PROFESSIONAL PUBLISHING
A Division of Central Law Training Ltd

© 1998 Peter Luxton and Margaret Wilkie

Published by
CLT Professional Publishing
A division of Central Law Training Ltd
Wrens Court
52/54 Victoria Road
Sutton Coldfield
Birmingham B72 1SX

ISBN 1 85811 165 X

Printed in Great Britain by Ipswich Book Company Ltd.

CONTENTS

PREFACE

IN its treatment of the law relating to commercial leases, this book aims to provide the practitioner with a modern, coherent, and practically-oriented account. The salient features of the subject are considered, and we have sought to highlight problem areas, to suggest solutions, and to give more extensive treatment to those aspects of the subject which are of particular current importance. The book deals with the property law and conveyancing aspects of commercial leases, and also, in recognition of their modern importance to the commercial property practitioner, it touches upon the relevant features of environmental, planning and insolvency law. Although this book is not a book of precedents, we have included a few short specimen clauses where appropriate, which we hope will be found useful.

The impetus for the writing of this book is the significant developments in both law and practice in this area which have occurred over the past decade. This period began with a recession which witnessed a period of unprecedented depression in the commercial property market, and which resulted in the insolvency of many tenants and in increasing numbers of claims against original tenants under the privity of contract doctrine. The unfairness of the operation of that doctrine in relation to leases had been highlighted by a Law Commission Report in 1988, but the effects of the recession focused attention sharply on the hardships which the doctrine caused. Peter Thurrock MP introduced a Private Members Bill in 1994 which sought to implement the core of the Commission's proposals; but, in the face of opposition from institutional landlords, it failed to make progress. The following year, he introduced a second Bill, which this time secured Government support. After various compromises had been made, and following only the briefest period of consultation, it reached the statute book in the shape of the Landlord and Tenant (Covenants) Act 1995. This Act is undoubtedly the most important piece of legislation affecting commercial leases since the Landlord and Tenant Act 1954. Although the new Act primarily affects the running of leasehold covenants in post-1995 leases, some of its provisions are of wider application; and litigation to resolve the uncertainties which the Act throws up is bound to ensue. At the time of writing, however, there have been no reported cases on the Act's central provisions, so that practitioners must at present take what steps they can, without judicial assistance, to avoid potential pitfalls. The book provides a wide-ranging coverage of the statute, and its practical aspects are considered from the point of view of sureties, as well as lessors and lessees.

Another consequence of the recession has been a marked shift in the balance of bargaining power away from landlords, which is reflected in the contents of commercial leases that are now being drawn up: see the report of the British Property Federation and Investment Property Databank, *Changes in Institutional Leases: a Response to Market Circumstances* (1996). Shorter leases seem to be the order of the day, with increased opportunities for tenants to break. With tenants wishing to escape from less favourable pre-recessionary leases, it is not surprising that litigation on break clauses has been rife over the last few years and has even reached the House of Lords (*Mannai Investment Co. Ltd v Eagle Star Life Assurance Co. Ltd* (1997)). The recession has also been the catalyst for much important case law on the impact on commercial leases of disclaimer, particularly the decision of the House of Lords in *Hindcastle Ltd v Barbara Attenborough Associates Ltd* (1996), and of voluntary arrangements. The decline in market rents has led to the consideration of the circumstances in which new leases settled by the court under the Landlord and Tenant Act 1954, Part II, should make provisions for downwards, as well as for upwards, rent review. Rent review is also affected by the Arbitration Act 1996.

The welter of case law in all areas of commercial leases continues, however, regardless of market conditions. In the last few years the House of Lords has given its opinion on the meaning of occupation for the purposes of the Landlord and Tenant Act 1954 (*Graysim Ltd v P&O Property Holdings Ltd* (1995)), and on the specific enforceability of keep-open covenants in commercial leases (*Co-operative Insurance Society Ltd v Argyll Stores (Holdings) Ltd* (1997)); other important decisions are to be found in the Court of Appeal (*e.g. Esselte AB v Pearl Assurance plc* (1996) on the Landlord and Tenant Act 1954) and in the High Court (*e.g. Rainbow Estates Ltd v Tokenhold Ltd* (1998) on the availability of specific performance for breach of a tenant's repairing covenant).

We wish to thank Carolyn Shelbourne and Alan Moran of the University of Sheffield, Mark Stallworthy of the University of East Anglia, and Rosalind Malcolm of the University of Surrey, for their kind assistance. We also give thanks to Jane Belford for her sterling work on the editorial side. Finally, we wish to thank our publishers, CLT Professional Publishing, for their indulgence in permitting us to make amendments at proof stage, which have enabled us to state the law (from sources available to us) as it stands on 19 March 1998, although we have been able to incorporate one or two later developments.

Peter Luxton
Margaret Wilkie

TABLE OF CASES

TABLE OF STATUTES

TABLE OF STATUTORY INSTRUMENTS

Chapter 1

LEASES GENERALLY

INTRODUCTION

This chapter considers the essential requirements for a lease and the formalities for the creation of legal and equitable leases. It distinguishes between a lease and a licence – a very important distinction with significant effects – and considers the different types of leases which may be created.

The nature and essential requirements of a lease

A lease is a contract which creates an estate in land.[1] There has been an increasing tendency in the cases to emphasise the contractual nature of a lease rather than to regard it simply as an estate in land. In *National Carriers Ltd* v *Panalpina (Northern) Ltd*[2] the House of Lords was prepared to accept that circumstances could arise in which the contractual doctrine of frustration could apply to a lease. More recent cases have held that a lease can be terminated, like a contract, by acceptance of a repudiatory breach.[3]

A lease may be legal or equitable. It will be legal if it grants a legal estate; it will be equitable if it is merely a valid contract[4] to grant such an estate of which equity will grant specific performance. A legal lease must generally be granted by deed[5]; but if it is a short lease (*i.e.* one for a term not exceeding three years which takes effect in possession at the best rent reasonably obtainable without taking a fine) it can be created without formalities.[6] A legal periodic tenancy may therefore arise merely by implication from the payment and acceptance of rent.

---

1 *Cricklewood Property & Investment Trust Ltd* v *Leighton's Investment Trust Ltd* [1945] AC 221, 233 (Lord Russell of Killowen); *Rye* v *Rye* [1962] AC 496 (HL).
2 [1981] AC 675.
3 *Hussein* v *Mehlman* [1992] 2 EGLR 87 (county court); *Chartered Trust plc* v *Davies* [1997] 49 EG 135 (CA).
4 *i.e.* one which complies with the formalities prescribed by the LP(MP)A 1989, s 2. The formalities do not apply to a contract to grant a short lease within LPA 1925, s 54(2): LP(MP)A 1989, s 2(5)(a).
5 LPA 1925, s 52(1).
6 LPA 1925, s 54(2).

Whereas a freehold estate is an estate in land of uncertain duration, an estate of less than freehold (a leasehold estate) is of a fixed and definite duration. In order to create a valid lease of any kind, therefore, the maximum duration of the term must be fixed and definite. In *Lace* v *Chantler*[7] a lease for the duration of the war was held to be invalid, and the House of Lords confirmed this principle in *Prudential Assurance Co Ltd* v *London Residuary Body*[8] where a Council had purported to grant a lease of land until such time as it was required for road widening. The document stated:

> "The tenancy shall continue until the said land is required by the Council for the purposes of the widening of Walworth Road ... and the Council shall give two months' notice to the tenant at least prior to the day of determination when the said land is so required...".

The purported lease was held to be bad for uncertainty of the term. The case also confirms that the principle of certainty of term applies equally to periodic tenancies.

A lease will not, however, be invalidated for uncertainty by the possibility of premature defeasance by notice, or the usual proviso for re-entry and forfeiture should the tenant default on payments of rent or be in breach of covenant.[9] Moreover, provided that a maximum duration is stated, it will not matter that the lease is made terminable on some event, such as the death of the tenant, within that maximum time. Although the maximum duration of a lease must be certain, it will still be valid if its commencement is uncertain but dependent upon some event, provided that the event has occurred at the time when it is sought to enforce it.[10]

Although the technical legal name for a leasehold estate is a term of years, it is specifically provided that this shall include also a term for less than a year or for a fraction of a year[11], so that it would be possible to have a lease for a term of one day only. A periodic lease is regarded as being a certain term for its period, which is automatically renewed at the end of that period for a further term unless either party gives notice to terminate it.

There must be an immediate reversion expectant upon the term demised. This may be a freehold reversion or a superior lease, in which case the term demised is a sub-lease. The term and the immediate reversion must be vested in different persons. In *Rye* v *Rye*[12] the two tenants in

7 [1944] KB 368.
8 [1992] 2 AC 386 (HL).
9 LPA 1925, s 205(1)(xxvii).
10 *Brilliant* v *Michaels* [1945] 1 All ER 121.
11 LPA 1925, s 205(1)(xxvii).
12 [1962] AC 496.

common of freehold premises were in partnership together. The premises were used for the partnership business and a sum of money allowed to them both for this. It was held that this arrangement could not have created a lease. Viscount Simonds said "it is meaningless to say that a man accepts from himself something which is already his own."[13]

A tenant has an estate in the land and so has the right to exclude anyone else, including the landlord, from the land during the subsistence of that estate. For this reason, the lease will usually expressly reserve rights of entry to the landlord for certain purposes, such as viewing the state of repair of the property, as he will not automatically have any rights of entry unless they are reserved. Without exclusive possession, there cannot be a lease and any entry granted to someone will merely amount to a licence. So in *Clore v Theatrical Properties Ltd*[14] a right to sell refreshments in a cinema did not create a lease but a licence.

Because of the regime of security of tenure and protected rents which existed for some time in the housing sector, and the possibility of a tenant obtaining a new business tenancy under the Landlord and Tenant Act 1954, Part II, many landlords have been anxious to grant licences of their premises rather than leases, thereby avoiding the effect of the various statutes which operate on leases. The courts have therefore had to interpret various agreements purporting to grant a licence rather than a lease. Such an agreement may try to give the impression that some essential characteristic of a lease, such as exclusive possession, is absent, whereas in reality the true nature and effect of the agreement is to create a lease with exclusive possession. The interpretation of each agreement will, of course, necessarily depend upon its own particular characteristics but it is possible to obtain some guidance from the considerable litigation which this area of the law has generated.

What the agreement calls itself will not be conclusive

In *Addiscombe Garden Estates Ltd v Crabbe*[15] a document which called itself a licence gave the trustees of a tennis club the exclusive use of tennis courts for a fee. Many of the terms, such as the obligation to repair, to allow the licensor to enter to view the state of repair of the property and to re-enter on non-payment of the fee, were more consistent with a lease, however, and the court held that a lease had in fact been created. In *Street v Mountford*[16], the leading House of Lords' authority considering the criteria

---

13 *Ibid,* at 505.
14 [1936] 3 All ER 483.
15 [1958] 1 QB 513.
16 [1985] AC 809.

for distinguishing between a lease and a licence, it was of no avail to the landlord that the agreement called itself a licence.

The courts must look to the reality of an agreement rather than to what it purports to effect

In *Street* v *Mountford*, Lord Templeman warned the courts that they must look out for "sham" agreements which did not accurately reflect the true arrangement between the parties. He said that wherever premises are granted for a term at a rent, there is a presumption that a lease has been created. He pointed out that what the parties term the arrangement is not therefore decisive:

> "The manufacture of a five-pronged implement for manual digging results in a fork even if the manufacturer ... insists that he intended to make and has made a spade".

The effect of the agreement in *Street* v *Mountford* was to give the occupier exclusive possession of a room for a term in return for weekly payments, which therefore gave her a lease.

An example of the type of "sham" agreement to which Lord Templeman was referring is to be found in *Antoniades* v *Villiers*[17], where the landlord granted occupation of a small one-bedroom flat to two people, reserving the right to himself to put someone else into the room so as to avoid their claim to exclusive possession. Clearly this was unrealistic and merely a device to attempt to negate their exclusive possession.

The presumption of a tenancy where premises are granted for a term at a rent may be rebutted if the arrangement is referable to some other agreement, or was never intended to create legal relations between the parties.

This too was contemplated in Lord Templeman's speech, and examples which he gave of occupancy attributable to an agreement other than a tenancy are service occupancies, occupancy by reason of an office-holding, or a purchaser going into occupation under a contract for sale.

A hospital surgeon or caretaker occupying premises incidentally to their work will be service occupants with a licence to occupy and not a tenancy. Although a service occupancy will generally be only a licence, it may also be possible to have a service tenancy where it is not essential for the employee to occupy the premises in order to carry out his work, and occupation of the premises is part of the consideration for his services. Obviously this is a matter of fact to be decided in each individual case. Occupation which is not absolutely essential to carry out the work but

17 [1990] 1 AC 417 (HL).

which enables the employee's duties to be more easily performed may still be a service occupancy and not a service tenancy.[18] In *Vandersteen* v *Agius*[19], however, the goodwill of an osteopathic practice was sold and the purchaser allowed to occupy two rooms in the premises where the practice was previously carried on. The purchaser was to make monthly payments for the goodwill over eight years. It was held that the purchaser's occupation was a tenancy as the purchase of the goodwill did not necessarily require possession of two rooms.

The same requirement for certainty is necessary for a service tenancy as for any other form of lease, and so if the services required of the occupant are uncertain and not capable of being quantified in money, the arrangement can only be a service occupancy and not a service tenancy.[20]

For circumstances negating the intention to create legal relations, Lord Templeman referred to Denning LJ's judgment in *Facchini* v *Bryson*[21] as "circumstances such as family arrangement, an act of friendship or generosity, or such like...". In the business context, absence of any rent payable may indicate a licence rather than a lease, although the Court of Appeal recognised in *Ashburn Anstalt* v *WJ Arnold & Co*[22] that a rent-free occupation could nevertheless still be a lease, and this is specifically stated in the definition of a lease in the Law of Property Act 1925.[23]

Where the tenant does not have exclusive possession of the premises, the arrangement will be a licence and not a lease

This is the ground upon which many attempts to claim a lease have floundered. A denial of exclusive possession is also a device which many landlords have used to avoid the creation of a lease.

A sufficient degree of control by the landlord (provided that it is not a sham as in *Antoniades* v *Villiers*) or occupation shared with someone else may negative exclusive possession. For example, in *Shell-Mex & BP Ltd* v *Manchester Garages Ltd*[24] a petrol company gave a licence of a filling station to a garage company which undertook to use its best endeavours to promote the sale of the petrol company's products. The employees of the petrol company frequently visited the filling station as they pleased and rights of access to the licensor were assumed and not expressly reserved in

---

18 *Norris* v *Checksfield* [1992] 1 EGLR 159, where the defendant, who was employed as a mechanic, occupied a bungalow in order to be more readily available for any urgent coach driving required for the plaintiff's business.

19 [1992] NPC 108.

20 *Barnes* v *Barratt* [1970] 2 QB 657.

21 [1952] 1 TLR 1386.

22 [1989] Ch 1 (CA).

23 LPA 1925, s 205(1)(xxvii).

24 [1971] 1 WLR 612.

the licence. It was held that the agreement was in substance a licence. In *Esso Petroleum Co Ltd* v *Fumegrange Ltd*[25] a filling station, shop and car wash were occupied by managers on behalf of Esso. The management was very much controlled by Esso however according to their manual of operating standards, and it was held that this degree of control negatived the exclusive possession necessary for a lease. In *Dresden Estates Ltd* v *Collinson*[26] a builder was granted the use of storage space. Some of the terms of the agreement, such as the right of the owners to enter and carry out repairs, were essentially similar to the terms of a lease, but the owner reserved the right to require the builder to transfer his belongings to other storage space of the owner's, and it was held that this was inconsistent with the grant of exclusive possession which is necessary for a lease.

Although the landlord's retention of a key to the premises will prima facie negative exclusive possession and so create a licence rather than a lease, the court may still find that retention of keys for another purpose, not related to shared possession, will not negative the existence of a tenancy.[27]

In *Venus Investments Ltd* v *Stocktop Ltd*[28], the judge stated that, whilst the principle of *Street* v *Mountford* applied equally to commercial property, no inference of exclusive possession could be made as regards commercial premises, although such an inference might more easily have been drawn had the premises been residential. On the facts, it was held that, in the absence of a reference to possession or to exclusive possession, or of a reservation to the landlord to enter or inspect, or of a right of re-entry, a licence had been created, as that was the intention of the parties.

A similar approach was adopted by the Court of Appeal in *Hunts Refuse Disposals Ltd* v *Norfolk Environmental Waste Services Ltd*,[29] which concerned the grant of an "exclusive licence" to use a site for the depositing of waste for 21 years. Hutchison LJ there expressed the view that, whilst the general principles of law as to whether an agreement constitutes a licence or a tenancy were the same, the terms of the agreement were not to be considered in a vacuum,

> "but rather with a proper regard to the context in which the issue arises. Thus while one would ordinarily expect that someone in occupation of a

---

25 [1994] 2 EGLR 90 (CA).
26 [1987] 1 EGLR 45 (CA).
27 *Family Housing Association* v *Jones* [1990] 1 All ER 385, where retention of the key was *inter alia* to inspect repairs and not to introduce another occupier.
28 [1996] EGCS 173, Tyrell QC, sitting as a deputy judge of the Queen's Bench Division; affirmed generally by the Court of Appeal: 14 May 1997 (unreported, Lexis Transcript).
29 [1997] 1 EGLR 16 (CA).

small house for a fixed term at a rent had exclusive possession, one would ... have no such preconceptions about a person given the right to tip rubbish on the excavated parts of a large plot of land on other parts of which it seems quarrying was continuing."

On the construction of the agreement, it was evident that the licensee's right over the site was a limited one, and that the grantor retained a right to enter the site. The proper inference was therefore that the grantee had merely a licence. The presence of other clauses in the agreement (such as a fully qualified covenant against assignment) were equivocal, in that they were consistent with either a licence or a tenancy, and they were therefore insufficient on their own to displace the inference of a licence.

Where the occupier shares possession with other occupiers, there will not be a joint tenancy under which they all collectively have exclusive possession unless the four unities for a joint tenancy are present. Thus in *AG Securities* v *Vaughan*[30] four different occupiers of a house were all given separate licence agreements under which they paid different fees for occupation which started on different dates. The House of Lords held that the four unities necessary to make them joint tenants, collectively enjoying exclusive possession, were not present and they were therefore only licensees.

The nature and effect of a licence

It will be evident from the preceding discussion of the essential characteristics of a lease that an arrangement which falls short of a lease may nevertheless be a licence to use or occupy premises and that licences may arise in a commercial context. It may therefore be appropriate to mention more specifically the characteristics of a licence, some of which have been referred to above.

A contractual licence is a contract allowing someone to occupy land or premises and it does not confer on the licensee any estate in the land. It is not therefore possible for the licensee to renew the arrangement under the Landlord and Tenant Act 1954, Part II, which applies only to business leases. Moreover, although the contractual terms of the licence are binding and enforceable between the parties to it, they will not usually be binding on third parties unless there is an estoppel[31] or a constructive trust[32] giving

---

30 [1990] 1 AC 417 (HL).

31 A case where a licence supported by estoppel was held to be binding on a third party volunteer is *Inwards* v *Baker* [1965] 2 QB 29. However, the doctrine of estoppel has developed considerably since 1965, and the more usual result of finding an estoppel nowadays is for the court to determine what actual interest in the land would satisfy the estoppel, which will generally be something more than just a licence.

32 A case where a constructive trust was held to protect a licensee against a third party (in that case a trustee in bankruptcy) is *Re Sharpe* [1980] 1 WLR 219.

rise to an equity which the courts will enforce. These are equitable concepts which operate on a person's conscience, and are therefore less likely to arise in the context of a business agreement, although it is by no means unknown.[33] Because a contractual licence does not create an interest in land[34], it cannot be an overriding interest under section 70(1)(g), Land Registration Act 1925. It is possible that a licence supported by an estoppel may gain protection under that paragraph, but the point remains to be decided.[35]

A licensee may or may not have exclusive occupation of the premises, and may or may not give consideration for the occupation. A full market consideration may be a factor, however, in favour of finding that the true nature of the agreement is a lease rather than a licence.

A licence may be terminated in the same way as any other contract. The parties may agree between themselves as to how and when it will be terminated, or it may be discharged by breach of a fundamental term according to the normal rules of contract. In *Dudley Port Warehousing Co Ltd v Gardner Transport & Distribution Ltd*[36] the plaintiffs had licensed part of some warehouse space to the defendants, who had undertaken to carry out certain work on the property but had failed to do so. It was held that, although this was a fundamental breach of a condition of the agreement, the defendants had elected to affirm the agreement by remaining in possession; the breach of condition was therefore to be treated as a breach of warranty which did not discharge the contract, and the licence fee was still payable.

DIFFERENT TYPES OF TENANCIES

Fixed-term tenancies

Most business leases will be for a fixed term, often for 20 or 25 years, and the term expires automatically at the end of the period. The tenant will of course have a right to agree a new lease with the landlord and to apply to the court if no agreement is reached, unless the parties have agreed that the

---

33 *DHN Food Distributors Ltd v Tower Hamlets LBC* [1976] 1 WLR 852 is a case where a contractual licence between two companies was held to give rise (*inter alia*) to a constructive trust which gave the licensee a right to compensation on compulsory purchase of the premises.
34 *Ashburn Anstalt v Arnold* [1989] Ch 1.
35 See Peter Gibson LJ in *Habermann v Koehler* (1997) 73 P & CR 515, 522.
36 [1995] EGCS 5.

Landlord and Tenant Act 1954, Part II, shall not apply and their agreement to opt out of the provisions of the Act has been authorised by the court.[37]

From the landlord's point of view, the long term will provide a continuing investment income, but there should be provisions for reviewing the rent from time to time to keep up with inflation. Rent-review clauses usually provide for a recalculation of the rent every five years.[38]

The tenant, who may be uncertain as to how his business venture will go, may want some flexibility in a long fixed-term lease. It may be possible to achieve this by a break clause which allows either party to serve notice on the other determining the lease after certain periods, such as seven years and 14 years in a 21-year lease. The date of the commencement of the fixed-term tenancy may vary from the date of execution of the lease. Although the legal estate cannot come into existence before the execution of the lease, the lease may backdate the term so that it starts at an earlier date than the date of the lease. The earlier date will apply for the calculation of the term, break clauses and rent reviews. The tenant's solicitor should ensure that the tenant is not made liable for rent and service charges for any period before the execution of the lease during which he was not in occupation of the premises.

If the tenant is taking a long term lease, he should also ensure that it will be easily assignable and that any user restrictions are not so strict as to make this difficult. He may of course also wish to reserve the right to sub-let, although should he exercise this, he should ensure that he retains a reversion of at least 14 months so that he remains a "competent landlord" for the purposes of the 1954 Act. In practice, assignments and sub-leases are usually made subject to the landlord's consent, in which case statute provides that the consent must not be withheld unreasonably.[39]

If the landlord wishes to retain a strict control over who occupies the premises, it may be more appropriate to provide that, before assignment, the tenant will first offer to surrender the term to the landlord. This will cause problems, however, if the tenancy is one within the Landlord and Tenant Act 1954, Part II.[40]

In leases created before 1 January 1996, the tenant's continuing liability under privity of contract for the default of an assignee of the lease was an additional factor which made a shorter lease more attractive to a tenant. The new regime introduced by the Landlord and Tenant (Covenants) Act 1995, however, ameliorates the tenant's position in this respect.[41]

---

37 *i.e.* under LTA 1954, s 38(4).
38 See Chap 9.
39 LTA 1927, s 19(1).
40 See Chap 12.
41 See Chap 5.

Option to renew

If the tenant takes a shorter term, he may be given the option to extend it by the landlord's granting him an option to renew. An option to renew the lease is a covenant which touches and concerns the land (or a landlord and tenant covenant in leases granted after 1995) and the benefit of it therefore passes to assignees of the term. The burden also passes to an assignee of the reversion but it must be registered as a Land Charge, Class C(iv) in unregistered title, or as a minor interest in registered title (unless binding as an overriding interest, which it is likely to be, as the tenant will probably be in actual occupation.[42])

The option should be drafted as clearly as possible as regards terms, such as provisions for agreeing a rent, and care should be taken to avoid the possibility of inadvertently creating a perpetually renewable lease.[43] The tenant will be able to exercise the option only if he has complied strictly with the terms of the lease. Thus in *West Country Cleaners v Saly*[44], the tenant was unable to exercise an option to renew because, although the premises were well kept, he had not redecorated every three years as provided for in the lease. Also, in *Bairstow Eves (Securities) v Ripley*[45] a tenant who had not repainted the premises in the last year of the term as covenanted was unable to exercise an option to renew, even though the premises were in good decorative repair and the landlord could only have recovered nominal damages.

Periodic tenancies

A periodic tenancy is one for a period, such as a year, a quarter, a month or a week, which automatically continues from one period to the next unless it is terminated by either party giving notice to quit to the other.[46] The period of a periodic tenancy is that by which the rent is expressed to be reserved, not that by which it is paid.[47] Therefore a tenancy which reserves a quarterly rent payable monthly in advance will be a quarterly, not a monthly, tenancy.

As well as arising by express agreement between the parties, a periodic tenancy may arise also by implication where a tenant occupies premises and pays a rent. In these circumstances, the type of periodic tenancy will be according to the periods of rent payments.

---

42 LRA 1925, s 70(1)(g).
43 See the discussion of perpetually renewable leases later in this chapter.
44 [1966] 1 WLR 1485.
45 [1992] 2 EGLR 47 (CA).
46 See Chaps 12 and 15.
47 *Adler v Blackman* [1953] 1 QB 146.

The period of a periodic tenancy will always be for a period not exceeding three years (although of course a periodic tenancy may continue for long beyond this time), so that such tenancies will usually be legal tenancies within the Law of Property Act 1925, section 54(2). The Landlord and Tenant Act 1954, Part II, applies to periodic tenancies, and the tenant may therefore obtain a new lease.

Tenancies at will

A tenancy at will arises where a tenant takes possession of land with the landlord's consent on the understanding that either of them may terminate the lease when he so wishes. Such a tenancy may be created expressly or impliedly. It will usually arise by implication where a tenant holds over at the end of a lease with the landlord's consent, or where a purchaser occupies premises before completion. It is not always easy to distinguish this type of tenancy from a licence, although it may be important to do so as time may run under the Limitation Act 1980 to extinguish a landlord's title in the case of a tenancy at will, whereas it will not do so if the occupier is merely a licensee.[48]

A tenancy at will may also arise by express agreement between the parties, and in these circumstances it may be difficult to distinguish it from a periodic tenancy. Thus in *Manfield & Sons Ltd v Botchin*[49] the owner of a shop had made unsuccessful applications to develop the premises. He agreed to allow someone to occupy them until such time as he was able to develop them, and the occupier did so, paying a yearly rent. It was held that the agreement had created a tenancy at will and not an implied yearly tenancy.

It was held in *Wheeler v Mercer*[50] that a tenancy at will which arose by operation of law was not a "tenancy agreement" upon which the Landlord and Tenant Act 1954 could operate. In *Hagee (London) Ltd v AB Erikson & Larson*[51] this was extended to an express tenancy at will which was held not to be a "tenancy agreement" for the purposes of the Act, and a tenant at will does not therefore have any right to a new tenancy under the Act. In *Hagee*, however, Lord Denning MR warned the courts to look carefully at any such agreement for a tenancy at will, which might in reality be an implied periodic tenancy, and so within the Act, disguised as a tenancy at will.

48 *Heslop v Burns* [1974] 1 WLR 1241.
49 [1970] 2 QB 612.
50 [1957] AC 416.
51 [1976] 1 QB 207.

Tenancies at sufferance

A tenancy at sufferance arises only by operation of law[52] where a tenant wrongfully holds over after the determination of a lawful term, *i.e.* without either any statutory right to do so or the landlord's consent.[53] The tenancy arises therefore from the failure of the landlord to take steps to regain possession. A tenant of business premises protected by Part II of the Landlord and Tenant Act 1954, for example, loses the right to a statutory continuation tenancy at the end of the term, if he does not serve a counter-notice to a landlord's notice to terminate under section 25. If such a tenant remains in possession after the termination date specified in the landlord's notice, his possession is as a tenant at sufferance. A tenant at sufferance is liable for voluntary, but not for permissive, waste[54]; he also has no right to emblements.[55]

A tenant at sufferance is not a trespasser, and so is not liable in damages for trespass; but the landlord may eject him without notice or sue for possession at any time; and the landlord may claim mesne profits for the occupation to that date. A re-entry by the landlord or his bringing of an action for possession causes the tenancy at sufferance to cease; and the claim for occupation for the period thereafter is in trespass. If the landlord accepts rent from a tenant at sufferance, the tenancy is thereby converted into a periodic tenancy. Although not a trespasser, a tenant at sufferance is in possession, and if he remains in possession for twelve years without paying rent, the title of the landlord is statutorily barred.[56]

A tenant who wrongfully holds over after the expiration of a notice to quit given by the landlord is liable to pay the landlord a statutory penalty in respect of the period of holding over after the notice to quit expires. If the tenancy is for a fixed term of years or a yearly periodic tenancy and the landlord serves notice to quit in writing, a tenant who wilfully[57] holds over is liable to pay double the yearly value of the land.[58] If the tenancy is of any other type determinable by notice and the landlord serves notice to quit either orally or in writing, the tenancy is extended by statute at double rent.[59]

---

52 *Meye v Electric Transmission Ltd* [1942] Ch 290.
53 *Remon v City of London Real Property Co* [1921] 1 KB 49, 58.
54 *Burchell v Hornsby* (1808) 1 Camp 360.
55 *i.e.* he has no right to reap growing crops after the tenancy has determined.
56 *Re Jolly* [1900] 2 Ch 616.
57 A tenant does not hold over wilfully unless he is aware that he has no right to possession: *French v Elliott* [1960] 1 WLR 40.
58 Landlord and Tenant Act 1730, s 1.
59 Distress for Rent Act 1737, s 18.

Tenancies by estoppel

If a lessor purports to grant a lease to a tenant but has no legal estate to support it, both parties (as well as their successors in title[60]) are estopped at common law from denying the existence of the lease.[61] A tenancy by estoppel does not require an express and unambiguous representation of title by the grantor, but is the product of the wider principle that precludes a grantor from disputing the validity or effect of his own grant.[62] A tenancy by estoppel usually arises through a mistake[63]; but it can arise even if both parties know that the landlord has no title[64], provided that they proceed on the assumption that he has.[65] A tenancy by estoppel can arise if the soi-disant lessor has merely an equitable interest in the land[66], but not if he has a legal estate in the land, albeit one which is less in extent than that purported to be granted.[67] The tenant may dispose of the tenancy by estoppel through assignment or in any other way.[68] The lessor is entitled to distrain the goods of the tenant[69], but not those of third parties (who are not bound by the estoppel).[70]

If, having granted a tenancy by estoppel, the lessor later acquires a legal estate in the land leased[71], the effect is to "feed the estoppel"[72], so that the tenant thereafter has a tenancy supported by the legal estate, *i.e.* a tenancy in interest, instead of a tenancy by estoppel. If a person who has

---

60 Except a bona fide purchaser for value from the grantor without notice of the earlier transaction: *Right d Jeffreys v Bucknell* (1831) 2 B & Ad 278, 283; *General Finance Mortgage and Discount Co v Liberator Permanent Benefit Building Society* (1878) 10 ChD 15.
61 *Cuthbertson v Irving* (1859) 4 H & N 742 (Martin B), affirmed (1860) 6 H & N 135 (see judgments of Willes and Blackburn LJJ).
62 *First National Provincial Bank plc v Thompson* [1996] Ch 231 (CA), (Millett LJ); *Goodtitle d Edwards v Bailey* (1777) 2 Cowp 597, 600–601 (Lord Mansfield CJ).
63 As in *Bell v General Accident Fire and Life Assurance Corporation plc* [1997] 29 April (unreported, Lexis Transcript) (CA), where one company in a group of associated companies purported to grant a lease of land the title to which was vested in another member of the group. A fresh appeal was later heard before a differently constituted Court of Appeal: [1998] 17 EG 144.
64 *Morton v Woods* (1869) LR 4 QB 293.
65 *Bruton v London and Quadrant Housing Trust* [1997] 4 All ER 970 (CA) (Millett LJ).
66 *Universal Permanent Building Society v Cooke* [1952] 1 Ch 102 (CA). See Pritchard, "Tenancy by estoppel" [1964] 80 LQR 370, 380.
67 In this case, the tenant will merely acquire whatever legal estate the lessor does have: *Hill v Saunders* (1825) 4 B & C 529.
68 *Gouldsworth v Knights* (1843) 11 M & W 337.
69 *Ibid.*
70 *Tadman v Henman* [1893] 2 QB 168.
71 Even if this is through the barring of the title of the paper owner by twelve years' adverse possession by the tenant by estoppel: Limitation Act 1980, s 15 and Sched 1: *Bell v General Accident Fire and Life Assurance Corporation plc* [1997] 29 April (unreported, Lexis Transcript) (CA) (Waite LJ).
72 *Rajapakse v Fernando* [1920] AC 892, 897 (Lord Moulton).

contracted to purchase a legal estate purports to grant a lease of it and later acquires the legal estate by conveyance subject to a mortgage, the conveyance and the mortgage are treated as simultaneous transactions indissolubly bound together, so that, whilst the estoppel is fed, the tenant takes subject to the prior rights of the mortgagee.[73]

Perpetually renewable leases

A perpetually renewable lease arises where a tenant is granted a lease for a fixed term with an option to renew the lease on exactly the same terms, including the option to renew. Such a lease effectively gives the tenant the right to renew the lease indefinitely.

These leases are converted by statute into leases for 2,000 years, terminable by the tenant only on giving ten days written notice to expire on a date when the lease would have expired had it not been converted to a term of 2,000 years.[74]

There is always a possibility that a perpetually renewable lease may have been created inadvertently, and the present attitude of the courts is therefore to construe an agreement if possible against its creation. Thus in *Marjorie Burnett Ltd* v *Barclay*[75] the relevant terms of the lease were:

> "If the tenant shall be desirous of taking a new lease of the demised premises after the expiration of the term hereby granted ... then the landlord will at or before the expiration of the term hereby granted ... grant to the tenant a new lease of the premises hereby demised for a further term of seven years ... at a rent to be agreed between the parties ... And such lease shall also contain a like covenant for renewal for a further term of seven years on the expiration of the term thereby granted".

It was held that the provision for the rent to be agreed between the parties, which was effectively a rent review, was inconsistent with a lease for 2,000 years and that the parties had failed to create a perpetually renewable lease.

The tenant of a perpetually renewable lease has always enjoyed one advantage which other tenants do not have. On assignment of the term, he is no longer liable to the landlord under privity of contract. For leases created after 1995, a tenant's liability is in any case limited by the Landlord and Tenant (Covenants) Act 1995.

---

73 *Abbey National Building Society* v *Cann* [1991] AC 56 (HL), rejecting the *scintilla temporis* doctrine and thereby effectively overruling *Church of England Building Society* v *Piskor* [1954] Ch 553. In that earlier case, the Court of Appeal had held that the estoppel had been fed in the *scintilla temporis* between the conveyance to the purchaser and his grant of the mortgage, with the result that the tenant took priority over the mortgagee.

74 LPA 1922, Sched 15, paras 5, 10(1)(i).

75 [1981] 1 EGLR 41 (Ch).

Reversionary leases

A lease, or a contract for a lease, will be void if the term which it purports to create is not to take effect in possession until more than 21 years later.[76] This does not affect an option to renew a lease contained in a lease for more than 21 years, however, as the option takes effect within 21 years of the termination of the lease which is the agreement containing it.[77]

Concurrent leases

Where a landlord who has granted a lease grants another longer lease of the same premises, he has effectively disposed of part of his reversion, and the lessee of the longer term becomes entitled to possession at the termination of the shorter term. From the moment that the lease is granted to him, he becomes the landlord of the tenant with the shorter term. Such a lease is sometimes referred to as a "reversionary" lease, being, in effect, a lease of part of the landlord's reversion, although it is in reality a concurrent lease and is not related to the reversionary lease described above.

Concurrent leases may be used as a means of creating second and subsequent mortgages on property, each subsequent mortgagee taking a demise of a term one day longer than the preceding mortgagee. However, legal charges have increasingly been used for this type of mortgage, being a simpler form of mortgage which can be protected by registration. Concurrent leases have been adopted by the Landlord and Tenant (Covenants) Act 1995 however as a means of giving a tenant or guarantor who has paid rent due from a defaulting assignee some recompense and means of control.[78]

FORMALITIES FOR CREATING A LEASE – LEGAL AND EQUITABLE LEASES

A lease is one of the two estates in land capable of subsisting at law after 1925[79]; but it will not subsist as a legal estate unless the formalities required for a legal estate have been complied with. It may nevertheless subsist in equity in certain circumstances. There are important differences between legal and equitable leases.

---

76 LPA 1925, s 149(3).
77 *Re Strand and Savoy Properties Ltd* [1960] Ch 582.
78 See Chaps 4 and 5.
79 LPA 1925, s 1(1).

Legal lease

In order to create or convey a legal estate in land, a deed must be used.[80] A deed must therefore generally be used to create a legal lease. There is a statutory exception, however, for a lease not exceeding three years, which provides that such a lease may be legal even if created by parol, provided that it takes effect in possession and is at the best rent obtainable (a market rent) without a fine.[81] Because all periodic tenancies are regarded as leases for the period specified (whether a week, a month, a quarter or a year), they fall within this statutory exception, and will be legal leases even though created orally. Similarly, all those periodic tenancies which arise impliedly from occupation and payment of rent will also be legal leases within the statutory exception.

It should be noted that statute requires a deed not only to create a legal estate but also to convey one.[82] The assignment of a lease must also therefore be made by deed, even if the lease is a legal lease not exceeding three years within the statutory exception.[83]

Equitable lease

Formalities

Even if the formalities necessary to create a legal lease have not been complied with, it is possible that there is a valid and enforceable contract to create a lease. In certain circumstances, equity will grant specific performance of a contract to create a lease, so that it may be regarded as an equitable lease – one enforceable in equity.

If a contract for a lease was made after 26 September 1989, it must comply with the formalities prescribed by the Law of Property (Miscellaneous Provisions) Act 1989, section 2. The contract must be in writing and signed by both parties, or alternatively it may be in two parts, one part signed by each party, and the parts exchanged. There is a growing body of litigation on this section as to what amounts to a signature for the purposes of the section, and whether collateral agreements between the parties are enforceable. This has been dealt with in Chapter 2, where contracts are considered as part of the conveyancing process.

A contract for a lease created before 27 September 1989 was governed

---

80 *Ibid.*, s 52(1).
81 *Ibid.*, s 54(2).
82 *Ibid.*, s 52(1).
83 *Crago v Julian* [1992] 1 All ER 744.

by the Law of Property Act 1925, section 40, which was superseded by the 1989 Act. Such a contract was enforceable if merely evidenced in writing, or if it was purely oral but there was a sufficient act of part performance. Some of these equitable leases may still survive. It is by no means certain that the equitable doctrine of part performance was abolished by the 1989 Act, which repealed section 40, as the doctrine did of course exist quite independently of the statute and section 40(2) merely provided that it should not be abrogated by the operation of section 40(1).[84]

In any event, the courts may be prepared to grant specific performance of a contract for a lease which does not comply with the 1989 Act if the plaintiff seeking to enforce it is able to invoke the equitable doctrine of proprietary estoppel. In *JT Developments v Quinn*[85] the landlords of a shop entered into negotiations with the tenants for a new lease on different terms. On the strength of the negotiations, the tenants spent money on the property. The landlords then sold the reversion to a third party. The negotiations preceded the 1989 Act and it was argued by the tenants that there was an oral agreement of which they could claim specific performance by reason of part performance. This argument was rejected by the Court of Appeal as no agreement had ever been concluded. It was held, however, that an estoppel had arisen, as the tenants had effectively been assured that a new lease would be granted, and had acted to their detriment on this assurance. Moreover, the lease which arose from the estoppel was binding on the purchasers of the reversion.

Enforceability and effect

The equitable remedy of specific performance will be available to enforce a contract for a lease only according to the normal rules for equitable intervention. If the plaintiff is at fault and is in breach of a term of the agreement, then equity will not assist him. Thus in *Coatsworth v Johnson*[86], the plaintiff was unable to obtain specific performance of a contract for a lease as he was in breach of one of the covenants which it contained. In *Warmington v Miller*,[87] the court refused to grant specific performance of a contract for a sub-lease, where there was a covenant against sub-letting in the head-lease, as to do so would have necessarily involved the tenant in a breach of covenant with a third party. Because equity will not act in vain, specific performance cannot be obtained of an agreement for a lease whose term has already expired by the date of the hearing.[88] Specific performance may, however, be granted of an agreement even for a very short lease, so

---

84 For a judicial expression of doubt as to this, see *Singh v Beggs* (1995) 71 P & CR 120 (CA).
85 (1991) 62 P & CR 33.

long as the action can be heard and the decree obtained before the term expires.[89] The court will not order specific performance against a purchaser if the vendor's title is bad, or is likely to be subject to litigation. The purchaser cannot be compelled to take the vendor's interest if it is a lesser interest or different in substance from what the vendor contracted to grant. A purchaser who contracted for the grant of a lease out of the freehold, for instance, cannot be compelled to accept a sub-lease.[90] The purchaser may, however, elect to take the vendor's lesser interest, with compensation for the difference.[91]

As the interest created by the enforceable contract is an equitable lease only, it will bind a purchaser of the reversion only if it is registered as a Land Charge, Class C(iv) (an estate contract) if the title is unregistered, or as a minor interest if the title is registered, although in the latter case it may become an overriding interest[92] if the equitable tenant is in occupation.

On assignment of a pre-1996 equitable lease, there is no privity of estate and although the benefit of covenants may be assigned, the burden of covenants touching and concerning the land will not pass to an assignee.[93] In a post-1995 agreement for a lease, the benefit and burden of covenants other than those expressed to be personal will pass.[94]

Finally, the Law of Property Act 1925, section 62, which operates to transfer rights appurtenant to the land in certain circumstances, will not apply to an equitable lease as it is not a "conveyance" of the legal estate. The section does, however, apply to the creation of a legal lease within section 54(2) of the same Act if it is in writing[95], and possibly even if it is purely oral.[96]

Because a legal periodic tenancy arises by implication where someone occupies premises and pays rent, if a person with an equitable lease occupies the premises and pays rent, he will have a legal periodic tenancy as well as an equitable lease; there will be two concurrent leases in the land. The legal periodic tenancy will be binding as a right in rem against a

---

86 (1886) 54 LT 520.

87 [1973] QB 877.

88 *Turner v Clowes* (1869) 20 LT 214.

89 Cf *Verrall v Great Yarmouth BC* [1981] QB 202 (Roskill J); *Winter Garden Theatre (London) Ltd v Millenium Productions Ltd* [1948] AC 173. Contrast *Lavery v Pursell* (1888) 39 ChD 508, where specific performance of a lease for one year was refused because (*inter alia*) the action could not be heard within that time.

90 *Madeley v Booth* (1845) 2 De G & Sm 718.

91 *Mortlock v Buller* (1804) 10 Ves Jun 292.

92 *i.e.* under LRA 1925, s 70(1)(g).

93 *Purchase v Lichfield Brewery Co* [1915] 1 KB 184.

94 LT(C)A 1995, ss. 3, 28(1).

95 *Wright v Macadam* [1949] 2 KB 744.

96 See Chap 3.

purchaser of the reversion if the title is unregistered, and as an overriding interest[97] if the title is registered. The question whether the equitable lease binds a purchaser of the reversion has already been discussed.

97 LRA 1925, s 70(1)(k).

Chapter 2

CONVEYANCING, ENVIRONMENTAL AND PLANNING CONSIDERATIONS

INTRODUCTION

It is assumed that the reader has a basic knowledge of the format of a conveyancing transaction and how this operates in relation to leasehold property. As far as conveyancing is concerned, therefore, this chapter does no more than highlight some of the main considerations which should additionally be borne in mind when dealing with commercial leasehold property.

A person taking leasehold premises will be either a tenant under a new lease, an assignee of an existing lease, or an under-lessee of part of a term of an existing lease. Each of these possibilities will be considered in turn.

A NEW LEASE

Preliminary considerations

Where the tenant is taking a new lease, there should be some scope for negotiation as to the terms, particularly in the current economic climate where the tenant is in a much stronger bargaining position than for many years. The effect of the various clauses to be found in leases is dealt with in the relevant chapters, and the inter-relation of the clauses discussed. For instance, clauses as to user, alterations and alienation will all be relevant factors in determining how easily disposable the lease is and will have an effect on rent review.

The tenant should consider carefully the extent of the demised premises and their physical state in relation to any repairing covenants. He should consider having a survey to discover any latent defects for which his repairing covenant may make him liable, and to ensure that the premises comply with any statutory requirements as to safety bearing in mind his proposed use of the premises. The lease may also include a covenant to comply with statutory requirements, in which case the survey should discover what work, if any, needs to be done to comply with them.

He should also consider if any easements necessary for his enjoyment and use of the premises will be properly granted,[1] and what easements or rights will be reserved over the demised premises to the landlord or other tenants.[2] If the demised premises are a unit in a larger block, service charges are important, and the tenant should enquire what services will be included, who will be responsible for administering them and how the charges are to be apportioned.

The tenant will also want to know how insurance is to be effected and what risks this will cover. If there is a block policy, he will want a copy of it and confirmation that notice of his interest will be given to the insurers and noted on the policy.

All these matters should be dealt with in the preliminary enquiries, and many of them are covered in the standard form of preliminary enquiries applicable to leasehold property.

Planning matters may also be raised in the preliminary enquiries as well as on the local search. These will be referred to in more detail later in this chapter. It should be noticed however that an authorised use under the lease does not imply that this is a lawful use for planning purposes.[3]

Contract

The usual commercial lease, which will be at a full market rent and no premium, will mostly be entered into without any prior contract. This is because the lease itself is the important document, which will determine in detail the legal relations between the parties. Any contract will merely provide that a lease is to be in the terms of the draft lease attached, and indeed Standard Condition 8.2.3. provides for this. There will usually be three copies of the draft lease – one to be kept by each of the parties and the third to be the "travelling draft lease" to which they may both make suggested amendments.

Nevertheless, a contract will be necessary if the grant of the lease is to be delayed. This could arise where it is to be conditional upon planning permission being obtained, or if it is to be subject to the court's authorisation of an agreement to exclude the Landlord and Tenant Act 1954, Part II. Any agreement must comply with the Law of Property

1 See Chap 3.
2 See Chap 3.
3 *Hill v Harris* [1965] 2 QB 601.

(Miscellaneous Provisions) Act 1989, section 2, unless it is an agreement for a short-term or periodic tenancy within the Law of Property Act 1925, section 54(2)[4], in which case it is exempted.[5]

The Law of Property (Miscellaneous Provisions) Act, 1989, section 2[6], requires a contract for the sale or other disposition of land to be in writing and signed by both parties, or in two parts, one part signed by each party, which are then exchanged as in the usual conveyancing transaction. A signature on a plan attached to a contract which was referred to in an unsigned letter was held not to be a sufficient signature for the purposes of the Act[7], and correspondence between solicitors was not sufficient to vary a completion date inserted into a contract satisfying the section.[8]

In order to avoid any possibility of the unintentional creation of a binding contract before exchange however, pre-contract correspondence should be expressly made "subject to contract." Negotiations for a lease should be made "subject to contract" or "subject to lease." In *Longman* v *Viscount Chelsea*[9] where it was expressly stipulated in correspondence that any agreement between the parties was "subject to lease", it was held that there could be no binding agreement until the lease and counterpart lease had been exchanged. Moreover, the signing and sealing of the lease did not constitute delivery of it as an escrow unless it was specifically stated to do so. In *Salomon* v *Akiens*[10] the tenant failed to apply to the court for a new lease under the 1954 Act as negotiations for a new lease were in progress with the landlord. The negotiations, however, were "subject to lease"; and when the landlord declined to proceed, even though the tenant had sent to him the counterpart lease and money due, it was held that there was no binding contract or estoppel which the tenant could enforce against the landlord.

In spite of the express requirement of section 2(1) of the 1989 Act for incorporation of all the terms of the contract into the written signed document, there is a growing body of case law where the courts have been prepared to find that a collateral agreement will nevertheless still be enforceable as it is not itself caught by the section. Thus in *Robert Leonard (Developments) Ltd* v *Wright*[11] an oral agreement was made between the vendor and purchaser of a leasehold flat that the price would

---

4   These are leases not exceeding three years which take effect in possession at a market rent and without a premium.
5   By LP(MP)A 1989, s 2(5).
6   Replacing LPA 1925, s 40.
7   *Firstpost Homes Ltd* v *Johnson* [1995] 4 All ER 355.
8   *McCausland* v *Duncan Laurie Ltd* [1996] 4 All ER 995.
9   (1989) 58 P & CR 189.
10 [1993] 1 EGLR 101.
11 [1994] NPC 49

include the furniture and appliances in the flat, which had been used as a show flat. It was held that this agreement, which was not contained in the contract itself, was enforceable as it was not itself a contract for the disposition of land. In *Tootal Clothing Ltd v Guinea Properties Ltd*[12] a separate written contract, whereby the landlord agreed to give the tenant £30,000 towards the cost of fitting out, was signed on the same day as the contract for a lease but not referred to in the lease contract. It was held nevertheless to be enforceable as a collateral contract, notwithstanding that the contract for the lease stated that it embodied the entire agreement between the parties. In *System Floors Ltd v Ruralpride*[13] a side letter dated the same date as three leases offering to accept a surrender of them was held to be binding on the landlord's assignee of the reversion notwithstanding that he had no knowledge of it and it was expressed to be personal to the tenant.[14]

Quite apart from these cases where "side agreements" have been found to be enforceable, the court may be prepared to grant specific performance of a lease if estoppel applies.[15]

A contract for a lease may be registered as a Land Charge, Class C(iv) if the title is unregistered, or protected as a minor interest if the title is registered, as it does in fact create an equitable lease. Registration protects it against a purchaser of the reversion, and so is particularly desirable if completion is to be delayed for any reason or in times of "gazumping". An enforceable contract for a lease takes effect as an equitable lease, the enforceability and effect of which is discussed more fully in Chapter 1.

The Costs of Leases Act 1958 provides that neither party to a lease shall be bound to pay the other's costs, unless there is an agreement in writing to the contrary. It is not unusual for the landlord's solicitor to provide that the tenant shall pay the landlord's costs in connection with the lease, however, and the tenant will usually pay the costs of engrossing the lease. Standard Condition 8.2.6. provides that the landlord (or "seller") is to engross both the lease and the counterpart. A limitation to the effect that the tenant will pay "reasonable" costs, and an estimate of what these are likely to be, is obviously a cautionary measure that a tenant's solicitor should take. The solicitor should be wary of giving any undertaking to pay such costs however unless he is first put in funds by his client. Even then, consideration should be given as to what is to happen if, for any reason, the lease is not completed.

12 (1992) 64 P & CR 452.
13 [1995] 1 EGLR 48.
14 For a further discussion of this case see pp. 106, 117.
15 *JT Developments* v *Quinn* (1991) 62 P & CR 33.

Conditional contract

An agreement for a lease may be made conditional upon some event, such as the vacation of the premises by another tenant. This will not infringe the requirement of certainty of term.[16]

The Landlord and Tenant Act 1954, section 38(4), provides a mechanism for the landlord and the tenant to agree that the provisions of the Act shall not apply to a business tenancy, but this agreement has to be approved by the court to be effective. A contract to grant a lease may be made expressly conditional upon such approval, or it may be possible to infer from the circumstances that an agreement is conditional upon approval being given. In *Cardiothoracic Institute* v *Shrewdcrest Ltd*[17] the court had approved agreed short-term tenancies outside the Act and the parties began negotiations for a third agreement. This was not concluded, however, before the end of the previous agreement; and the tenant, who remained in possession of the premises, claimed that he had an implied periodic tenancy which was protected under the Act. It was held that there was an inference that the third agreement would also be conditional upon the court's consent to the exclusion of the Act.

In the *Shrewdcrest* case, the condition was precedent to the formation of a contract. The true interpretation of some conditions, however, is that there is a binding contract which is avoided in certain circumstances. Examples of this type of agreement are a contract subject to planning permission being obtained[18] or subject to the reversioner's consent being obtained to the assignment of a lease.[19] Any such agreement should be made as clear as possible and a time specified for the condition to be fulfilled. If no time is specified, then it will be a reasonable time. If the condition is too vague (such as "subject to a satisfactory mortgage"[20]) the term may be void for uncertainty.

Because the true construction of this type of contract is that there is a valid agreement which may be avoided if certain conditions are not fulfilled, any such condition may be waived by the party who benefits from it. So, in *Batten* v *White*[21], where the vendor repudiated an agreement to sell subject to the purchaser's obtaining planning permission, the purchaser was able to waive the condition and obtain an order for specific performance even though planning permission had not been obtained.

16 *Brilliant* v *Michaels* [1945] 1 All ER 121.
17 [1986] 1 WLR 368.
18 *Batten* v *White* (1960) 12 P & CR 66.
19 *Property & Bloodstock* v *Emerton* [1968] Ch 94.
20 *Lee-Parker* v *Izzet* (No 2) [1972] 1 WLR 775.
21 (1960) 12 P & CR 66.

The landlord's title

The law with regard to the tenant's right to call for deduction of the landlord's title is most unsatisfactory. Unless expressly stipulated, the tenant has no right to call for deduction of the freehold title at all, either in unregistered or registered land.[22] The tenant's solicitor should resist this state of affairs wherever possible, particularly where the tenant is to pay a premium, or intends to spend sums of money on alterations or fitting out the premises. In any event, inability to see the freehold title leaves the tenant uncertain as to what restrictive covenants there may be affecting the property which will, of course, be binding on him. It will also mean that he will not be able to use the lease as security for a loan, should he wish to do so. Even if this does not concern the tenant, it may affect an assignee who requires a loan, thereby making the premises less easily disposable. If the landlord's freehold title is mortgaged, then the mortgagee's consent to a lease may be required, and the tenant should know that this has been granted. The standard form of preliminary enquiries for leasehold property asks for information on the reversionary title, whether the lease is a head-lease or a sub-lease, and the names and addresses of any superior lessors.

Where the lease exceeds 21 years, it will be registrable substantively at HM Land Registry, and Standard Condition 8.2.4. provides that the "seller" landlord is to deduce a title (the freehold title from which the lease derives) which will enable the lease to be registered with title absolute. The Land Registry will make a note of any lease in the Charges Register of the freehold title, and the tenant's solicitor should require that the landlord deposits his land certificate with the Registry on completion of the lease so that a corresponding note may be made on the land certificate. A lease of 21 years or less will be an overriding interest under the Land Registration Act 1925, section 70(1)(k), and additionally under section 70(1)(g) if the tenant is in occupation or in receipt of the rents and profits of a sub-lease.

The lease

The contents of a lease and the effect of the various clauses in a lease are considered in detail in the appropriate chapters of this book. In a pre-1996 lease, privity of contract means that the original tenant remains liable to the original landlord on the covenants in the lease throughout the term[23], unless the lease contains some restriction on such continuing liability. The tenant may have been able to include a proviso that his contractual liability should

---

22 LPA 1925, s 44(2) as regards unregistered title. As regards registered title, LRA 1925, s 110, does not apply to a lessee.
23 See Chap 5.

cease on assignment with the landlord's consent to an assignee of whom the landlord has approved. This might well, depending upon the wording of the surety's covenant, have the effect of discharging also the liability of any surety. In a post-1995 lease, the original tenant's liability under the covenants in the lease will usually cease upon assignment, although the landlord may be able to demand from such original tenant that he enter into an authorised guarantee agreement guaranteeing the liability of his immediate assignee only.[24]

Completion of the lease

Before the lease is finally completed, the usual pre-completion conveyancing searches should be made. These include a Land Charges search in bankruptcy (or a full Land Charges search if the freehold title is unregistered), a search at HM Land Registry if the title is registered, and a company search if the landlord is a company. Both the lease and the counterpart should be executed by the landlord and the tenant respectively, and dated on completion, when the lease is handed over to the tenant and the counterpart to the landlord. Care should be taken to insert the date on which the term is to commence, and from which rent is to be payable, if these are different from the date of the lease itself.

After completion, the lease and the counterpart will require stamping, and the lease will require registration with the Land Registry if its term exceeds 21 years. It may also be necessary under the terms of the lease to give notice of the lease to any mortgagee of the landlord's.

ASSIGNMENT OF A LEASE

The assignor and assignee of a lease cannot, upon an assignment, themselves vary the terms of the lease. The lessor will need to be a party to any deed varying such terms; and, of course, even if the lessor is willing to agree to a variation, he may demand consideration, and will invariably require to be indemnified as to his costs. An assignment will follow more closely the usual purchase procedure and will normally be preceded by exchange of contracts. The usual preliminary enquiries and local searches should be made. If planning permission is required, the contract should be made conditional upon this being granted. In this event, it might also be prudent to make the contract conditional on there being no unacceptable conditions attached to planning consent.

---

24 See Chap 5.

Title

Like the lessee under an open contract, the assignee cannot call for the freehold title to be deduced. He is entitled to see only a copy of the lease which is being assigned to him and all assignments for the last 15 years. If the leasehold title is registered with title absolute, however, this means that the Registrar has seen, and approved, the freehold title out of which the lease is granted, so that the assignee has no cause for concern. His risks in not seeing the freehold title are otherwise much the same as those of the lessee.[25]

From the assignor's point of view, he should furnish a copy of the lease with the draft contract and provide specifically that the assignment is subject to its terms. Standard Condition 8.1.2. provides that the assignee, having been provided with the documents embodying the terms of the lease, is deemed to know of these and to accept them.

A breach of covenant by the assignor will amount to a defective title, to which the assignee may object unless his right to do so is negated by a special condition in the contract of sale. To avoid the objection that a repairing covenant may not have been strictly complied with, it is not unusual to provide that the assignor shall not be liable for any breach of covenant as to the condition of the premises, even though the assignor assigns with a guarantee of title which implies that the lease is subsisting and that there is no breach of covenant which could make it liable to forfeiture[26]. The standard form of preliminary enquiries for leasehold property asks about any breach of covenants by either the lessor or the lessee.

The lease will almost certainly require the landlord's consent to any assignment. Standard Condition 8.3.2. provides that the assignor is to apply for this at his expense, and to use all reasonable efforts to obtain it, whilst the assignee is to furnish references and information reasonably required in this connection. Standard Condition 8.3.4. provides that either party may rescind the contract if the landlord's consent to the assignment is not forthcoming three days before the date for completion. This applies even if there is some doubt as to the reasonableness of the landlord's refusal of consent.

25 Considered *supra*.
26 Standard Condition 4.5.2 states that if there is no provision as to title in the contract, then the seller transfers with full title guarantee, but 4.5.3 makes this subject to all matters to which the property is sold subject.

The assignment

Even if the lease itself is within the Law of Property Act 1925, section 54(2), and so may be created by word of mouth, any assignment of it must be made by deed.[27] If the title to the lease is registered, the assignment may simply be a transfer of the whole of the registered title.

On assignments made before 1 July 1995, where the assignor assigned as "beneficial owner", statute implied covenants for quiet enjoyment and further assurance, and that the assignor had a right to convey.[28] If the assignment was for value, it was additionally implied that the lease was valid and in force and that all the tenant's covenants had been performed.[29]

In the case of a disposition of land (including the grant or assignment of a lease) made on or after 1 July 1995, the Law of Property (Miscellaneous Provisions) Act 1994, provides that a person who sells "with full title guarantee" gives covenants similar to the right to convey and further assurance, and also a covenant that the land is free from incumbrances other than those of which he does not know, or cannot reasonably have known. Additionally, on the assignment of a lease, a further covenant is implied that the lease is still subsisting and not liable to forfeiture for breach of covenant. The covenant as to incumbrances is modified to cover only incumbrances imposed by the grantor or anyone since the last disposition for value where the transfer is made "with limited title guarantee". The covenants do not apply, however, to any matters which the disposition is expressly made subject to, or of which the grantee knew at the time of the grant.

If the assignment is of a pre-1996 lease, the lessee (because of his continuing liability under the covenants contained in the lease) should take an express indemnity from the assignee for future breaches of covenant. Standard Condition 4.5.4. provides for such an indemnity. Even if no express indemnity covenant is entered into, such a covenant is implied by statute: in unregistered title if the assignment is for value[30], and in registered title whether it is for value or not.[31] In *Middlegate Properties Ltd v Bilbao*[32] it was held that an assignee's indemnity covenant could apply to continuing breaches of covenant, such as a repairing covenant, which commenced before assignment and should not be construed as applying only to breaches after assignment. An assignee should therefore seek to limit his indemnity to breaches of covenant occurring while he is the tenant.

---

27 *Crago v Julian* [1992] 1 WLR 372.
28 LPA 1925, s 76(1)(A), Sched 2, Part I.
29 *Ibid.*, s 76(1)(B), Sched 2, Part II; LRA 1925, s 24(1)(a).
30 LPA 1925, s 77.
31 LRA 1925, s 24.
32 (1972) 24 P & CR 329.

If the assignment is of a post-1995 lease, no indemnity covenant is required (and no statutory covenant is implied), since the tenant's liability under the lease generally ends upon assignment. He can be liable thereafter only under any authorised guarantee agreement which he enters into.[33]

The normal pre-completion searches need to be made before completion of the assignment, and after completion any stamp duty paid and the transfer registered, assuming the title is registered. If the leasehold title is not registered, it will be registrable if there is more than 21 years of the term left.

THE GRANT OF A SUB-LEASE

Many of the considerations that apply to the grant of a lease will apply also to the grant of a sub-lease, and the tenant's solicitor should be prepared to negotiate any unfavourable terms. The enquiries and searches to be made on behalf of the sub-lessee will be much the same.

A sub-lessee is not entitled to call for deduction of the freehold title.[34] He may require production of the head-lease out of which the sub-lease is to be granted, and of any assignments going back for 15 years. Standard Condition 8.2.4. (that the seller will deduce title to the purchaser so as to enable him to register a lease of over 21 years with title absolute) applies to a sub-lease in the same way as it applies to a lease, however. If, therefore, the lessor himself is not able to deduce title to the freehold, he should expressly exclude this condition. It will apply of course only if a contract is used which incorporates the Standard Conditions, and a sub-lease is usually granted, in the same way as a lease, without any prior contract.

The sub-lessee should ask to see the receipt for the last insurance premium and instalment of rent paid under the head-lease. He should require an assurance that the covenants under the head-lease have been performed. The head-lessor's consent will usually be necessary for a sub-lease and Condition 8.3.2. (as to obtaining consent) and 8.3.4. (as to the right of either party to rescind if consent is not forthcoming) apply.

It is very important that the covenants in the sub-lease correspond with those in the head-lease. Otherwise the sub-lessor may find that he is sued by the head-lessor for a breach of covenant in the head-lease for which he has no recourse against the sub-lessee. The sub-lessee should take a covenant from the sub-lessor to pay the rent due under the head-lease and

---

33 See further Chap 5.
34 LPA 1925, s 44.

to observe and perform the covenants in the head-lease. An example of this would be a covenant:

> "To pay the rents reserved by the lease under which the landlord holds the demised premises and to perform and observe the tenant's covenants therein contained but only insofar as the superior lessor shall require the same to be performed and observed and except insofar as the same are to be performed and observed by the tenant under this lease."

At common law, if a tenant of a lease for a fixed term purports to grant a sub-lease for a term expiring after the expiration of his own lease, the purported sub-tenancy takes effect by way of assignment. No tenancy by estoppel can arise unless the soi-disant lessor has no legal estate at all or merely an estate in equity.[35] In *William Skelton & Son Ltd v Harrison & Pinder Ltd*[36], however, a tenant who had a tenancy protected by Part II of the Landlord and Tenant Act 1954, in error purported to grant a sub-lease for a period which expired one month after his own contractually agreed term. It was held that this took effect as a sub-lease rather than an assignment because section 24 of the 1954 Act conferred on the tenant the right to hold over. There was therefore the possibility that the head-lease could endure longer than the sub-lease; and this possibility of a reversion was sufficient to support the sub-lease. The decision must now be considered to be in doubt since it has since been established that the grant of a sub-lease causes the head-lease to lose any protection it may have had under Part II in respect of the premises sub-demised.[37]

THE ASSIGNMENT OF A SUB-LEASE

The same considerations apply on the assignment of a sub-lease as on the assignment of a head-lease. Statute provides, however, that the purchaser shall assume that all covenants have been performed and rent paid under the sub-lease and any superior lease on production of the last receipt for rent due.[38]

---

35 *Universal Permanent Building Society v Cooke* [1952] 1 Ch 95, 102 (CA); *First National Bank plc v Thompson* [1996] 1 All ER 140, 147; *St Giles Hotel Ltd v Microworld Technology Ltd* [1997] 27 EG 121, 122.
36 [1975] QB 361.
37 *Graysim Holdings Ltd v P & O Property Holding Ltd* [1996] 1 AC 329 (HL); see also *Esselte AB v Pearl Assurance plc* [1997] 2 All ER 41 (CA), where it was held that the tenant's rights and obligations under Part II of the 1954 Act are lost immediately the tenant ceases to occupy the premises.
38 LPA 1925, s 45(3).

OCCUPATION PRIOR TO COMPLETION OF A LEASE, SUB-LEASE OR ASSIGNMENT

Although a tenant may be anxious to move into premises before completion, to take advantage of pre-Christmas trade for example, it is likely to prejudice his negotiating position, so that it may not ultimately be in his best interests. From a landlord's point of view, however, he could allow the tenant to occupy the premises as a tenant at will or a licensee. A tenancy at will may be created expressly[39] and will be outside the protection of Part II of the 1954 Act.[40] A licensee will not have any interest in the land, and a purchaser who takes possession before completion is within one of the categories of occupation which Lord Templeman specifically mentioned in *Street* v *Mountford*[41] as not raising any presumption of a tenancy; but merely calling the arrangement a licence will not preclude the creation of a tenancy if this is the true relationship between the parties. Even if a lease is created, the tenant will not enjoy the protection of the 1954 Act if the lease is for a term certain unless it is for a term exceeding six months.[42]

Condition 5.2.2 of the Standard Conditions of Sale expressly provides that a purchaser who occupies premises before completion does so as a licensee and not a tenant. If the tenant does take possession before completion, he would be very unwise to spend money on improvements. Quite apart from the risk that the transaction may not proceed to completion for some reason, any such improvements would not qualify for compensation under the Landlord and Tenant Act 1927, and may not be within the disregard in any rent-review clause.[43]

Where there is no formal agreement for a lease (as is usually the case) and the tenant is allowed into possession under the terms of a letter, it is advisable to regard any such letter as an agreement for a disposition of an interest in land and so within the Law of Property (Miscellaneous Provisions) Act 1989, section 2(1). It should therefore include all the terms upon which possession is given and be signed by all the parties, including any guarantor. For the landlord's protection, the letter should state that the tenant is a licensee or a tenant at will (as neither of these is protected under the Landlord and Tenant Act 1954) and takes possession at his own risk. It should state the purpose for which possession is granted (for alterations or trading) and require the term of the lease, when ultimately

---

39 *Manfield & Sons Ltd* v *Botchin* [1970] 2 QB 612.
40 *Javad* v *Aquil* [1991] 2 EGLR 82.
41 [1985] AC 809.
42 LTA 1954, s 43(3).
43 See further Chaps 7 and 9.

granted, to be back-dated to the date when possession was taken. The letter should include an undertaking by the tenant to complete the lease within a certain time, or on the earlier satisfaction of any condition upon which the grant of the lease is dependent (a superior landlord's licence to sub-let or a court order that the lease is to be contracted out of the 1954 Act). The letter should provide for the immediate termination of the licence if the tenant breaches any of its conditions, or a condition upon which the grant of the lease is dependent becomes impossible. It should also provide that the licensee occupies the premises at his own risk. Even though no implied term of fitness for purpose is implied into a lease or a contract for a lease, such a provision might be implied into a licence.[44] From the licensor's point of view, the licence should therefore expressly exclude any implied warranty or condition by the licensor as to the fitness or suitability of the premises for their intended purpose.[45]

ENVIRONMENTAL CONSIDERATIONS

Environmental assessments in the planning process

The European Community's Directive on Environmental Assessment[46] required that the environmental effects of certain developments should be considered before planning consent was granted. The Directive was introduced into the planning procedure by the Town and Country Planning (Assessment of Environmental Effects) Regulations 1988 as amended[47] and there is now a further statutory power to make regulations on environmental assessment under the Planning and Compensation Act 1991, section 15.

The Regulations divide potentially environmentally damaging developments into two categories listed in Schedules 1 and 2. Schedule 1 includes large projects, such as aerodromes and land fill sites, where the environmental impact must be assessed as part of the planning procedure. An environmental assessment is required for Schedule 2 projects, however, only where the nature, size or location of the project makes it likely that it

---

44 *Wettern Electric Ltd v Welsh Development Board* [1983] QB 796.
45 See further McDougall, "Completion: speeding the process" [1994] 37 EG 144.
46 EEC/85/337 as amended by EEC/97/11.
47 SI 1988 No 1199, as amended by the Town and Country Planning (Assessment of Environmental Effects) (Amendment) Regulations 1990 (SI 1990 No 367); 1992 (SI 1992 No 1494); and 1994 (SI 1994 No 677). See also Town and Country Planning (Environmental Assessment and Permitted Development) Regulations 1995, SI 1995 No 417, and Town and Country Planning (Environmental Assessment and Unauthorised Development) Regulations 1995, SI 1995 No 2258.

will have a significant effect on the environment. A circular issued by the Department of the Environment[48] gives guidance on whether Schedule 2 projects should be environmentally assessed. The grounds for an assessment are that the project has more than merely local significance, is in a sensitive or vulnerable location, or that it is unusually complex and could have potentially adverse effects. The circular also provides a list of quantitative thresholds. Schedule 2 comprises a long list of projects under generic headings such as agriculture, energy, food, rubber industry, processing of metals, glass-making, extractive industry, chemical industry, textile, leather and wood and paper industries, knackers' yards and industrial estate development.

Where a project falls to be environmentally assessed, the applicant for planning permission must produce an **environmental statement** to the local planning authority at the same time as the planning application. Certain bodies, such as the Nature Conservancy Council, the Countryside Commission, and the Environment Agency, must be notified of the proposed development and consulted about it. The environmental statement must then include a statement describing the development and assessing its likely impact on "human beings, flora, fauna, soil, water, air, climate, the landscape, the interaction between any of the foregoing, material assets and the cultural heritage."

If it is not clear whether a development falls within Schedule 2 or not, an applicant can apply to the local planning authority to determine whether an environmental statement is necessary. The authority has three weeks in which to make a decision. If a planning application is submitted without a statement where the authority thinks a statement should be submitted, it must notify the applicant of this requirement within three weeks. The Secretary of State has a general power to require an environmental statement on any appeals to him.

Where an environmental statement is required, the planning authority has 16 weeks to consider the application instead of the usual eight weeks.

Contaminated land

Definition and identification of contaminated land

A regime for identifying and registering contaminated land was laid down in the Environmental Protection Act 1990. Parts of the Act were never brought into force, however[49], and were subsequently repealed by the

---

48 Environmental Assessment: Implementation of the EC Directive 15/88 WO 23/88.
49 Notably s 143 requiring local authorities to set up a register of contaminated land in their area.

Environment Act 1995, which substantially amended the 1990 Act. Parts of the 1995 Act itself dealing with contaminated land have not yet been implemented, and it is possible that there may be further amendments before they become effective. The following text describes the amendments made by the Environment Act 1995, but it should be borne in mind that this is not yet operative.

If implemented as it stands, the Environmental Protection Act 1990, Part IIA[50], will require all local authorities to survey and identify land in their area which may be contaminated. The registration of such land under the controversial section 143 of the 1990 Act (which was never implemented by the necessary Regulations) has now been abandoned, but there is a requirement to register remediation notices or agreements and appeals and convictions relating to contaminated land and to special sites for which the Environment Agency is primarily liable. It will not be possible to identify all contaminated land from such registers, but the Environmental Information Regulations 1992 require a local authority to provide information on environmental matters to the public, which could assist a prospective purchaser or lessee. Many local authorities had started to prepare registers of contaminated land in anticipation of section 143 becoming effective, and therefore have considerable information. Enquiries could additionally be made of neighbours and previous owners of the land if there is reason to suspect that the land may have been contaminated by a previous use. Where a company has previously owned the land, an inspection of the company records may assist, and ultimately an environmental survey. If the lessee or assignee feels that there is a serious risk of contamination from a previous use of the premises, or of neighbouring premises, then he should argue for the lease to include a break clause to become operative if the premises become unsuitable through contamination for his proposed user.[51] There is no implied covenant as to fitness of premises for any particular use,[52] and an environmental survey should be obtained if there is any doubt.

Contaminated land is defined in the 1995 Act as land which may, by reason of substances in, on or under it, cause significant harm or pollution (not necessarily significant) of controlled waters. Harm is defined as "harm to the health of living organisms or other interference with the ecological systems of which they form part" or "harm to human property." The test for contamination is to be applied in the context of the use to which the land is put, and is not an absolute standard of fitness for

50 Inserted by Environment Act 1995.
51 See Tromans & Turrall-Clarke, *Contaminated Land* (1994) Sweet & Maxwell.
52 *Manchester Bonded Warehouse Co Ltd* v *Carr* (1880) 5 CPD 507, where the floors of a warehouse gave way under the weight of the tenant's flour.

all purposes. It is therefore possible that land which is harmful for some users, and therefore contaminated, may not be for other users. Pollution of controlled waters means "the entry into controlled waters of any poisonous, noxious or polluting matter or any solid waste matter."

Special sites are sites which, by reason of substances in, on or under the land are likely to cause "serious" harm or "serious" water pollution, and responsibility for these lies with the Environment Agency and not the local authorities.

Remediation of contaminated land

Where the local authority, which is under a duty to inspect land within its area from time to time, has identified contaminated land, it must determine what remedial action is required. A period of three months for consultation with the "appropriate person" is then allowed to reach an agreement as to the work to be carried out. If no agreement is reached, it must serve a remediation notice requiring the work to be carried out in a reasonable time. The primary liability for remediation is with the polluter, and the polluter is the appropriate person upon whom the notice should be served. If, however, no notice can be served on the polluter (because he cannot be found or identified after "reasonable enquiry"), then it may be served on the owner or occupier of the land, who may also be liable. The owner is the person who receives, or would receive if the land were let, the rack rent, but the Act does not define the meaning of "occupier." Guidance (currently in draft form only) will be provided by the Department of the Environment as to which of them is to be primarily liable and as to apportioning the cost of remediation between them.

Where the contamination on land has emanated from another site, the polluter on the originally contaminated site will be primarily liable for its remediation. If he cannot be found, however, the owner or occupier of the site to which the contamination spread will be liable, although he will not be liable for any further contamination spreading from his land to the land of a third party unless he has caused or knowingly permitted its spread. A purchaser of a originating site will not be liable for contamination of an infiltrated site if he was unaware of it, unless he had in some way caused or knowingly permitted the contamination to spread.

In the case of special sites (where serious harm or serious pollution of controlled waters may be caused) the Environment Agency is responsible for serving the remediation notice, but no three month consultation period is necessary. The Environment Act 1995 designates the Environment Agency as the body to take over various regulatory functions, such as water control from the National Rivers Authority, waste disposal from the local authorities and atmospheric pollution control from HM Inspectorate of Pollution. It is responsible for the operation of the integrated pollution control regime introduced by the Environmental Protection Act 1990.

There are provisions for appeal from remediation notices served by a local authority to the magistrates' court, and from the Environment Agency to the Secretary of State. There are criminal sanctions for failing to comply with a remediation notice, and the local authority or the Environment Agency may carry out the specified work themselves and recover the reasonable cost of this from the person served.

It is doubtful if clearing contaminated land would fall within the scope of the usual repairing covenant, although asbestos removal could possibly do so. A covenant to comply with any statutory requirements or notices might make a tenant liable for cleaning contaminated land however, and even if the landlord is liable, such work might fall within the scope of a service charge ultimately payable by the tenant.

The tenant's activities on the land

The implied covenants against waste and to use the premises in a tenant-like manner may afford the landlord a remedy in preventing the tenant from carrying on any contaminating activities on the land, and an express covenant not to do anything which would cause a nuisance or annoyance to the landlord or to neighbouring landowners would presumably cover not only contamination to the leased land but also to neighbouring land from the flow of air, water or soil.

Certain activities such as the use of hazardous or radioactive substances, atmospheric emissions, waste management, integrated pollution control and the discharge of trade effluent into sewers or rivers, require licences or consents under the relevant legislation. There is usually a criminal sanction for failure to obtain any necessary licence or consent, but a landlord may also be liable for permitting an unauthorised use if he fails to stop it. In leases of industrial premises therefore it is wise to include a covenant by the tenant, such as the one below, to comply with any legislation and obtain any necessary licences.

> "At all times to observe and comply with the provisions of or imposed under any statute licence or registration regulating or permitting the use of the demised premises for the purpose for which they are for the time being used and the requirements of any competent authority in that connection and at the expense of the tenant to do all that is necessary to obtain maintain and renew all licences and registrations required by law for the use of the demised premises for that purpose."

A landlord might also consider taking a covenant from a tenant not to dispose of waste on the premises so as to cause, or to increase any existing, contamination on the land. Any such covenant should be supported by a right of entry to take samples in order to ensure that the covenant is not being breached.[53]

The enquiries which a landlord makes of a tenant to ascertain what likely contamination may arise from the user of the land should also be made of any proposed assignee or sub-lessee. Enquiries should cover any previous convictions under the Health and Safety at Work legislation or for waste disposal, the precautions he proposes to take with regard to industrial processes, and the training and skill of his employees.[54]

PLANNING CONSIDERATIONS

Since the Town and Country Planning Act 1947, a system for the public management and control of land has operated. It has been the responsibility of local government to manage land in the best economic and social interests of their communities. Since then, various other allied responsibilities, such as the designation and preservation of conservation areas, listed buildings and tree preservation orders, have been included in land administration. There has been a growing recognition of the scarcity value of land in urban areas and the requirement for careful planning for the needs of a community. More recently, environmental issues have warranted consideration, sometimes emanating from the European Union.

The development plan

The 1947 Act required local planning authorities to prepare a development plan for their areas which had to take into account social, economic and environmental considerations. This requirement is now contained in Part II of the Town and Country Planning Act 1990, as amended by the Planning and Compensation Act 1991.

The current provisions require non-metropolitan county councils to produce a structure plan for the whole county designating areas generally for types of user such as education, recreation or housing. The plan must include a written statement on general policies for the development and use of land. Additionally, a local plan must be prepared by non-

---

53 For suggestions and drafts of various covenants which might protect a landlord from contaminative user of land by a tenant, see Tromans & Turrall-Clarke, *Contaminated Land* (1994) Sweet & Maxwell, Appendix A.

54 See *ibid,* Appendix A, for a suggested environmental questionnaire.

metropolitan local planning authorities which must indicate in more detail proposed land use consistent with the overall structure plan. In the case of metropolitan councils, the council must prepare a unitary plan, which includes both the elements of the structure plan outlining general policy and the more specific details of the local plan. A minerals local plan and waste local plan should also be prepared by the county councils or metropolitan councils.

Definition of development

With some exceptions, there is now a general requirement to obtain planning permission for any development. Section 55(1) of the 1990 Act states that "development means the carrying out of building, engineering, mining or other operations in, on, over or under land, or the making of any material change in the use of any buildings or other land". The definition therefore encompasses two types of activity – one being operations carried out on the land and the other relating to a change in the user of the land.

Planning permission for development

Section 70(2) of the 1990 Act requires a local planning authority to have regard to the development plan and to "any other material considerations" in determining planning applications.

Section 54A of the 1990 Act[55] requires the authority to determine (*inter alia*) any planning applications in accordance with the development plan "unless material considerations indicate otherwise." The development plan will also be relevant for the modification or discontinuance of any planning permissions. The effect of section 54A is that there is a presumption in favour of granting planning consent for a development which is consistent with the development plan, but a presumption against consent for a development which is inconsistent with the plan.

The Secretary of State for the Environment has produced a number of Planning Policy Guidance Notes (known as PPG's) and circulars to assist authorities in determining planning applications, and PPG1 (revised in 1997) states that:

> "An applicant who proposes a development which is clearly in conflict with the development plan would need to produce convincing reasons to demonstrate why the plan should not prevail."

The "material considerations" referred to in section 70(2) have been widely interpreted to include any consideration relating to the use and

---

55 Inserted by Planning and Compensation Act 1991, s 26.

development of land. In *R* v *Westminster City Council, ex parte Monahan*[56] the Court of Appeal accepted that the financing of a proposed development was a material consideration in granting planning permission for another development nearby. In that case, a development in Covent Garden which involved the demolition of buildings, some of them listed, was permitted in order to finance an extension to the Royal Opera House.

The courts take the view that the determination of planning applications is essentially the job of the local planning authorities, and they will not upset a decision made by an authority unless it is *ultra vires*, or, under the *Wednesbury* principle[57], it is so unreasonable that no reasonable authority could ever have come to it.

In *Bendles Motors Ltd* v *Bristol Corporation*[58] Lord Parker CJ expressed personal reservations about the decision of the Minister that a small egg-vending machine placed on the forecourt of a garage amounted to a change of use which required planning permission, but nevertheless said:

> "This court can only interfere if satisfied that it is a conclusion that he could not, properly directing himself as to the law, have reached."

Planning enforcement

A local authority may issue an enforcement notice in respect of a development without planning permission, or for a breach of condition attached to a planning consent. PPG 18 (1991) provides that such notices should only be issued, however, if the authority consider it to be necessary in the interests of planning. Failure to comply with such a notice is a criminal offence. A stop notice may be served with an enforcement notice if the circumstances warrant bringing the unauthorised development to a rapid halt, or in the event of an appeal against an enforcement notice, it may be used to suspend the operation of either kind of development, but compensation is payable for this if an appeal is successful. Quite independently of this procedure, a local authority may apply for an injunction to restrain an unauthorised development under section 187B, Town and Country Planning Act 1990.

In addition, there are two further notices which may be served: the planning contravention notice where the local planning authority believes there has been a breach of planning control, and the breach of condition notice where a condition has not been observed.

---

56 [1988] JPL 107.
57 Established in *Associated Picture Houses Ltd* v *Wednesbury Corporation* [1948] 1 KB
    223.
58 [1963] 1 WLR 247.

Planning agreements or obligations

Under the Town and Country Planning Act 1990, section 106, it was possible for a local planning authority and a developer to enter into a planning agreement which did not fall within the normal planning procedure. Agreements under the section have been made in the past whereby a developer conveyed open space land to the authority in return for planning permission to develop other land. Such agreements were criticised as effectively allowing developers to buy planning consent, and section 12, Planning and Compensation Act 1991, replaced the section with a new section 106. Any planning agreements made before 25 October 1991 are still valid however and governed by the old law.

The new section allows a developer to enter into a planning obligation, either by agreement or by unilateral undertaking. The obligation may require the developer to use the land in a specified way, or may specify operations or activities to be carried out on the land to be developed or on other land. Payments to the authority may be required for matters not connected with the development, or, apparently even planning objectives. A new section 106A allows a person under a planning obligation to apply to the local authority for its discharge or modification, and a new section 106B allows for an appeal against their decision to the Secretary of State.

In *Wimpey Homes Holdings Ltd* v *Secretary of State for the Environment*[59] Wimpey unilaterally undertook to transfer open space land to the authority and to make a payment for its maintenance. It was held that the money payment was within section 106 as amended, but that the transfer of title to other land was not as it did not impose any restriction on the land which was the subject of the application. Whilst money payments unconnected with the site to be developed are therefore within the new section 106, it would appear that the transfer of open space land in lieu is not.

The scope and weight to be attached to planning obligations was considered by the House of Lords in *Tesco Stores Ltd* v *Secretary of State for the Environment*[60] where Tesco had unilaterally undertaken to provide funding for a new link road not near to the proposed development. The Secretary of State, in refusing Tesco's application, decided that the link road was not necessary for, or reasonably related to, the proposed development. The House of Lords said that any planning obligation which has a connection with the proposed development which is not *de minimis* must be taken into consideration in the planning decision. However, the weight to be given to such an obligation is entirely a matter for the

59 [1993] 2 PLR 54.
60 [1995] 1 WLR 759.

planning authority provided that they act within the *Wednesbury* principle. In the *Tesco* case, the Secretary of State was entitled to attach little weight to the planning obligation offered by Tesco. In practice, this may mean that a local authority is more likely to attach more weight to an obligation imposed by itself than one which is offered by the developer.

The Town and Country Planning (General Permitted Development) Order 1995

This Order[60a] (known as the GPDO) sets out in Schedule 2 various developments which may be carried out without planning permission. These include (*inter alia*) minor operations such as the erection of gates and fences of a certain height, the construction of an access to a highway (not being a trunk or classified road) in connection with a development[61], and the provision of temporary buildings or structures.[62] The Town and Country Planning (Use Classes) Order 1987[62a] provides that a change of use to another use in the same Use Class, or to a use in another Use Class if it is not a material change of use, will not amount to development. Additionally, the GPDO 1995 provides that certain changes of use between Use Classes, or certain material changes within a Class, will be permitted development.[63] These are discussed more fully below.

A local authority may restrict the application of the Order in its area by an Article 4 Direction. A local search will reveal whether any such Direction has been made or not.

Simplified planning zones

Under sections 82–87 of the 1990 Act, a local planning authority may designate an area as a simplified planning zone (SPZ). The authority may then make a scheme, operative for ten years, applicable to the whole or part of the zone, and specifying types of development for which planning consent is not necessary within the area of the scheme. The scheme may be a general one under which there is general consent to development, or a specific one giving consent to only certain types of development. The Secretary of State has indicated that such zones might be used for the development of large tracts of land, such as old railway sidings. They could be used to give consent to new industrial parks or the redevelopment of an old industrial estate.

60a SI 1995 No 418.
61   Part 2, Sched 2.
62   Part 4, Sched 2.
62a SI 1987 No 764, as amended by SI 1991 No 1567.
63   Part 3, Sched 2.

Certificates of lawfulness of an existing use or development

For a long time there has been something similar to a limitation period for proceedings for infringements of planning law. After a certain time, both operational and user development were to be regarded as "established use" which then became immune from proceedings for infringement.

The Planning and Compensation Act 1991, section 10[64], has extended and amended the procedure whereby an owner could apply for a certificate of established use. Any person may now apply to a local planning authority for a certificate of lawfulness of an existing operational development or use, or a certificate of lawfulness of a proposed operational development or use. In both cases, the onus of proof is on the applicant to furnish sufficient evidence of the grounds for such certificate. If the evidence presented is satisfactory, the planning authority must issue the certificate and they do not have any discretion in the matter. A certificate as to the *proposed* use or development will be appropriate where the activity would not constitute development (such as a change from an established use to one in the same class), or would be a permitted development under a GPDO, or it is consistent with an existing planning permission.

Section 4 of the 1991 Act[65] sets out the time limits after which a development is to become lawful. It confirms that the time for operational development is four years after the *substantial* completion of the work. It is also four years where there is a change of user to a single private dwellinghouse. The period for development by change of user other than this is ten years however, as is the period for breach of a condition attached to a planning consent. Any development for which planning permission is obtained must be started within five years of the consent.

A solicitor acting for a client where there may be some doubt as to the lawful use of premises should take advantage of the certification procedure and not merely rely upon a statement from a planning officer. *In Western Fish Products Ltd v Penwith DC and Secretary of State for the Environment*[66], developers acted upon assurances from a planning officer as to the established use of a site. The Court of Appeal held that the assurances were not binding on the authority, and Megaw LJ said:

> "An estoppel cannot be raised to prevent the exercise of a statutory discretion or to prevent or excuse the performance of a statutory duty."

---

64 Inserting new ss 191–194 into 1990 Act.
65 New s 171B(3) of 1990 Act.
66 [1978] JPL 623.

Conditions attached to planning permissions

A planning permission may be granted with conditions attached, and an outline planning permission will invariably have conditions attached for which reasons should be stated. Any such conditions must be fair and reasonable, relate to the permitted development, and be imposed for planning purposes and not for any ulterior motive. Conditions which do not comply with these requirements may be quashed.

A solicitor acting for a prospective tenant should ensure that any such conditions do not impede the tenant's proposed user of the premises. In *GP & P Ltd* v *Bulcraig & Davies*[67] solicitors acting for tenants paid £333,193 in compensation when a planning permission for office use, subject to a condition restricting part to use as offices for the printing trade only, made it impossible to dispose of the lease.

In *Le Roux* v *Pictons*[68] solicitors were liable in negligence to their clients when they received only one page of a two-page planning permission, the second page disclosing that the use of a restaurant had to finish at 11.00 pm, which was extended to midnight on Fridays and Saturdays. It was therefore impossible for the clients to develop the upstairs part of the premises as a function room as they had intended to do.

In practice, a local planning authority will often attach conditions, such as landscaping, to a planning consent in order to reach a compromise between the applicant and those opposing the application. Conditions for the restoration of land after mineral workings or relating to land fill sites are usual. The 1991 Act has made it possible for an authority to serve a breach of condition notice on someone who fails to comply with any condition, and there is no appeal against such a notice. It is a criminal offence to fail to comply with a notice within the time specified, which must not be less than 28 days.

Development involving building etc operations

Section 55 defines building operations as including demolition, rebuilding, and structural alterations or additions to buildings. The word "includes" used in the section indicates that the definition is illustrative rather then exhaustive. "Building" includes also structures and erections. Section 55(2) exempts from the definition alterations affecting the internal, but not materially affecting the external, appearance of a building, although such alterations may of course require approval under the Building Regulations

---

67 [1988] 1 EGLR 138 (CA).
68 [1994] EGCS 168.

1991[68a] if they are structural alterations. An underground extension does however require planning consent.

To obtain planning consent, the applicant (who need not necessarily be the owner of the land) should first apply for an outline planning consent. This avoids the applicant incurring the expense involved in producing detailed plans for a development which may not receive approval at all. If the outline consent is granted, it will be subject to reserved matters, and detailed plans must be submitted for approval by the local planning authority in respect of these matters.

The development must be commenced within five years of the outline permission, or within two years of the final approval of the reserved matters, whichever is later.

Development involving any material change of use

This second head of development must be read subject to the Town and Country Planning (Use Classes) Order 1987.[68b] This Order deregulates the development process by exempting certain changes of user from the requirement to obtain planning permission. Section 55(2)(f) of the 1990 Act therefore states that it shall not amount to development where buildings or other land, or part of them, used for a purpose in any Class are to be used for another purpose in the same Class. Even a change of user from one Class to another Class will not necessarily be development unless it amounts to a "material change in the use". It has already been mentioned that, on the application of the *Wednesbury* principle, the courts regard themselves as having only a very limited jurisdiction to intervene in planning decisions.[69]

It was sometimes the practice, when granting planning permission for a change of use under the 1972 Order (which preceded the 1987 Order) to make it subject to a condition that it would not apply to any other user in the Class. The Secretary of State's Circular[70] makes it clear that such a practice under the new Order would be considered unreasonable.

The Town and Country Planning (General Permitted Development) Order 1995[71], provides additionally that certain specified changes of user from one Use Class to another, or material changes of use within a Use Class, are "permitted development". Examples of these are A2 (financial services to the public) to A1 (shop), and B2 (general industrial use) to B1 (business use) or to B8 (storage and distribution).

68a SI 1991 No 2768, as amended.
68b SI 1987 No 764, as amended by SI 1991 No 1567.
69 See *Bendles Motors Ltd v Bristol Corporation* [1963] 1 WLR 247.
70 13/87, para 12.
71 SI 1995 No. 418, Sched 2, Part 3.

It is a matter for the tenant to decide if his proposed use of any premises will be lawful under the planning law.[72] The tenant should bear in mind, however, that a change of use within a class will only be lawful if the original use has been implemented. A tenant of a new building for which planning consent has been granted for one class use might need to apply again for planning consent for another user.[73]

The Use Classes

In addition to deregulation, the 1987 Order sought to recognise changes in business user. For example, the rapidly developing "high-tec" industries have more in common with office user than with other manufacturing industries. The increase in numbers of hot food take-away businesses, which could be a nuisance in more residential areas, made it desirable to put this in a separate class from shops, so that consent is necessary to a change of use from, say, a greengrocer's shop to a fish and chip shop. Consent is also necessary to change from use as a shop to an office offering financial services to the public, so that planning authorities have some control over the disappearance of retail shops in town centres.

Class A1 covers various retail shops and A2 financial, professional and other services for the public appropriate for a shopping area. A3 covers the consumption of food and drink on the premises and hot food off the premises.

Class B1 covers office use not within Class A2 and research and development of products or processes. This includes light industrial purposes with no adverse effects in a residential area. B2 is general industrial use (and now includes the former Classes of special industrial uses B3 and B4–B7). Class B8 is storage and distribution; but retail warehouses selling directly to the public are within A1, even if a small part of the floor space is used for storage.

Class C covers residential use, including Class C1 (hotels and hostels), C2 (residential institutions where care or treatment is provided and residential educational facilities), and Class C3 (dwellinghouses).

Class D1 comprises non-residential social and community uses, such as museums and libraries. Class D2 comprises assembly and leisure centres, such as cinemas and sports centres.

In addition to the Classes, there are certain uses not included in any of the Classes known as *sui generis*. Some of these are specified in the Order and include a theatre, amusement arcade, launderette, the sale or display of motor vehicles and the sale of fuel for motor vehicles, a taxi or car-hire

---

72 *Hill v Harris* [1965] 2 QB 601.
73 *Kwik Save Discount Group v Secretary of State for Wales* [1981] JPL 198.

business, a scrapyard or knacker's yard. Additionally, uses involving hazardous substances in notifiable quantities could make a use within B1 a *sui generis* use and may trigger a requirement for hazardous substance consent under the Planning (Hazardous Substances) Act 1990.

Abandonment of use

Where a use has been abandoned, planning permission is necessary to resume it. It will depend upon the circumstances in each case whether there has in fact been an abandonment of the use or not. The actual act of abandonment itself however is not a material change of use.

In *Trustees of the Castell-y-Mynach Estate* v *Secretary of State for Wales*[74], a case involving the resumption of a residential use of a derelict house, the Divisional Court gave judicial notice to a submission of counsel that factors which could be taken into account in deciding whether or not there had been an abandonment were the physical state of the premises, the period of non-user, any intervening use and the owner's intentions.

Sub-division of premises

A sub-division of a larger unit into smaller units within the same Class will not amount to development. Sub-division of a unit with a user outside the Order might, however, be development. It may also be necessary, in this context, to consider the principal user and any ancillary user.

Possible drafting implications of the Order

The most substantial change of user permissible without consent, not being a material change of use, is the change from A2 (offices for financial services) to B1 (general offices), which can then be changed to use for light industrial purposes. If a landlord wishes to prevent this, he should consider a user clause prohibiting a change from one Use Class to another.

From a tenant's point of view, a B1 light industrial use could conceivably be used to argue that office-user would be permitted with a resulting adverse effect on a rent-review clause. So for use within this Class, a user clause should specify exactly which use is permitted and not simply refer to the Class.

The new Order is not comprehensive any more than the 1972 Order, so that the problem which arose in *Wolff* v *Enfield LBC*[75] could arise again. The user clause in the lease permitted "use for any purpose within Class

---

74 [1985] JPL 40.
75 [1987] 1 EGLR 119 (CA).

III" of the 1972 Order. It was held that the user as a non-teaching service unit for Middlesex Polytechnic was not within the Class. Rent had to be assessed by reference to Class III use only however, which resulted in a lower rent.

It is possible that, in time, if change of use within the Classes becomes habitual, it might be regarded as unreasonable for a landlord to refuse consent to a change of user under a qualified covenant against this. Possibly a refusal of consent to assign on these grounds might also be deemed unreasonable in the same way.

Given the wider uses within certain Classes, it would seem preferable to state verbatim in the lease what user is permitted rather than to rely upon the shorthand reference to user within certain Use Classes.

A clause requiring the tenant to furnish full information as to occupation and user of premises might well assist the landlord in establishing exactly which Use Class has been applicable to demised premises.

Interpretation of reference in user clause to Use Class

The Interpretation Act 1979 provides that a reference to a statute shall be a reference to that statute as amended. It might be arguable however that the 1987 Order (amended in 1991) revises the 1972 Order so drastically as not to qualify as an amendment.

The Act applies in any event only so long as there is no contrary intention expressed. Leases usually contain an interpretation clause, so that this would have to be construed so as to decide whether any reference is to the 1987 Order or to its 1972 predecessor.

A typical interpretation clause in a lease might be:

> "Any reference to a statute (whether specifically named or not) shall include any amendment or re-enactment of such statute for the time being in force and all instruments, orders, notices, regulations, directions, bye-laws, permissions and plans for the time being made, issued or given thereunder or deriving validity therefrom."

In *Brett v Brett Essex Golf Club Ltd*[76] it was held that, although it might be reasonable to interpret any reference to a statute to the statute as amended, each clause must be construed in its context. In that case, a reference to the Landlord and Tenant Act 1954, section 34, was construed as a reference to the section in its original form before it was amended by the Law of Property Act 1969. Presumably it would be open to a court to construe a reference to a Use Class similarly.

---

76 [1986] 1 EGLR 154 (CA).

Chapter 3

CONTENTS OF THE LEASE

FORM OF THE LEASE

Most leases of commercial property are lengthy, as they have to cover many areas of agreement between the parties. To abbreviate the lease as much as possible and to avoid argument, the lease will usually define certain terms such as "the demised premises" and "service charge". In a long and complex lease of, say, a unit in a shopping precinct, there may be two or three pages of definitions which precede the commencement of the lease. A less complicated lease will usually contain definitions at the beginning of the lease.

In order to make the lease as comprehensible as possible and to keep the provisions relating to a particular aspect together, it may be advisable to use schedules to the lease. Rights granted to the tenant and reservations excepted to the landlord should be set out in schedules. Additionally, separate schedules may deal with matters such as rent review, insurance, service charges and regulations for the management of a shopping precinct. It is possible that the actual body of the lease, including the parties, the term, the rent and the parcels, will be no more than two or three pages, and will leave all other matters, including the tenant's and the landlord's covenants, to be set out in schedules.

Obviously the extent to which schedules are used is a matter for the preference of the individual draftsman, but they may assist in making the document easier to read, and quicker to refer to on some particular point.

The formal parts of a lease are:
- *the premises* (containing the operative words, *e.g.* "grant", "demise" or "let"; the parcels, being a description of the demised premises and of the easements and other rights granted with the property; and exceptions and reservations);
- *the habendum* (the length of the term);
- *the reddendum* (the rent reserved);
- *the covenants* (of both landlord and tenant); and
- *the provisos, options and declarations.*

If the detailed content of some or all of these is consigned to schedules, the body of the lease may be very short, and may simply state that, in consideration of the rent reserved, the demised premises are granted to the tenant for a specified term.

THE RESERVATION OF THE RENT (*REDDENDUM*)

The *reddendum* reserves the rent, stating what the rent is, when it is to be paid, and whether it is to be paid in arrears or in advance. It is implied by the common law that rent will be payable in arrears unless it is specifically provided that it shall be payable in advance, which most leases do. Most commercial leases will include provisions for rent review, and the *reddendum* will specifically reserve future rents payable under these rent reviews. The process of rent review is often quite complex and specific and will usually be set out in a schedule to which the *reddendum* will refer.

THE PARCELS

The demised premises will be set out in the parcels clause. This may, however, simply refer to a definitions clause in which the demised premises are described, or more probably refer to a schedule to the lease containing a description of the demised premises. If only a brief description is needed, as perhaps where the property is a single building and curtilage with its own address, or where it is registered with a separate title at HM Land Registry, then a definition clause might be sufficient. A more complex property, such as a unit in part of a building, may require a more lengthy description which would be better set out in a schedule. Whichever method is adopted, the description of the demised premises should be set out in sufficient detail and clarity to identify the premises, and may or may not refer to a plan. A plan is not necessary unless the property to be demised is part of a title registered at HM Land Registry, when it will be necessary to submit a plan to obtain registration of a separate title where the lease is for more than 21 years.

If the demised premises are a single self-contained building, then reference to the land contained in the Land Registry title number, or the previous deed of conveyance, will probably be sufficient. If it is a unit in a larger building or development, or even a shared building, then a plan will be almost essential to define not only the demised premises, but also such common rights as access, parking and dustbin areas. Any plan included in the lease should be signed by both parties, and in the case of a company, by two directors or a director and the secretary.

In any event, if a plan is used, it should be made clear in the parcels clause if it is merely for identification ("the property shown edged red on the plan attached for the purpose of identification only") or whether the plan is an accurate scale drawing of the property ("the property edged red and more particularly delineated on the plan attached hereto"). In the event of any disparity between the wording of the parcels clause and the plan, the parcels clause takes precedence over the plan if the former wording is used, but the plan takes precedence if the latter is used.

The extent of the demise of a unit in a building

It will be particularly important to decide, and to define clearly, what is included in the demised premises, where the demise is part of a building, as it will affect such matters as liability to repair, access and possible liability for trespass. There are different ways of arranging for the repair of structural and other parts of the building, and the parcels clause will have to be drafted carefully to reflect the intended arrangement.

The first possibility is that the landlord will retain all the common parts and structural and load-bearing parts of the building, including any main walls of this description within the demised premises, and undertake to repair these. He will recoup the cost of repair as part of the service charge payable by all the tenants.[1] Such an arrangement may be achieved by a careful definition of the "demised premises" and "the Building" as follows:

"The demised premises means the internal surfaces of all walls (both internal and external) floors ceilings bounding or within the said premises and the windows and door frames and doors thereof and the glass in such window frames but excluding all load bearing structural walls and any walls separating the demised premises from any other part of The Building or any other premises and excluding all sewers pipes ducts [etc] within the demised premises other than those which solely serve the premises"

"The Building means the building known as [address] including the boundary walls and fences thereof the yards and forecourts and corridors and the roof and roof area and other areas not included in the demise of any premises and the foundations thereof and all load bearing structural walls."

The second possible arrangement is that all external walls of the building are included in the demise, but vertical and horizontal walls adjoining other demised premises are party walls with cross rights of support. The two owners are then jointly liable for the maintenance of the party walls. The following clause would reflect such an arrangement:

---

1 See Chap 11.

"There is included in this demise the entirety of all external boundary walls but a moiety only severed vertically of walls between the demised premises and other parts of the Building and a moiety only severed horizontally of floors and ceilings between the demised premises and other parts of the Building and all such dividing walls floors and ceilings shall be deemed to be party walls."

Obviously, whichever mode of division is adopted should be maintained throughout the building and reflected in all the leases.

In the absence of any express provision to the contrary, it was said in *Graystone Property Investments Ltd* v *Margulies*[2] that it is "almost invariable conveyancing practice" that the horizontal part of any unit is between the floor space and the underside of the floor above, that is, it includes the ceiling and the joists supporting the floor above. This may be very important for the installation of services requiring pipes and cables. In *Graystone*, the parcels clause described the property as being "formed on the first floor of the block". There were some false ceilings and the tenant wanted to use the space above them to form a mezzanine floor. The landlord objected, arguing that this space was not part of the demise. The Court of Appeal was strongly influenced by the fact that the false ceilings were only in some rooms and not throughout. It accepted the general rule in *Sturge* v *Hackett*[3] that in the absence of any definite indication in the wording, external walls will belong to the demised premises. To have included in the demise the space between the walls up to ceiling level only (including the false ceilings) would have resulted in the landlord retaining a number of irregularly shaped voids. It was therefore held that the word "formed" was not sufficient to displace the usual practice of a demise up to the underside of the floor above.

If the demise of top floor premises includes the roof, then the tenant will be free to develop the roof space, which will be deemed to belong to the roof.[4] If there is a possibility that the landlord will want to add further units to the building one day, then the roof should be excluded from the demise and the right expressly reserved to the landlord.

Express grant of easements and rights appurtenant to the demised premises

Following on from the description of the demised premises in the parcels clause will be a description of any easements or rights to be granted with the demise and any exceptions and reservations. Both of these are likely to

2 [1984] 1 EGLR 27 (CA).
3 [1962] 1 WLR 125.
4 *Haines* v *Florensa* [1990] 1 EGLR 73.

be found in separate schedules to the lease so as to keep the main part of the lease uncluttered.

Again, if the demise is of a self-contained building, these are not likely to be extensive or complicated, but the demise of a unit in a building will probably involve extensive rights and reservations. The tenant should be granted easements ensuring access, the supply of services through other parts of the building, and a right to enter on to other demised premises to carry out repairs.

An example of such a schedule granting rights to the tenant might be:

> "1. The right at all times during the term for the tenant its servants licensees and invitees in common with others authorised by the landlord—
>
> (a) to pass and repass over the common parts of the Building;
>
> (b) to the free passage and running of gas electricity water and soil and other services to and from the demised premises through and along the conduits forming part of the Building but not included in the demised premises and the right to make connections thereto;
>
> (c) to support and protection for the demised premises from the remainder of the Building;
>
> (d) after reasonable prior written notice by appointment during normal business hours (except in an emergency) to enter upon any part of the Building not hereby demised with or without workmen for the purpose of carrying out any repairs renewals maintenance or authorised alterations to the demised premises or any part thereof or the services thereto the tenant causing as little damage as possible and making good any damage so caused."

The schedule of reservations should include reciprocal rights of support, services and access for repairs reserved to the landlord and other tenants of the building.

It is probably wiser to list the rights which are intended to pass with the property rather than to add general words such as "together with the appurtenances thereto belonging", as this may have the effect of conferring rights which were never intended to pass. In *William Hill (Southern) Ltd v Cabras Ltd*[5], the lease demised the premises "together with appurtenances thereto." This was held to pass the right to display two signs over the door at ground floor level, which did not belong to the tenant. The lease also contained a general clause against the grant of easements, but this was held to be insufficient to allow the grantor to derogate from his grant by detracting from the specific grant of appurtenances.

Quite apart from any specific grant of access to adjoining premises, section 1(1), Access to Neighbouring Land Act 1992, gives a person a right of access to adjoining premises to carry out works reasonably necessary

---

for the preservation of his premises where it would be impossible, or substantially more difficult, to do so without access. This includes work to drains and cables, and to a party wall.[6]

In granting rights of access, one should consider potential annoyance to other tenants and possible security risks, and it may therefore be appropriate to limit such rights to certain hours. Unloading, particularly, may cause inconvenience to other tenants, and some restrictions on this may be desirable. In the development of a large site or shopping precinct, such matters may be dealt with in Regulations drawn up for the management of the centre which the tenant covenants to observe. It may be advisable to limit rights to access "on foot and with or without motor vehicles." This wording was sufficient in *White* v *Richards*[7] to exclude juggernauts from a narrow unmetalled roadway.

It should be remembered that the owner of a servient tenement, such as a right of access over which others enjoy an easement, is not liable for its upkeep[8] so that provision should be made in the lease for contribution to the upkeep of any access (if this is not to be done by the landlord and the cost recovered as part of the service charge). The following covenant by the tenant would cover this situation:

> "to contribute a fair proportion according to use of the cost of repairing and maintaining the access ways yards and gardens coloured blue on the plan attached hereto."

Although there will generally be no implied obligation on the landlord to maintain any access way, there may be an implied obligation to take reasonable care to maintain an access which is essential for enjoyment of the demised premises.[9]

It may be necessary to consider whether a right of access to a fire escape needs to be reserved or granted. Care should be taken to see that this is granted or reserved as an easement and not as a licence.[10] It will be binding upon future owners of the "servient" premises only if granted as an easement.

A new lease granted under the 1954 Act will include a right of way if this was appurtenant to the holding under the old lease, as is seen in *Nevill Long & Co (Boards) Ltd* v *Firmenich & Co*[11], where a right of way

---

6 *Dean* v *Walker* [1996] NPC 78.

7 [1993] RTR 318.

8 *Holden* v *White* [1982] QB 679.

9 *Liverpool City Council* v *Irwin* [1977] AC 239. The House of Lords' decision in this case was based on a requirement to give business efficacy to the grant of leases of flats in a building. The landlord's obligation is not an absolute one, however, but an obligation only to take reasonable care to maintain the access ways.

10 *IDC Group Ltd* v *Clarke* [1992] 2 EGLR 184 (discussed *infra*).

11 (1983) 47 P & CR 59.

appurtenant to the holding was held to be included in the new lease. It will not be appurtenant to the holding if the right of way was granted to the tenant under an entirely separate grant of the right of way itself, however, as in *Land Reclamation Co Ltd v Basildon DC*[12], where a right of way over a road was granted for a seven-year term quite separately from the lease of the holding, and was not therefore appurtenant to it.

The tenant should be granted an easement to use all services passing through other parts of the building or estate, subject to a similar reservation to the landlord and other tenants of services passing through the demised premises (see *supra*). This should include not only services presently installed, but any future services to be installed within 80 years.[13]

The tenant may also require the use of sanitary facilities. It was recognised in *Miller v Emcer Products Ltd*[14] that the use of a lavatory could be a valid easement and it is preferable that such rights are granted as easements in order to bind future owners. Even if the use of sanitary facilities is only granted to the tenant as a licence, it may amount to derogation from the landlord's grant to revoke the licence during the currency of the lease.[15]

Parking facilities may be covered by the inclusion in the demised premises of parking places in a central car park in the building or grounds. An alternative to individual parking spaces being included in the demise would be for the landlord to retain the car park and to grant easements over certain spaces to the tenants. The case of *Copeland v Greenhalf*[16] suggested that the right to park a car in a particular place could satisfy the requirements for an easement, and this has been confirmed by the Court of Appeal in *London & Blenheim Estates Ltd v Ladbroke Retail Parks Ltd*[17]. Alternatively, the tenant may be granted a licence to park in a common parking area, although presumably here some limitations as to the number and types of vehicles would have to be included. Following the principle of *White v Richards*[18], the wording of an easement of parking expressed to be for cars might not cover vans or lorries, and the tenant should consider whether car parking is sufficient.

The tenant will almost certainly want to put up a plate or advertising signs, and possibly directions to premises on an industrial estate. There is

---

12 [1979] 2 All ER 993.
13 Eighty years being the limit for the grant of a future interest in land: Perpetuities and Accumulations Act 1964, s 1.
14 [1956] Ch 304.
15 *Creedon v Collins* (1964) 191 EG 123.
16 [1952] Ch 488.
17 [1994] 1 WLR 31.
18 [1993] RTR 318 (mentioned *supra*).

unlikely to be any problem with regard to this if the sign is attached to the demised premises, although it will have to comply with the Town and Country Planning (Control of Advertisements) Regulations 1992 and the tenant must comply with any covenants in the lease as to alterations and user which could affect the right to put up signs, in addition to any covenant specifically dealing with it. If the sign is to be erected on a building or land not included in the demise however, then the tenant will require an easement for this. An example of this might be:

> "the right at all times to display and maintain in the entrance foyer or other entrance door a suitable sign of a size and kind first approved in writing by the landlord showing the tenant's trading name and directions for access to the tenant's premises."

The tenant should reserve the right to vary the sign. If the sign is to be affixed to the tenant's demised premises, then the landlord may wish to take a covenant from the tenant that he will first obtain the landlord's approval to the type and size of the sign.

Many, if not all, of the rights mentioned here could have been granted to the tenant by a licence. It is important to remember the difference between a licence and an easement. A licence is an agreement between two parties (the landlord and the tenant in this context) which is usually revocable and will only bind third parties in certain circumstances. An easement is an incorporeal hereditament – an interest in land which subsists through different ownerships – and, if legal or overriding, binds third parties. All easements derive from a grant, whether it is an express, implied or presumed grant. If there is no grant, but merely a licence, an easement will not have been created. This was the ruling in *IDC Group Ltd v Clarke*[19], which concerned a right of passage through a connecting door in a party wall to use a fire escape. Although granted in a deed and therefore capable of being a legal easement, it was held in essence to be a licence as this was how it described itself. The subsequent owner of the premises could not therefore claim damages against the successor in title of the adjoining premises when the connecting doorway was blocked up.

Implied grant of easements on a demise

As well as easements expressly granted in the lease, easements may be impliedly granted in certain circumstances, and the landlord should be particularly wary of this when granting a lease of part of premises. It is advisable to include a clause negating the inadvertent grant of easements in this way. The following clause would have this effect:

19 [1992] 2 EGLR 184.

"Nothing contained in this lease shall impliedly confer upon or grant to the tenant any easement, right or privilege other than those hereby expressly granted."

As well as easements of necessity such as access[20], the law may imply such easements as are deemed to be intended to give business efficacy to an agreement. These will generally be rights of support to a building, but may include other rights which satisfy the requirements for an easement. Thus, in *Wong* v *Beaumont Property Trust Ltd*[21], the tenant of restaurant premises in a basement was required by health regulations to have adequate ventilation. This necessarily entailed a ventilation shaft in the wall of the landlord's premises, and it was held that the tenant acquired an easement for this as it was necessary to give business efficacy to the lease of the premises, which could not be used as a restaurant without it.

The Court of Appeal decision in *Nickerson* v *Barraclough*[22] suggests that an express exclusion clause can also exclude easements of necessity.

Easements may also be impliedly granted to a tenant under the rule in *Wheeldon* v *Burrows*[23] if they were enjoyed by the demised property immediately prior to the demise and were continuous, apparent and reasonably necessary for the enjoyment of the demised premises. The rule applies to an agreement for a lease as well as a lease by deed.[24]

Probably most dangerous for a landlord, the Law of Property Act 1925, section 62, operates to pass with a conveyance of land all rights, liberties and privileges appurtenant to and enjoyed with it at the time of the conveyance. The section was intended to be a word-saving conveyancing section, but can in fact result in rights previously enjoyed only by licence becoming fully fledged easements. Thus in *Wright* v *Macadam*[25] a weekly tenant used a shed for storing coal. The landlord granted her a one-year lease in writing. It was held that section 62 operated to give the tenant an easement of storage. The lease was a legal lease[26], and therefore a "conveyance."[27] The section does not apply, however, to a contract for a lease, which is not a "conveyance" within the section. It will apply only if the demised premises and the servient tenement were separately occupied immediately prior to the lease[28], and will not apply if it is expressly

---

20 *Liverpool City Council* v *Irwin* [1977] AC 239.
21 [1965] 1 QB 173.
22 [1981] Ch 426.
23 (1879) 12 Ch D 31.
24 *Borman* v *Griffith* [1930] 1 Ch 493.
25 [1949] 2 KB 744.
26 LPA 1925, s 54(2).
27 *Ibid*, s 205(1)(ii) (definition).
28 *Long* v *Gowlett* [1923] 2 Ch 177 confirmed by the House of Lords in *Sovmots Investments Ltd* v *Secretary of State for the Environment* [1979] AC 144.

excluded. If it can be shown that there was a common intention or agreement to exclude the section, then it may be possible to obtain rectification of the lease after execution to exclude it.

Exceptions and reservations from the demised premises

Exceptions and reservations will also be included in the parcels clause of the lease, although again this may be done by reference to a schedule to the lease. Many of these will be the reciprocal rights which have been granted to the tenant, to which reference has already been made, including the right to use drains, pipes and services passing through the demised premises and any which may be installed within an expressed period of 80 years.[29] It is, important, however that they should be included, as the general principle that a grantor may not derogate from his grant will preclude any implied reservation except for easements of necessity, which may be limited to rights of access, and possibly intended easements.

In addition to the reservation of reciprocal rights, the landlord may wish to reserve the right to enter and view the state of repair of the premises or any landlord's fixtures (although where the landlord has covenanted to repair this right will be implied), or to erect a notice advertising the premises during the last six months of the tenancy. A precedent for the former right of entry, (which may be extended to include other tenants of the landlord's in the same building), might be:

> "To permit the landlord [and other tenants of the landlord's whose premises adjoin the demised premises] and its [and their] agents and workmen at any time during the term at reasonable hours in the daytime and upon prior notice to enter upon the demised premises for the purpose of inspecting the state of repair of the premises and the landlord's fixtures thereon."

A covenant by the tenant permitting the landlord to advertise the premises might be:

> "For a period of six months immediately preceding the determination of this lease to permit a noticeboard to be exhibited on some conspicuous part of the demised premises intimating that the same are to be let or sold."

If the lease is a sub-lease, the right should be reserved to the head-lessor to enter in order to comply with any of the covenants in the head-lease. The following clause would achieve this:

> "Any rights given to the landlord of entry upon the demised premises for the purpose of inspecting or executing any works to on or from the demised premises shall be deemed also to be given to every superior landlord and to

---

29 The limitation to a lawful period of perpetuity (which may comprise a specified period not exceeding 80 years) is necessary to comply with the rule against perpetuities: Perpetuities and Accumulations Act 1964, s 1(1).

agents workmen and others authorised by the landlord and any superior landlord."

If there is a possibility that the landlord will want to develop either the demised premises or adjoining premises at some time in the future, then the acquisition of any easement of light should be expressly negatived. Under the Prescription Act 1832, a tenant may acquire an easement of light against his landlord by twenty years' user; and he will do so if the right to build is not expressly reserved to the landlord. The right to erect scaffolding should be expressly reserved too, as this may otherwise be a trespass to the demised premises. It may in any event be an actionable nuisance, or an interruption of the landlord's express or implied covenant for quiet enjoyment.[30]

It would seem from *Haines v Florensa*[31] that if the landlord has included the roof in the demise of a top floor unit, he will not be able to build on any additional floors. If the landlord has this in mind as a possibility, then the roof and roof space should be excluded from any specific demises and the right to build up or convert the roof space specifically reserved.

THE TERM OF THE LEASE (*HABENDUM*)

The date on which the term granted by a tenancy commences (the term date) might not be the date of execution of the lease. Although the legal estate cannot come into existence before the date of execution of the lease (the execution date), the lease may back-date the term so that it is expressed to start before the execution date. If the tenant has been permitted to go into possession before the execution date, it may be appropriate to back-date the term to the date upon which the tenant moved into possession, so that the tenant's obligations (including the obligation to pay rent) run from that earlier date. Back-dating of the term may also be useful in order to ensure that the term can be expressed as a whole number of years.

A provision in a lease which relates to the measurement of time will prima facie be construed by reference to the term date.[32] Thus, subject to a contrary indication in the lease, the earlier date (the term date) will apply for the calculation of the term, the date of earlier termination under break-clauses[33], and the review date for rent reviews. Where the term commences before the date of execution and the tenant has not been in possession

---

30 *Owen v Gadd* [1956] 2 QB 99.
31 [1990] 1 EGLR 73 (mentioned *supra* note 4).
32 *Trane (UK) Ltd v Provident Mutual Life Assurance* [1995] 1 EGLR 33 (Ch).
33 *Bird v Baker* (1858) 1 E & E 12.

during the whole of the intervening period, the tenant's solicitor should ensure that the tenant is not made liable under the terms of the lease for the payment of rent or other sums, such as a service charge, for any period before the date on which the tenant took possession.

A provision in a lease (or in a statute) which depends upon the commencement of the legal estate will however be governed by whichever is the later of the term date or the execution date.[34]

Subject to indications to the contrary, a lease for a term of a particular length specified to commence "from" a particular date will commence at midnight at the end of that date. This principle seems to go back to the days when rent was traditionally paid in arrears, so that one would expect a term "from" Lady-day to include the Lady-day at the end of the term in order to include the tenant's obligation to pay the final quarter's rent due on that quarter-day.[35] Applying this principle, under a lease for a term of three years "from 29 September 1997", the expressed date (29 September 1997) is not included within the term; but 29 September 2000 is. The term of such a lease therefore expires at midnight at the end of 29 September 2000. To avoid doubt, it is best in all circumstances to state that the term commences "on" (or, less elegantly, "on and from", or "from and including") a particular date.

Nowadays rent is usually expressed to be payable in advance, and the court is more willing to infer from this and from other provisions in the lease that a lease expressed to commence "from" a particular day, commences at the first moment of that day.[36] The traditional presumption has, for instance, been held to be raised only where the date begins a term of a specified length. It does not apply, therefore, where the lease grants a term "from" a specified date "to" another specified date; here, the presumption is that both of these dates are included within the term.[37] Thus a term granted from 29 September 1997 to 28 September 1998 commences at the stroke of midnight at the beginning of 29 September 1997 and ends at the stroke of midnight at the end of 28 September 1998.

---

34 *Cadogan v Guiness* [1936] Ch 515.
35 See *Meadfield Properties Ltd v Secretary of State for the Environment* [1995] 1 EGLR 39 (Ch).
36 *Ladyman v Wirral Estates Ltd* [1968] 2 All ER 197 (Fisher J); *Whelton Sinclair v Hyland* [1992] 2 EGLR 158 (CA), (both concerning the validity of notices served under LTA 1954, Part II).
37 *Meadfield Properties Ltd v Secretary of State for the Environment* [1995] 1 EGLR 39.

COVENANTS

Some covenants will be implied into a lease without any express agreement between the parties. These covenants are implied by reason of the relationship of landlord and tenant and do not depend upon any particular wording as do the covenants for title in a conveyance. A "covenant" can only be implied into a lease by deed (being itself a contract by deed), but the same obligations will be implied into a lease not made by deed.[38]

Implied covenants of landlord

Covenant of non-derogation from grant

The covenant that a grantor may not derogate from his grant has a general applicability in property law and "embodies in a legal maxim a rule of common honesty"[39] that "a grantor having given such a thing with one hand is not to take away the means of enjoying it with the other."[40] The covenant underlies the principle that continuous and apparent quasi-easements pass to the grantee of part of a tenement.[41] It also explains why a vendor of part of a plot of land, or a lessor who retains premises adjoining those he has leased, may not generally claim by way of implied reservation an easement over the part retained. The only easements which a vendor or lessor may claim by way of implied reservation are easements of necessity, which may be limited to rights of access where there is no other means of access to the premises[42], and mutual easements of support of adjacent buildings.[43]

The doctrine of non-derogation from grant is not, however, restricted to easements.[44] A landlord will be in breach of his implied covenant of non-derogation from grant if, having granted a lease for a particular purpose, he uses the land retained by him "in such a way as to render the land granted or demised unfit or materially less fit for the particular purpose for which the grant or demise was made."[45] The implied covenant extends to the acts of the landlord's successors in title. In *Aldin v Latimer Clark*

---

38 *Baynes & Co v Lloyd & Sons* [1895] 2 QB 610.
39 *Harmer v Jumbil (Nigeria) Tin Areas Ltd* [1921] 1 Ch 200, 225, per Young LJ.
40 *Birmingham, Dudley and District Banking Co v Ross* (1888) 38 Ch D 295, 313, per Bowen LJ. See also *Johnston & Sons Ltd v Holland* [1988] 1 EGLR 264, 267 (Nicholls LJ); *Moulton Buildings Ltd v City of Westminster* (1975) 30 P & CR 182, 186 (Lord Denning MR).
41 *Wheeldon v Burrows* (1879) 12 Ch D 31.
42 *Nickerson v Barraclough* [1981] Ch 426 (CA).
43 *Richards v Rose* (1853) 9 Exch 218.
44 *Browne v Flower* [1910] 1 Ch 219, 224.
45 *Ibid*, at 225.

Muirhead & Co[46], the landlord had leased premises for use only as a timber yard which required a free flow of air to the timber. An assignee of the landlord was unable to build on the landlord's adjoining premises, so blocking the free flow of air, as to do so would have been to derogate from the grant.

A landlord who has leased units in a row or block or premises to different tenants may be in breach of the covenant of non-derogation from grant implied into the lease of tenant A if he does nothing to stop tenant B from committing acts of nuisance that make the premises materially less fit for the particular purpose for which the lease was granted to tenant A.

In *Chartered Trust plc* v *Davies*[47], the landlord had leased to the defendant a unit at the rear of a small shopping mall. The defendant carried on trade there selling puzzles and executive toys. The landlord subsequently leased the adjoining unit to another tenant who traded as a pawnbroker. Because only one customer at a time was permitted into the pawnbroker's shop, there were frequently six or more people waiting outside. Such persons were not likely to have the money to spend in the defendant's shop, and their presence along the passageway (which formed the only access to both units) tended to deter other persons from using it, thereby depriving the defendant of passing trade. The landlord maintained control over the common parts of the shopping mall; it had rule-making powers in relation to the development, and charged the tenants a service charge to finance the necessary management. Henry LJ emphasised that the central point was that it was clear from the circumstances surrounding the lease at the time that it was granted to the defendant, that the landlord was marketing not just a separate and independent retail unit, but a shop in its place in a shopping arcade. That was the particular purpose for which the premises had been leased. In these circumstances, the Court of Appeal held that the landlord was in breach of the covenant of non-derogation from grant because of its failure to stop the nuisance that rendered the defendant's premises materially less fit for the purpose for which they had been let. The court also rejected the landlord's argument that the defendant had the remedy of herself bringing an action against the pawnbroker. Henry LJ pointed out that litigation "is too expensive, too uncertain and offers no proper protection against, say, trespassing and threatening members of the public."

The covenant of non-derogation from grant will not be breached if the acts of the landlord, or his successor in title, whilst detracting from the profitability of the tenant's business, do not actually render the premises

---

46 [1894] 2 Ch 437.
47 [1997] 49 EG 135 (CA).

materially less fit for the purpose for which they were let. In *Port v Griffith*[48], the landlord had let shop premises for the specified use of the sale of wools and trimmings. He subsequently let adjoining premises for use as a tailor's and dressmaker's shop including the sale of cloth and trimmings. This did not interfere with the tenant's actual enjoyment of his property, and so was held not to amount to a breach of the covenant not to derogate from his grant.

By analogy, a landlord could probably not be held to be liable for breach of the implied covenant where tenants in a shopping centre suffer loss of profit owing to the closure in breach of covenant of the centre's "anchor" store.[49] A prospective tenant of a unit in a shopping centre might therefore consider trying to obtain from the landlord an express covenant, where the anchor store closes, to use his best endeavours to re-let the premises as soon as is reasonably practicable.

The covenant of non-derogation from grant will also not be breached if the tenant's user of the premises is extraordinarily sensitive (provided, of course, that the premises have not been leased expressly for the sensitive purpose).

Covenant for quiet enjoyment

A lease confers exclusive possession on the tenant, and a landlord's covenant for quiet enjoyment is designed to protect such possession, as well as to prevent substantial interference by the landlord, or by those claiming under the landlord, with the tenant's ordinary lawful enjoyment of the premises. Like the covenant not to derogate from his grant, the covenant for quiet enjoyment will be implied into the lease if it is not actually expressed. Since the Law of Property (Covenants for Title) Act 1994, this covenant is not implied by a grant or assignment "with full title guarantee". It is, however, implied by the common law[50], but to avoid all doubt, it may be advisable for the tenant to take an express covenant. One of the advantages of an express covenant is that it may cover the acts of a head-lessor as well as the immediate landlord if the definition clause in the lease includes such a person.[51] Many formal leases will however include an express covenant, making it dependent upon the tenant's obligations as follows:

> "That the tenant paying the rent and observing and performing the tenant's covenants herein contained shall be permitted peaceably to hold and enjoy

---

48 [1938] 1 All ER 295; applied in *Romulus Trading Co Ltd v Comet Properties Ltd* [1996] 2 EGLR 70.
49 See further Chap 8.
50 *Budd-Scott v Daniell* [1902] 2 KB 351.
51 *Queensway Marketing Ltd v Associated Restaurants Ltd* [1988] 2 EGLR 49 (CA).

the premises herein demised without interruption or disturbance by the
landlord or any person claiming under or in trust for the landlord."

The covenant extends to physical interference with the demised premises
and the acts complained of may also give the tenant grounds for an action
in tort for nuisance, or possibly even trespass. In the case of residential
premises, the acts may amount to harassment which is an offence giving
rise to an action for criminal compensation.[52]

Examples of breach of the covenant are the erection of scaffolding
outside the tenant's shop interfering with his business[53] (although not the
erection of a fire escape outside the tenant's window[54] which was held
merely to be an interference with his privacy rather than his enjoyment of
the premises), extensive construction work over a considerable period on
the landlord's adjoining premises[55], and the tiling of a roof terrace on the
flat above so that the tenant of the flat below suffered constant noise from
footsteps on the terrace.[56]

Although the covenant extends to the lawful acts of a person claiming
under the landlord, it will not extend to the unlawful acts of such a
person[57], although the tenant might well have an action in tort against such
a person. Nor will the implied covenant extend to the acts of a person with
a superior title to the landlord, such as the freehold owner, or a
predecessor in title.[58]

The wording of an express covenant for quiet enjoyment may however,
extend the covenant to the acts of a sub-tenant's head-lessor, as well as to
the acts of the sub-lessor itself. In *Queensway Marketing Ltd* v *Associated
Restaurants Ltd*[59] a covenant for quiet enjoyment by a sub-lessor was held
to extend to the acts of its lessor as the "landlord" in the sub-lease was
defined as including any superior lessor. This could also be achieved by
adding the words "or by title paramount" to the foregoing covenant. If,
however, the covenant is not so extended, or if it is merely an implied
covenant, it will cover the acts only of the landlord, and not those of the
landlord's superiors in title.[60]

The tenant's remedies for breach of the covenant are damages and an
injunction. The damages may cover loss of income because the tenant is

---

52 Protection from Eviction Act 1977, s 1.
53 *Owen* v *Gadd* [1956] 2 All ER 28.
54 *Browne* v *Flower* [1911] 1 Ch 219.
55 *Mira* v *Aylmer Square Investments Ltd* (1990) 22 HLR 182.
56 *Sampson* v *Hodson-Pressinger* [1982] 1 EGLR 50 (CA). For more recent cases involving
   noise, see *Baxter* v *Camden LBC* [1997] 20 June (unreported, Lexis Transcript)(CA), and
   Southwark LBC v *Mills* [1998] *The Times* 11 March (Laddie J).
57 *Sanderson* v *Berwick on Tweed Corporation* (1834) 5 QBD 547.
58 *Celsteel Ltd* v *Alton House Holdings Ltd (No 2)* [1987] 1 WLR 291.
59 [1988] 2 EGLR 49 (CA).
60 *Celsteel Ltd* v *Alton House Holdings Ltd (No 2)* [1986] 1 WLR 666; affirmed [1987] 1
   WLR 291.

unable to sub-let at a rent owing to interference by the landlord's construction operations.[61]

Implied covenants of tenant

As to state of the demised premises

Commercial leases are usually fairly lengthy documents which will make specific provision for the repair of the demised premises and, if the demised premises are a unit in a larger building, for the building of which they form part. This will be the position in a fixed-term tenancy.

In the absence of any express covenant by the tenant to repair, the tenant will only be liable for waste and to use the premises in a tenant-like manner. All tenants are liable for voluntary waste (acts of commission), which, as well as wanton destruction, may also include ameliorating acts, although the landlord's damages for any such acts are likely to be minimal. Fixed-term tenants and most periodic tenants are also liable for permissive waste, which is damage to the premises caused by neglect. A weekly tenant is not liable however and his only implied obligation is to use the premises in a tenant-like manner.[62]

Waste is a tortious act, so the landlord may sue a third party, with whom he has no contractual relationship at all, for damages for waste.[63]

Implied obligation to allow landlord to enter and view the state of repair

There is generally no obligation on a tenant to allow the landlord entry to the demised premises, as the tenant has exclusive possession. Where, however, the landlord has covenanted to repair, or there is an implied obligation on the landlord to carry out repairs, then there is a corresponding implied covenant by the tenant to allow the landlord to enter and view the state of repair.[64]

Obligation to pay rates and taxes

The tenant, as occupier of the premises, will be liable to pay any rates and taxes levied on the occupier of the premises unless, of course, the terms of the lease provide otherwise. Most commercial leases will include an express covenant by the tenant to pay rates and taxes.

---

61 *Mira v Aylmer Square Investments Ltd* (1990) 22 HLR 182.
62 *Warren v Keen* [1953] 2 All ER 1116.
63 See Chap 7.
64 *Mint v Good* [1950] 2 All ER 1159.

Implied condition that the tenant will not deny the landlord's title

A denial of the landlord's title by the tenant is a ground for forfeiture, even if the denial is contained in a pleading in an action involving a third party[65]. Relief against forfeiture is still available to a tenant in such an action.[66]

The usual covenants

Sometimes a contract for a lease will simply provide that the lease is to include "the usual covenants." This is not a shorthand phrase for a specific list of covenants, and the covenants which will be "usual" will vary from one period to another and according to the type of premises leased. In *Chester* v *Buckingham Travel Ltd*[67], Foster J heard evidence from conveyancing experts as to what covenants might be usual for a lease of garage premises. An agreement for a lease with "the usual covenants" had been made some years before but the lease had never been executed. Foster J considered the earlier case of *Hampshire* v *Wickens*[68] but decided that in the period since 1878, when that case had been decided, it had become possible to add to the covenants which had then been considered usual. In addition to the tenant's covenants to pay rent, rates and taxes and to deliver up the premises in repair at the end of the term, he found that covenants not to alter the premises, not to cause a nuisance or annoyance or to interfere with easements, and not to use the premises for any purpose other than a garage and workshop without the landlord's consent were also usual in the circumstances. The lease in this case was of premises which were part only of larger premises. He held that a covenant not to assign without the landlord's consent was not a usual one, but a proviso for re-entry for non-payment of rent or for breach of any other covenant was.

Express covenants

Most commercial leases will contain a number of express covenants by the tenant and some by the landlord. The effect of the typical covenants found in commercial leases will be considered in later chapters of this book.

PROVISOS, OPTIONS AND DECLARATIONS

The lease will always contain a proviso for forfeiture in the event of non-payment of the rent or breach of any of the tenant's covenants. Without

---

65 *W G Clark (Properties) Ltd* v *Dupre Properties Ltd* [1992] 1 All ER 596.
66 LPA 1925, s 146(2).
67 [1981] 3 All ER 386.
68 (1878) 7 Ch 555.

such a proviso, the landlord has no right of forfeiture.[69]

There may also be a proviso for the cessation or suspension of rent in the event of the premises being destroyed or being rendered unusable. Without such a proviso, rent is still payable.

There may be declarations as to party walls between the tenant's and the landlord's adjoining premises and declarations as to how and what shall constitute service of notices under the lease. Sometimes provision is made for the resolution of any disputes by arbitration, and this is usually so in the case of a dispute on rent review.

The lease may also contain a break clause allowing the tenant to terminate the lease by notice after a certain time[70], or options for the tenant to renew the lease or to purchase the landlord's freehold reversion.[71]

EXECUTION OF THE LEASE

In order to create a legal lease, the document must be a deed, and so has to be signed or otherwise validly executed and delivered as a deed by all parties to it in the manner prescribed by law.[72]

For a document to be validly executed as a deed by an individual, it must be both signed by him as a deed in the presence of a witness who attests the signature[73] and also delivered as a deed by him or by a person authorised to do so on his behalf.[74]

For a document to be validly executed as a deed by a corporation, it must be executed by the corporation and make it clear on its face that it is intended to be a deed. Execution may be effected by affixing the common seal[75]; alternatively, it may be effected by the signature of a director and the secretary, or by two directors, and expressed (in whatever form of words) to be executed by the company.[76] A document executed by a company which makes it clear on its face that it is intended by the person or persons making it to be a deed has effect, upon delivery, as a deed; and it is presumed, unless a contrary intention is proved, to be delivered upon its being so executed.[77]

---

69 Forfeiture is considered in Chap 13.

70 See Chap 12.

71 See Chap 1 and pp. 113–114 *infra*.

72 LP(MP)A 1989, s 1(2); Companies Act 1985, s 36A (inserted by Companies Act 1989, s 130(2)). The formalities contained in both of these sets of provisions apply to documents executed after 31 July 1990.

73 Alternatively, it may be signed as a deed at his direction and in his presence and the presence of two witnesses who each attest the signature: LP(MP)A 1989, s 1(3).

74 LP(MP)A 1989, s 1(3).

75 Companies Act 1985, s 36A(2).

76 *Ibid*, s 36A(4).

77 *Ibid*, s 36A(5).

An agent may deliver an instrument as a deed for another (whether an individual or a corporation) without the need for the authorisation to be itself by deed.[78]

FIXTURES ON THE DEMISED PREMISES

Fixtures are chattels which lose their identity as chattels and become part of the premises. It is not always easy to decide whether any particular object is or is not a fixture, but there are two tests which may be applied to assist in determining this.

First, is the object physically attached to the premises or to the land? If it is, then *prima facie* it will be a fixture. This is particularly so if it cannot be removed without substantially damaging the premises. If the chattel stands on the land by its own weight, however, then *prima facie* it will not be a fixture. For example, printing machines standing on the floor of a factory were held not to be fixtures, despite being connected to an electricity supply on the premises.[79]

This test is not, however, conclusive. If the object is attached, it is then necessary to ask, secondly, for what purpose it was attached. Was it attached to improve the building, or was it attached merely for the better enjoyment of the chattel? In *Leigh v Taylor*[80] tapestries were fixed to a wall; but it was held that they did not become fixtures as they had been attached, not in order to improve the building, but rather so that they could be enjoyed. A contrary conclusion was reached in *D'Eyncourt v Gregory*[81], where garden ornaments and statues forming part of the landscaping of a garden, although not attached at all, were held to be fixtures because they were an essential feature of the garden.

In the recent case of *Elitestone Ltd v Morris*[82], the House of Lords followed a three-fold classification of objects on land in *Woodfall, Landlord and Tenant*[83], which recognises that certain objects may become part of the realty not by becoming fixtures but by being part of the hereditament itself. In that case, a bungalow which had been built some 50 years previously was not attached to the land, but merely rested on the land on brick piers. It was, however, impossible to remove the bungalow as a unit; and any attempt to do so would have resulted in its destruction.

---

78 LP(MP)A 1989, s 1(1)(c).
79 *Hulme v Brigham* [1943] KB 152; see also *TSB Bank plc v Botham* [1996] EGCS 149 (CA).
80 [1902] AC 187.
81 (1866) LR 3 Eq 382.
82 [1997] 2 All ER 513.
83 Release 36 (1994) Vol 1, 13/83, para 13.131.

Lord Lloyd said that:

> "a house which is constructed in such a way that it cannot be removed at all, save by destruction, cannot have been intended to remain as a chattel. It must have been intended to form part of the realty."[84]

Lord Clyde referred to the possibility in such cases of a chattel becoming part of the "inheritance" in Scots law, and both their Lordships approved Blackburn J's example in *Holland v Hodgson*[85] that

> "blocks of stone placed one on the top of another without any mortar or cement for the purpose of forming a dry stone wall would become part of the land, though the same stones, if deposited in a builder's yard and for convenience sake stacked on the top of each other in the form of a wall, would remain chattels."

Both their Lordships also rejected the plaintiff's contention that the licence fee paid for the land and not for the bungalow prevented the bungalow from becoming part of the land. Although intention as to the purpose of annexation or otherwise is relevant, the intention must be judged objectively and "no man can make his property real or personal by merely thinking it is so."[86]

In the *Elitestone* case, the House of Lords reversed the Court of Appeal, which had held that the bungalow was a chattel. One of the reasons for the Court of Appeal's decision had been its drawing an analogy with a large shed resting on land[87] and a market-garden greenhouse which the vendor of property had used for his business[88], both of which had been held to be chattels and so removable.

Removal of tenant's fixtures

It has always been recognised that it could be unfair to deprive a tenant of expensive fixtures which he may have attached to the demised premises, and which have therefore become part of the property. For this reason, a tenant may remove certain tenant's fixtures, including trade fixtures, at the end of a lease.

Trade fixtures are those objects which the tenant has attached to the premises for the purposes of his trade or business, and they have been very liberally construed by the courts in favour of a tenant. They have been held to include plant and machinery and shop fittings, extractor fans[89] and

---

84 *Elitestone Ltd v Morris* [1997] 2 All ER 513, 519.
85 (1872) LR 7 CP 328, 335.
86 *Dixon v Fisher* (1843) 5 D 775, 793, per Lord Cockburn.
87 *Webb v Frank Bovis Ltd* [1940] 1 All ER 247.
88 *Deen v Andrews* [1986] 1 EGLR 262.
89 *Mancetter Developments Ltd v Garmanson Ltd* [1986] QB 1212.

petrol pumps[90] (even though these last were bolted to the petrol tanks below, as they were capable of being severed from the tanks without damage).

The tenant must make good any damage caused by the removal of the fixtures and will be liable for the tort of waste if he does not do so.[91]

The tenant may remove tenant's fixtures at any time before the termination of the tenancy, and within a reasonable time after its termination. This is the position if the lease provides expressly that he may remove them at the end of the tenancy, or if the notice required to terminate the tenancy is very short, as in the case of a tenancy at will, or a weekly tenancy. It was said in *Smith v City Petroleum Co Ltd*[92] that where a week's notice was all that was required to terminate a tenancy, so that it was impossible for the tenant to remove the fixtures before the tenancy terminated, then he could still remove them within a reasonable time afterwards. If he fails to do so, however, the fixtures become the property of the landlord and cannot be claimed by a subsequent tenant who takes over the business.

The provision to allow the tenant to remove tenant's fixtures is usually inserted by way of exception in the part of the lease which requires the tenant to yield up the premises at the end of the term. It would appear in a tenant's covenant as follows:

> "To yield up the demised premises at the expiration or sooner determination of the term together with all additions and landlord's fixtures but excepting all tenant's fixtures."

In *New Zealand Government Property Corporation v HM & S Ltd*[93], the tenants of Her Majesty's Theatre in the Haymarket had installed seating and other fixtures during the currency of a 72-year lease which terminated on 30 September 1970. The tenants remained in occupation at the end of the lease and applied for a new tenancy under the 1954 Act, which was granted in 1973 to run for 21 years from 1 October 1970. In 1977 it was necessary to determine a new rent under a rent-review clause in the new tenancy, and a dispute ensued as to whether the tenants' fixtures should be taken into account for this purpose. If the tenants had lost the right to remove the fixtures, so that they had become landlord's fixtures, then it was proper that they should be taken into account as part of the demised premises in determining the open market rent. If, however, they remained tenants' fixtures, then they should be disregarded. It was held that a tenant

---

90 *Smith v City Petroleum Co Ltd* [1940] 1 All ER 260.
91 *Mancetter* above, discussed fully in Chap 7.
92 [1940] 1 All ER 260.
93 [1982] QB 1145.

has a right to remove fixtures at any time during which he remains in possession of the demised premises, including the period of a new lease under the 1954 Act. The fixtures therefore remained tenants' fixtures and fell to be disregarded for the purposes of a rent review. Lord Denning MR also expressed the opinion that the "improvements" to be taken into account in fixing a rent on a new tenancy under the Act were improvements by the tenant to the landlord's fixtures and not to the tenant's fixtures.

RECTIFICATION

If both parties to the lease recognise that it contains a mistake, they can correct it themselves by contractual agreement or by jointly executing a deed of rectification; but if one party resists, an action for rectification will be necessary. The equitable remedy of rectification may be obtained where the lease contains a mutual mistake in that it fails (whether through incompetence of drafting or some other mistake) to give effect to the parties' common intention.[94] The mistake may be a failure to give effect to the terms of a prior contract; but the availability of rectification is not dependent upon the existence of an antecedent contract that is both complete and valid.[95] On the other hand, "a continuing common intention is not sufficient unless it has found expression in outward agreement"[96], which might be appropriately described as an accord.[97]

---

94 *Jervis v Howle & Talke Colliery Co Ltd* [1937] 1 Ch 67 (Clauson J); *City of Westminster Properties (1934) Ltd v Mudd* [1959] Ch 129; *Co-operative Insurance Society Ltd v Centremoor Ltd* [1983] 2 EGLR 52, 55 (Dillon LJ). Particular care needs to be taken when the lease is prepared from a precedent to adapt the terms as necessary: a cautionary tale is *Boots the Chemist Ltd v Street* [1983] 2 EGLR 50 (Falconer J). Here the parties had agreed a term for 25 years with five-yearly rent reviews, but the lease provided for reviews in the seventh and 14th years; this came about because the travelling draft lease was insufficiently adapted from a lease for a term of 21 years which had itself provided for rent review in the seventh and 14th years. Nowadays, the danger is often in failing to amend a precedent contained on a computerised data-base. Much of the litigation on rectification of leases involves rent-review clauses, which may reflect both the importance of such clauses to the parties and the comparative ease with which mistakes can creep into rent provisions particularly where they need to be dove-tailed with similar provisions in sub-leases: see, *e.g. Yorkshire Metropolitan Properties Ltd v Co-operative Retail Services Ltd* [1997] EGCS 57 (Neuberger J). The mistake can arise from an attempt to express in a form of words what might more clearly be expressed in a simple formula: *London Regional Transport v Wimpey Group Services Ltd* [1986] 2 EGLR 41, 42 (Hoffmann J).
95 *Joscelyne v Nissen* [1970] 2 QB 86.
96 *Ibid* at 98, (Russell LJ, approving, subject to this qualification, the dictum of Simonds J in *Crane v Hegeman-Harris Co Inc* [1939] 1 All ER 662, 664); *Frederick Rose v William H Pim Junior & Co Ltd* [1953] 2 QB 450, 461–2 (Denning LJ).
97 *Yorkshire Metropolitan Properties Ltd v Co-operative Retail Services Ltd* [1997] EGCS 57 (Neuberger J), a case of mutual mistake.

Rectification can sometimes be obtained where the mistake is unilateral. If one party, A, is aware[98] both that the lease does not contain what has been mutually agreed and that the other party, B, is labouring under the mistake that it does, but, instead of bringing the mistake (which is to A's advantage) to the notice of B, A allows B to execute the lease, A will be estopped from resisting B's action for rectification on the ground that the mistake was unilateral and not common.[99]

When the court is asked to rectify an instrument, the extent of the rectification (though not necessarily the exact words) must be clearly ascertained and defined by evidence contemporaneous with or anterior to the instrument[1]; no evidence of *ex post facto* intention can be admitted.[2] The standard of proof is at least the normal civil standard, namely the balance of probabilities, but it has been pointed out that "the use of a variety of formulations used to express the degree of certainty ... is not very helpful and may, indeed, be confusing."[3] The courts have said that they are looking for convincing proof[4], and that the evidence to support the claim must be "of the clearest and most satisfactory description."[5] The standard of proof may therefore be higher according to the nature of the facts to be established (which may often involve deciding between strongly conflicting evidence) and the circumstances of the case.[6] Rectification will be ordered only of the instrument giving effect to the bargain between the

---

98 A will have imputed to him the knowledge of his agent: *Kemp v Neptune Concrete Ltd* [1988] 2 EGLR 87, 90 (Purchas LJ), applying a dictum of Browne-Wilkinson V-C in *Strover v Harrington* [1988] 1 All ER 769, 779.
99 *Thomas Bates & Son v Wyndham's (Lingerie) Ltd* [1981] 1 WLR 505 (rectification of lease granted inserting an arbitration clause previously agreed). In that case, Buckley LJ (at 515) indicated that fraud is not required: relief depends "more on the equity of the position". In deciding this, Buckley LJ preferred the view of Pennycuick J in *Roberts (A) & Co Ltd v Leicestershire County Council* [1961] Ch 555, 570, to that expressed by Russell LJ in *Riverplate Properties Ltd v Paul* [1975] Ch 133, 140, who had considered that sharp practice was essential. See also *Central & Metropolitan Estates v Compusave* [1983] 1 EGLR 60; and *Kemp v Neptune Concrete Ltd* [1988] 2 EGLR 87, 90, where Purchas LJ expressed the requirement as "unconscionable behaviour."
1 *Bradford (Earl) v Romney (Earl)* (1862) 30 Beav 431; *Central & Metropolitan Estates v Compusave* [1983] 1 EGLR 60, 64 (Gerald Godfrey QC, sitting as a deputy judge of the Chancery Division), a case of unilateral mistake, but the rule applies equally to cases of common mistake.
2 *Kemp v Neptune Concrete Ltd* [1988] 2 EGLR 87, 90 (Purchas LJ), a case of unilateral mistake.
3 *Thomas Bates & Son v Wyndham's (Lingerie) Ltd* [1981] 1 WLR 505 (Buckley LJ), a case of unilateral mistake.
4 *Equity & Law Life Assurance Society Ltd v Coltness Group Ltd* [1983] 2 EGLR 118, 119 (Whitford J), a case of mutual mistake.
5 *Fowler v Fowler* (1859) 1 De G&J 250, per Lord Chelmsford LC.
6 *Thomas Bates & Son v Wyndham's (Lingerie) Ltd* [1981] 1 WLR 505 (Buckley LJ).

parties: in no circumstances will rectification be ordered of the bargain itself.[7]

Rectification is a discretionary remedy that may in appropriate circumstances be refused, or awarded only if the plaintiff submits to terms laid down by the court. The plaintiff's claim for rectification is rarely barred by the fact that the mistake occurred through his own negligence, or through that of his agent[8]; but the plaintiff's conduct can be taken into account in determining the terms of the order. The point is well-illustrated in *Central Metropolitan Estates* v *Compusave*.[9] The parties had agreed a rent for the first five years of a 20-year term and had agreed that thereafter it was to be subject to review, but had not specified any formula. The lease mistakenly contained no rent-review clause, and the landlord sought rectification against the tenant (who had been aware of the mistake). The court was prepared to grant the remedy, and ordered that the lease be rectified by the insertion of a rent-review provision (to operate at the end of the fifth year of the term) for a "fair and reasonable rent" to be fixed by the court. As the mistake arose through the landlord's own negligence, however, the order was made on the terms that the rectified lease also included a tenant's right to break at the end of the fifth year.

A right to rectification passes to successors in title of the landlord[10] or the tenant. The right to rectification being a mere equity, it does not, where the title is unregistered, bind a purchaser for value (even of a mere equitable interest[11]) without notice[12]; but, if the title is registered, it may be binding as an overriding interest if the plaintiff is in actual occupation.[13] A landlord bringing rectification proceedings should join as a party to the

---

7 *Harlow Development Corporation* v *Kingsgate (Clothing Productions) Ltd* (1973) 226 EG 1960.

8 *Weeds* v *Blaney* [1978] 2 EGLR 84 (CA) (rectification of a conveyance of a freehold); *Boots the Chemist Ltd* v *Street* [1983] 2 EGLR 50.

9 [1983] 1 EGLR 60.

10 LPA 1925, s 63(1); *Boots the Chemist Ltd* v *Street* [1983] 2 EGLR 50 (Falconer J), in that case, a successor in title of the landlord.

11 *Taylor Barnard Ltd* v *Tozer* [1984] 1 EGLR 21, 22 (Judge Thomas, sitting as a deputy judge of the Chancery Division), where the landlord's right to rectify was, however, held to be binding on the purchaser of the lease under a contract to assign; since, although the purchaser had no notice of the equity when he entered the contract, he had not at that date paid the purchase money in full, and so was not a purchaser for value: *Tourville* v *Naish* (1734) 3 P Wms 307.

12 *Smith* v *Jones* [1954] 1 WLR 1089 (Upjohn J); *Equity & Law Life Assurance Society Ltd* v *Coltness Group Ltd* [1983] 2 EGLR 118.

13 LRA 1925, s 70(1)(g); *Blacklocks* v *JB Developments (Godalming) Ltd* [1982] Ch 183; see Farrand [1983] Conv 169, 257; Barnsley, "Rectification, Trusts and Overriding Interests" [1983] Conv 361.

action any person who joined in the lease as guarantor; failing which the court may award the landlord his remedy only upon his giving an undertaking not to enforce against the guarantor the lease as rectified.[14]

---

14 *Stavrides v Manku* [1997] EGCS 58 (Vinelott J), where crucial parts of the rent-review clause had mistakenly been left blank.

Chapter 4

PARTIES TO A LEASE AND SURETIES

THE PARTIES TO A LEASE

Definition of the parties

The lease will start, as any other deed, by setting out the parties. There will usually be an interpretation clause somewhere in the lease which will provide that:

> "In this Lease, unless the context indicates otherwise, the masculine shall include the feminine, the singular shall include the plural, and words denoting a person shall include a corporation or other entity."

A lease will usually define the parties by stating that the terms "landlord" and "tenant" shall, where the context so admits, include their successors and assigns. This will be particularly important for the passing of the benefit of non-touching and concerning covenants in pre-1996 leases; and, in *Griffith v Pelton*[1], the benefit of an option to purchase the reversion on a lease passed to an assignee of the tenant where the lease stated:

> "The lessee" which expression shall include her executors, administrators and assigns where the context so admits.

In *Queensway Marketing Ltd v Associated Restaurants Ltd*[2] a sub-tenant successfully sued its immediate landlord for a breach of a covenant for quiet enjoyment in the sub-lease caused by the actions of the head-lessor. The lease contained a covenant for quiet enjoyment by "the landlord or any person or persons lawfully claiming through, under, or in trust for the landlord", and further provided that "the landlord" included "the successors in title of the landlord, and shall be deemed to include the superior lessors." It was held that the express covenant in the sub-lease extended to the actions of a superior lessor.

One of the essential characteristics of a lease (as has previously been mentioned[3]) is a reversion immediately expectant upon the term granted,

---

1 [1958] Ch 205.
2 [1988] 2 EGLR 49 (CA).
3 See Chap 1.

and the House of Lords held in *Rye v Rye*[4] that the tenant and the reversioner must be different persons. It is not therefore possible for A to grant a valid lease to himself: "it is meaningless to say that a man accepts from himself something which is already his own"[5], and such a grant would be both "fanciful and whimsical."[6] It is similarly not possible for A and B to grant a lease of property to themselves as joint tenants.[7] Even if a leasehold estate were created in such circumstances, there would be nothing to prevent its at once merging into the higher estate from which it had sprung.[8] Quite apart from this, Viscount Simonds has pointed out the difficulties that would arise were an estate to be created[9]:

> "Even a bare devise implies certain covenants at law; but to such an estate as this no covenants can be effectively attached. Nor can the common law remedy of distress operate to enable the lessor to distrain on his own goods. Again, at law in the absence of some special provision the lessee is entitled to exclusive possession of the demised premises. What meaning is to be attributed to this where the lessee is also the lessor?"

The Court of Appeal has held that it is also not possible for a nominee to grant a valid lease in favour of his principal on the ground that, as a lease is a contract, it is subject to the rule that there cannot be a valid contract between a principal and his nominee concerning the property which is the subject-matter of the nomineeship.[10] In a dissenting judgment, however, Millett LJ considered that such a grant would be valid at common law. In his view, the objection that the nominee would be precluded in equity from enforcing the leasehold covenants against his principal was not a substantive bar, but merely a procedural one.[11]

A may grant a lease of his own land to himself and B jointly.[12] Similarly, A and B, the joint owners of land, may validly lease it to A only.[13] In either case, the covenants, whether express or implied, entered into by A with

4 [1962] AC 496.
5 *Ibid,* at 505 (per Viscount Simonds).
6 *Grey v Ellison* (1856) 1 Giff 438, 444 (Stuart V-C).
7 *Rye v Rye* [1962] AC 496, in which the House of Lords rejected the argument that the position at common law had been changed by LPA 1925, s 72(3).
8 *Ibid,* at 505 (Viscount Simonds).
9 *Ibid,* at 505.
10 *Ingram v IRC* [1997] 4 All ER 395 (CA), following *Kildrummy (Jersey) Ltd v IRC* [1990] STC 657 (Court of Session). On the reasoning of the majority, it also follows that a principal could not grant a valid lease in favour of his nominee.
11 *Ingram v IRC* [1997] 4 All ER 395, 423–428, especially 424, referring to *Hirachand Punamchand v Temple* [1911] 2 KB 330. Another analogy might be drawn with *Re Kay's Settlement* [1939] Ch 329. It should be noted that the Court of Appeal in *Ingram v IRC* granted the executors leave to appeal to the House of Lords.
12 LPA 1925, s 72(1), since a lease is in this context a "conveyance", and the sub-section applies to "personal property, including chattels real."
13 *Ibid,* s 72(4).

himself and B are enforceable as if they had been entered into with B alone.[14]

Different legal entities as landlord

If the landlord dies, the reversion will vest in his personal representatives, who will then vest it in the person entitled under his will or on his intestacy. The personal representatives and the person entitled will have the same rights and obligations as an assignee of the reversion.[15]

If the landlord is two or more persons, then the most desirable situation from the tenant's point of view is that they should covenant jointly and severally; but statute provides for this effect[16], so far as a contrary intention is not expressed.[17]

If the landlord is a company, a company search will disclose its financial position, whether the property is vested in it and not in a parent company, and if it has the power to grant a lease.

Different legal entitles as tenant

Individual

If the tenant is an individual, the term will pass to his personal representatives on his death (who will vest it in the person entitled under his will or on his intestacy) or to his trustee in bankruptcy if he should become insolvent. Neither of these devolutions will involve a breach of a covenant against assignment.

The trustee in bankruptcy may disclaim the lease[18] or he may assign it. Any assignment by him is however subject to any covenant which the lease may contain against assignment without consent.

Co-owners

If the tenant is two or more co-owners, covenants should be made by them jointly and severally so that the landlord may sue all or any of them, although the legal title cannot be vested in more than four co-owners.[19]

Partners

The most usual situation where there are co-owner tenants is where

14 *Ibid*, s 82(1).
15 See Chap 5.
16 LPA 1925, s 81(1).
17 *Ibid*, s 81(3).
18 See Chap 14.
19 LPA 1925, s 34, as amended by Trusts of Land and Appointment of Trustees Act 1996, Sch 2, para 3.

partners take a lease. Although the Partnership Act 1890, section 9, provides that all partners are liable for the partnership debts, it is desirable to include any partners in whom the legal estate is not vested as parties to the lease as guarantors. From the landlord's point of view, it saves his having to prove the partnership and that the premises are partnership property in any action by him, and liability can be clearly stated to be both joint and several. From the tenants' point of view, if one of the partners in whom the legal estate is vested dies, the landlord would find it difficult to object to an assignment vesting the lease in a partner whom he had previously accepted as a guarantor. It might also be preferable to have a partner liable as a tenant rather than as a guarantor, as it appears that payment by a guarantor might be regarded as payment under a contractual obligation rather than of rent, and that acceptance of any sum by the landlord from the guarantor might not therefore discharge the tenants' liability, in which case the landlord (subject to the possibility of waiver) would not be precluded from subsequently seeking to forfeit the lease in respect of the breach.[20]

From the tenant's point of view, there are disadvantages in having the lease in the name of one partner only. In the event of his death, the property will devolve through his personal representatives instead of passing automatically to the surviving partners by the right of survivorship. Also the provisions in the Landlord and Tenant Act 1954, section 41A, as to the service of notices with regard to a new tenancy, will not apply.

A provision for relaxation of any covenant requiring consent to an assignment in the case of assignment to a partner is desirable from the tenant's point of view to allow for changes in the partnership. The landlord may be reluctant to agree to this, however, as it could be used as a means of evading the consent covenant altogether – two assignments could effectively change the ownership completely. Difficulties with regard to obtaining consent to assign may possibly be avoided anyway by one partner allowing the partnership to use the premises, or to share the premises with him. Such an arrangement would still be a breach of a covenant against parting with possession of the whole or any part of the premises – a very usual addition to a covenant against assigning or subletting. It will not be a breach of a covenant against assignment if one partner remains in possession after dissolution of a partnership unless there is an assignment to that partner alone.

---

20 See *London & County (A & D) Ltd* v *Wilfred Sportsman Ltd* [1971] Ch 764 (CA); *Milverton Group Ltd* v *Warner World Ltd* [1995] 2 EGLR 28 (CA); and *Romain* v *Scuba TV* [1996] 2 All ER 377 (CA), discussed further *infra* and in Chap 5.

Where a partnership has been dissolved, the court can, if necessary, compel joint-tenant trustees of the legal estate to join with a surviving partner to serve a counter-notice for a new lease under the 1954 Act, as pointed out in *Harris v Black*.[21] In that case, however, the two partners had quarrelled and were occupying separate parts of the premises, and in these circumstances the court declined to compel the unwilling partner to take on the commitments of a new lease which he did not want.

Company

If the tenant is a company, an effective assignment may be achieved by a sufficient disposition of the company shares to pass control. If the landlord wishes to maintain control, there should be a provision in the lease that disposition of a certain proportion of the company's shares is deemed to be an assignment. As in the case of a trustee in bankruptcy, the vesting of the lease in a liquidator will not amount to an assignment without consent; although any assignment by the liquidator is subject to any requirement to obtain consent. A usual safeguard for the landlord is to provide that in the event of liquidation of the company the landlord is to have a right of re-entry.[22]

Service of notices on parties to a lease

Any notice required to be served upon (*inter alia*) a landlord or tenant or other person, is deemed to have been served if it is left at the person's last known place of abode or business, or sent by registered post (or recorded delivery by amendment to the section) to his place of abode or business and is not returned by the Post Office.[23] The notice will be sufficient if it designates the person as lessee or lessor even if it does not actually name him. This is a very useful section which most leases will incorporate by reference to the section, and a usual clause effecting this would be:

> "The provisions of Section 196 of the Law of Property Act 1925, as amended by the Recorded Delivery Service Act 1962, shall apply to any notice required or given under this lease."

SURETIES

If the landlord is uncertain as to the financial standing of the tenant, or the tenant is a limited company, the landlord may require a surety or several

---

21 (1983) 46 P & CR 366.
22 See Chaps 13 and 14.
23 LPA 1925, s 196.

sureties for the tenant's liabilities under the lease. The surety will contract directly with the landlord, usually in the form of a covenant. A person who is a surety for the original tenant from the date the lease is granted will usually covenant in the lease itself, and will therefore be a party to the lease. A surety for a later tenant will usually covenant with the landlord in the licence to assign. At other times, a surety who substitutes for an existing surety will usually do so in a separate deed of suretyship.

A solicitor who is acting for a tenant should consider whether he can act also for the tenant's intended surety or sureties. If the tenant is a company and the intended surety is either one of its directors or is otherwise involved in its business in some way, there would not seem to be any problem, as no conflict of interest would arise. If the surety is not, however, there may be a conflict of interest between the surety and the company, and the surety should be advised to seek independent legal advice. The same situation could potentially arise between any tenant and his surety. Even where there is no conflict of interest, the solicitor should ensure that he advises both clients personally and does not rely upon the tenant to inform the surety of his obligations.[24] A letter, or written memorandum of the interview, should be kept on the file to avoid any doubt as to this in the future.

Guarantees and indemnities

The expression "surety" is used to embrace two distinct types of obligations: namely, a contract of guarantee and a contract of indemnity.

Under a contract of guarantee, the surety (called the guarantor) covenants to perform the obligations in the lease entered into by his principal in the event of the latter's default. A guarantor's obligations are therefore merely secondary or collateral to the obligations of his principal: if the principal is discharged, so is the guarantor. A contract of guarantee must be in writing or evidenced in writing and signed by the guarantor or his agent[25], although it is possible that it may be varied later merely orally.[26]

Under a contract of indemnity, the surety covenants to perform himself the obligations of the tenant for whom he is a surety. A surety's obligations under a contract of indemnity are therefore primary in nature: he is a principal debtor under the contract of indemnity, and the discharge of the tenant for whom he is a surety does not necessarily discharge the surety himself. A contract of indemnity can also be created orally or

---

24 See *Barclays Bank plc v O'Brien* [1994] 1 AC 180 (HL).
25 Statute of Frauds 1677, s 4.
26 *Re a Debtor (No 517 of 1991)* [1991] *The Times,* 25 November.

otherwise informally. In practice, however, many surety covenants blur the distinction between the two types of obligations, and often state that the "guarantor" is to be liable as a "principal debtor." The Landlord and Tenant (Covenants) Act 1995 expressly provides that an authorised guarantee agreement may impose liability on the tenant entering into it as sole or principal debtor.[27]

A surety's contract may also subject him to obligations which are independent of those imposed on the tenant. A surety often covenants to take a lease in his own name in the event of disclaimer. A covenant of this type is considered further below.

Duration of surety's liabilities

The extent and duration of a surety's liabilities under a guarantee or indemnity depend upon whether the lease is an old lease or a new lease for the purposes of the Landlord and Tenant (Covenants) Act 1995.

Pre-1996 leases

In a pre-1996 lease, a landlord who has extracted from the tenant a covenant to pay the rent and to observe and perform the obligations in the lease throughout the term might seek to impose a commensurate liability on that tenant's surety. There is nothing in the 1995 Act to restrict the duration or extent of a contract of guarantee or indemnity of a tenant's obligations under a pre-1996 lease.[28] It is, however, in the surety's interests that his covenant expressly limits his liability to the period during which the term is vested in the tenant for whom he is acting as guarantor.[29] In *Johnsey Estates Ltd* v *Webb*[30] the guarantor's covenant was limited for "so long as the term hereby granted is vested in the tenant", and the guarantor was held not liable for the subsequent default of an assignee. If the landlord is not prepared to accept this limitation on the surety's liability, an alternative might be to limit the guarantee until such time as a substitute can be found. It might be very difficult, however, to find a substitute willing to guarantee

---

27 LT(C)A 1995, s 16(5)(a).
28 Although the 1995 Act does affect an agreement entered into by the surety after 31 December 1995 to take a new lease: see further *infra*.
29 If the lease contains a covenant requiring the landlord's consent to assign, it might be argued that if a landlord has approved an assignee whom the guarantor had no opportunity of approving, it should be the landlord, and not a surety, who should bear any loss occasioned by the assignee's default. Such an argument has, however, been rejected when put forward by a prior tenant: *Norwich Union Life Insurance Society* v *Low Profile Fashions Ltd* [1992] 1 EGLR 86; and it is unlikely to receive a more favourable reception if argued by a surety.
30 [1990] 1 EGLR 80 (Ch).

the tenant in the same way for the whole of the term of the lease.

Subject to an agreement to the contrary, the surety is liable only during the contractual term. He is not liable during any extension of the tenancy under the 1954 Act[31], unless his covenant expressly provides that his liability is to continue during any statutory continuation of the term.[32] Similarly, he will not be liable in respect of any new lease granted under the 1954 Act.

As there is no privity of estate between a surety and the lessor, the benefit of a surety covenant cannot pass to the lessor's assignee by virtue of the Law of Property Act 1925, section 141. In *P & A Swift Investments* v *Combined English Stores Group plc*[33], however, the House of Lords held that a surety covenant touches and concerns the land, so that the benefit of the covenant passes to an assignee of the reversion without the necessity for any separate assignment. Lord Templeman drew a cricketing analogy[34]:

> "A surety for a tenant is a quasi tenant who volunteers to be a substitute or twelfth man for the tenant's team and is subject to the same rules and regulations as the player he replaces. A covenant which runs with the reversion against the tenant runs with the reversion against the surety."

In that case, it was held that an assignee of the lessor could recover from the surety a sum equivalent to the unpaid rent. Shortly after, in *Coronation Street Industrial Properties Ltd* v *Ingall Industries*[35] the House of Lords said that its earlier decision meant that all the obligations in a surety covenant touched and concerned the land; and it was held that the assignee of the reversion could enforce against the surety a covenant to take a new lease after disclaimer.[36]

Post-1995 *leases*

Since in a post-1995 lease, the tenant's liability on the leasehold covenants ends on a lawful assignment of the term[37], so does the liability of his surety.[38] It is therefore not possible in a post-1995 lease for a landlord to obtain from a surety a covenant to endure beyond such time. An assigning tenant may, however, be required (where the lease so provides) to enter into

---

31 *Junction Estates* v *Cope* (1974) 27 P & CR 482.
32 *A Plesser & Co Ltd* v *Davis* [1983] 2 EGLR 70 (QB).
33 [1989] AC 632 (HL), approving *Kumar* v *Dunning* [1989] QB 193.
34 *P & A Swift Investments* v *Combined English Stores Group plc* [1989] AC 632, 637.
35 [1989] 1 WLR 304 (HL).
36 *Ibid,* where Lord Templeman, continuing his analogy from the earlier case, said that "[a]s a result of the disclaimer the tenant retires mortally wounded and the surety is the substitute."
37 LT(C)A 1995, s 5.
38 *Ibid,* s 24(2).

an authorised guarantee agreement (AGA), guaranteeing the observance and performance of the covenants in the lease for the period that his immediate assignee has the term vested in him.[39]

There is nothing in the 1995 Act to prohibit the surety of a tenant who is assigning a post-1995 lease from guaranteeing the AGA if he wishes to do so. Whether the surety agreement can impose an obligation on him to provide a sub-guarantee in such circumstances is, however, by no means clear. A sub-guarantee of this sort can be particularly important where the tenant is a company with few assets, and the real covenant strength lies in the covenants entered into by its sureties, often its directors or its parent company. If it were to be held that the Act invalidates a surety covenant to the extent that it obliges the surety to enter into a sub-guarantee, the landlord should protect its position by insisting that the directors or the parent company join in the lease, not (as they might have done in a pre-1996 lease) as sureties, but as co-tenants.[40]

The point has caused a difference of opinion among commentators, and will no doubt receive judicial clarification in due course. In the meantime, the better view appears to be that such a ploy is unnecessary, as the 1995 Act does not invalidate a surety's obligation to sub-guarantee any AGA into which the tenant might subsequently enter.[41] Assuming that such an

---

39 *Ibid*, s 16.

40 See letter by Phillip Taylor, [1996] 1 EG 53.

41 The leading proponents of invalidity are Cullen & Potterton, in "Must a surety guarantee an AGA?", [1996] 19 EG 118. For the purposes of their analysis, it may be helpful to divide their argument into a series of lettered propositions They argue: (a) that a tenant is released from liability on the tenant covenants in the lease on a lawful assignment (s 5), and that where the tenant is thereby released, so is his surety (s 24(2)); (b) that a covenant by a tenant to enter into an AGA is a tenant covenant; and therefore (c) that a covenant by a surety to sub-guarantee any AGA is automatically released on assignment (s 24(2)). They further argue (d) that it is not possible to surmount this restriction indirectly by making the surety's entering into a sub-guarantee a condition precedent to the tenant's right to assign, as this would run foul of the anti-avoidance provision (s 25) as an attempt to exclude, modify or frustrate the operation of the Act, or to impose a liability on the tenant beyond that permitted by the Act itself. In a response to this, Adams, "Another view of AGAs", [1996] 32 EG 68, agrees with propositions (a) and (b), but not with (c). He points out that, whilst the tenant's obligation to enter into an AGA is a tenant covenant, any AGA which the tenant in fact enters into is not, since the tenant ceases to be the tenant on assignment, and so it is not a covenant "falling to be complied with by the tenant of premises demised by the tenancy" (s 28(1)). Since the Act does not therefore prohibit an obligation to sub-guarantee an AGA, he further argues that proposition (d) is also wrong, and that a condition precedent in the terms envisaged by Cullen & Potterton would not be struck down by s 25. For a review of both sides of the argument, see Fogel & Slessenger, *The Blundell Memorial Lectures 1996: Current Problems in Property Law,* 1996, RICS Conferences and Training, at 24–28, who conclude that it is in their view unlikely that the courts would adopt the Cullen & Potterton construction, and who point out that it is clear from the Parliamentary speech of the Bill's promoter, Peter Thurnham MP (*Hansard,* House of Commons, 14 July 1995, col 1243) that the proposed legislation was not intended to weaken the covenant strength of leases subject to its provisions.

obligation is valid, it has been suggested that, from the tenant's point of view, it is desirable that the tenant as well as the landlord is made a covenantee of the surety's covenant to provide a sub-guarantee, as this strengthens the tenant's hand should the guarantor later proves unwilling to provide the sub-guarantee (which is a distinct possibility if he no longer has an interest, *e.g.* if he is no longer a director of the tenant company).[42]

Agreement to take a new lease in the event of disclaimer

As has been mentioned, the contract of guarantee or indemnity is often supplemented by an independent obligation, typically a covenant by the surety to accept, on a written request made by the landlord, the grant of a new lease in his own name on the same terms for the unexpired reside of the existing lease in the event that his principal becomes insolvent and the lease is disclaimed or surrendered by the liquidator or trustee in bankruptcy.[43] This has been variously described as a contingent obligation, the contingency being a timeous demand made by the lessor[44]; and as a conditional contract, which becomes unconditional, binding and specifically enforceable upon the landlord's request.[45] From the moment the landlord makes its request, the surety is treated in equity as if a lease had been executed in proper form[46], and he becomes liable to pay the rent due under it.[47]

A suitable provision dealing with both disclaimer and surrender is a covenant by the tenant to procure a covenant by the surety with the landlord:

> "That in the event of this Lease being disclaimed or surrendered by a liquidator or trustee in bankruptcy, the Guarantor shall, if so requested by the Landlord (which request shall be made in writing and in the case of a surrender within three months thereof and in the case of a disclaimer within three months of the Landlord's receiving notice thereof), accept from, execute and deliver to the Landlord a counterpart of a new lease of the demised premises for a term commencing on the date of the disclaimer or surrender and continuing for the then unexpired residue of the term of this Lease and such lease shall be subject to the same covenants, conditions and provisos (including those relating to the payment of rent and re-entry) as are contained in this Lease and the costs of the Landlord in connection with the

---

42 Adams, "Another view of AGAs" [1996] 32 EG 68.
43 See further Chap 14.
44 *Coronation Street Industrial Properties Ltd v Ingall Industries Ltd* [1989] 1 WLR 304 (HL) (Lord Jauncey).
45 *Re a Company (No 00792 of 1992) ex p Tredegar Enterprises Ltd* [1992] 2 EGLR 39, 40 (Mummery J).
46 *Walsh v Lonsdale* (1882) 21 Ch D 9.
47 *Re a Company (No 00792 of 1992) ex p Tredegar Enterprises Ltd* [1992] 2 EGLR 39 (Mummery J).

grant of such new lease (including the reasonable costs and expenses of the Landlord's solicitors) shall be paid by the Guarantor."

This obligation to take a new lease (particularly from the date of disclaimer) is less significant following the decision of the House of Lords in *Hindcastle v Barbara Attenborough Associates Ltd*[48], which, overruling earlier cases of long-standing, held that, whilst disclaimer ends the liability of the insolvent tenant, it does not end the liability of his surety.[49] If the surety is required to pay under his contract of guarantee, he is entitled to apply for a vesting order.[50] A landlord can therefore choose whether to compel the surety to take up a fresh lease under his independent contractual undertaking to do so, or merely to demand the rent from the surety as it falls due, leaving it to the surety to apply to have the lease vested in him.

The landlord should be aware of the differences which can result from this choice. An agreement by a surety to take a lease in his own name is a contract for a lease, and whether a lease he takes up pursuant to such an agreement is a new lease or an old lease for the purposes of the Landlord and Tenant (Covenants) Act 1995 depends, not upon the date of the disclaimed lease itself, but upon the date that the surety agreement was entered into.[51] Therefore, even if the disclaimed lease was an "old lease" for the purposes of the 1995 Act, if the surety entered into its obligations after 31 December 1995, any fresh lease which is granted to the surety pursuant to such obligations will be a "new lease", and the landlord will not have the benefit of continuing contractual liability against the surety. In contrast to this, it seems that a vesting order does not create another lease, but merely vests in the applicant the residue of the term of the disclaimed lease. If the disclaimed lease was an old lease for the purposes of the 1995 Act, a surety who takes a vesting order will incur liability under it as an old lease, even if he became a surety after 31 December 1995.[52]

Sureties of an assignee

A landlord may also seek to include a covenant in the lease that on assignment to a company, guarantees for rent will be given by at least two

---

48 [1997] AC 70.

49 See further Chap 14.

50 Insolvency Act 1986, ss 181 (liquidation), 320 (bankruptcy). The application may be refused if the surety has covenanted to take a new lease: *Re AE Realisations (1985) Ltd* [1988] 1 WLR 200.

51 LT(C)A 1995, s 1(3)(a).

52 See Chap 14 *infra*. " See also "The Landlord and Tenant (Covenants) Act 1995: where does it fall short of its presumed intent? Part 2", Fogel & Slessenger, *The Blundell Memorial Lectures 1996: Current Problems in Property Law*, 1996, RICS Conferences and Training, at 42–44. Cf *Beegas Nominees Ltd v BHP Petroleum Ltd* [1997] 25 March (unreported), Lexis Transcript (Lindsay J); affirmed in part [1998] EGCS 60 (CA).

directors. An example of this is where a tenant's (fully) qualified covenant not to assign contains the following proviso:

> "Provided that if an intended assignee shall be a limited company then upon the Landlord's request at least two (or more if the Landlord shall reasonably require) of the directors of such intended assignee shall join in the deed of assignment as sureties for such company in order jointly and severally to covenant with the Landlord as sureties that such company will observe and perform the covenants of the Lease (including the covenant to pay rent) and to indemnify the Landlord against all losses damages costs and expenses arising by reason of any default by the company."

The tenant should try to resist any such requirement as it may well impede assignment.

Surety's rights and liabilities

If there has been an assignment or a series of assignments of a pre-1996 lease, the landlord may be able to recover any rent arrears or other sums due under the lease not merely from the current tenant or its surety, but (where there is privity of contract) from the original or any intermediate tenant or from the surety of any such tenant. The cases establish that an earlier tenant[53] or surety[54] from whom the landlord recovers in this way, is itself entitled to recover such sums by way of indemnity in its own right from the tenant in default. Since ultimate liability clearly lies with the tenant in default, such claim appears to be an application of the general principle:[55]

> "that if A and B are liable to a creditor for the same debt in such circumstances that the ultimate liability falls on A, and if B in fact pays the debt due to a creditor, then B is entitled to be reimbursed by A, and likewise is entitled to take over by subrogation any securities or rights which the creditor may have against A..."

Within the context of the developing law of restitution, recovery in such cases appears to be based upon the unjust enrichment of the current tenant, who would otherwise have had the benefit of exclusive possession under the lease without having to comply with all the obligations which the lease imposes. In addition to the direct claim, therefore, the plaintiff is entitled to be subrogated to the landlord's rights against the defendant, which in these circumstances would include the right of distress.

53 *Selous Street Properties Ltd v Oronel Fabrics Ltd* [1984] 1 EGLR 50 (QB), applying *Moule v Garrett* (1872) LR 7 Exch 101.
54 *Selous Street Properties Ltd v Oronel Fabrics Ltd* [1984] 1 EGLR 50.
55 *Re Downer Enterprises Ltd* [1974] 1 WLR 1460, 1468, per Pennycuick V-C, following the principle stated by Lord Selbourne LC in *Duncan Fox & Co v North & South Wales Bank* (1880) 6 App Cas 1, 10.

The cases, however, have gone further and have held that an original tenant[56] or its surety[57] is entitled to an indemnity from the surety of the tenant in default. This result, which has been described as a requirement of "justice and common sense"[58], has been explained on the footing that, as between the original tenant and its surety on the one hand, and the surety for the tenant in default on the other, the latter should be primarily liable.[59] The principle is very broad, and gives to any earlier tenant or its surety its own right to recover by way of indemnity from any intermediate tenant or its surety down the line.[60] In addition to such claim in its own right, such earlier tenant or surety may be subrogated to the landlord's claim against the defendant. Any intermediate tenant or surety who has to pay such indemnity is entitled to recover such payment in turn from any subsequent assignee or surety.

A surety who is required to pay out on his guarantee may recover by way of indemnity such sum, and it would seem any sums spent reasonably defending the claim[61], from the tenant whose obligation he has guaranteed.[62] He may also recover by way of contribution from any co-surety for the same tenant, even if their obligations arose at different times and under different documents.[63]

The consequence for the surety of the tenant in default can therefore be very severe if it cannot recover from its principal – which may well be insolvent – since it will be primarily liable vis-à-vis all earlier tenants and their sureties. McLoughlin has, however, contended that this result runs contrary to the normal rule that, where there is more than one surety, their liability *inter se* is equal. In his view, if the original tenant's surety had to pay the landlord in full, he should be entitled to recover from the defaulting tenant's surety only a contribution, which (if there are no intermediate sureties against whom a claim for contribution can be brought) will be 50 per cent.[64]

Default notice

The Landlord and Tenant (Covenants) Act 1995, section 17, has improved

---

56 *Becton Dickinson UK Ltd v Zwebner* [1989] QB 208, followed in *Re a Debtor (No 21 of 1995)* [1995] (unreported). See the criticisms of the earlier case in McLoughlin, "The expanding liability of sureties" [1989] Conv 292.
57 *Selous Street Properties Ltd v Oronel Fabrics Ltd* [1984] 1 EGLR 50 (QB).
58 *Kumar v Dunning* [1989] QB 193 (in relation to a claim by the original tenant).
59 *Becton Dickinson UK Ltd v Zwebner* [1989] QB 208.
60 *Selous Street Properties Ltd v Oronel Fabrics Ltd* [1984] 1 EGLR 50 (QB).
61 *Baxendale v London, Chatham & Dover Railway Co* (1874) LR 10 Exch 35, 44.
62 *Re Fox, Walker & Co, ex p Bishop* (1880) 15 Ch D 400 (CA).
63 *Scholefield Goodman & Sons Ltd v Zyngier* [1986] AC 562 (PC).
64 McLoughlin, *Commercial Leases and Insolvency*, 2nd ed, (1996) Butterworths, at 160.

the position of a former tenant[65] and its guarantor[66] (under a pre-1996 lease), and of a former tenant who has entered into an authorised guarantee agreement[67] and its guarantor[68] (under a post-1995 lease). Such a former tenant or guarantor is not liable under the agreement to pay any amount in respect of a fixed charge payable under the covenant unless the landlord serves on him a notice within six months from the date the charge becomes due.[69] The notice (which may be conveniently termed a default notice) must inform the former tenant or guarantor that the charge is now due and that in respect of the charge the landlord intends to recover from the former tenant or guarantor such amount as is specified in the notice and (where payable) interest calculated on such basis as is so specified.[70] "Fixed charge" means rent, a service charge[71] and any amount payable under a tenant covenant of the tenancy providing for the payment of a liquidated sum in the event of a failure to comply with any such covenant.[72]

In *Cheverell Estates Ltd* v *Harris & Haddon*[73], which concerned a pre-1996 lease, the assignee tenant was bankrupt owing £15,000 in rent arrears and other charges. The landlord served a statutory default notice on each of the two guarantors of the original tenant, but not on the original tenant itself. The defendants argued that they could not be liable as guarantors since there was no longer any unsatisfied liability on the part of the principal debtor. This argument was rejected, the court holding that the separate arrangements in section 17 for former tenants and guarantors was a sufficient indication that the service of a notice on a guarantor was not intended to be subject to the service of a notice on its principal debtor.[74]

The courts have yet to consider whether a former tenant or guarantor under a pre-1996 lease upon whom the landlord has served a default notice and recovered the sums due, would be entitled to recover such sums by way of indemnity from an intermediate tenant or guarantor upon whom the landlord has served no default notice. It would seem that this would not be a defence to an action brought by the plaintiff in its own right under the principle enunciated in *Selous Street Properties* v *Oronel Fabrics Ltd*[75],

65 LT(C)A 1995, s 17(1)(b).
66 *Ibid*, s 17(3).
67 *Ibid*, s 17(1)(a).
68 *Ibid*, s 17(3).
69 *Ibid*, s 17(2) (former tenant) s 17(3) (former tenant's guarantor).
70 *Ibid*, s 17(2)(a)(b) (former tenant), s 17(3)(a)(b) (former tenant's guarantor).
71 As defined by LTA 1985, s 18 (the words "of a dwelling" being disregarded for this purpose).
72 LT(C)A 1995, s 17(6).
73 [1998] 2 EG 127 (QB); noted Cooklin, (1997) 11 *The Lawyer* (30 September) 12.
74 Cf *City of Westminster Assurance Co* v *Registrar of Companies* [1996] 28 June (Millett J), where the possible discharge of a guarantor in such circumstances was considered.
75 [1984] 1 EGLR 50 (QB).

since the claim would not be in respect of a fixed charge payable under the covenant with the landlord; but that it would be a defence to an action based on subrogation to the landlord's rights against the defendant. If six months have not yet elapsed, however, the plaintiff might be in time himself to serve a default notice on the defendant through subrogation.

Other steps to protect surety

A surety may seek to improve his position in the event of his principal's default by extracting covenants in his favour from the landlord and from his principal either in the lease (where he is the original surety) or in a separate surety covenant. A surety should take a covenant from the landlord to serve upon him copies of all notices or proceedings which the landlord serves upon the tenant, and to give him notice of any breach of covenant. Apprising the surety of any breaches in respect of which the landlord intends to forfeit may enable the surety to put pressure on his principal to remedy any breaches swiftly. It will not, however, put the surety into the position of himself being able to seek relief from forfeiture, since such right is available only to the tenant or to the holder of a derivative interest. A surety can overcome this weakness, however, by extracting from his principal an irrevocable authority to act as his agent for the purpose of seeking relief from forfeiture.

A guarantor (whether under a pre-1996 or a post-1995 lease) who is required to pay a fixed charge to the landlord after he has been served with a section 17 default notice is entitled to have the landlord grant him an overriding lease.[76] It is important to bear in mind, however, that such a default notice is not served on the guarantor of the current tenant[77]; so that, if the current tenant defaults and his guarantor is made to pay, the latter has no right to an overriding lease. It is therefore still important for a surety to extract a covenant from his principal to assign the lease to the surety in such circumstances upon the surety's written demand. The lease should be checked for any restrictions on assignment which might be

---

76 LT(C)A 1995, ss 19–20. A surety under a pre-1996 lease who is made to indemnify an earlier surety or tenant may not, however, obtain an overriding lease, since the payment is not "of an amount which he has been required to pay in accordance with section 17 ...": LT(C)A 1995, s 19(1). *Sed quere*, whether this is so only where the plaintiff brings the action in its own right under the principle in *Selous Street Properties Ltd v Oronel Fabrics Ltd* [1984] 1 EGLR 50 (QB). It might be argued that a defendant surety who satisfies an indemnity claim does acquire a right to an overriding lease if he had been served with a s 17 default notice and the claim for the indemnity had been brought by way of subrogation to the landlord's rights.

77 This does not include a former tenant of a post-1995 lease who is liable under an AGA, upon whom no demand for a fixed charge can be made without the prior service of a s 17 notice: LT(C)A 1995, s 17(1)(a), (2).

breached by any assignment pursuant to the surety's demand, or even by the demand itself. If, however, the surety's right to demand an assignment is contained in the surety covenant itself, the landlord, being a party to such covenant, would probably be estopped from contending that any such demand when made comprises an automatic breach of a restriction on alienation in the lease. If the lease contains a covenant against assignment without the landlord's consent, there is always the possibility that the landlord might refuse consent; but it will probably be more difficult for him to object reasonably to having as a tenant someone whom he was prepared to accept as a guarantor. The surety's position is made fully secure if the landlord expressly covenants not to object to an assignment to a surety in such circumstances.

Any surety whose liability is not discharged by the disclaimer of the lease may apply for a vesting order.[78] This is dealt with in Chapter 14.

The landlord's position

If the landlord has a choice of seeking to recover rent arrears from one or more of several guarantors, he should bear in mind that any guarantor who pays the sums due after having been served with a section 17 default notice[79] has the right to claim an overriding lease.[80] In choosing upon whom to serve the section 17 notice, the landlord is also effectively choosing which one or more of the sureties he would be prepared to have as a future tenant. Therefore, although there may be a strong temptation to serve default notices on all the sureties, the landlord might prefer not to serve any surety whom he would not wish to have as a tenant.

If the landlord intends to forfeit the lease for non-payment of rent, he should consider carefully the possible effect of his recovering an equivalent sum from a guarantor. The danger is that if the guarantor's payment ranks as rent, it will discharge the existing tenant's obligation to pay, and there will then be no subsisting breach in respect of which the landlord can forfeit. On this matter, unfortunately, there is some difference of judicial opinion. In *London & County (A & D) Ltd* v *Wilfred Sportsman Ltd*[81], Russell LJ stated that any sum which the guarantor pays is not itself rent, but rather a payment under the guarantor's own obligation; the payment would therefore not itself preclude the landlord from taking steps to forfeit in respect of the breach. If this is correct, it means that (subject to the

---

78 Insolvency Act 1986, ss 181, 320.
79 This therefore excludes the existing tenant's guarantor (unless it is the former tenant under a post-1995 lease who has entered into an AGA).
80 LT(C)A 1995, ss 19–20.
81 [1971] Ch 764 (CA).

possibility of waiver[82]), a landlord may proceed to forfeit for breach of covenant to pay rent even after recovering an equivalent sum from a guarantor.[83] In *Milverton Group Ltd v Warner World Ltd*[84], however, Hoffmann LJ opined that the distinction between the rent payable by the tenant and the contractual obligation of the guarantor could not survive the decision of the House of Lords in *P&A Swift Investments v Combined English Stores Group plc*.[85] Most recently, in *Romain v Scuba TV*[86], Evans LJ adopted an intermediate view. He appeared to accept that a landlord's claim against a guarantor is not one for arrears of rent, but considered that – at least where the guarantor expressly undertook the same obligations as the lessee – the payment by the guarantor discharged the lessee's obligation also. On balance, therefore, it would appear that the payment of rent by a guarantor[87] also discharges the existing tenant's obligation to the landlord, who thereby loses the right to forfeit the lease for that breach. If the landlord wishes both to forfeit the lease and to recover from the surety, he should therefore ensure that he elects to forfeit by issuing and serving possession proceedings before seeking to recover from the surety. The landlord will also need to ensure that any refusal to accept rent from the tenant (so as to avoid waiving the right to forfeit) does not discharge the surety; this point is considered further below.

Discharge of sureties

A surety may be discharged by an express deed of release executed by the landlord. The release may be in consideration of a monetary sum, part of which may be intended to discharge rent arrears or other accrued obligations under the lease. Although a deed is not necessary when the release is for a consideration, it is nevertheless always desirable in order to avoid argument about whether payment of a debt clearly due is sufficient consideration to discharge the surety from future liabilities.[88]

The landlord must appropriate any consideration received for the surety's release towards the obligations under the lease; but he is not obliged to appropriate it or any part of it in discharging existing

---

82 Discussed *infra*.

83 This could be either a previous tenant under a post-1995 lease who had entered into an AGA, the guarantor of such a tenant's liability, or the guarantor of an earlier tenant under a pre-1996 lease).

84 [1995] 2 EGLR 28 (CA).

85 [1989] AC 632 (HL).

86 [1996] 2 All ER 377 (CA).

87 Including payment by a former tenant under an AGA.

88 *Milverton Group Ltd v Warner World Ltd* [1995] 2 EGLR 28, 31 (Hoffmann LJ). The problem is the rule in *Pinnel's case* (1602) 5 Co Rep 117a, approved in *Foakes v Beer* (1884) 9 App Cas 605 (HL).

obligations or future obligations in the order in which they fall due. In the absence of any agreement as to appropriation between the landlord and surety, the landlord may choose to appropriate the payment towards the last instalments of rent which fall due at the end of the term, even if this is many years into the future. He is, however, obliged to credit those who discharge such future obligations with interest (at a commercial rate, compounded after tax with annual rests) from the date such payment is received until the date on which the obligation to which it was appropriated falls due.[89] In *Milverton Group Ltd v Warner World Ltd*[90], where these principles were laid down, two of the sureties were released by deed upon the payment to the landlord of some £50,000. At that time, one quarter's rent under the lease (£19,500) was in arrears, and the landlord had demanded such sum from the sureties in question. The judge at first instance concluded that the reference to such demand in the deed of release was an implied appropriation of that amount to the existing arrears. The Court of Appeal affirmed his judgment, and held that the original tenant was not entitled to demand that the landlord appropriate the balance (£30,500) towards the two immediately succeeding quarters' rent.

Accidental discharge

A surety may be discharged, not merely by an intentional act on the part of the landlord (by a deed of release) but also accidentally. Any act of the landlord which might prejudice the position of the guarantor and to which he does not consent will discharge that guarantor. Any release of the tenant's liability or any substantial variation in the terms of the lease which might increase the guarantor's liability will therefore release any guarantor who did not agree to it.[91] The discharge of his liabilities under the guarantee will also discharge a guarantor from any liability to take a new lease in the event of disclaimer; since such an obligation, although in nature independent, will be regarded as ancillary to his obligations as guarantor.[92]

The guarantor will not be discharged by a variation which is insubstantial, or if it is self-evident without inquiry that the variation cannot prejudice him.[93] Conduct which merely affects the cost of complying with the obligations in a lease will not discharge a guarantor, *e.g.* a variation of the lease which results merely in an increase in intensity of occupation by the tenant for the time being will not be a material

---

89 *Milverton Group Ltd v Warner World Ltd* [1995] 2 EGLR 28, 32 (Hoffmann LJ).
90 [1995] 2 EGLR 28 (CA).
91 *Holmes v Brunskill* (1877) 3 QBD 495.
92 *Selous Street Properties Ltd v Oronel Fabrics Ltd* [1984] 1 EGLR 50, 61 (Hutchison J).
93 *Metropolitan Properties Co (Regis) Ltd v Bartholomew* [1996] 1 EGLR 82, 83 (Millett
    LJ), paraphrasing the words of Cotton LJ in *Holmes v Brunskill* (1877) 3 QBD 495, 505.

variation merely because it may increase the service charge or the cost of keeping the demised premises in repair.[94] On the other hand, an agreement between the landlord and the tenant under which the latter is given extended time to pay will discharge a guarantor, since such forbearance might result in an increase in the guarantor's ultimate liability.[95]

In the absence of any provision to the contrary in the guarantee agreement, a guarantor is discharged by a material variation to which he is not a party only if it is entered into by, and affects, the person whose liability he has guaranteed. The liability of the surety for an original tenant under a pre-1996 lease is not, therefore, discharged by a variation entered into only by the landlord and an assignee[96], because such a variation affects the liability only of the parties to it[97]; and so, since the original tenant's liability is not increased, neither is that of his surety. In such circumstances, even the original tenant's joining in as a party to the licence will not affect him or discharge his surety; in the absence of an indication to the contrary, it will be presumed that the parties intended that the variation should affect only the estate in the hands of the assignee, and not the contractual liability of the outgoing tenant or his surety.[98]

There are three established ways by which a landlord may avoid a surety's accidental discharge. One method is for the surety to confer an irrevocable authority on the tenant to enter into an agreement with the landlord which is to bind the surety.[99] Another method is for the guarantee covenant to provide expressly that the surety is to be liable as a principal debtor. In a pre-1996 lease, a principal debtor clause – if appropriately worded – can convert what would otherwise be a guarantee into an indemnity, so as to enable the landlord to recover from the surety even though the tenant itself has been discharged.[1] An AGA under a post-1995 lease may contain a "principal debtor" clause: statute expressly permits such agreement to impose on the tenant "any liability as sole or principal debtor in respect of any obligation owed by the assignee under the relevant covenant."[2] In post-1995 leases, however, a principal debtor clause is of reduced significance because an agreement cannot be an AGA to the extent

---

94 *Metropolitan Properties Co (Regis) Ltd v Bartholomew* [1996] 1 EGLR 82, 83 (Millett LJ), where the variation permitted the assignee company only to share the use of the premises with another company in the same group.

95 *Overend, Gurney & Co Ltd (liquidators) v Oriental Financial Corp Ltd (liquidators)* (1874) LR 7 HL 348 (HL).

96 *Metropolitan Properties Co (Regis) Ltd v Bartholomew* [1996] 1 EGLR 82 (CA).

97 *Friends' Provident Life Office v British Railways Board* [1996] 1 All ER 336 (CA); LT(C)A 1995, s 18. *Selous Street Properties Ltd v Oronel Fabrics Ltd* [1984] 1 EGLR 50 has been overruled on this point.

98 *Metropolitan Properties Co (Regis) Ltd v Bartholomew* [1996] 1 EGLR 82.

99 Lewison, *Drafting Business Leases*, 5th ed, (1996) FT Law & Tax at 266.

1 See Halsbury's Laws, (4th ed, reissue 1993), Butterworths, para 307.

2 LT(C)A 1995, s 16(5)(a).

that it purports "to impose on the tenant any liability, restriction or other requirements (of whatever nature) in relation to any time after the assignee is released from [the relevant covenant] by virtue of this Act."[3] The only value in a principal debtor clause in an AGA, therefore, is to prevent the discharge of the surety in circumstances (such as a variation of the lease, forbearance or the giving of time) which, whilst not releasing the current tenant, would normally discharge a guarantor. A final method of avoiding the accidental discharge of a surety is to provide expressly in the lease that the surety is not to be released by any act of forbearance, or variation of the lease[4], but only by an express release from the landlord.

Many surety covenants adopt a belt-and-braces approach and use both the last two methods. A suitable clause is one by which the tenant covenants to obtain a covenant from the surety with the Landlord:

> "That no variation of the terms of this Lease (including any reviews of the rent payable hereunder) or any assignment of this Lease nor any neglect, delay or forbearance of the Landlord in attempting to obtain payment of the rents or the amounts required to be paid by the Tenant or in enforcing the performance or observance of any of the Tenant's obligations under this Lease shall release, determine or in any way lessen or affect the liability of the Guarantor as principal debtor under this Lease or otherwise prejudice or affect the right of the Landlord to recover from the Guarantor to the full extent of this guarantee."

Even in the absence of such a provision, however, the compromise of a court action may not amount to a forbearance which will release the surety. Thus, in *Colin Estates Ltd* v *Buckley*[5], various disputes between the landlord and tenant were compromised by the promised payment of £10,000 by the tenant under a consent order. The tenant became insolvent and it was held that the compromise payment, being a sum in settlement of claims for rent and breach of other covenants, was payable by the surety.

If the landlord wishes to retain an action for recovery of rent from the surety in addition to forfeiture proceedings, the lease should also state that refusal of rent from the tenant where a right of re-entry has arisen will not release the surety. An appropriate means of achieving this is a tenant's covenant to procure a covenant from the surety with the landlord:

> "That a refusal by the Landlord to accept rent tendered by or on behalf of the Tenant at a time when the Landlord is (or would after the service of a notice under the Law of Property Act 1925, section 146, have been) entitled to re-enter the demised premises shall not release, determine, discharge or in any way lessen or affect the liability of the Guarantor."

---

3 *Ibid*, s 16(4)(b).
4 As in *Selous Street Properties Ltd v Oronel Fabrics Ltd* [1984] 1 EGLR 50.
5 [1992] 2 EGLR 78 (CA).

Substitution of sureties

A lease may provide for the liability of the existing sureties to be ended if the tenant gives notice to the landlord and substitute sureties are provided. It is important that the landlord ensures that such a clause is drafted so that the liability of existing sureties is not terminated merely by the tenant's notice.[6]

The landlord should also include a provision in the lease for the tenant to inform him of the death or bankruptcy of the surety and to provide a substitute in these circumstances. Thus the tenant might covenant:

> "In the event of the Guarantor (or, if more than one, any one or more of the guarantors) dying or becoming insolvent, the Tenant shall forthwith in writing notify the Landlord of such event and shall, if the Landlord shall so request, deliver to the Landlord within three months of such notification a deed containing covenants by another acceptable guarantor being covenants identical to those entered into by the guarantor who has died or become insolvent."

---

6 Cf *Grovewood (LE) Ltd v Lundy Properties Ltd* (1995) 69 P & CR 507 (Ch D); noted, Haley, "A surety covenant: common sense and construction" [1994] JBL 383.

Chapter 5

ENFORCEABILITY OF LEASEHOLD COVENANTS

This chapter considers the extent to which covenants in the lease are enforceable by, or binding upon, the original parties to the lease, their successors in title, those holding derivative interests, and adverse possessors. In the examples in this chapter, L1 refers to the original landlord, L2 to his immediate assignee, and so on. Similarly, T1 refers to the original tenant, T2 to his immediate assignee, and so on.

As between the original parties to the lease, there exists both privity of contract and (before either of them has assigned) privity of estate. The doctrine of privity of contract means that all the covenants in the lease, regardless of whether they relate to the land leased, are enforceable by and against each of the original parties to the lease. The rights and liabilities of the parties after assignment of the lease or reversion (or both), however, differ according to whether the lease was entered into before 1 January 1996 (an old lease) or after 31 December 1995 (a new lease).[1] The provisions of the Landlord and Tenant (Covenants) Act 1995 relating to the transmission of the benefit and burden of leasehold covenants apply only to new leases.[2] Two regimes relating to the transmission of such covenants therefore need to be considered.

LEASES CREATED BEFORE 1 JANUARY 1996

Original parties

Continuing liability after assignment

After either of the original parties has assigned its estate to a third party, the privity of estate which exists between the original parties comes to an

---

1 See generally Fancourt, *Enforceability of Landlord and Tenant Covenants,* 1st ed (1997) Sweet & Maxwell.

2 LT(C)A 1995, s 1; LT(C)A 1995 (Commencement) Order, SI 1995 No 2963.

end. Unless the lease provides otherwise, however, each of the original parties to the lease remains liable on the covenants in the lease under the doctrine of privity of contract throughout the remainder of the contractually agreed term. Therefore, after T1 has assigned the lease to T2, T1 will remain liable to L1 for breaches of the tenant's covenants in the lease which occur even after the assignment, *i.e.* even after T1 has put it out of his power to comply with the covenants in the lease.[3] Similarly, even after L1 has assigned his reversion to L2, L1 will remain liable to T1 on the landlord's covenants in the lease. In practice such continuing liability is of greater concern to the tenant. There are two reasons for this. First, most of the obligations in a typical commercial lease are tenant's obligations.[4] Secondly, in practice, the covenant which is most likely to be enforced against an original party after assignment is the original tenant's covenant to pay rent.

This is why a pre-1996 lease usually contains, not merely a provision specifying the rent to be paid, but also a covenant by the tenant to pay the rent throughout the term. In the absence of such a covenant, the obligation to pay the rent would be enforceable by the landlord for the time being against the tenant for the time being; but, being merely an incident of the estate, would not be enforceable by L1 against T1 after T1 has assigned to T2. A covenant by T1 to pay the rent throughout the term, however, means that, under general principles, T1 remains liable on the covenant even after assignment to T2.

If, therefore, T2 (or a later assignee) defaults in the payment of the rent, L1 is entitled to recover it from T1. T1 cannot require L1 to sue the defaulting tenant first, because (as between T1 and L1) T1's liability remains a primary one: T1 cannot argue that, after assignment, he is merely a surety for the performance by the defaulting tenant.[5]

If T1 is required to pay L1, he may be able to recover such payment from his immediate assignee, a later intermediate assignee or (if a subsequent assignee) the tenant in default.[6] He may also be able to recover from the defaulting tenant's surety.[7] In practice, however, L1 will generally proceed initially against the defaulting tenant and any surety it may have provided. L1 will therefore usually seek to recover from T1 only where the tenant for the time-being is insolvent and either did not provide a surety,

3 If, therefore, having assigned the lease, T1 were to go bankrupt or into liquidation, L1 would be entitled to prove in the bankruptcy or liquidation for the loss of T1's covenant: cf *Stanhope Pension Trust Ltd v Registrar of Companies* [1993] 2 EGLR 118 (Ch).
4 See Law Com No 174 (1988), para 2.1.
5 *Baynton v Morgan* (1882) 22 QBD 74.
6 This is considered more fully below.
7 *Becton Dickinson UK Ltd v Zwebner* [1989] QB 208, followed at first instance in *Re a Debtor (No 21 of 1995)* (unreported). See further Chap 4.

or provided one who cannot now pay. In these circumstances, either T1 or an intermediate assignee from him may be left with a liability which cannot be recovered.

Attempts to restrict continuing liability

Where possible, the tenant under a pre-1996 lease should have sought to limit its liability on the covenants in the lease to the period during which it remains the tenant under the lease. A suitable form of wording might be a proviso to the tenant's covenants such as one in the following form. In this and in the following precedents, clause x prohibits assignment without the landlord's consent, and clause y requires the tenant to procure that the assignee (and any surety for the assignee) enters into direct covenants with the lessor:

> "Provided that the liability of [the name of the original tenant] under the Tenant's covenants contained herein shall cease in respect of breaches which occur after an assignment by him of this Lease if:
> (a) at the date of such assignment [the name of the original tenant] shall not be in breach of any of the Tenant's covenants contained herein; and
> (b) such assignment comprises the whole of the property demised by this Lease and is made in accordance with clauses x and y hereof."

If the tenant of a pre-1996 lease could not obtain such immediate cessation of liability upon assignment, he might have sought to include a clause to limit his liability only in respect of breaches which occur during his own time as tenant and during the time as tenant of his immediate assignee. This provides some limited safeguard for T1 since T1 can at least select his own prospective assignee, and therefore check such person's creditworthiness. Such a limitation might be expressed thus:

> "Provided that the liability of [the name of the original tenant] under the Tenant's covenants contained herein shall cease in respect of breaches which occur after an assignment (the relevant assignment) of this Lease by his immediate assignee (the relevant assignee) but only if:
> (a) at the date of the relevant assignment neither [the name of the original tenant] nor the relevant assignee shall be in breach of any of the Tenant's covenants contained herein; and
> (b) both the assignment to the relevant assignee and the relevant assignment comprise the whole of the property demised by this Lease and are made in accordance with clauses x and y hereof."

Failing this, where the lease contains a qualified covenant against assignment without the landlord's consent, T1 might have sought to include a clause in the lease under which L1 covenanted with T1 to take reasonable care to ensure that a later assignee was financially able to meet the rental

and service payments due under the lease. A breach of such a covenant by
L1 would free T1 from liability for subsequent breaches. An express
covenant, however, is required: the court will not be willing to imply any
such term into the lease.[8]

The extent of T1's continuing liability after assignment depends upon
the terms of the contract which he entered into in the lease. If T1 assigns a
lease which contains provision for rent review, T1 is liable to pay any
higher rent agreed in accordance with the formula so laid down between
the landlord and T1's assignee, since this was envisaged in T1's contract.[9]

T1's contract cannot, however, be varied by an agreement between the
landlord and T1's assignee without T1's consent. In *Friends' Provident
Life Office* v *British Railways Board*[10], pursuant to a deed of variation
which relaxed the alienation and user covenants in the lease, the annual
rent was increased from £12,000 payable quarterly in arrears to £35,000
payable quarterly in advance. The assignee defaulted, and the landlord
claimed the increased rent from the original tenant, T1. The Court of
Appeal, referring to the distinction between contract and estate clarified by
the House of Lords in *City of London Corporation* v *Fell*[11], held that no
variation of the terms of the lease agreed between L and T2 could affect
T1's continuing contractual liability. T1 was therefore liable to make good
the arrears only to the extent of the £12,000 specified in the lease.

If a variation between T1's assignee and the landlord is so substantial as
to change the fundamental nature of the lease, T1 might be discharged
from liability on the basis that a new lease has arisen which causes the old
lease to be surrendered by operation of law.[12] In the *Friends' Provident*
case, Beldam LJ said that a variation which affects the estate will always
effect a surrender and re-grant irrespective of the parties' intentions: this
will occur, therefore, if there is a change in the length of the term or in the
physical extent of the premises leased. Other changes, however, such as
those in the case before him, could operate merely as a variation of the

---

8 *Norwich Union Life Insurance Society* v *Low Profile Fashions Ltd* [1992] 1 EGLR 86
   (CA).
9 As in *Centrovincial Estates* v *Bulk Storage Ltd* (1983) 46 P & CR 393, which is still
   supportable on this narrower ground.
10 [1996] 1 All ER 336; overruling on this point the broader ratio of Harman J *Centrovincial
   Estates* v *Bulk Storage Ltd* (1983) 46 P & CR 393 (that T1 puts his assignee into the
   position of being able to vary the terms of T1's contract with the landlord) and the later
   cases so far as they applied it, viz *Selous Street Properties Ltd* v *Oronel Fabrics Ltd* [1984]
   1 EGLR 50, and *GUS Property Management Ltd* v *Texas Homecare Ltd* [1993] 2 EGLR
   63. See also LT(C)A 1995, s 18.
11 [1994] AC 458 (HL).
12 See Chap 12.

existing lease if this was what the parties intended. A variation in the basis of calculating the rent does not amount to a change in the estate.[13]

A tenant who could not obtain any other reduction in liability might therefore have sought to include a term in the lease limiting his continuing liability to pay the rent to the amount of rent payable at the time of the assignment. The tenant might have sought the inclusion of a proviso like the following:

> "Provided that after an authorised assignment of this Lease the liability of [the name of the original tenant] under the Tenant's covenants herein contained to pay rent that falls due after such assignment shall not exceed such amounts as would have fallen due had the rent after such authorised assignment continued to be payable at the rate payable at the date of such authorised assignment.
> In this clause "authorised assignment" means an assignment by [the name of the original tenant] that:
> (a) is made at a date when [the name of the original tenant] shall not be in breach of any of the Tenant's covenants contained herein; and
> (b) comprises the whole of the property demised by this Lease and is made in accordance with clauses x and y hereof."

Continuing liability during extension of the lease under the Landlord and Tenant Act 1954, Part II

When the contractual term of a fixed-term tenancy subject to the Landlord and Tenant Act 1954, Part II, expires, the tenant's estate is prolonged subject to a statutory variation as to the mode of determination.[14] The "tenancy" so continued, however, is the tenancy only of the person who is the tenant at that time. If such person is not T1, T1 is not thereby made liable to L1 for breaches of covenant committed by any assignee of the lease during the period of holding over. Any continued liability through privity of contract under a pre-1996 lease will arise only where the original parties agree that it should continue after the expiry of the contractual term.[15]

If, therefore, the landlord under a pre-1996 lease wished to continue the liability of T1 during such period, he must have stipulated for this expressly in the lease. A simple method of extending the tenant's liability in this way was by extending the definition of "term" as follows:

> "The expression "the said term" shall where the context admits include not only the term hereby granted but also the period of any holding over or any extension thereof whether by statute or at common law."

---

13 *J W Childer Trustees Ltd v Anker* [1995] EGCS 116.
14 LTA 1954, s 24(1); see Chap 15.
15 *City of London Corporation v Fell* [1994] AC 458 (HL).

This form of wording will suffice to make the original tenant liable for the contractual rent during the period of holding over by an assignee; and this will probably include liability to pay any higher rent settled under a rent-review clause. It is not, however, sufficient to make the original tenant liable for the difference between the contractually agreed rent and any higher rent provided for in an interim rent order.[16] If, therefore, the landlord wished to make the original tenant liable to pay any increase resulting from such an order, he would have needed to ensure that the lease also contains a covenant by the tenant on the following lines:

> "The tenant hereby covenants to pay (without deduction or set-off) any additional rent which may become payable under the lease during any period of holding over by virtue of any interim rent order made under the Landlord and Tenant Act 1954 or any enactment or statutory modification thereof."

The tenant should have resisted the inclusion of such a clause vigorously.

Restricted ability to sue after assignment

Although liability under a pre-1996 lease continues after assignment, the assignor loses, after assignment, the right to sue on those covenants which "touch and concern" the land leased.[17] In the case of the assignment of the reversion, this principle is laid down by the Law of Property Act 1925, section 141(1).[18] This sub-section refers to covenants which have reference to the subject-matter of the lease; but this has the same meaning as "touch and concern". In the case of the assignment of the lease, the principle was laid down in *Spencer*'s case[19], under which there passes to the assignee the benefit of those tenant's covenants which "touch and concern" the land.

One original party and the assignee of the other

The issues here are whether L2 (or a subsequent assignee of the reversion) can sue or be sued by T1; and whether T2 (or a subsequent assignee of the lease) can sue or be sued by L1. If there is privity of covenant between the parties (which, in pre-1996 commercial leases, there commonly is), a contractual action may lie; this will be considered later in this chapter. For the present, however, the only rights and liabilities that will be considered are those which arise from the relationship of landlord and tenant itself.

---

16 *Herbert Duncan Ltd v Cluttons* [1993] 1 EGLR 93 (CA).
17 For the meaning of "touch and concern", see *infra*.
18 *Arlesford Trading Co Ltd v Servansingh* [1971] 1 WLR 1080, discussed *infra*.
19 (1583) 5 Co Rep 16a.

Can L2 sue T1?

The assignment of the reversion by L1 to L2 does not create privity of contract between L2 and T1.[20] It does, however, create privity of estate. This is by virtue of the Law of Property Act 1925, section 141, which annexes to the reversionary estate, upon its assignment by the lessor, the benefit of every lessee's covenant "having reference to the subject-matter" of the lease.

The requirement that the covenant have reference to the subject-matter of the lease has been held to be a mere reformulation of the older terminology, which required the covenant to "touch and concern" the demised premises.[21] This means that there does not pass to L2 the benefit of all the covenants contained in the lease. There will pass to L2 the benefit only of those covenants which affect the parties in their capacities as lessor and lessee. The benefit of covenants of a purely personal nature will not pass.

The distinction between those covenants with run with the land and those which do not (personal covenants) has been criticised as purely arbitrary and, for the most part, quite illogical.[22] In practice, however, most covenants (including all the most important covenants commonly found in leases) satisfy the "touching and concerning" test. These include covenants by the lessee to pay the rent[23], to repair[24], to spend a specified sum annually on repairs or to pay any shortfall to the lessor[25], to insure the premises against fire[26], not to assign or sub-let without the lessor's consent[27], to restrict user[28], and to restrict sales of goods to those produced by the lessor only.[29]

Examples of personal covenants, the benefit of which does not pass to L2 by virtue of an assignment of the reversion, include the performance of personal services by the lessee, and a covenant by T1 not to carry on a similar trade within a specified radius.[30] A personal covenant therefore

---

20 *Re King* [1963] 1 Ch 459.
21 See *e.g. Caerns Motor Services Ltd* v *Texaco Ltd* [1995] 1 All ER 247, 257, (Judge Paul Baker QC, sitting as a judge of the Chancery Division).
22 *Grant* v *Edmundson* [1931] 1 Ch 1, 31.
23 *Parker* v *Webb* (1693) 3 Salk 5.
24 *Martyn* v *Clue* (1852) 18 QB 661.
25 *Moss' Empires Ltd* v *Olympia (Liverpool) Ltd* [1939] AC 544.
26 *Vernon* v *Smith* (1821) 5 B & Ald 1.
27 *Goldstein* v *Sanders* [1915] 1 Ch 549.
28 *Wilkinson* v *Rogers* (1864) 2 De GJ & Sm 62; *Lynnthorpe Enterprises Ltd* v *Sidney Smith (Chelsea) Ltd* [1990] 2 EGLR 131 (CA).
29 *e.g.* a solus agreement: *Caerns Motor Services Ltd* v *Texaco Ltd* [1995] 1 All ER 247 (ChD).
30 *cf Thomas* v *Haywood* (1869) LR 4 Exch 311.

remains enforceable by L1 against T1 even after L1 has assigned the reversion to L2.

The benefit of a "touching and concerning" covenant passes to L2 under the Law of Property Act 1925, section 141, even if the covenant does not refer to successors in title.[31]

Section 141(1) states that the benefit of every covenant in the lease having reference to the subject-matter thereof passes with the reversionary estate to the assignee. This clearly includes the right to sue for breaches of covenant which occur after the assignment of the reversion. It has, however, been held that the sub-section also passes to the assignee the right to sue for breaches of covenant which occurred before the assignment.[32] If, therefore, rent is in arrears at the time L1 assigns the reversion to L2, the right to sue for those arrears passes to L2; L1 loses the right to sue for them, even though the rent in arrear accrued due during his own time as landlord.[33] This might appear harsh on L1; but it should be borne in mind that, if rent is in arrear, L1 can use this in order to try to obtain a higher price for the assignment to L2. If L2 does not wish to take on the right to sue T1 for already accrued arrears, he might consider reaching an agreement with L1 whereby, on the assignment of the lease to L2, L2 assigns such right as a chose in action to L1.[34]

In respect of "touching and concerning covenants", the sub-section also operates to prevent L1, after assignment to L2, from suing T1 under the doctrine of privity of contract. The right to sue on such covenants also passes to L2. In *Arlesford Trading Co Ltd* v *Servansingh*[35], T1 committed breaches of covenant (non-payment of rent) and then (while L1 was still the landlord) assigned the lease to T2. L1 then assigned the reversion to L2. It was held that section 141(1) enabled L2 to sue T1 in respect of those breaches. This shows the far-reaching effect of the sub-section, because at no time was there either privity of contract or of estate between L2 and T1.

In the *Arlesford Trading Co Ltd* case, T1 had himself committed the breaches. The question which then arises is whether L2 can sue T1 for breaches committed by T2 during L2's time as reversioner. From the foregoing analysis, it would appear that the answer should be no, since when L1 assigns the reversion to L2, he loses (under section 141) the right to sue T1 on touching and concerning covenants, and section 141(1) cannot pass to L2 a right against T1 which L1 does not himself possess.

31 *Caerns Motor Services Ltd* v *Texaco Ltd* [1995] 1 All ER 247 (Ch).
32 *Re King* [1963] Ch 459.
33 *London and County (A & D) Ltd* v *Wilfred Sportsman Ltd* [1971] Ch 764.
34 As had occurred in *Kataria* v *Safeland plc* [1998] 5 EG 155 (CA).
35 [1971] 1 WLR 1080.

Strangely, however, this important question appears never to have been addressed directly in a reported case[36]; and two alternative arguments might be put forward to support the view that, in such circumstances, L2 should be able to recover from T1. First, it might be contended that section 141 effects a statutory assignment to L2 of L1's contractual rights against T1. Secondly, it might be argued that, when L1 assigns the reversion to L2, L1's contractual rights against T1 are assigned, not under section 141, but by implication.[37] In support of this latter argument, it should be noted that an implied assignment (necessarily outside section 141) of the benefit of a guarantor's indemnity covenant has been held to take place on the assignment of the reversion[38]; and that the benefit of even personal covenants can pass by implied assignment.[39]

Section 141(1) is not limited in application to assignments. It provides that rent and the benefit of the tenant's touching and concerning covenants go, by virtue of section 141(1), "with the reversionary estate in the land ... immediately expectant on the term granted by the lease ...". It therefore enables such covenants to be enforced by, for instance, the lessor's mortgagee in possession, or the grantee of a reversionary lease.

Can T1 sue L2?

This is governed by the Law of Property Act 1925, section 142(1), which states that the obligation under a lessor's covenant having reference to the subject-matter of the lease passes with the reversionary estate to bind the assignee, and it may be enforced by the person in whom the term is from time to time vested. The expression "having reference to the subject-matter of the lease" has the same meaning as in section 141(1), *i.e.* it imports a "touching and concerning" requirement.[40]

Lessor's covenants that touch and concern, and therefore fall within section 142(1), include covenants to repair or insure the demised premises, to give the tenant quiet enjoyment, not to serve a notice to quit a periodic

---

36 The question did not arise in *City of London Corporation v Fell* [1994] AC 458 since the reversion was still vested in the original landlord. In *Beegas Nominees Ltd v BHP Petroleum Ltd* (1997) 25 March, Lindsay J (unreported), the court proceeded (apparently without argument) on the basis that an assignee of the reversion of a pre-1996 lease could recover the rent arrears (accrued by the present tenant) from intermediate tenants with whom the assignee had neither privity of estate nor (apparently) privity of contract. See appeal at [1998] EGCS 60 (CA).
37 *Quere,* whether assignment might be effected (expressly or by implication) under LPA 1925, s 136.
38 *P & A Swift Investments v Combined English Stores Group plc* [1989] AC 632 (HL).
39 *Griffith v Pelton* [1958] Ch 205.
40 See *Hua Chiao Commercial Bank Ltd v Chiaphua Industries Ltd* [1987] AC 99, 106 (Lord Oliver) (PC).

tenancy during its first three years[41], to rebuild on the demised premises[42], not to build on adjoining land[43], and to renew the lease.[44] Lessor's covenants that do not touch and concern include covenants to sell the reversion to the lessee at the option of the lessee[45], to give the lessee a right of pre-emption on the sale of the reversion, and to repay a security deposit.[46] At the end of the lease, therefore, the tenant cannot recover the deposit from L1's assignee, but only from L1 itself. The risk for the tenant is that L1 may by then be insolvent or (in the case of an individual) have died and his estate have been wound up, or (in the case of a company) have gone into liquidation.

A collateral agreement qualifying a covenant that touches and concerns the land contained in a lease itself touches and concerns the land and so runs with the reversion by virtue of section 142, thereby binding successors in title to the reversion irrespective of notice. Such a collateral agreement might relate to the suspension of the right to serve a notice to quit[47], the acceptance of an alternative method of satisfaction of a touching and concerning covenant[48], and an undertaking to remedy defects and to give the tenant a rent-free period while any remedial work remains uncompleted.[49] Similarly a side letter provided by the landlord on the grant of three leases giving the tenant a right to break has been held to be binding on the assignees of the reversion under section 142 even though the letter had not been disclosed to them, and even though the benefit of the side letter was expressed to be personal to the original tenant.[50]

Section 142(1) does not in terms annex to the term the benefit of the lessor's covenants. This means that, even after assignment of the lease to T2, T1 retains the right to sue L2 for breaches of the lessor's covenants which occurred while T1 was tenant.[51]

Section 142(1) imposes the liability of "touching and concerning" covenants upon L2, so that L2 is liable in respect of breaches which occur during his own time as landlord. The sub-section does not, however,

---

41 *Breams Property Investment Co Ltd v Strougler* [1948] 2 KB 1.
42 *Easterby v Sampson* (1830) 6 Bing 644.
43 *Ricketts v Enfield Churchwardens* [1909] 1 Ch 544.
44 *Richardson v Sydenham* (1703) 2 Vern 447; *Weg Motors Ltd v Hales* [1962] Ch 49. For a discussion of options to renew, see Chap 1.
45 *Woodall v Clifton* [1905] 2 Ch 257.
46 *Hua Chiao Commercial Bank Ltd v Chiaphua Industries Ltd* [1987] AC 99.
47 *Breams Property Investment Co Ltd v Strougler* [1948] 2 KB 1, 7-9.
48 *Grace Rymer Investments Ltd v Waite* [1958] Ch 831, 847.
49 *Lotteryking Ltd v AMEC Properties Ltd* [1995] 2 EGLR 13 (Lightman J).
50 *Systems Floors Ltd v Ruralpride Ltd* [1995] 1 EGLR 48 (CA).
51 *City & Metropolitan Properties Ltd v Greycroft Ltd* [1987] 1 WLR 1085.

operate to render L2 liable for breaches which occurred before the assignment of the reversion to him.[52]

Like section 141(1), section 142(1) is not restricted to assignments. It enables the tenant to enforce the benefit of the landlord's touching and concerning covenants against the immediate reversioner or mortgagee in possession.

Can L1 sue T2?

L1 can sue T2 on "touching and concerning" covenants. This is the rule of common law laid down in *Spencer*'s case.[53]

Can T2 sue L1?

T2 can sue L1 on "touching and concerning" covenants.[54] T2 will not, however, acquire the right to sue L1 for breaches which occurred *before* the assignment to T2.[55]

Enforceability between the assignees of original parties

It will again be assumed for present purposes that there is no separate express covenant between the assignees.[56]

Can L2 sue T2?

Although there is no privity of contract between L2 and T2, there is privity of estate. L2 acquires the right to sue for breach of the tenant's covenants by virtue of the Law of Property Act 1925, section 141(1). The liability of the tenant's covenants passes to T2 at common law. Therefore L2 can sue T2, whether T2 commits the breach before or after the assignment of the reversion to L2. T2 will not, however, be liable for breaches which occurred before the assignment of the lease to him.

Can T2 sue L2?

Although there is no privity of contract between L2 and T2, there is privity of estate. T2 can sue on "touching and concerning" covenants under *Spencer*'s case[57]; and L2 is liable for breach of such covenants under the Law of Property Act 1925, section 142(1). Therefore T2 can sue L2, but

---

52 *Duncliffe v Caerfelin Properties Ltd* [1989] 2 EGLR 38.
53 (1583) 5 Co Rep 16a.
54 *Spencer*'s case (1583) 5 Co Rep 16a.
55 *City & Metropolitan Properties Ltd v Greycroft Ltd* [1987] 1 WLR 1085. This is in marked contrast to the rights which L2 acquires against T1 under s 141(1).
56 The effect of such a covenant is considered *infra*.
57 (1583) 5 Co Rep 16a.

only in respect of breaches committed after the assignment of the lease to T2.[58] Furthermore, L2 will not become liable for breaches which occurred before the assignment of the reversion to him.[59]

Action for damages against intermediate assignee

Under the foregoing principles, an intermediate assignee of the lease (T2) is not liable for breaches committed by a subsequent assignee (T3). The reason is that, after assignment of the lease, there is no longer privity of estate between the intermediate assignee and the landlord. Furthermore, since the intermediate assignee was not a original party to the lease, it is not liable under the doctrine of privity of contract.

Where landlord has direct covenant with intermediate assignee

A landlord under a pre-1996 lease might have secured the inclusion of a clause that contained a qualified covenant against assignment and which provided that as a condition of the landlord's giving consent the assignor would procure that the intended assignee enter into a direct covenant with the landlord to pay the rent and to observe and perform all the tenant's covenants in the lease during the remainder of the term. An intermediate assignee who has entered into such a covenant under a pre-1996 lease will thereby remain liable for breaches committed even after it has assigned the lease. Such a clause was frequently seen in pre-1996 commercial leases.[60]

The landlord must, however, have taken care in drafting the clause.

First, clear words are necessary to make an assignee liable for breaches which occur after he has parted with the term. The clause will, however, be construed in the context of the lease as a whole. Thus an assignee who covenanted "to pay the rent reserved in the lease" was held liable for rent which accrued due after he had assigned, because the lease itself provided for the payment of rent "during the term hereby granted."[61] A better drafted pre-1996 lease will have removed any element of uncertainty by requiring the assignee to covenant to pay the rent expressly "during the remainder of the term hereby granted."

Secondly, in the case of a qualified covenant against assignment, the consent must not be unreasonably withheld.[62] Under a pre-1996 lease, the parties cannot circumvent this by specifying the circumstances in which

---

58 cf *City & Metropolitan Properties Ltd v Greycroft Ltd* [1987] 1 WLR 1085.
59 *Duncliffe* v *Caerfelin Properties Ltd* [1989] 2 EGLR 38.
60 See Chap 6.
61 *Estates Gazette Ltd v Benjamin Restaurants Ltd* [1995] 1 All ER 129 (CA); reversing [1993] 4 All ER 367 (QB).
62 LTA 1927, s 19(1)(a).

refusal is to be regarded as reasonable.[63] At least in the case of consent to assign (as opposed to consent to sub-letting), however, the court would probably accept that consent conditional upon the assignee's entering into a direct covenant is reasonable if it is provided for in original lease.[64]

Alternatively, the landlord could draft a clause which would make the obtaining of a direct covenant from a prospective assignee a condition precedent to the tenant's right to assign. The idea has been held valid in the context of offer-to-surrender clauses.[65] Section 19(1)(a) is side-stepped because it bites only when the tenant has a right to assign; whereas, by making the right to assign subject to a condition precedent, the tenant's right to assign does not arise unless and until the specified procedure is complied with. This was the method usually adopted in pre-1996 leases.[66]

If the landlord has not made any provision in the lease to obtain a direct covenant from an assignee, the demand for such a covenant would be subject to section 19(1)(a) scrutiny. It would probably be treated as an unreasonable refusal on the ground that it is a demand for a collateral advantage. It should be remembered that the Landlord and Tenant Act 1988 has strengthened the position of the tenant: it is now for the landlord to show that the refusal was reasonable[67], and the tenant may have a tortious claim for damages for breach of statutory duty.[68]

It has been held that if the landlord by an accord and satisfaction releases his current tenant from all liability under the lease, this will also release an earlier tenant from its contractual liability to the landlord.[69] The reason for this is that, if the earlier tenant were not released and had to make payment to the landlord, it would have its own independent right of indemnity against the current tenant, who would not therefore have been effectively released.

Rights as between original tenant and subsequent assignees *inter se*

If there is a breach of a tenant's covenant after T1 has assigned the lease, the landlord (as has been explained) may have a choice of actions. First, he can bring an action against the tenant for the time-being (*i.e.* the tenant who has committed the breach). Secondly, if the landlord is the original

---

63 *Balfour v Kensington Garden Mansions Ltd* (1932) 49 TLR 29.
64 See further p 146.
65 *Adler v Upper Grosvenor Street Investments Ltd* [1957] 1 WLR 227, and see pp 136–137.
66 See pp. 136–137.
67 LTA 1988, s 1(6).
68 *Ibid*, s 4.
69 *Deanplan v Mahmoud* [1993] Ch 151 (Judge Paul Baker QC sitting as a judge of the High Court).

party to the lease, *i.e.* L1, he can brings an action for damages for the breach against the original tenant, T1. Thirdly, the landlord may have a right of action against an intermediate assignee, if such intermediate assignee entered into a separate covenant with him to observe and perform all the covenants in the lease.

Assume therefore that L1 remains the landlord throughout. At some time in the past, T1 assigned the lease to T2, and T2 in turn later assigned to T3. T3 has now breached a covenant in the lease. If L1 sues T1 for the breach and T1 pays the sums due, T1 may have up to four different courses of action open to him.

First, T1 may be able to recover an indemnity from his immediate assignee, T2, under any indemnity covenant provided by T2.[70] Secondly, T1 might be able to recover directly from T3 under the restitutionary principle exemplified in the rule in *Moule v Garrett.*[71] Thirdly, T1 may be subrogated to any claim that the landlord would have had against T2 (under a direct covenant[72]) or against any surety of T2 or T3.[73] The weakness of a subrogated claim is that the defendant can use against the plaintiff any defence that would have been available to him had the action been brought by the landlord. This might now include the fact that the landlord has not served a default notice upon the defendant[74], and it may indeed be too late to do so. Fourthly, if T1 took a covenant from T2 to pay the rent and to observe and perform the covenants in the lease together with a right of re-entry for breach thereof, T1 has an equitable right of re-entry. This enables him, in such event, to re-take the lease even against a subsequent assignee, except one without notice.[75] As such a right of re-entry is a means of providing T1 with security for the indemnity payment, the defendant may seek relief.[76]

Indemnity covenants

It is necessary to distinguish between implied and express indemnity covenants.

In an assignment for valuable consideration of the entire land comprised in a pre-1996 lease, there is implied a covenant by the assignee

---

70 T2 might then be able to recover in turn from T3 in one of the four ways described in the text.

71 (1872) LR 7 Exch 101.

72 T1 in principle may also have a subrogated claim against T3, but *Moule v Garrett* provides a direct and more secure means of proceeding against T3.

73 *Becton Dickinson (UK) Ltd v Zwebner* [1989] QB 208.

74 LT(C)A 1995, s 17; T2 or its surety might argue this, but no default notice would need to be served on T3 or its surety.

75 *Shiloh Spinners Ltd v Harding* [1973] AC 691.

76 *Ibid.*

with the conveying parties.[77] This is a covenant that the assignees, or persons deriving title under them will duly pay the rent due and observe and perform all the covenants and conditions in the lease, and that they will keep the conveying parties indemnified against all proceedings, costs, claims and expenses on account of their omission to pay the rent or any breach of the said covenants and conditions.[78] Where there is an assignment of part, a parallel covenant is implied, which imposes corresponding obligations in relation to the apportioned rent and the covenants and conditions which relate to the land assigned.[79] Similar covenants are implied in assignments of pre-1996 leases with registered title.[80] "Valuable consideration" has been held to include the assignee's taking on the obligations in the lease;[81] the statutory covenant will therefore be implied even if the assignment is not made in consideration of the payment of a premium. In practice, the statutory covenant arises upon nearly every assignment of a pre-1996 lease.

Because of the principle that under a pre-1996 lease T1 continues to be liable on the covenants in the lease for the whole of the term, even for breaches committed after assignment, T1 will generally seek an express indemnity covenant from his immediate assignee, T2. When T2 assigns, he will in turn naturally seek an indemnity covenant from his assignee, T3, and so on. This means that there can be a chain of indemnity covenants. There is, therefore, as between the original tenant and successive assignees, an order of priority. If obliged to pay, the original tenant can recover from his immediate assignees, who can in turn recover from their immediate assignees, and so on further down the line.[82] A break in the chain, caused (for instance) by the death or insolvency of an intermediate assignee, can therefore leave the immediately preceding assignee with a liability which cannot be recovered, unless recourse can be had to the rule in *Moule* v *Garrett* or to any claim by way of subrogation.

An intermediate tenant can assign the benefit of an express or implied indemnity covenant to an earlier tenant to enable the earlier tenant to recover from a later tenant with whom he has no direct contractual relationship. If the present tenant is in rent arrears, and the landlord recovers the arrears from T1, T1's right of indemnity against T2 is worthless if T2 is also insolvent. If, however, T3 remains solvent, it is possible for T2 to assign to T1 the benefit of its indemnity covenant

---

77 LPA 1925, s 77(1)(C).
78 *Ibid*, Second Sched, Part IX.
79 *Ibid*, s 77(1)(D) and Second Sched, Part X.
80 Land Registration Act 1925, s 24.
81 *Johnsey Estates Ltd* v *Lewis & Manley (Engineering) Ltd* [1987] 2 EGLR 69.
82 *Selous Street Properties Ltd* v *Oronel Fabrics Ltd* [1984] 1 EGLR 50.

against T3 to enable T1 to recover from T3.[83] If T2 is in administration, T2's administrator may be prepared to do this for a consideration. It is clear, however, from *RPH Ltd v Mirror Group (Holdings) Ltd*[84], where these circumstances occurred, that T1 cannot compel T2's administrator either to require T3 to pay the rent to the landlord, or to assign the indemnity covenant[85] to it, since there is no direct legal nexus between the indemnity covenants given by T3 and T2. If T2 had been in liquidation instead of in administration, T1 would probably have been able successfully to negotiate an assignment with the liquidator, who would have been under a duty to realise T2's assets, and the only way in which the indemnity covenant could have been turned to account would have been by its assignment to T1.

The rule in Moule v Garrett

Although, as has been seen, as between L1 and T1, T1 cannot argue he is merely a surety for the assignee responsible for the default, as between T1 and such assignee the latter is primarily liable. The restitutionary principle underlying the rule is that where the plaintiff has been compelled to pay to a creditor a sum for which the defendant is primarily liable, the plaintiff can recover such sum from the defendant. In *Moule* v *Garrett* itself, T1 had assigned to T2, and T2 had later assigned to T3. T3 defaulted in the payment of the rent to L1, who compelled payment from T1. T1 brought an action directly against T3, who, not being T1's immediate assignee, had given no indemnity covenant, express or implied to T1. The court nevertheless relied on the foregoing principle to give judgment for T1.

Although the court in *Moule* v *Garrett* itself considered the principle to based upon an implied contract, the more modern view is to treat the rule in *Moule* v *Garrett* as a rule of law. The importance of the difference is that the parties cannot agree to exclude a rule of law. This was held in *Re Healing Research Trustee Co Ltd*[86], where T2 defaulted in the payment of the rent, and L1 called upon T1 to pay. T2 contended that, since the assignment of the lease to it contained a clause excluding the statutory indemnity covenant[87], the rule in *Moule* v *Garrett* was also ousted. The court rejected this argument, evidently holding that the rule is one of law. An assignee of a lease cannot, therefore, even by express exclusion of the statutory indemnity

---

83 As occurred in *Selous Street Properties Ltd v Oronel Fabrics Ltd* [1984] 1 EGLR 50, 61 (Hutchison J).
84 [1993] 1 EGLR 74.
85 In *RPH Ltd v Mirror Group (Holdings) Ltd* [1993] 1 EGLR 74, this was the covenant implied by LRA 1925, s 24.
86 [1991] BCLC 716.
87 *i.e.* that contained in Part IX of Second Sched to LPA 1925.

covenants, exclude his liability under *Moule* v *Garrett* to indemnify an earlier assignee who has been (or is being) compelled to pay.

Particular rights

Lessee's right to renew the lease

A right conferred on a lessee to renew a commercial lease at the end of the term is less common nowadays, since the tenant of such a lease has a basic statutory right to renew at the end of the term.[88] A right to renew a lease conferred upon the lessee by the lease itself has been held to touch and concern the land, and therefore to run with the lease (to benefit T1's assignees) and with the reversion (to burden L1's assignees).[89] In *Beesly* v *Hallwood Estates Ltd*[90], however, it was held that an option to renew the lease is an estate contract for the purposes of (what is now) the Land Charges Act 1972. Therefore, although an option to renew the lease does touch and concern the land, such a right will not bind a purchaser for money or money's worth of a legal estate (which L2 will generally be) unless protected by registration as a Land Charge, Class C(iv). In registered land, the position is different, because, if the tenant is in actual occupation, his option to renew the lease will be binding on L2 as an overriding interest.[91]

Lessee's option to purchase or right of pre-emption

The lease may confer upon T the right to purchase the reversion (*i.e.* the interest of L), or (in the case of a right of pre-emption) the right to purchase the reversion if L wishes to sell or otherwise dispose of his reversion. Such rights do not touch and concern the demised premises because the rights affect the parties, not in their capacities as landlord and tenant, but only as vendor and purchaser. They do not therefore run with the lease or with the reversion.[92] This means that, unless the lease restricts the right to the period during which T1 is tenant, T1 is entitled to exercise the option against L1 even after T1 has assigned to T2. If, however, L1 has itself assigned the reversion to L2, T1 can sue L1 only for damages for breach of covenant. T1 may enforce the option against L2 if the option has been protected by the

---

88　LTA 1954, Part II.

89　*Richardson* v *Sydenham* (1703) 2 Vern 447.

90　[1960] 1 WLR 549, 557; affirmed in *Taylor Fashions Ltd* v *Liverpool Victoria Trustees Co Ltd* [1982] QB 133 (where, however, equitable estoppel applied), and in *Phillips* v *Mobil Oil Co Ltd* [1989] 3 All ER 97.

91　LRA 1925, s 70(1)(g); *Webb* v *Pollmount Ltd* [1966] Ch 584.

92　*Woodall* v *Clifton* [1905] 2 Ch 257 (option); *Charles Frodisham & Co Ltd* v *Morris* (1974) 229 EG 961, 962 (pre-emption).

appropriate form of registration. In land with unregistered title, the option will not bind L2 unless it is registered as a Land Charge, Class C(iv), even if L2 knew of the existence of the option when taking the assignment.[93] In land with registered title, the option should be protected by entry of a minor interest, failing which it may nevertheless gain protection as an overriding interest if the tenant is in actual occupation.[94]

Assignment of personal rights

Although the benefit of an option to purchase or right of pre-emption cannot pass to T1's assignee by annexation, it may pass to T2 in some other way. Each of these rights is a chose in action which can (unless in terms restricted) be assigned to a third party and exercised by it. Such a right may therefore be assigned to T2, either contemporaneously with the lease, or even subsequently.

Whilst an assignment is best effected expressly, the courts seem willing to find that an assignment of such rights has been effected impliedly. In *Griffith* v *Pelton*[95], the option to purchase the reversion was conferred upon "the lessee", which term was defined in the lease to include the tenant's executors, administrators and assigns. The Court of Appeal held that this showed that the original parties intended that the option should be exercisable by T1's assignees as well; and, furthermore, that a mere assignment of the term was to operate as an assignment of the benefit of the option. Since most leases define the term "lessee" to include (inter alia) an assignee, this principle is of potentially wide application.[96]

It was suggested in *Griffith* v *Pelton* that, by a parallel process, the burden of such a covenant could pass to L2. Even if this is correct, however, an option to purchase the reversion or a right of pre-emption would need (at least in the case of land with unregistered title) to be protected by registration.

---

93 *Midland Bank Trust Co Ltd* v *Green* [1981] AC 513 (HL).
94 LRA 1925, s 70(1)(g).
95 [1958] Ch 205. See also *Re Button's Lease* [1964] Ch 263.
96 In *Kumar* v *Dunning* [1989] QB 193 (CA), however, Browne-Wilkinson V-C commented that he had considerable difficulty in understanding what *Griffith* v *Pelton* did decide.

LEASES CREATED AFTER 31 DECEMBER 1995

The Landlord and Tenant (Covenants) Act 1995[97], which came into force on 1 January 1996, broadly enacts the recommendations made by the Law Commission in 1988[98] that the basic principle governing the running of covenants in a lease is that they should be enforceable only by and against the persons who are the landlord and the tenant for the time being.[99]

The application of the Act

The changes relating to the running of covenants and restrictions on the parties' liabilities apply only to new leases. A new lease is a lease granted on or after 1 January 1996, unless the grant was pursuant to a contract entered into, to an order of the court made, or to the exercise of an option (including a right of first refusal) granted, before that date. A new lease also includes a variation (on or after 1 January 1996) of an existing tenancy that takes effect as a deemed surrender and regrant.[1]

The result that there remain in force two distinct sets of rules relating to the running of leasehold covenants: in essence, one for new leases, and another for pre-1996 leases and other leases which are excluded from the scope of the Act. In this chapter, as elsewhere in this work, unless the context indicates otherwise, a post-1995 lease refers to a lease subject to the provisions of the Act relating to the enforceability of leasehold covenants.

The running of leasehold covenants

Section 3 provides that the benefit and burden of all landlord and tenant covenants[2] are annexed and incident to the demised premises and of the

---

97 On the Act generally, see Luxton, "The Landlord and Tenant (Covenants) Act 1995: its impact on commercial leases", [1996] JBL 388; Fogel & Slessenger, "The Landlord and Tenant (Covenants) Act 1995: where does it fall short of its presumed intent?", *The Blundell Memorial Lectures 1996: Current Problems in Property Law*, 1996, RICS Conferences and Training; Bridge, "Former tenants, future liabilities and the privity of contract principle: the Landlord and Tenant (Covenants) Act 1995", (1996) 55 CLJ 313; Davey, "Privity of contract and leases – reform at last", (1996) 59 MLR 78.
98 Landlord and Tenant Law: Privity of Contract and Estate, Law Com No 174.
99 *Ibid*, para 4.1.
1 LT(C)A 1995, s 1.
2 These are covenants falling to be complied with by the landlord or by the tenant (respectively) of premises demised by the tenancy: LT(C)A 1995, s 28(1).

reversion, and pass on an assignment of the premises or of the reversion.[3] Furthermore, an assignee does not have, by virtue of the Act, any liability or rights under the covenant in relation to any time falling before the assignment.[4] Rights can, however, be expressly assigned.[5]

The rule established in *Re King*[6] that, where a lessor assigns the reversion at a time when rent is in arrears, the right to sue for such rent passes, upon the assignment, to the assignee, does not apply to post-1995 leases, as the right to sue on the covenant to pay rent will be severed, with only the right to sue for future breaches passing under the section to the assignee.[7] Nevertheless, although the existing rent arrears would not be owed to L2, it appears that they would still rank as rent arrears enabling L2 (where the lease contains a proviso for re-entry) to forfeit for the breach.[8]

In post-1995 leases, tenant covenants are made expressly enforceable by (and landlord covenants enforceable against) any immediate reversioner or mortgagee in possession.[9] This reproduces the position under pre-1996 leases.[10]

Covenants that run

The distinction between "touching and concerning" covenants and others, had been judicially criticised as being "purely arbitrary" and "illogical"[11], and the Law Commission had recommended its abolition.[12] It is clear that the Act intends that this distinction be expunged: hence the wide meaning given to a landlord covenant and a tenant covenant[13] and the express statement that the Act applies "whether or not the covenant has reference to the subject matter of the tenancy".[14]

The Act does not, however, operate, "in the case of a covenant which (in whatever terms) is expressed to be personal to any person, to make the

---

3 *Ibid*, s 3(1).

4 *Ibid*, s 23(1).

5 *Ibid*, s 23(2).

6 [1963] Ch 459, interpreting LPA 1925, s 141(1); see also *London & County (A&D) Ltd* v *Wilfred Sportsman Ltd* [1971] Ch 764.

7 LT(C)A 1995, s 23(1). This puts the law into the position favoured by Denning LJ in his dissenting judgment in *Re King* [1963] Ch 459.

8 cf *Kataria* v *Safeland plc* [1998] 5 EG 155 (CA) (pre-1996 lease under which L2 had assigned the right to sue for accrued arrears to L1, but was held entitled to forfeit the lease for their non-payment).

9 LT(C)A 1995, s 15.

10 LPA 1925, ss 141(1), 142(1).

11 *Grant* v *Edmondson* [1931] 1 Ch 1, 28, per Romer LJ.

12 Law Com No 174 (1988), para 4.3; and see *Hua Chiao Commercial Bank Ltd* v *Chiaphua Industries Ltd* [1987] AC 99.

13 LT(C)A 1995, s 28(1).

14 *Ibid*, s 2(1)(a).

covenant enforceable by or (as the case may be) against any other person".[15] This seems to admit the possibility that (as in the case of pre-1996 leases[16]) the burden of a covenant entered into by the tenant can be expressed to be personal to the particular tenant only, whilst the benefit of such covenant can run with the reversion (and vice versa). The parenthesised phrase, "in whatever terms" indicate that a covenant can be "expressed" to be personal even if it does not actually state: "This is a personal covenant ...". It remains unclear, however, what other terms might be a sufficient expression. If a lease which normally refers to the parties as "landlord" and "tenant" contains a covenant which is entered into (or the benefit of which is taken) by one of the parties in its own name, rather than by the generic description, this might be treated as a sufficient expression of the covenant to be personal to such party.

It is more difficult to ascertain whether, in the absence of a clear statement in the lease, the court will be able to determine whether a covenant is "personal" or otherwise by reference to the nature of the obligations which it imposes. In the case of pre-1996 leases, the personal quality of a covenant was merely one factor in determining whether or not it touched and concerned the land. In *P&A Swift Investments v Combined English Stores Group plc*[17], Lord Templeman specified four criteria to determine whether a covenant touches and concerns the land. His third criterion was that "[t]he covenant is not expressed to be personal (that is to say neither being given only to a specific reversioner nor in respect of the obligations only of a specific tenant)."

In contrast to this, in post-1995 leases the expression that the covenant is personal is to be the sole criterion by which the running of covenants is to be determined. If the covenant cannot by its nature be complied with by anyone other than the particular person who entered into it, there would be no sense in treating it as anything other than a personal covenant. In a pre-1996 lease, for example, a covenant by a tenant to repair his own property adjoining that leased to him might touch and concern the land so as to run on the landlord's side; but it could hardly be considered to touch and concern the land so as to run on the tenant's side, since it could be complied with only by the original tenant in his capacity as owner of the adjoining land.[18] It would therefore make sense, in a post-1995 lease, to

---

15 *Ibid*, s 3(6)(a).

16 *Systems Floors Ltd v Ruralpride Ltd* [1995] 1 EGLR 48 (CA).

17 [1989] AC 632 (HL).

18 cf *Dyson v Forster* [1909] AC 98 (HL); contrast *Dewar v Goodman* [1909] AC 72 (HL). The Court of Appeal in *Kumar v Dunning* [1989] QB 193 considered these authorities to be irreconcilable, and preferred to follow *Dyson v Forster*. *Kumar v Dunning* was itself expressly approved by the House of Lords in *P&A Swift Investments v Combined English Stores Group plc* [1989] AC 643.

treat such a covenant as personal on the tenant's side so as to be enforceable by the landlord (or his successor in title) only against the original tenant. It must be admitted, however, that this approach appears to revive in a different guise the touching and concerning distinction which the Act has sought to abolish. If this approach is not adopted, however, the distinction between personal and non-personal covenants must depend upon a covenant's form rather than its substance. In time, this may itself throw up anomalies every bit as objectionable as those which were well documented under the old "touching and concerning" requirement.

Tenant's liability after assignment

The underlying principle of the Act is that a tenant's liability as lessee should cease (except in relation to existing breaches of covenant[19]) when he assigns the lease.[20] The Law Commission did not, however, favour the complete abolition of the doctrine of privity of contract in relation to leases because it appreciated that there were circumstances in which it might be appropriate for a party to be liable for future breaches. The Act implements this recommendation by introducing the authorised guarantee agreement.

Authorised guarantee agreements

An assigning tenant may be required to become a guarantor of his immediate assignee under an authorised guarantee agreement (AGA)[21] if the lease contains either an absolute or a qualified covenant against assignment, if the consent of the landlord (or some other person) is made subject to a condition that the tenant is to enter into such an agreement, and if the tenant enters into the agreement pursuant to that condition.[22] An agreement is not an AGA to the extent that it purports to make the assignor a guarantor for any person other than the immediate assignee, or to impose any liability or obligation on the assignor after the immediate assignee is released from liability.[23] Subject to this, an AGA may require the tenant to enter into a new tenancy in the event of the tenancy's being disclaimed after assignment, but only if the term of such tenancy expires no later than the term of the tenancy assigned, and if the tenant covenants which it contains are no more onerous than those of that tenancy.[24]

With the abolition of the continuing contractual liability of tenants

---

19 LT(C)A 1995, s 24(1).
20 *Ibid,* s 5(2).
21 *Ibid,* s 16(1).
22 *Ibid,* s 16(3).
23 *Ibid,* s 16(4).
24 *Ibid,* s 16(5)(c).

under post-1995 leases, intending lessors will be keen to ensure that they can obtain an AGA from a tenant who wishes to assign, and so will generally insist that the lease contain an absolute or qualified covenant against assignment. If the prohibition upon assignment is absolute, it is likely to have a depressing effect on the rent; so a prospective lessor is likely to impose the obligation in one of two ways. First, he may seek to impose an initial absolute prohibition upon assignment, but mitigate its effects by giving the tenant a qualified right to assign if it complies with the condition precedent of entering into an AGA. Secondly, in the case of a commercial lease, the prospective lessor may use the new power to specify what is to comprise a reasonable refusal of consent to assign[25] by ensuring that the lease states that it shall be reasonable for him to refuse consent to assign to a tenant who declines to enter into an AGA.

Since a tenant cannot be liable under an AGA after his immediate assignee has assigned the lease under a lawful assignment, a tenant might seek to end its liability under such agreement by using the device of two assignments in quick succession, *i.e.* T1, who really intends to assign to T3, might do so via an intermediate assignee (T2) – perhaps a company in the same group. There is nothing in the Act to prohibit assignments designed to nullify the value of an AGA; but a prospective lessor can reduce the effectiveness of such a scheme by ensuring that the lease contains a qualified covenant against assignment. It will be reasonable for the landlord to refuse consent to assign if, for instance, T2 is not of sufficient financial standing.[26]

The liability of a tenant under an AGA is that of a guarantor; and the Act expressly declares that the rules of law relating to guarantees (and in particular those relating to the release of sureties) are, subject to its terms, applicable in relation to any authorised guarantee agreement as in relation to any other guarantee agreement.[27]

Assignments made in breach of covenant or by operation of law

A tenant's own liability under the covenants in the lease will continue, despite assignment, if the assignment is made in breach of covenant or occurs by operation of law. In these instances (which the Act calls "excluded assignments") the assignor's liability continues until there is a later assignment which is not an excluded assignment.[28] If, therefore, T1 assigns to T2 in breach of a covenant against assignment, and if T2 later

---

25 LT(C)A 1995, s 22, inserting new s 19(1A) into the LTA 1927.
26 *Air India v Balabel* [1993] 2 EGLR 66.
27 LT(C)A 1995, s 16(8). For further discussion of the position of a former tenant under an AGA, see Chap 4.
28 LT(C)A 1995, s 11(2).

assigns to T3 with L's consent, T1 will remain liable under the tenant covenants in the lease until the assignment to T3. In circumstances such as these, there is potential for the application of a restitutionary claim such as that exemplified in *Moule v Garrett*.[29] It would enable T1, if he were required to make payment to L under the covenants in the lease for the default of T2 while T2 was tenant, to recover from T2. Furthermore, if when L consents to the assignment to T3, L extracts an AGA from T2, L can also demand that T1 enter into a similar agreement with L, also guaranteeing the performance of the covenants by T3.[30]

A landlord's continuing liability after assignment of the reversion

A landlord who assigns the reversion in the whole[31] of the premises may apply to be released from the landlord's covenants; if he is so released, he also ceases to be entitled to the benefit of the tenant's covenants as from the assignment.[32] The application for release of a covenant to any extent is made by serving a notice on the tenant either before the assignment is made or within four weeks of its being made.[33] The Bill originally permitted only pre-assignment applications; but it was amended to permit applications after assignment to enable a landlord to assign without having to reveal details to the tenant in advance.[34] The notice must inform the tenant both of the proposed assignment (or of the fact that the assignment has already taken place) and of the request for the covenant to be released to that extent.[35]

The covenant is released if the tenant fails to serve a notice of objection on the landlord within four weeks of the landlord's service of the notice of application, or if he serves on the landlord a notice in writing consenting to the release (and, if he had previously served a notice objecting to it, stating that that notice is withdrawn).[36] Any release made in accordance with this procedure is treated as occurring at the time of the assignment.[37] In some instances, therefore, release will be retrospective. If the tenant does serve a notice of objection within four weeks, the landlord may apply

---

29 (1872) LR 7 Ex 101.
30 LT(C)A 1995, s 16(6).
31 There are similar provisions by which a landlord who assigns part of the premises can obtain a release in relation to the part assigned: LT(C)A 1995, s 6(3).
32 LT(C)A 1995, s 6(2).
33 *Ibid,* s 8(1)
34 See debate at Committee Stage: 565 HL Official Report (5th series) col 368, 21 June 1995.
35 LT(C)A 1995, s 8(1).
36 *Ibid,* s 8(2)(a) and (c).
37 *Ibid,* s 8(3).

to the court (a county court)[38] for a declaration that it is reasonable for the covenant to be so released.[39]

If a former landlord remains bound by a tenant covenant after assignment, he may nevertheless apply to be released on a later assignment of the reversion.[40]

PROVISIONS APPLICABLE TO ALL LEASES

Sections 17–20 of the Landlord and Tenant (Covenants) Act 1995 apply to all leases, regardless of when they were entered into.

Default notices

Section 17 restricts the liability of a former tenant who is liable to pay a fixed amount (whether under an authorised guarantee agreement or, in a pre-1996 lease, under the covenants in the lease).[41] The former tenant is not liable to pay such charge unless, within six months of its becoming due, the landlord serves upon him a notice in writing informing him that the charge is now due and that the landlord intends to recover from him such amount (with interest where payable) as is therein specified.[42] Identical provisions apply *mutatis mutandis* to restrict the liability of a former tenant's guarantor.[43] A fixed charge means[44] rent, a service charge[45], and any amount payable under a tenant covenant which provides for the payment of a liquidated sum in the event of failure to comply with any such covenant.[46]

Variation of covenant

Section 18 expressly states that a former tenant cannot be liable under an authorised guarantee agreement (or, in a pre-1996 lease, under a covenant) for any increased amount which may be payable under the covenants as a

---

38 *Ibid*, s 8(4)(c).
39 *Ibid*, s 8(2)(b).
40 *Ibid*, s 7(2).
41 *Ibid*, s 17(1)
42 *Ibid*, s 17(2).
43 *Ibid*, s 17(3). See further Chap 4.
44 *Ibid*, s 17(4).
45 As defined in s 17(4)((b).
46 See *e.g. Jervis* v *Harris* [1996] 1 All ER 303 (CA), affirming *Hamilton* v *Martell Securities Ltd* [1984] Ch 266.

result of a variation effected after he has assigned.[47] This section was evidently intended to abrogate the broader principle contained in *Centrovincial Estates v Bulk Storage Ltd*[48], where, Harman J held T1 liable to pay the higher rent upon the principle that T1, by assigning the lease, is to be treated as putting T2 into the position of being able to vary the terms of the lease so as to vary the L1-T1 contract.

This broader principle has, however, now been rejected by the Court of Appeal in *Friends Provident Life Office v British Railways Board*.[49] The court there evidently anticipated the new section, which merely states the existing position at common law.

Overriding lease

Sections 19 and 20 provide an extended use for concurrent leases. Under the old law, whilst a former tenant who had been made to pay rent arrears which accrued due after assignment had a right to recover such payment from the tenant in default, he had no other right against the tenant in default.

Under the new Act, a former tenant or a guarantor (the claimant) who has been made to pay in accordance with section 17, is entitled to have the landlord grant him an overriding lease of the premises demised,[50] which means a tenancy of the reversion for a term equal to the remainder of the term of the existing tenancy plus three days,[51] and containing (subject to any agreed modifications) the same covenants as the existing tenancy.[52] A claim to an overriding lease must be made by notice in writing to the landlord within 12 months of the payment's being made.[53] Within a reasonable time of receiving the request, the landlord must grant and deliver an overriding lease to the claimant;[54] if he fails to do so, the claimant has a right to recover damages against him for breach of statutory duty.[55] The claimant must thereupon deliver to the landlord a

---

47 LT(C)A 1995, s 18(2), (3).
48 (1983) 46 P & CR 393; [1983] 2 EGLR 45.
49 [1996] 1 All ER 336.
50 LT(C)A 1995, s 19(1).
51 *Ibid*, s 19(2)(a), which also provides that if the landlord's reversion on the existing tenancy is less than three days, the period is reduced so far as is necessary to avoid displacing such reversion.
52 *Ibid*, s 19(2)(b). A covenant in the existing lease is not, however, to be reproduced to the extent that it is expressed to be a personal covenant (*ibid*, s 19(3)) or is spent: s 19(4)(b). If rights and liabilities in the existing lease are determined by reference to its commencement, the corresponding covenant in the overriding lease is to framed by reference to the same commencement date: *ibid*, s 19(4)(a).
53 *Ibid*, s 19(5).
54 *Ibid*, s 19(6)(a).
55 *Ibid*, s 20(3).

duly executed counterpart (or else lose all rights otherwise exercisable under the overriding lease)[56] and is liable for the landlord's reasonable costs.[57]

If more than one person has been made to pay the existing tenant's arrears, each has a right to request an overriding lease. The basic principle is that the overriding lease is to be granted to the first such person to make the request.[58] If, however, two or more requests are made on the same day, a request by a former tenant is to be treated as made before that of a guarantor; and, subject to that, the request of a person whose liability under the covenant commenced at the earliest date is to be treated as made first.[59]

There can exist more than one overriding lease.[60] If A and B are both made to pay for the default of the existing tenant, T, and A puts in notice first and obtains an overriding lease from L, B may nevertheless also obtain an overriding lease, so that A becomes B's landlord under B's reversionary lease.

ENFORCEABILITY OF COVENANTS IN SUB-LEASES

There is no privity of estate between a head-landlord (L) and his immediate tenant's (T's) sub-tenant (S), and the creation of a sub-lease does not itself create privity of contract between L and S. L might, nevertheless be able to ensure compliance by S with the covenants in the head-lease in one of four ways.

Action on a direct covenant with S

L can enforce a covenant in the sub-lease against S if L (or his predecessor in title) is a direct covenantee. L may be able to secure this if the head-lease contains a covenant by T not to sub-let without L's consent, such consent being conditional upon T's securing from S a direct covenant with L to observe and perform all the covenants and conditions in the head-lease (other than those relating to the payment of rent) during the term of the sub-lease. If a landlord can secure a direct covenant from S in these terms, it can bring a direct action against S for breach of the covenants in the head-

---

56 *Ibid*, s 20(3).
57 *Ibid*, s 19(6)(b).
58 *Ibid*, s 19(7).
59 *Ibid*, s 19(8). Special provision is made for withdrawals: s 19(9).
60 *Ibid*, s 19(11).

lease. A landlord should therefore ensure that the lease contains an express covenant in a suitable form.[61]

The sub-lease may contain covenants entered into by S with T which also benefit L, such as a covenant by S with T to permit T and the superior landlord to enter the premises for the purpose of ascertaining the state of repair, and (in the event of S's failing to comply with any notice to repair) to permit T and the superior landlord to enter the premises to execute such repairs and to pay the costs of such repairs. L can enforce such a covenant, however, only if the covenant is made with him; the Law of Property Act 1925, section 56, does not enable him to enforce it merely by virtue of the fact that the covenant benefits him.[62]

Action against T

L may be able to ensure compliance indirectly. Because T remains liable on the covenants in the head-lease after sub-letting (T does, after all, remain the tenant), T will invariably extract from S a covenant in the sub-lease that S will observe and perform all the covenants in the head-lease. Although L cannot himself sue on such covenants in the sub-lease, he can proceed against T for breach of the covenants in the head-lease; and T will in turn sue S on the sub-lease.

Forfeiture of head-lease

If there is a breach of the covenants in the head-lease, L may be able (assuming there is a proviso for re-entry for breach) to forfeit the head-lease. If the head-lease is forfeited, any sub-lease falls with it; although S (as well as T) may be able to claim relief from forfeiture. The possibility of forfeiture ensures that S takes an interest in seeing that the covenants in the head-lease are complied with.

Enforcement of restrictive covenants

Under the doctrine of *Tulk* v *Moxhay*[63], L may be able to enforce against S (by means of an injunction), covenants in the head-lease which are of a negative or restrictive nature. Such covenants relate mainly to user; but the doctrine has been held applicable to a covenant against sub-letting, enabling L to obtain a mandatory injunction against S and T, requiring S to surrender up to T a sub-lease granted by T in breach of a covenant against

---

61 See the precedent on p 149 *infra*.
62 *Amsprop Trading Ltd v Harris Distribution Ltd* [1997] 2 All ER 990 (Neuberger J).
63 (1848) 2 Ph 774.

sub-letting in the L-T head-lease.[64]

Restrictive covenants in a lease cannot be registered as land charges;[65] under *Tulk* v *Moxhay*, therefore, the burden of a restrictive covenant in a head-lease (whether made before 1926 or after 1925) binds all sub-lessees except one who can establish that he is a bona fide purchaser for value of the legal estate without notice.

Under an open contract, a prospective sub-lessee is entitled to inspect the head-lease. A sub-lessee will therefore be treated as having constructive notice of restrictive covenants in the head-lease, and so will be bound by them.[66] It is therefore vital for a solicitor acting for a prospective sub-lessee to insist upon the right to inspect the head-lease. Failure to do so could render the solicitor liable to an action in negligence should the sub-lessee suffer resulting loss.

A prospective sub-lessee is not, however, under an open contract, entitled to inspect the title to the freehold.[67] A solicitor acting for an intending sub-lessee must nevertheless ensure that restrictive covenants affecting the freehold title are disclosed, as they will be binding on a sub-lessee under *Tulk* v *Moxhay*, provided (in the case of post-1925 covenants) they are protected by registration.

ENFORCEABILITY OF LEASEHOLD COVENANTS AGAINST ADVERSE POSSESSORS

After 12 years' adverse possession, the title of the owner of the estate adversely possessed is barred.[68] If a person has 12 years' adverse possession against land which is leased, only the title of the lessee is barred, not the title of the reversioner.

Land with unregistered title

In land with unregistered title, subject to one qualification, L cannot enforce against the adverse possessor (A) the covenants in the lease, nor sue A for the rent which the lease reserves. The reason is that, in unregistered land, the statute of limitation does not operate as a parliamentary

---

64 *Hemingway Securities Ltd* v *Dunraven Ltd* [1995] 2 EGLR 61.
65 LCA 1972, s 2(5).
66 *Hill* v *Harris* [1965] 2 QB 601.
67 LPA 1925, s 44.
68 Limitation Act 1980.

conveyance, *i.e.* the estate of A is not the former estate of T.[69] There is therefore no privity of estate between L and A, and neither is there privity of contract. A has an independent estate whose length is co-terminous with that of T's, which has been barred. Since therefore A is not L's lessee, no action of forfeiture can be brought against A, and it might appear that L must wait until the expiration of the term of T's (barred) lease before being able to claim possession against A.

In practice, however, L's position may be stronger that this. First, L's lease with T may contain both a covenant by T (whether absolute or qualified) not to part with possession (whether voluntarily or involuntarily) and a right of re-entry for breach of covenant. In such circumstances, A's adverse possession is a breach of covenant by T, which enables L to bring an action for possession. Such a right, being that of L rather than that of T, is not barred by the statute of limitation. In an action by L against T to forfeit the lease, A (not having privity of estate with L) cannot claim relief from forfeiture.[70] This indicates the importance to a landlord of extracting from the prospective tenant a suitable covenant against parting with possession. Neither a covenant against assignment, nor a covenant against sub-letting, would be breached by an act of adverse possession. Secondly, the House of Lords has held that, even after the statute of limitation has barred T's title, T still retains the power to surrender his lease to L, thus enabling L to obtain possession against A.[71] Collusion between L and T can therefore have the desired result for L. Thirdly, restrictive covenants in the L-T lease (which are not registrable) will be binding on A because A cannot establish the defence of bona fide purchaser for value of a legal estate in the land without notice: A acquires title, not by purchase, but by operation of law.[72]

Land with registered title

In land with registered title, the Land Registration Act 1925 provides that, after adverse possession for 12 years, T's title is held in trust for A. Thus, at the end of that period, A can apply to the Land Registry to be registered as proprietor. Between the expiry of the period of 12 years adverse possession and the registration of A's title, T holds his estate upon trust for A.[73]

---

69 *Tichborne v Weir* (1892) 67 LT 735 (L unable to sue A for breach of repairing covenant in T's lease).
70 *Tickner v Buzacott* [1965] Ch 426.
71 *Fairweather v St Marylebone Property Co Ltd* [1963] AC 510.
72 *Re Nisbett & Potts' Contract* [1905] 1 Ch 391.
73 LRA 1925, s 75(1).

It might appear from this that, in land with registered title, the combined effect of the statute of limitation and the Land Registration Act 1925 is indeed to pass to A, upon registration, the same estate in the land as was formerly vested in T.[74] Upon registration, A would therefore be placed into the position of assignee of T's lease, so that L and A would be entitled to enforce against each other the covenants in the lease. L would, of course, still be entitled to bring an action for forfeiture for breach of a covenant against parting with possession; but A, having privity of estate with L, could presumably claim relief from forfeiture. Furthermore, T would not, in the case of registered land, have an estate which he could surrender in order to enable L to claim possession.

The better view, however, is that A does not acquire by registration the same estate as T. Although in *Spectrum Investment Co v Holmes*[75] the adverse possessor was registered with a leasehold title, it is understood that usual Land Registry practice is to register an adverse possessor with a qualified freehold title, which thereby excepts from the register the claims of the landlord when the lease determines.[76]

Until the adverse possessor acquires a registered title, his rights under the Limitation Acts (whether acquired or in course of being acquired) are protected as an overriding interest.[77]

74 *Spectrum Investment Co v Holmes* [1981] 1 WLR 221.
75 *Ibid.*
76 See Cooke, "Adverse possession – problems of title in registered land", (1994) 14 *Legal Studies* 1, 9.
77 LRA 1925, s 70(1)(f) and (g).

Chapter 6

RESTRICTIONS ON DISPOSITION

INTRODUCTION

A t common law, a lessee has complete freedom to dispose of the term in any way he wishes, *e.g.* by assignment, sub-lease, mortgage, or by parting with possession. In the context of leases of commercial property, the only restrictions upon this freedom of disposition are those which may be contained in the lease itself.

Types of restriction

Covenant

The lease may contain a covenant by the tenant not to assign, sub-let, mortgage, charge, or part with possession or occupation. This is the most common type of restriction on disposal. In older leases, the restriction upon disposition was frequently framed in the "traditional three-limbed form"[1] of a covenant against **"assignment, underletting or parting with possession."**

Condition or limitation

The lease may be expressed to be subject to a condition subsequent, *i.e.* upon the tenant's assigning, sub-letting or parting with possession, or attempting to do any of these things. Alternatively, the lease may be expressed to be determinable, *e.g.* it may provide that it is to continue "for so long as" or "while" the tenant does not (or does not attempt to) assign, sub-let or part with possession.

Extent of restriction

A covenant restricting disposition can take one of three forms: absolute, qualified or fully qualified. An *absolute* covenant against assignment is one in which the tenant simply covenants not to assign. A *qualified* covenant against assignment is one in which the tenant covenants not to assign without the landlord's consent. A *fully qualified* covenant against assignment is one in which the tenant covenants not to assign without the

---

1 *Marks v Warren* [1978] 2 EGLR 41, per Browne-Wilkinson J.

landlord's consent, such consent not to be unreasonably withheld.

An absolute covenant by the tenant against disposition might take the form of a covenant:

> "Not to assign transfer charge underlet or part with or share possession or occupation of all or any part or parts of the demised premises."

A covenant against assignment does not prohibit a declaration of trust.[2] Occupation and the carrying on of a business by all or any of the beneficiaries under the trust is treated for the purposes of the Landlord and Tenant Act 1954, Part II[3], as equivalent to the occupation or carrying on of a business by the tenant.[4] The tenant may therefore retain security of tenure as a business tenant even after it has removed from the premises.[5] The landlord might therefore consider obtaining a covenant from the tenant

> "Not to hold all or any part or parts of the demised premises on trust."

Where the lease is granted to two or more persons jointly, they will inevitably hold the estate upon trust, and a covenant against holding the property upon trust would need to provide an exception to allow for this.

Construction of restrictions on disposition

A restriction on disposition is construed strictly against the lessor.[6] A strict construction means "that the court should be reluctant to adopt a wider or more generous construction as opposed to a narrower or more literal construction and that if a covenant can have two meanings, the ambiguity is to be resolved in favour of the tenant."[7] A covenant against sub-letting part is therefore not breached by a sub-letting of the whole[8] and a general restriction upon assignment will be construed to comprise only legal (and

---

2 *Gentle v Faulkner* [1900] 2 QB 267.

3 LTA 1954, s 23.

4 *Ibid*, s 41(1).

5 See further Lewison, *Drafting Business Leases,* 5th ed (1996) FT Law & Tax, at 232.

6 *Church v Brown* (1808) 15 Ves Jun, 258, 265 (Lord Eldon LC). Since most leases contain a proviso for re-entry, a strict construction may be justified on the ground that breach of the covenant will usually entail a forfeiture: *Russell v Beecham* [1924] 1 KB 525, 539 (CA) (Atkin LJ). Even in the absence of a proviso for re-entry, however, a strict construction is appropriate on the basis of non-derogation from grant: *Cook v Shoesmith* [1951] 1 KB 752, 755 (CA) (Somervell LJ). See further Crabb, *Leases: Covenants and Consents,* 1st ed (1991) Sweet & Maxwell, at 7–9.

7 *Yorkshire Metropolitan Properties Ltd v Co-operative Retail Services Ltd* [1997] EGCS 57, per Neuberger J.

8 *Field v Barkworth* [1986] 1 All ER 362. The decision in *Grove v Portal* [1902] 1 Ch 727, suggests that the courts would similarly treat a covenant against the assignment of part as not being breached by an assignment of the whole; but see Crabb, *Leases: Covenants and Consents,* 1st ed, (1991), Sweet & Maxwell, at 12.

not equitable) assignments.[9] A general restriction upon assignment will also prohibit only voluntary assignments, meaning assignments in which the lessee is a voluntary assignee: involuntary assignments fall outside its scope. Such a general restriction will not, therefore, include an assignment by way of compulsory purchase[10], or the taking of the lease by the tenant's judgment creditor in execution[11], or the vesting of the lease in the lessee's trustee in bankruptcy[12], or in his personal representatives upon death.[13] Similarly, the ouster of the tenant by an adverse possessor against the tenant's will does not, it would seem, breach a covenant against parting with possession.[14] If, therefore, the lessor wishes to restrict dispositions in such cases, the wording of the covenant must be widened in the appropriate manner.

However, "strict construction does not mean departing from the ordinary meaning of the words used, unless, of course, the ordinary meaning produces a capricious or unlikely result."[15] The court does not therefore always adopt the narrowest possible meaning. Thus a covenant against under-letting the whole is breached by the grant of two under-leases which between them comprise the whole[16]; a covenant merely against underletting or parting with possession will be breached by an assignment that necessarily involves a parting with possession[17]; a mortgage by sub-demise breaches a covenant against sub-letting[18]; and a covenant against parting with possession probably also precludes a parting by way of sub-letting.[19]

The courts recognise the importance of clear precedents to those drafting leases, and (whilst they must attempt to find the meaning of the

---

9 *Gentle v Faulkner* [1900] 2 QB 267 (declaration of trust); *M'Kay v M'Nally* (1879) 4 LR Ir 438, 451 (Palles CB) (contract to assign).

10 *Slipper v Tottenham and Hampstead Junction Railway Co* (1867) LR 4 Eq 112, 114 (Lord Romilly MR).

11 *Doe d. Mitchinson v Carter* (1798) 8 Term Rep 57 (Lord Kenyon CJ); unless the lessee consents to judgment being entered against him in order to defeat the restriction on assignment: see the further proceedings in *Doe d Mitchinson v Carter* (1799) 8 Term Rep 300. See further Crabb, *Leases: Covenants and Consents*, 1st ed, (1991), Sweet & Maxwell, at 21–22.

12 *Re Riggs* [1901] 2 KB 16 (Wright J); *Re Griffiths* [1926] 1 Ch 1007 (Romer J).

13 *Seers v Hinds* (1791) 1 Ves 294 (Lord Thurlow LC).

14 *Doe v Payne* (1815) 1 Stark. 86 (Lord Ellenborough); but the covenant probably is breached if the tenant is turned out willingly: *Doe v Rickarby* (1803) 5 Esp. 4. See further Crabb, *Leases: Covenants and Consents*, 1st ed, (1991), Sweet & Maxwell, at pp 18–19.

15 *Yorkshire Metropolitan Properties Ltd v Co-operative Retail Services Ltd* [1997] EGCS 57, per Neuberger J.

16 *Chatterton v Terrell* [1923] 1 AC 578 (HL), applied in *Yorkshire Metropolitan Properties Ltd v Co-operative Retail Services Ltd* [1997] EGCS 57; cf *Roberts v Enlayde Ltd* [1924] 1 KB 335 (CA).

17 *Marks v Warren* [1978] 2 EGLR 41.

18 *Sergeant v Nash & Co* [1903] 2 KB 304 (CA).

19 *Russell v Beecham* [1924] 1 KB 525.

words used from the context in which they appear) they do not strive to distinguish long-established decisions of the higher courts on words which are virtually identical.[20]

Effect of disposition in breach of a restriction

A lease does not come to an end merely because there is a disposition by the tenant which breaches either a condition or a limitation, or a covenant which provides for the lease to terminate upon its breach. The landlord must take steps to forfeit the lease, and before he can do this he must serve a notice under the Law of Property Act 1925, section 146.[21]

An assignment of the lease in breach of a covenant or condition is effective to vest the term in the assignee, albeit subject to the landlord's right to proceed to terminate the lease in accordance with the statutory requirements.[22] The notice under section 146 should therefore be served on the assignee.[23]

As an alternative to seeking to forfeit the lease for the tenant's assigning or sub-letting in breach of a disposition covenant, the landlord may be able to obtain a mandatory injunction to compel the assignee or sub-lessee to re-assign or surrender[24], either on the ground that he induced a breach of contract, or because he can be treated as having taken with notice of the restriction, which therefore binds him under the principle of *Tulk* v *Moxhay*.[25]

The running of disposition covenants

A covenant not to assign without the lessor's consent "touches and concerns" the land[26] and the benefit and burden of it therefore run on the assignment of the term and the reversion of a pre-1996 lease. The same is undoubtedly true of any absolute or qualified covenant against any type of disposition or parting with possession. A covenant restrictive of disposition in a post-1995 lease runs with the lease and the reversion unless expressed to be personal.[27]

---

20 *Yorkshire Metropolitan Properties Ltd* v *Co-operative Retail Services Ltd* [1997] EGCS 57 (Neuberger J).
21 See Chap 13.
22 *Old Grovebury Farm Ltd* v *W Seymour Plant Sales & Hire (No 2) Ltd* [1979] 1 WLR 1397. See also *Sanctuary Housing Association* v *Baker* [1998] 9 EG 150 (CA) (landlord's consent to assign obtained by fraud).
23 See Chap 13.
24 *Hemingway Securities Ltd* v *Dunraven Ltd* [1995] 1 EGLR 61 (Ch.).
25 (1848) 2 Ph 774.
26 *Williams* v *Earle* (1868) LR 3 QB 739.
27 LT(C)A 1995, s 3(6).

Consent "subject to licence"

Since a landlord's consent to a disposition is a unilateral act, the words "subject to licence" do not have an automatic suspensive effect, and the court may still infer from the landlord's correspondence and conduct that a licence has been granted.[27a]

QUALIFIED COVENANTS AGAINST DISPOSITION

In some instances, statute intervenes to turn a qualified covenant into a fully qualified covenant, *i.e.* it implies into the covenant an additional qualification that the lessor's consent is not to be unreasonably refused. It should be noted that the following statutory provisions apply only to covenants that are in terms already qualified. None of them applies where the covenant against disposition is absolute.

Law of Property Act 1925: consent to mortgage

Where a licence is required to sub-demise by way of legal mortgage, such licence is not to be unreasonably refused.[28] Further, where a licence to assign is required on a sale by a mortgagee, such licence is not to be unreasonably refused.[29]

Landlord and Tenant Act 1927

Because of its generality, the most important statutory provision is the Landlord and Tenant Act 1927, section 19(1)(a). This applies to leases that contain a covenant, condition or agreement against assigning, underletting, charging or parting with possession of the demised premises (or part thereof) without licence or consent. Such covenant, etc, is, notwithstanding any express provision to the contrary, deemed to be subject to a proviso to the effect that such licence or consent is not to be unreasonably withheld.

As mentioned above, this provision applies only to qualified covenants, not to covenants that are absolute. Furthermore, it applies only to covenants against disposition. For the impact of the Act on covenants restrictive of improvements, see Chapter 7; and for its impact on user covenants, see Chapter 8.

27a *Next plc v National Farmers' Union Mutual Insurance Co Ltd* [1997] EGCS 181 (Morland J), applying the principle stated in *Prudential Assurance Co Ltd v Mount Eden Land Ltd* [1997] 1 EGLR 37 (discussed in Chapter 7).
28 LPA 1925, s 86(1).
29 *Ibid*, s 89(1).

Parties cannot generally specify what is a reasonable refusal

The general rule is that the parties to the lease cannot weaken the impact of section 19(1)(a) by trying to specify in the lease the circumstances in which a refusal is to be regarded as reasonable. Statute has recently abrogated this rule in respect of a post-1995 lease of commercial premises, where the parties are permitted to specify the circumstances in which a refusal to consent to an *assignment* is reasonable.[30] The narrowness of the abrogation should be noted. Even under a post-1995 lease of commercial premises, the parties cannot specify what is reasonable refusal to consent to any disposition other than an assignment. A qualified covenant against sub-letting or parting with possession, for instance, remains subject to section 19(1)(a).

The general rule was laid down in *Balfour* v *Kensington Garden Mansions Ltd.*[31] There a lease of a flat contained a qualified covenant by the tenant against sub-letting. The covenant was, however, subject to a proviso that the landlord could require, as a condition of consent, that the proposed sub-lessee enter into a direct covenant with the lessor to perform and observe the covenants in the head-lease. It was further provided that "non-compliance with such condition shall be deemed a reasonable ground for refusing such consent." The court held that the final proviso was void and therefore to be disregarded in deciding what was reasonable. On the facts the court held the landlord's refusal unreasonable: first, because the sub-lessee would already be bound to pay the rent under the sub-lease to his immediate landlord; and, secondly, since there had been a fall in the rents since the lease had been granted, no sub-lessee could be expected to covenant to pay the lessor a rent higher than that reserved in the sub-lease.

A similar approach was adopted in *Re Smith's Lease*[32], where a fully qualified covenant against disposal was expressed to be subject to the proviso that a refusal of consent should not be deemed unreasonable merely because the lessor at the time of refusal also offered to accept a surrender; and, in the event of such an offer being made, the lessee was to surrender the tenancy. The proviso was held ineffective (and the refusal was held unreasonable).

Some older leases provide that:

> "The landlord shall not unreasonably refuse consent in respect of a respectable and responsible person."

---

30 LT(C)A 1995, s 22, inserting a new s 19(1A) into LTA 1927.
31 (1932) 49 TLR 29.
32 [1951] 1 All ER 346.

"Respectable" in this context appears to refer to a person's general reputation; whereas "responsible" relates to a person's financial ability to pay the rent and observe and perform the other covenants in the lease. It has been suggested that such a qualification also falls foul of section 19(1)(a).[33] In *Moat v Martin*[34], however, a clause in terms similar to this, but with the word "unreasonably" omitted, was upheld on the basis that the section did not invalidate a provision whereby the landlord conceded more than the statute required of him. The clause meant that the landlord could not object to any proposed assignee who was respectable and responsible, even though the landlord might, but for the proviso, have reasonably objected on other grounds.

Assignment of post-1995 commercial leases

The Landlord and Tenant (Covenants) Act 1995 contains an important concession for landlords of non-residential tenancies, in that, by adding a new sub-section to the Landlord and Tenant Act 1927, section 19[35], it effectively enables the parties to specify what is reasonable refusal to consent to an assignment. As has already been pointed out, this relaxation applies only to qualified restrictions on assignment; it does not, for example, enable the parties to specify what is a reasonable refusal to consent to a sub-letting.

Under the modification to the 1927 Act, the parties to a post-1995 commercial lease may by agreement specify the circumstances in which the landlord may withhold his licence or consent to an assignment of the demised premises, or the conditions subject to which any such licence or consent may be granted.[36] A landlord who refuses consent in reliance on such circumstances (where they exist) or gives his consent subject to such conditions, will not be treated as refusing consent unreasonably or as imposing unreasonable conditions.[37] In most cases, such circumstances or conditions will be contained in the lease; but, in any event, they must be agreed before the tenant applies for the landlord's consent to assign.[38] Once such application has been made, any non-specified circumstances or conditions on which the landlord relies will continue to be subject to the reasonableness scrutiny of the 1927 Act.

---

33 See Crabb, *Leases: Covenants and Consents*, p 36.
34 [1950] 1 KB 175.
35 This is a new s 19(1A) inserted into LTA 1927 by LT(C)A 1995, s 22.
36 LTA 1927, s 19(1A)(a), (b).
37 *Ibid*, s 19(1A) (i), (ii).
38 *Ibid*, s 19(1B).

Condition precedent as a way around section 19(1)(a)

Even before the partial relaxation of the rule that the parties cannot themselves agree what is a reasonable refusal to consent, they were nevertheless free to impose restrictions upon disposition by means of the condition precedent. The lease will initially impose an absolute prohibition upon disposition, but provide that the tenant can acquire a (fully) qualified right of disposition if it complies with certain conditions or if a specified state of affairs exists.

The use of a condition precedent in relation to restrictions on disposition was upheld in *Adler v Upper Grosvenor Street Investments Ltd*.[39] The covenant began in the usual form of a qualified covenant not to assign; but this was subject to a proviso that if the tenant should wish to assign he had first to offer voluntarily to surrender the lease, and the landlord could accept such offer within 21 days. Such a clause was held valid on the basis that the sub-section bites only when the lessee has a right to assign (albeit qualified by consent); whereas under an *Adler*-type clause such a right did not arise until the tenant had first made an offer to surrender and such offer had not been accepted by the landlord. The validity of such a clause was affirmed in *Bocardo SA v S & M Hotels Ltd*.[40]

The use of the condition precedent as a means of avoiding the Landlord and Tenant Act 1927, section 19(1)(a) sometimes arose (as in the *Adler* case itself) in the context of offer-to-surrender clauses. However, the impact of the Landlord and Tenant Act 1954, section 38(1), as interpreted in *Allnatt London Properties Ltd v Newton*[41], has reduced the value of offer-to-surrender clauses in commercial leases.[42]

Despite the opportunity which is now afforded to specify in a commercial lease what is to constitute a reasonable refusal to consent to assign, it appears that many practitioners are continuing to use the condition precedent as a means of protecting the landlord's position upon assignment.[43] In a post-1995 lease, the device is commonly used to extract obligations, notably to require an assigning tenant to enter into an authorised guarantee agreement, and to require an assignee to provide guarantors. Conditions precedent frequently deny the tenant the right to assign unless it is established that the value of the landlord's reversion would not be diminished, that there is no material breach of any covenant

39 [1957] 1 WLR 227.
40 [1980] 1 WLR 17.
41 [1981] 2 All ER 290, affirmed [1984] 1 All ER 423.
42 For a full discussion of offer-to-surrender clauses, see Chap 12.
43 See Acheson, "Too little too late" [1997] 3 EG 132; Sands, "Life post-privity" [1996] 7 EG 54.

(particularly of a repairing covenant), and that the assignee meets various financial criteria (*e.g.* that its net annual profits over a specified number of years is at least a specified multiple of the total annual financial obligations under the lease, that its debts do not exceed a specified proportion of its asset value, and that the last figure is itself a specified multiple of the annual rent).[44]

Landlord and Tenant Act 1927: building leases

It is clearly important for the tenant of a building lease not to be restricted in its ability to assign or sub-let, since this is a means by which the tenant is enabled to recoup on its investment.[45] To ensure that such tenants are free to dispose, there is special statutory provision in the shape of the Landlord and Tenant Act 1927, section 19(1)(b). This paragraph, which applies only to building leases of at least 40 years, subjects a qualified disposition covenant, condition or agreement to the proviso that no consent is required for an assignment, underletting, charging or parting with possession effected more than seven years before the end of the term, provided that written notice is given to the lessor within six months after the transaction is effected. For the purpose of paragraph (b), a building lease is a lease made in consideration of the erection, substantial improvement, addition or alteration of buildings.

Paragraph (b) does not apply if the landlord is a government department, or local, public, or other statutory authority. Thus, for instance, local authorities involved in building schemes in the inter cities may retain control over them.[46]

A provision in a building lease may make the landlord's consent conditional upon the obtaining of both a guarantor of the obligations of the assignee and also a direct covenant from the assignee to observe and perform the covenants in the lease. Such provision is not invalidated by section 19(1)(b).[47]

Demand by lessor of payment for consent to disposition

Expenses of giving licence

The Landlord and Tenant Act 1927, section 19(1)(a), expressly states that the implied proviso does not preclude the right of the landlord to require

---

44 Acheson [1997] 3 EG 132 at 133.
45 Yates and Hawkins, *Landlord and Tenant Law*, 2nd ed (1986) at 301.
46 *Ibid.*
47 *Vaux Group plc* v *Lilley* [1991] 1 EGLR 60.

payment of a reasonable sum in respect of any legal or other expenses incurred in connection with the licence or consent. This means that a demand for such a payment is not to be taken as an unreasonable refusal to consent to the disposition. It is generally advisable, however, to provide for this in the lease expressly. A covenant by the tenant to pay the landlord's costs of consenting to the disposition may well be one of several covenants entered into by the tenant relating to the landlord's costs (including, for instance, the costs of a section 146 notice). A covenant (or the part of a covenant) relevant for present purposes is as follows:

> "To pay and indemnify the Landlord against all reasonable costs, charges, fees, disbursements and expenses properly incurred by the Landlord, including (but not restricted to) those payable to solicitors ... in relation to any application for consent to [assign, sub-let, part with possession, etc] whether or not such consent is granted (except in the circumstances where the Landlord is obliged not to withhold consent unreasonably and the withholding of such consent is held to be unreasonable) and whether or not the application for consent is withdrawn."

Demand for other payments

If the landlord demands some other form of payment as a condition of giving its consent to assign, underlet, etc, there are two possible effects. First, such demand may constitute an unreasonable refusal to consent under the Landlord and Tenant Act 1927, section 19(1)(a). Secondly, it may be contrary to the Law of Property Act 1925, section 144, which applies to all leases containing a covenant, condition or agreement against assigning, underletting, or parting with possession, or disposing of the land or property leased without licence or consent. This section deems such restriction to be subject to a proviso that no fine or other sum of money in the nature of a fine shall be payable for such consent; but this does not preclude the right to require payment of a reasonable sum in respect of legal or other expenses incurred in relation to such licence or consent.

For several reasons, section 144 is of limited practical effect. It states that the lease may contain an express provision to the contrary, so it is easily avoided. Like the Landlord and Tenant Act 1927, section 19(1)(a), it does not apply to absolute covenants against assignment, etc. It does not refer, and has been held not applicable, to dispositions of part of the premises only. Finally, it merely inserts the proviso into the lease: it does not make the demand itself unlawful. Provided, therefore, that the demand is not otherwise unlawful (*e.g.* it is not made fraudulently, or under duress or undue influence), if the tenant pays the sum demanded, it cannot be recovered.[48]

48 *Andrew v Bridgman* [1908] 1 KB 596.

The only substantial effect of section 144 therefore is that, if the landlord demands a fine that is not provided for in the lease itself, the tenant is relieved of the need to obtain the lessor's consent to assign or otherwise dispose of the property. The lessee can simply go ahead and assign, etc, without consent.[49] It also means that, before the fine has been paid, the tenant can withdraw from any agreement to pay it.

It has been judicially stated that the section points to a sum of money that is to go irrevocably into the pocket of the lessor.[50] This includes a demand for a higher rent[51], but not a demand that a prospective assignee enter into a direct covenant with the lessor.[52] The section has, however, been interpreted widely, and has also been held to include a landlord's demand for a tie in an assignment of a lease of a public house.[53] Where there has been a serious breach of a repairing covenant, a demand as a condition of consent to assign that a prospective assignee deposit a sum of money as security against the cost of the repairs, is probably not a demand for a fine within section 144.[54] If, however, the lessor demands that the prospective assignee pay him a specified sum to enable the lessor himself to effect the repairs, such demand might well be caught by the section. Apart from section 144, however, these demands must still satisfy the reasonableness test of the Landlord and Tenant Act 1927, section 19(1)(a).[55]

THE LANDLORD AND TENANT ACT 1988

This statute was passed as a result of two Law Commission Reports that concluded that the law did not adequately protect tenants who wished to dispose of their leases and also led to unacceptable delays in conveyancing.[56] There were several specific problems. First, in most cases, a tenant had no action in damages against a landlord who had refused consent to assign unreasonably.[57] This was because the standard form of restriction on assignment or other disposition was a covenant by the tenant only; the saving that consent would not be unreasonably withheld was

---

49 *Ibid.*
50 *Re Cosh's Contract* [1897] 1 Ch 9. See also Chap 8 for the cases on the meaning of "fine" in the LTA 1927, s 19(3).
51 *Jenkins v Price* [1907] 2 Ch 229, 234.
52 *Waite v Jennings* [1906] 2 KB 11.
53 *Gardner & Co v Cone* [1928] Ch 955.
54 *cf Orlando Investments Ltd v Grosvenor Estate Belgravia* (1990) 59 P & CR 21 (where the issue was not raised).
55 *Supra.*
56 Law Com Nos 141 (1985) and 161 (1987).
57 *Treloar v Bigge* (1874) LR 9 Ex 151.

merely a proviso to the tenant's covenant, not an independent covenant by the landlord. Where, therefore, the landlord had in fact covenanted not to withhold consent unreasonably, the tenant could bring an action against him for breach of covenant where the consent was unreasonably withheld.[58] Secondly, the landlord might not make his decision or communicate it to the tenant very speedily. Thirdly, the landlord did not have to give reasons for his refusal, thus making it difficult for the tenant to know if the refusal was unreasonable or not. Finally, the burden of proof was on the tenant, *i.e.* it was for the tenant to establish that the refusal was unreasonable, not for the landlord to prove that it was reasonable. Although an assignment or other disposition in breach of covenant is effective to vest the legal estate in the assignee or disponee[59], few prospective purchasers would be willing to risk going ahead where consent had not been forthcoming.

The position is now changed as a result of the Landlord and Tenant Act 1988. In the first few years after it was passed, it generated little litigation, as the recession made commercial property more difficult to let, so that landlords generally preferred to permit an assignment rather than risk the insolvency of an existing tenant. More case law on the Act is, however, appearing as the commercial property market improves.

Scope

The Act applies to tenancies whenever made which contain (whether expressly or by statutory implication) a fully qualified covenant against assignment, underletting, charging or parting with possession. It therefore applies to qualified covenants that are made *fully qualified* by the Landlord and Tenant Act 1927, section 19(1)(a); but it does not apply to absolute covenants prohibiting disposition. It applies to applications for consent made on or after 29 September 1988.[60]

Application by tenant and landlord's notice

If the tenant serves upon the landlord a written application for consent to the transaction, the landlord owes the tenant a duty within a reasonable time to give consent, unless it is reasonable not to give it.[61] Giving consent subject to an unreasonable condition does not satisfy this duty.[62] The

---

58 *Ideal Film Renting Co v Nielson* [1921] 1 Ch 575; Law Com No 141 (1985), paras 8.62–8.68 (pp 85–86).
59 *Old Grovebury Farm Ltd v W Seymour Plant Sales & Hire (No 2) Ltd* [1979] 1 WLR 1397 (considered *supra*).
60 LTA 1988, s 5(4).
61 *Ibid*, s 1(3).
62 *Ibid*, s 1(4); but in *BRS Northern Ltd v Templeheights Ltd* [1997] EGCS 180, the landlord gave two reasons for refusing consent to assign, one good and one bad. Neuberger J held that, both at common law and under the LTA 1988, the presence of a bad reason did not vitiate a refusal founded upon a sound independent reason.

landlord must also serve a written notice of his decision on the tenant. Where consent is withheld, such notice must specify the reasons for withholding it. Where consent is given subject to conditions, the notice must specify the conditions.[63]

Where the tenant is applying for consent to sub-let, his written application need not contain the terms of the sub-lease: it is enough if the landlord is furnished with sufficient particulars so that he would *prima facie* know the substance of the true nature of the transaction. A landlord supplied with such particulars, however, might reasonably impose a condition that his consent is subject to further approval of the sub-lease.[64]

The reasonableness or otherwise of a landlord's withholding of consent is to be judged solely by reference to the circumstances existing and known to the landlord at the time he makes his decision. Furthermore, evidence of matters occurring or emerging subsequently is not admissible for the purpose of supporting reasons already advanced. In *CIN Properties Ltd* v *Gill*[65], the landlord refused consent to assign in November 1989. The court held inadmissible as part of the landlord's evidence the accounts of the tenant's proposed assignee company for the year ending September 1990. In the pre-1988 Act case of *Bromley Park Garden Estates Ltd* v *Moss*[66], the majority of the Court of Appeal took the view that, in considering whether a refusal was reasonable, the court was entitled to consider reasons other than those which the landlord had specified to the tenant when refusing consent, provided that such reasons had influenced the landlord at the time he decided to withhold consent. Following the Act, it would seem that the only reasons that the court will consider are those specified in the landlord's written notice; this point was, however, expressly left open for future consideration in *Kened Ltd* v *Connie Investments Ltd.*[67] The Act appears to provide for only one such notice.

Reasonable time

Although the landlord must give his decision to the tenant within a reasonable time, the Act does not specify what period is to be considered reasonable. It would seem, however, that anything more than a few weeks will be regarded as unreasonable. In *Midland Bank plc* v *Chart Enterprises Inc*[68], on the facts, ten weeks' delay was held unreasonable. In *Dong Bang*

---

63 *Ibid*, s 1(3).
64 *Warren* v *Marketing Exchange for Africa Ltd* [1988] 2 EGLR 247; *Dong Bang Minerva (UK) Ltd* v *Davina Ltd* [1995] 1 EGLR 41 (Ch) (appeal on a narrower point dismissed: [1996] 2 EGLR 31 (CA)).
65 [1993] 2 EGLR 97 (QB).
66 [1982] 1 WLR 1019.
67 [1997] 1 EGLR 21, 23 (Millett LJ) (CA).
68 [1990] 2 EGLR 59.

Minerva (UK) Ltd v Davina Ltd[69], a period of 28 days from the landlord's receipt of the application and references was held to be a reasonable time where the tenant had a lease with 40 years left to run and where the application was for consent to sub-let on a five-year contracted-out tenancy. In that case it was also held that time can start to run even though the landlord has not been given a satisfactory undertaking as to costs.

Burden of proof

The burden of proof has been reversed by the Act. It is now for the landlord to show that a refusal was reasonable, that conditions attached to a consent were reasonable, and that his notice was served within a reasonable time.[70]

Tortious claim for damages

A landlord who is in breach of his obligations under the Act is liable to the tenant in damages for breach of statutory duty.[71] If, for instance, the tenant were to lose a sale to an assignee because of an unreasonable refusal, the tenant could sue the landlord for damages for the lost sale. Again, if, as a result of a delayed consent, a tenant has to sell to an assignee at a reduced price, the tenant can sue the landlord for the difference in price. Such action is additional to any other course of action the tenant may have, *e.g.* assigning to a willing assignee without consent, or applying to the court for a declaration that consent has been unreasonably withheld.

What Constitutes a Reasonable Withholding of Consent?

The Landlord and Tenant Act 1988 is of no assistance in ascertaining when a withholding of consent is reasonable. All it states is that, for the purposes of the Act, "it is reasonable for a person not to give his consent to a proposed transaction only in a case where, if he withheld consent and the tenant completed the transaction, the tenant would be in breach of covenant."[72] This, however, is clearly circular. As a result, the existing case law on what is reasonable or unreasonable continues to apply.

General approaches

The case law is not entirely consistent, and several different approaches

---

69 [1995] 1 EGLR 41 (Ch) (not dealt with on the appeal: [1996] 2 EGLR 31 (CA)).
70 LTA 1988, s 1(6).
71 *Ibid*, s 1(4).
72 *Ibid*, s 1(5).

have been advanced. The most influential is probably that advocated by Warrington LJ in *Re Gibbs & Houlder Bros & Co Ltd's Lease*,[73] that an objection to a disposition is reasonable only if it concerns either the personality of the proposed assignee, or his proposed user of the property. In that case the landlord refused consent on the ground that the proposed assignee was an existing tenant of adjoining property leased by the landlord, and that, if the assignment were approved, the assignee would determine the lease of the premises held under his existing lease, and that the landlord would find those premises difficult to re-let. The refusal was held unreasonable. A broader view was, however, taken in *Bickel v Duke of Westminster*[74] where it was suggested that reasonableness depends simply on the circumstances of each case, and that the authorities lay down, not rules of law, but mere propositions of good sense.

There is also authority to support the proposition that a landlord may reasonably refuse consent on a ground which was within the reasonable contemplation of the parties at the time the lease was made. The reverse of this is that a refusal of consent is unreasonable if it does not affect the subject-matter of the contract that forms the relationship between the landlord and the tenant. This was the view expressed in *Re Gibbs & Houlder Bros & Co Ltd's Lease*[75] by Sargant LJ. If the landlord withholds consent on such a ground, it follows that the landlord is seeking to obtain for himself a collateral advantage, *i.e.* an advantage not conferred upon him by the lease.

In *Bromley Park Garden Estates Ltd v Moss*[76], a restaurant with a flat above had been leased to different persons on separate leases. The flat was let subject to a qualified covenant against assignment. A few months before the lease of the flat expired, the tenant sought to assign; but the landlords refused, eventually arguing that this was in the interests of good estate management, *i.e.* that they would obtain a higher rent if the flat were let together with the restaurant. In substance, the landlords' argument was based upon the personality of the proposed assignee, but the court held the refusal unreasonable because the interests of estate management were wholly outside the intention to be imputed to the parties at the time the lease was granted. This can be contrasted with *Crown Estate Commissioners v Signet Group plc*[77], where estate management was accepted as a reasonable ground for refusing consent to assign (and also to make alterations and to a change of use).

---

73 [1925] Ch 575 (CA).
74 [1977] QB 517 (CA).
75 [1925] Ch 575 (CA).
76 [1982] 1 WLR 1019.
77 [1996] 2 EGLR 200.

The court may be able to find that the bargain between the parties goes beyond what is expressly stipulated in the lease, *i.e.* that particular terms are to be implied into the lease, or that the parties made a collateral agreement. There was no evidence of this in the *Bromley Park* case (*supra*); but a collateral contract may explain *Premier Confectionery (London) Co Ltd* v *London Commercial Salesrooms Ltd.*[78] It is, however, arguable that a collateral contract, if made after 26 September 1989, would be void unless in a form which complies with the Law of Property (Miscellaneous Provisions) Act 1989, section 2.

In order to preclude the implication of additional terms or collateral contracts, the lease may provide that the terms contained in the lease embody its entire terms. A suitable form of wording is a statement that:

> "This Lease sets out the entire agreement between the parties and such agreement is not collateral to any other agreement or arrangement."

In *International Drilling Fluids Ltd* v *Louisville Investments (Uxbridge) Ltd*[79], Balcombe LJ summarised the relevant law in a series of propositions, the essence of which is as follows:

> The purpose of a qualified covenant against assignment is to protect the landlord from having his premises used in an undesirable way or by an undesirable tenant or assignee.
>
> Thus the landlord is not entitled to refuse consent on grounds other than those which relate to the relationship of landlord and tenant in regard to the subject-matter of the lease.
>
> It is not necessary for the landlord to prove that the conclusions that led him to refuse consent were justified if they were conclusions that might have been reached by a reasonable man in the circumstances. This principle was confirmed in *Air India* v *Balabel*,[80] where it was held that it remains unnecessary for the landlord to justify as a matter of fact the matters upon which he relies.[81]
>
> It may be reasonable to refuse consent on the ground of the purpose for which the proposed assignee intends to use the premises, even if that purpose is not expressly forbidden in the lease.[82]
>
> While the landlord need usually consider only his own relevant interests in deciding whether to refuse consent, there may be cases where a refusal of consent will cause disproportionate harm to the tenant compared with the resulting benefit to the landlord. In such cases, refusal may be unreasonable.[83]
>
> Subject to the foregoing, the reasonableness of a refusal is in each case a question of fact, dependent upon all the circumstances.

78 [1933] Ch 904; discussed in Chap 8.
79 [1986] Ch 513.
80 [1993] 2 EGLR 66 (CA).
81 See also *Beale* v *Worth* [1993] EGCS 135 (CA).
82 *Bates* v *Donaldson* [1896] 2 QB 241. See further Chap 8.
83 See Chap 8 for further discussion of the *International Drilling* case in relation to this point.

Although these propositions were set out in the context of a qualified covenant against assignment, they would appear to be equally relevant to qualified covenants restrictive of other types of disposition. In *Straudley Investments Ltd v Mount Eden Land Ltd*[84] they were applied *mutatis mutandis* to qualified covenants against sub-letting, and the Court of Appeal added two further guidelines. The first is that it would normally be reasonable to refuse consent if such refusal is necessary to prevent the tenant from acting to the prejudice of the landlord's existing rights. The second is that it would normally be unreasonable to impose a condition which would increase or enhance the control which the landlord is entitled to exercise under the terms of the lease.

Consent subject to conditions

Where the lease is silent

The imposition of a condition is unreasonable if it seeks to obtain for the lessor a collateral advantage, *i.e.* one not contemplated in the lease. In *Premier Rinks Ltd v Amalgamated Cinematograph Theatres Ltd*,[85] the demand that an assignee of a sub-lease enter into a covenant not to use the premises for a specified purpose was held an unreasonable refusal to consent where the sub-lease permitted such user. Similarly, in *Straudley Investments Ltd v Mount Eden Land Ltd*[86], the landlord stated that he would consent to sub-let only on the condition (not provided in the head-lease) that the sub-lessee pay a sum by way of rent deposit into an account in the joint names of the landlord and the tenant. This was held to comprise a demand for a collateral advantage, so that the landlord was in breach of his duty under the Landlord and Tenant Act 1988 not to impose an unreasonable condition. In *Roux Restaurants Ltd v Jaison Property Development Co Ltd*[87], a landlord who refused consent to assign unless the tenant entered into a deed of variation of the lease was held to have refused unreasonably.

By contrast, consent conditional upon the assignee's providing security for the completion of repairs was held not to constitute an unreasonable withholding of consent in *Orlando Investments Ltd v Grosvenor Estate Belgravia*.[88] There were serious and long-standing breaches of a repairing covenant in the lease, and the landlord was entitled to have the covenant complied with. The demand was not, therefore, a collateral advantage.

84 [1996] EGCS 153 (CA).
85 [1912] WN 157.
86 [1996] EGCS 153.
87 [1996] EGCS 118.
88 (1990) 59 P & CR 21.

Where the lease provides

Whether a landlord can satisfy the reasonableness test by specifying in the lease what conditions may be imposed has not (except in the case of an assignment of a post-1995 commercial lease) been clearly resolved. According to the approach based on the reasonable contemplation of the parties at the time the lease is made[89], consent that is made subject to a condition is never an unreasonable refusal to consent if the condition is provided for in the lease. This view is, however, difficult to square with *Balfour* v *Kensington Garden Mansions Ltd*[90], where a consent to sub-let subject to conditions was held unreasonable even though such conditions were specified in the lease. Such approach, however, might now be considered outmoded. In practice, many commercial leases provide that the lessor is to be entitled to demand that an assignee enter into a direct covenant to observe and perform the covenants in the lease and to provide a guarantor. Alternatively, a future court might treat the *Balfour* case as limited to consent to sub-let and to its special facts: as was stated in the case itself, no sub-tenant could be expected to covenant to pay the rent provided for in the head-lease when this was higher than that payable under the sub-lease.

Examples of reasonable or unreasonable withholding of consent

Disponee's proposed user
This is a common instance of withholding of consent, and is dealt with further in the discussion of restrictions upon user.[91]

Standing, status or personality of disponee

It is reasonable to refuse consent to assign to an assignee who is unlikely to be able to comply with the financial obligations imposed by the lease, *i.e.* the payment of rent and service or other charges.[92] A landlord may request references and a sight of the assignee's accounts.[93]

   In *Olympia & York Canary Wharf Ltd* v *Oil Property Investments Ltd*[94], the lease, which contained a fully qualified covenant against

89 Discussed *supra*.
90 (1932) 49 TLR 29; discussed earlier in this chapter.
91 See further Chap 8.
92 *Air India* v *Balabel* [1993] 2 EGLR 66 (CA).
93 *British Bakeries (Midlands) Ltd* v *Michael Testler & Co Ltd* [1986] 1 EGLR 64; *Ponderosa International Developments Inc* v *Pengap Securities (Bristol) Ltd* [1986] 1 EGLR 66.
94 [1994] 2 EGLR 48 (CA). The effect of the break clause in this case, however, must be considered in the light of *Max Factor Ltd* v *Wesleyan Assurance Society* [1996] 2 EGLR 210 (CA), discussed in Chapter 12.

assignment, conferred on Enterprise Petroleum Ltd (EPL) – the original tenant – and upon that company only, the right to determine the lease at the end of the tenth year of the term (*i.e.* on 8 March 1995). EPL assigned to Olympia in 1987, which in 1992 wished to assign back to EPL. The landlord had no objection to EPL *per se*. It nevertheless refused to grant consent on the ground that, if EPL determined the lease, it was likely (in view of the slump in the commercial property market) that the premises would not be let for a year or more, that the rent would be reduced by more than half, and that the value of its reversion would fall. It was clear that a reasonable landlord could come to the same conclusions, and the court held that the injunction that the landlord had obtained against an assignment to EPL was to continue until after 8 March 1995.

In *Re Cooper's Lease*[95], a tenant with no security of tenure himself wished, three years before the expiry of his lease, to sub-let to an oculist. The landlord, fearing that the oculist would have security of tenure under the Landlord and Tenant Act 1954, Part II, was unwilling to consent to the sub-letting unless there was an application to the court for such protection to be excluded. The refusal to consent was held reasonable.

In *West Layton v Ford*[96], a landlord was also held reasonable in refusing consent to sub-let to a person who would thereby obtain security of tenure. The lease, made in 1971, was of a butcher's shop, with a flat above. The lease contained a covenant by the tenant not to sub-let the flat except on a service tenancy to an employee or on a fully-furnished tenancy. In 1971, occupiers of fully-furnished tenancies did not have security of tenure under the Rent Acts, but they obtained such protection in 1974. The tenant sought consent to sub-let to a furnished tenant in 1977. The court, looking to the intention rather than to the letter of the covenant, found that its purpose was to preserve the letting's commercial character, *i.e.* to ensure that the shop and the flat could be re-let as a single unit. The landlord was therefore held reasonable to refuse consent.

If, as in *West Layton v Ford,* the landlord is letting property which has mixed business and residential occupation, he might therefore be well advised to insist that there is a covenant against sub-letting part, and that such covenant is absolute. Alternatively, the landlord might be prepared to permit sub-letting of the residential part on terms which ensure that the residential sub-tenant does not acquire security of tenure. This might be achieved by a proviso to a restriction on sub-letting in the following form:

> "Provided that if the Tenant wishes to sub-let the residential part of the demised premises on an assured shorthold tenancy the Tenant shall be

95 (1968) 19 P & CR 541.
96 [1979] QB 593.

permitted to create such a sub-lease only if he obtains in advance of such sub-letting the Lessor's consent in writing, such consent not to be unreasonably withheld."

It has been held unreasonable to refuse consent to sub-let to a foreign diplomat, merely on the ground that diplomatic immunity would prevent the landlord from obtaining possession were the head-lease to be determined.[97] It has been suggested, however, that refusal to consent to an *assignment* to such a person would probably be reasonable, because an assignment creates privity of estate.[98]

Refusal by a landlord to consent on the ground of the disponee's gender or race may contravene the sex discrimination[99] or race relations[1] legislation. There is a saving in each case if the premises are small (as there defined), are occupied by the person refusing consent or a close relative (as there defined) who shares part of the accommodation with other residents who are not members of his or her household.

Existing breaches of covenant

If these are serious, they may justify a withholding of consent[2], or the imposition of conditions.[3] Trivial breaches, however, do not justify a refusal to consent.[4]

CONDITIONS COMMONLY IMPOSED ON A SUB-LETTING

The landlord will often require a tenant to covenant in the lease that, should the tenant wish to sub-let, he will obtain the landlord's consent to certain matters and ensure that the sub-lease contains specified terms and covenants.

Lessee's covenant to obtain direct covenant by sub-lessee with the (head-)lessor

The tenant may covenant that, before applying for consent to sub-lease, he

<hr/>

97 *Parker v Boggan* [1947] KB 346 (where moral pressure was considered sufficient).
98 Crabb, *Leases: Covenants and Consents* (1991) Sweet & Maxwell, at 94–5.
99 Sex Discrimination Act 1975, s 31.
1 Race Relations Act 1976, s 24.
2 *Goldstein v Sanders* [1915] 1 Ch 594.
3 *Orlando Investments Ltd v Grosvenor Estate Belgravia* [1989] 2 EGLR 74 (CA).
4 *Farr v Ginnings* (1924) 44 TLR 249, where the landlord's attempt to use trivial breaches to persuade the tenant to surrender was treated as an attempt to secure a collateral advantage; also *Beale v Worth* [1993] EGCS 135 (CA); *Straudley Investments Ltd v Mount Eden Land Ltd* [1997] EGCS 175 (Ch).

will submit a licence to sub-let to the landlord, such licence to contain a covenant by the sub-tenant with the (head-)landlord to observe and perform all the covenants and conditions in the (head-)lease (other than those relating to rent). This ensures privity of covenant between the head-landlord and the sub-tenant, and enables the landlord to proceed for breach of covenant, if necessary, directly against the sub-tenant. A form of covenant by the tenant is:

> "Before any permitted underletting, to procure that the under-tenant enters into a direct covenant with the Landlord to observe and perform all the tenant's covenants and other provisions contained in this Lease (other than those relating to the payment of rent)."

If the landlord wishes to prevent the sub-tenant himself creating a sub-lease (*i.e.* a sub-under-lease), he may insist that such covenant includes a direct covenant with the landlord not to sub-let.

Lessee's covenant to grant sub-lease at a rack rent without a premium

The tenant may covenant that the sub-lease is not to be granted at a premium or a fine, and that the rent payable under the sub-lease is to be a rack rent and, in any event, is not to be less than the rent at that time payable under the head-lease. Such a covenant is clearly designed to ensure that, if the lease of the head-tenant were to terminate before that of the sub-lease, the head-landlord would thereafter gain maximum financial benefit from the sub-letting. Were the tenant to grant the sub-lease at a premium or a fine, the rent under the sub-lease would, as a consequence, clearly be less than a rack rent. A suitable precedent might be a covenant by the tenant:

> "Not to underlet the whole of the demised premises in consideration of a fine or at a premium or at a rent less than whichever shall be the higher of the rent payable under this Lease and the open market rental value of the demised premises at the time of such underletting."

If the open-market rent of the premises has fallen since the lease was granted, any sub-lease granted by the tenant will probably command a lower rent than that payable under the head-lease. This had occurred in *Blockbuster Entertainment Ltd* v *Leakcliff Properties Ltd*[5], where the landlord's consent was required to sub-let. The landlord argued that it was reasonable to refuse consent to sub-let because a sub-letting at a reduced (hard-core) rent would alert a potential purchaser of the reversion that it was worth less than the present rent (including the froth) payable under the head-lease, with a consequential reduction in the market value of the

---

5 [1997] 1 EGLR 28 (Ch).

landlord's reversion. Neuberger J rejected this argument, which he described as "unattractive", because it would effectively enable a lessor who intended to dispose of his reversion in the future, and who anticipated that the market was going to rise, to compel his tenant to postpone any sub-letting for an indeterminate period.

Lessee's covenant to ensure that any sub-lease contains proviso for re-entry

Like any well-drawn lease, the sub-lease will invariably contain a proviso for re-entry – it is, after all, in the tenant's (*i.e.* the sub-lessor's) own interests. In the event that the sub-tenant should become an immediate tenant of the landlord at some time, however, the landlord has an interest in ensuring that the sub-lease does contain such a proviso. It might take the form of a covenant by the tenant:

> "to procure that every permitted under-lease contains a proviso for re-entry on breach of any covenant by the under-tenant."

Lessee's covenant regarding rent review in sub-lease

The lessee may be required to covenant that any sub-lease is to contain provisions for rent review in terms parallel to those contained in the head-lease, and that the dates specified for rent review in the sub-lease are to be identical to those specified for rent review in the head-lease. But for this, there might be a rent review in the head-lease which increases the rent under the head-lease without there being a similar review of rent in the sub-lease. This would increase the chance that the head-tenant might not be able to pay the rent under the head-lease. This can be provided for by the addition of the following words to the foregoing covenant:

> "and to provide in any such under-letting for the rent thereunder reserved to be reviewed at the same time or times and upon the same basis as is hereunder provided for the review of the rent hereby reserved."

This will not in itself be sufficient, however, to give the landlord any voice in the setting of the rent in the sub-lease at review. The landlord might therefore wish to add words such as the following:

> "but not to agree any reviewed rent with the under-tenant nor any rent payable on a renewal thereof without the prior written consent of the Landlord (such consent not to be unreasonably withheld)."

The landlord might, of course, prefer to retain even greater control over the rent-review procedure under the sub-lease, *e.g.* if the sub-lease is to give the sub-lessor the power to select either an expert or arbitrator at review, the landlord might wish to make his own written consent necessary before the sub-lessor can make such decision, and to ensure that he is entitled to make his own representations to such independent person.

Lessee's covenant not to surrender or vary the terms of the sub-lease

The lessee may covenant that any sub-lease granted is not to be surrendered or its terms varied without the landlord's consent. A suitable covenant is:

> "Not to vary the terms or to accept a surrender of any permitted under-lease without the Landlord's prior written consent (such consent not to be unreasonably withheld)."

Lessee's covenant to have sub-lease excluded from the Landlord and Tenant Act 1954, Part II

Occasionally, the landlord requires a covenant by the tenant to have the sub-lease excluded from the protection of the Landlord and Tenant Act 1954, Part II.[6] Such a clause might be drafted thus:

> "Before the grant of any underlease, to obtain an order of the court under section 38(4) of the Landlord and Tenant Act 1954 authorising an agreement excluding in relation to such intended under-lease the provisions of sections 24 to 28 of that Act."

6 See Chap 15.

Chapter 7

ALTERATIONS

The landlord will wish to retain some control over the physical layout of the demised premises; and, to this end, most leases contain a covenant by the tenant not to make alterations, such covenant being in form either absolute or qualified (*i.e.* not to make alterations without the landlord's consent). Before considering these covenants in more detail, however, it should be noted that there are other factors which may affect a tenant's freedom to make alterations to the premises, and these will be considered first.

IMPLIED OBLIGATIONS WHICH MAY PREVENT ALTERATIONS

Waste

There is an implied obligation on all tenants not to commit waste, and the lease will sometimes contain an express covenant by the tenant to this effect.

Different types of waste

The law recognises different types of waste. Voluntary waste involves positive acts which change and damage the premises, so diminishing the value of the reversion. Equitable waste is an extreme form of this, where the acts are committed maliciously. There will also be an implied covenant against ameliorating waste; but as this consists of acts which improve the premises, the landlord is unlikely to have any remedy in damages or by way of an injunction. An example of ameliorating waste where an injunction was refused is *Doherty* v *Allman*[1], where a tenant with a 999-year lease converted a barracks into cottages by the erection of easily removable partitions.

---

[1] (1878) 3 App Cas 709.

Tortious liability for waste

In most cases, the implied liability for waste and the implied contractual obligation to use the premises in a tenant-like manner[2] will be co-extensive. An act of waste gives rise to a liability in tort, however, which may be relevant where there is no contractual relationship between the landlord and the person committing the waste. In *Mancetter Developments Ltd* v *Garmanson Ltd*[3], the first defendant, a company, purchased fixtures from the liquidator of a tenant of factory premises and occupied the premises, although no assignment of the lease was ever made and the company was probably only a licensee. The second defendant, a director who controlled the first defendant, ordered the removal of extractor fans and pipes installed by the tenant, as a result of which large holes were made in the walls. By a majority, the Court of Appeal found the making of the holes in removing trade fixtures to be waste; and Dillon LJ considered that this was also a breach of an implied contractual obligation to make good any damage caused by removing tenant's fixtures. The first defendant went into liquidation, so that any implied contractual obligation against it was of no assistance to the landlord. The landlord was held entitled to recover damages for waste from the second defendant, however, as he was a director who had given instructions to carry out the acts which amounted to waste and so comprised a tort.

Implied covenant to use the premises in a tenant-like manner

An additional obligation implied into all tenancies (unless expressly excluded) is an implied contractual obligation of a tenant to use and deliver up the premises in a tenant-like manner. In *Marsden* v *Edward Heyes Ltd*[4], this obligation was implied into an oral yearly tenancy, and was held to have been broken when the tenant of a dwelling-house and shop removed a wall, staircase and fireplace in order to convert the premises into an enlarged shop.[5]

---

2 See *infra*.
3 [1986] QB 1212.
4 [1927] 2 KB 1.
5 See Chap 10 for a discussion of waste and the implied obligation to use the premises in a tenant-like manner.

OTHER PROVISIONS OF THE LEASE WHICH MAY AFFECT THE TENANT'S RIGHT TO MAKE ALTERATIONS

It is possible that some other covenant contained in the lease may prevent the tenant from carrying out alterations. For example, a covenant not to cause a nuisance or annoyance to neighbouring occupiers could be infringed by an alteration which interfered with a neighbouring property's right to light or to access.[6]

In *Heard v Stuart*[7], the tenant (a tailor), sub-let for bill-posting the wall of a house which faced the main entrance to a church. As well as being held to be a breach of the covenant not to make any alterations to the premises' external appearance, this was held to be a breach of other covenants in the lease: namely, a covenant not to do anything that would be an annoyance to the neighbourhood, and (evidence being given that the wall was part of the demised premises) of a covenant to keep in repair. Joyce J thought that there might also have been a breach of a covenant to use the premises only for the business of a tailor, and of a covenant not to assign or part with the possession of any part of the demised premises.

Easements

There may be a covenant not to do anything which would interfere with the landlord's access to light or with other easements. Such a covenant might be breached by alterations involving additions to the demised premises. Interference with an easement will of course amount to a nuisance for which an action for damages and an injunction may lie in any event.

User covenants

Another covenant likely to be breached by an alteration is a covenant relating to user.[8] In the absence of any user covenant, however, alterations carried out to enable the premises to be used differently will not necessarily amount to a breach of a repairing covenant or to waste. In *Hyman v Rose*[9], alterations were made to enable the tenant to use a chapel as a cinema, and the changed user, which was not inconsistent with the lease, was held by

---

6 See the clause set out on p 196 *infra*.
7 (1907) 24 TLR 104.
8 See Chap 8.
9 [1912] AC 623.

Lord Loreburn LC to be the "governing factor". The lease did not contain a covenant against the alterations; but the principle of the case might conceivably be relevant in considering whether a landlord has unreasonably refused consent to alterations.[10]

Covenant not to commit waste

As well as the implied obligation not to commit waste, there may be an express covenant in the lease. An example of this would be a covenant by the tenant:

> Not to commit or permit or suffer any waste, spoil or destruction in or upon the demised premises or any part thereof.

The lease under consideration in *F W Woolworth & Co v Lambert*[11] contained conflicting covenants. There was a covenant not to commit waste and a covenant not to make alterations without the landlord's consent. Romer LJ considered that the covenant not to commit waste, which precluded the acts for which consent was sought, must be read subject to the covenant allowing alterations with the landlord's consent.

Restrictive covenants

In addition to covenants contained in the lease, there may also be restrictive covenants on the freehold title which affect a lessee or sub-lessee.[12] It may, however, be possible to obtain an order for their modification or discharge.[13]

STATUTORY REQUIREMENTS WHICH OVERRIDE COVENANTS AGAINST ALTERATIONS

Statutes may provide that certain premises must comply with health and safety regulations. A lease will often contain a covenant by the tenant to comply with any statutory requirements, such as the following covenant:

> "To comply with all obligations imposed by and do or cause to be done and executed all such works as under or by virtue of any Act of Parliament or

---

10 See *infra*.
11 [1937] 1 Ch 37.
12 See Chap 8.
13 See Chap 8.

regulations made thereunder for the time being in force shall be properly directed or necessary to be done or executed upon or in respect of the demised premises or any part thereof by the lessee, tenant or occupier and at all times to keep the lessor indemnified against all claims, demands and liability in respect thereof."

In the absence of such a covenant, the statute may provide for the court to vary or set aside any clause in a lease which prohibits necessary alterations. Several statutory provisions allow for this.

The Factories Act 1961, section 169, provides that where the owner or occupier of a building, of which the whole or part is let as a factory, is unable to carry out structural or other alterations required to comply with the Act because of the terms of the agreement under which it is let, he may apply to the county court. The county court may set aside or modify the terms of the agreement after hearing evidence. Section 170 allows the court to apportion the expenses of the alterations between the parties, and to determine the lease if either party requests this.

The Offices, Shops and Railway Premises Act 1963, section 73, allows a person who is required by a notice served under the Act to carry out structural or other alterations, but who is prevented from doing so by the terms of a lease or agreement, to apply to the county court to modify or set the terms aside. The court has power, in doing so, to apportion the expense between the landlord and the tenant and to make adjustments in the rent if it sees fit.

The Fire Precautions Act 1971, section 28, provides that a person who is prevented from carrying out structural or other alterations to comply with the requirements of this section may apply to the county court for an order to set aside or modify any terms of a lease or agreement to enable him to do so. As before, the court may apportion the expense or adjust the rent.

The Telecommunications Act 1984, section 96, not yet in force, provides that any alterations to a leased building in connection with the provision of a telecommunications system shall be subject to the lessor's consent, such consent not to be unreasonably withheld. The question of unreasonableness is to be decided bearing in mind all the circumstances, and on the premise that a person should not unreasonably be denied access to a telecommunications system. The section applies to a lease for a year or more, and to an agreement for a lease, taking effect after the section came into force, although there is provision for the Secretary of State to apply it retrospectively.

The Environmental Protection Act 1990, section 78G[14], provides that a remediation notice may require a person to do things by way of

---

[14] Added by Environment Act 1995, s 57; see SI 1995 No 1983, art 3.

remediation notwithstanding that he is not entitled to do those things. Any person whose consent is required to do such things must grant or join in granting such rights as will enable them to be done.

The Disability Discrimination Act 1995, section 16, provides that, where an employer or trade organisation occupies premises under a lease and proposes to make an alteration to comply with its duties under the Act, the lease is deemed to contain a provision entitling the employer or trade organisation to apply to the lessor for consent to make the alteration, and to make the alteration with the written consent of the lessor (such consent not to be unreasonably withheld). The lessor is entitled to make his consent subject to reasonable conditions.[15] Section 27 makes similar provision where the occupier under a lease is a provider of services.

TRESPASS TO OTHER PREMISES

The extent of the demised premises

A further preliminary matter which should not be overlooked with regard to alteration covenants is the extent of the demised premises. Will the tenant's alteration constitute a trespass to adjoining property which is not part of the demised premises? Are the walls and roof of the premises included in the demise, or do they belong to the landlord or to someone else? In *Haines* v *Florensa*[16], the Court of Appeal held that the tenant of a top-floor flat, whose demise expressly included the roof and roof-space, could extend the roof-space by raising the height of the roof, as the air-space above it belonged to him. This alteration was an improvement to which the landlord's consent could not be unreasonably withheld.[17]

If the demised premises are part only of a building belonging to the landlord, it is quite probable that the walls and roof are not included in the demise, and therefore belong to the landlord or even to another tenant.[18] In leases of a unit in a building, structural and common parts of the building usually belong to the landlord.

The tenant is not entitled to make any alterations which involve a trespass. In *Frederick Berry Ltd* v *Royal Bank of Scotland*[19], it was held that the tenant of a third floor who had covenanted not to exhibit signs had no

---

15 S 16 is modified if the employer or trade organisation occupies the premises under a sub-lease or sub-tenancy: Disability Discrimination (Sub-leases and Sub-tenancies) Regulations 1996, SI 1996 No 1333, regs 3, 4.

16 [1990] 1 EGLR 73.

17 See *infra*.

18 See Chap 3.

19 [1949] 1 KB 619.

right to put up a name-plate at the main entrance of a building on a wall which was not part of the demised premises. If he required this facility, it should have been expressly granted to him as an easement.[20]

Trespass or nuisance in the carrying out of alterations

The actual process of carrying out alterations may also involve a trespass or a nuisance if it interferes with an easement. This could arise, for instance, where the alterations cannot be carried out without erecting scaffolding covering other parts of the building. In *Owen* v *Gadd*[21], the erection of scaffolding over the door and window of a shop to carry out repairs to premises above was a nuisance, and also a breach of the implied covenant for quiet enjoyment.

From the tenant's point of view, it is obviously best to cover such situations by expressly including in the lease easements of access for the purpose of carrying out such alterations. The leases of units in a building will often contain a covenant by the tenant to allow the landlord and other tenants access for the purpose of carrying out repairs and alterations.[22]

The Access to Neighbouring Land Act 1992 allows the court to make an order for access on to neighbouring premises in certain circumstances for preservation work. The court may also make an order for access for alterations or improvements which the preservation work "incidentally involves" if the court deems it to be fair and reasonable to do so. For non-residential premises, a reasonable consideration may be required for this.

THE FORM OF A COVENANT AGAINST ALTERATIONS

Like any other agreement, the form of a covenant against alterations may be infinitely variable. Should a dispute arise, it is the actual covenant contained in the lease which the court will have to interpret. Although the covenants are often drafted on the basis of precedents used before, there may be variations which will result in different interpretations.

The meaning of "alterations"

In *Bickmore* v *Dimmer*[23], Stirling LJ held that the term "alterations" should

---

20 See Chap 3.
21 [1956] 2 QB 99.
22 See clause on p 258.
23 [1903] 1 Ch 158.

be limited to alterations which would affect the form and structure of a building. Thus in *LCC v Hutter*[24], the erection of an electrically-illuminated advertisement on the facade of the premises on twelve iron brackets cemented into 23 holes cut into the stonework amounted to a breach of a covenant: "**not to cut or maim any of the principal walls ... or make or permit to be made any alterations in the elevation of the building.**" Conversely, in *Joseph v LCC*[25], the erection of a lit advertisement on struts which were easily removed was held not to be an alteration.

A further point of difference between the last two cases was that in *LCC v Hutter* the advertisement, which was one for gin for which the tenant had rented out the space, was in no way related to his business; whereas in *Joseph v LCC* the advertisement was in furtherance of the tenant's business. The courts have shown themselves ready to construe a covenant, or in some cases to imply a covenant, which gives business efficacy to a lease. Such a construction would make the tenant in *Joseph v LCC* a candidate for more sympathetic treatment.

In *Lilley & Skinner Ltd v Crump*[26], it was necessary to decide whether making two openings in a wall between premises was an "alteration" (which was prohibited only without the landlord's consent), or was a cutting or maiming (which was absolutely prohibited). Rowlatt J. held that it was an alteration. In *Joseph v LCC*[27], it was said that an alteration meant an alteration to the fabric of the building.

The meaning of "structure"

It may not always be entirely clear what is included in the "structure" of a building, so that a covenant "**not to cut or maim any of the principal walls or timbers, roof or foundations**" is a clearer and more comprehensive form of covenant than one which is simply "**not to make any structural alterations.**"

It is quite usual for covenants against alterations to distinguish between structural alterations, against which there may be an absolute covenant, and minor alterations, which may be carried out with the landlord's consent. An example of such a covenant would be:

> Not the cut, maim or injure or suffer to be cut, maimed or injured any of the structure or the roofs, walls, timbers, wires, pipes, drains, appurtenances, fixtures or fittings thereof, and not without the previous consent in writing

---

24 [1925] Ch 626.
25 (1914) 111 LT 276.
26 (1929) 73 SJ 366.
27 (1914) 111 LT 276.

of the landlord to make or suffer to be made any alteration or addition to
the demised premises of any part thereof.

There is no legal definition of the word "structure", although it was
considered by the Court of Appeal in the context of the Housing Act 1961,
section 32[28], in its application to dwellinghouses in *Campden Hill Towers
Ltd v Gardner*.[29] There, Megaw LJ expressed the opinion that it might be
part of a building which affected the safety of it, or would materially affect
its use as a dwellinghouse. In *Irvine v Moran*[30], Forbes QC sought to follow
this approach and said that the structure of a dwellinghouse consists of
"those elements which give it its essential appearance, stability and shape"
and is "a material or significant element in the overall construction",
although not necessarily load-bearing.

Covenants against alterations are onerous covenants which will be
construed against the landlord; so that, in any case of doubt, "structure" is
likely to be interpreted in favour of the tenant.

Because of the negative nature of a covenant against alterations, a tenant
will not be liable for its breach owing to the work of an independent
contractor which the tenant did not authorise or of which he had no
knowledge.[31]

"Elevation" of a building

A covenant may expressly prohibit alterations to the "elevation" of a
building, which in *Joseph v LCC*[32] was held to mean the front view of it.

ABSOLUTE AND QUALIFIED COVENANTS: THE LANDLORD AND TENANT ACT 1927, SECTION 19(2)

A covenant against alterations may be absolute (where the tenant covenants
not to carry out alterations at all), or qualified (where the tenant covenants

---

28 Now LTA 1985, s 11.
29 [1977] QB 823.
30 [1991] 1 EGLR 261.
31 *Hagee (London) Ltd v Co-operative Insurance Society Ltd* (1992) 63 P & CR 362. The
 covenant in this case was one not to cut or maim walls and timbers The independent
 contractor had been instructed by the tenant to renew the air conditioning, and in the
 course of the work, cut the joists without the tenant's knowledge.
32 (1914) 111 LT 276.

not to carry out alterations without first obtaining the landlord's consent, which will usually be required to be in writing).[33] If the covenant is in qualified form, it will almost always be caught by the Landlord and Tenant Act 1927, section 19(2).

Section 19(2) provides that a covenant, condition or agreement in a lease against the making of "improvements" without licence or consent, is deemed, notwithstanding any express provision to the contrary, to be subject to a proviso that such licence or consent is not to be unreasonably withheld. Such proviso allows the landlord to require, as a condition of such licence or consent, the payment of a reasonable sum in respect of damage to or diminution in the value of the premises or any neighbouring premises belonging to the landlord, and of any legal or other expenses properly incurred in connection with such licence or consent. Furthermore, in the case of an improvement which does not add to the letting value of the holding, such proviso allows the landlord to require as a condition of such licence or consent, where reasonable, an undertaking on the part of the tenant to reinstate the premises in the condition in which they were before the improvement was executed.

The county court has the same jurisdiction as the High Court to make a declaration that a licence or consent to the making of an improvement to the demised property or any part thereof has been unreasonably withheld.[34] In practice, therefore, most applications are made to the county court.

"Improvements"

The usual form of covenant found in leases is one against the making of "alterations", or "alterations and additions"; the covenant is not generally worded to prohibit "improvements" *eo nomine*. Section 19(2) will, however, apply to a qualified covenant against alterations, in whatever terms, if "the proposed alterations are in fact capable of being deemed to be improvements."[35]

The courts have interpreted the expression "improvements" liberally and in a way which favours the tenant. In *Balls Brothers Ltd v Sinclair*[36], the tenant under a lease which contained a covenant not to make any alteration or addition without the written consent of the landlord was refused consent to, move a staircase. Luxmoore J took the view that the covenant was within section 19(2). As the sub-section protected the landlord's interests by providing for reinstatement and for a reasonable sum to be payable to him

33 An example of a qualified covenant against alterations is set out on pp 160–161 *supra*.
34 LTA 1954, s 53(1).
35 *F W Woolworth & Co Ltd v Lambert* [1937] Ch 37, per Lord Wright MR.
36 [1931] 2 Ch 325.

for any diminution in value, "improvement" was to be looked at from the point of view of the tenant.

This approach was taken by the majority of the Court of Appeal in both *F W Woolworth & Co Ltd v Lambert*[37] and in *Lambert v F W Woolworth & Co Ltd.*[38] These cases involved the same set of circumstances. The plaintiffs, who held a lease of shop premises from the defendant lessors, also held a tenancy of other premises at the rear of the demised premises, which had been leased to them by another landlord. The plaintiffs wished to extend their shop into the latter premises by joining the two sets of premises together. The alterations that were needed to achieve this would involve the demolition of a wall at the rear of the demised premises and the removal of a staircase. It was proposed to move the main staircase and staff accommodation into the adjacent premises at the rear. The lease which the plaintiffs held from the defendants contained a covenant against making any structural alterations without the previous written consent of the lessors.

The facts were considered by the Court of Appeal on two separate occasions. On the first of these, the views of the court as to the meaning of "improvements" were *obiter*, since it was held that, even if the alterations ranked as improvements, it had not been established that the landlord's consent had been withheld unreasonably. In both cases, the majority of the Court of Appeal considered that, for the purposes of section 19(2), "improvements" meant improvements from the point of view of the tenant. Applying this interpretation to the facts before them, the majority in each case considered that the proposed alterations would indeed be improvements within the sub-section. The dissenting judges in each case were Greene LJ and Greer LJ respectively, who each felt that the alterations could not fall within section 19(2) because they could not be improvements to the "demised premises" which were the subject-matter of the covenant. In their view, the proposed work would be an "improvement" only if it were permissible (which they believed it was not) to take into account the additional use of the premises adjoining.

Burden of proof under section 19(2)

The Landlord and Tenant Act 1988 does not apply to qualified covenants against alterations. The onus of proving an unreasonable refusal is therefore on the tenant.

In the first *Woolworth* case[39], the landlords had demanded a sum of

---

37 [1937] Ch 37.
38 [1938] Ch 883.
39 [1937] Ch 37.

£7,000 for their consent to the alterations. The tenants applied to the court for a declaration that the landlords' consent had been unreasonably withheld; this application was dismissed as the tenants failed to satisfy the court that the demand for such a sum was unreasonable. The court held, moreover, that it had no jurisdiction to decide what would have been reasonable by referring the matter to an official referee unless both parties agreed to this. The wording of the sub-section does not confer this remedial right upon the court; in this it differs from section 19(3), which relates to user, which expressly contemplates a determination by the court of what is a reasonable sum.

In the second *Woolworth* case[40], the landlords refused consent to the alterations without giving any reasons, and this was held to be unreasonable. This would seem in part to shift the burden of proof of unreasonableness from the tenant to the landlord.

Undertaking to reinstate

The lease may contain an express covenant by the tenant to reinstate the premises at the end of the lease, *i.e.* a covenant to "deliver up" the premises at the end of the term in the same state as they were in at the commencement of the term. If there is a breach of such a covenant contained in a pre-1996 lease, the lessor may claim damages for the breach either from the original tenant (through privity of covenant) or (this being a "touching and concerning covenant") from the person who is the lessee when the obligation to reinstate arises, even if the alterations were made by a predecessor in title. It is a matter of construction whether the covenant to reinstate at the end of the term obliges the tenant to reinstate if the term is determined earlier by means, for instance, of a break clause. An obligation to reinstate will be imposed whenever the term determines if the covenant is expressed to be one "to keep and deliver up." To meet the costs of reinstatement in the event of the tenant's becoming bankrupt or going into liquidation before the expiration of the term, the landlord should consider backing up the tenant's covenant to reinstate with either a security deposit or an insurance policy. If the lease does not contain an express covenant to reinstate, none will be implied.[41]

Even if the lease does not contain an express covenant by the tenant to reinstate, the landlord asked to give his consent under a qualified covenant against alterations may still be able to make an undertaking by the tenant to reinstate the premises a condition of giving his consent. If the proposed alteration would not be an improvement, the landlord can impose whatever

---

40 [1938] Ch 883.
41 *Never-Stop Railway (Wembley) Ltd* v *British Empire Exhibition (1924) Inc* [1926] Ch 877.

conditions he wishes, since the Landlord and Tenant Act 1927, section 19(2), does not apply. If the proposed alteration would be an improvement, section 19(2) does apply, and it allows the landlord to require such an undertaking where this would be reasonable and the improvement does not add to the letting value. The Law Commission has suggested that the requirement that the improvement does not add to the letting value of the premises should be abolished, as the landlord may want the premises restored to their original layout in order to occupy them himself, in which case the letting value is irrelevant.[42] In a pre-1996 lease, an undertaking given by the tenant as a condition of obtaining consent will not, however, be binding upon his successors in title unless the landlord and the tenant agree that it should become a term of the lease. If it is not made a term of the lease, the landlord will be able to bring an action for breach against an assignee of the tenant who gave the undertaking only if the assignee enters into a direct covenant with the landlord to reinstate. In a post-1995 lease, the undertaking to reinstate will bind the tenant's successors in title since it will rank as a "tenant covenant" within the Landlord and Tenant (Covenants) Act 1995. A covenant to reinstate given by a head-lessee to the head-lessor will never bind a sub-tenant; the head-lessor should therefore seek a direct covenant to reinstate from a sub-tenant.

In *James v Hutton & J Cook & Sons Ltd*[43], it was held that damages recoverable by a landlord for breach of an undertaking to reinstate should be assessed according to the usual rule of compensation for damages for breach of contract. In that case, a tenant had put in a new shop window; but there was no evidence that this was less desirable than the original one, nor was there any indication that the landlord did in fact intend to reinstate the old shop window. The damages recoverable were limited to the diminution in the value of the reversion; and, there being no such diminution, the damages that the landlord recovered were only nominal.

Reasons for refusing consent

A landlord's reasons for refusing consent to improvements may be many and varied. In the second *Woolworth* case[44], Slesser LJ said that "many considerations, aesthetic, historic or even personal, may be relied upon as yielding reasonable grounds for refusing consent." He pointed out that the wider the court's interpretation of "improvement", the more important it becomes to protect a landlord who has grounds for objecting.

---

42 *Codification of the Law of Landlord and Tenant: Covenants restricting dispositions, alterations and change of user*, Law Com No 141, (1985) paras 8.42–8.43.
43 [1950] 1 KB 9.
44 [1938] Ch 883, 907.

Although the Landlord and Tenant Act 1927, section 19(2), specifically allows the landlord to have the premises reinstated if the improvement diminishes the letting value, this presumably does not mean that an undertaking to reinstate in other circumstances would necessarily be unreasonable.

Conditions attaching to consent

Conditions imposed on the granting of consent, like the grounds for refusing consent, may also take account of a wide range of matters, and are not limited to those contemplated by section 19(2) itself.

The licence granting consent to alterations will almost certainly include conditions as to how, and possibly when, the work is to be done. It will usually require the plans and specifications to be approved by the landlord, and will require the tenant to obtain planning permission and approval under the Building Regulations if necessary. It will often require the tenant to carry out the work in a workmanlike manner within a certain time, and not in such a way as to cause a nuisance or annoyance to nearby owners or occupiers. The tendency is for alteration covenants to become more comprehensive, so that the covenant itself may specify these requirements as conditions for consent. Such a covenant might be one:

> "To carry out approved alterations for which consent is given in a good and workmanlike manner, with materials of good quality, and to the satisfaction of the landlord."

In order not to fall outside the statutory provisions entitling him to compensation for improvements[45], the tenant should ensure that the licence is not drafted so as to oblige him to carry out the improvements in a contract for valuable consideration supplied by the landlord.

Consent "subject to licence"

If the landlord intends to consent subject to the drawing up of a formal licence by his solicitors, he should exercise great care in communicating his intention to the tenant. The risk for the landlord is that a letter to the tenant indicating the landlord's intention might itself be construed as the requisite licence; and the landlord will therefore be precluded from introducing conditions or terms in the formal licence which were not specified or envisaged in the earlier letter. If the body of the letter confers consent, merely heading it "subject to licence" will not suspend its operation.

---

45 LTA 1927, Part I, discussed *infra*.

This principle was applied by the Court of Appeal in *Prudential Assurance Co Ltd* v *Mount Eden Land Ltd*[46], where the landlord's managing agents, in response to the tenant's application for consent to make certain alterations, sent the tenant a letter headed "Subject to Licence." The letter confirmed that the landlord gave its consent subject to a formal licence being entered into by the tenant, and further stated that in the event of acceptance the writers would arrange for the landlord's solicitors to prepare the necessary licence. The issue was whether the words of the heading prevented the remainder of the letter from operating as a consent. The court adopted a distinction drawn by Harman J in *Venetian Glass Gallery Ltd* v *Next Properties Ltd*[47], between negotiations between persons who were legal strangers and the unilateral act of a party to a pre-existing legal relationship. In the former case, the use of an expression such as "subject to contract" worked the magic of automatically suspending legal relations despite any apparent conflict with an otherwise firm commitment contained in the body of the document. In the latter case, the heading was to be read together with the text in order to discover the true intention of the writer. A landlord's giving consent to alterations fell into the latter category. On the facts of the case, the only way to reconcile the heading and the body of the letter was to treat the letter as giving conditional consent.

IMPROVEMENTS AND COMPENSATION FOR IMPROVEMENTS UNDER THE LANDLORD AND TENANT ACT 1927, PART I

The Landlord and Tenant Act 1927, Part I, introduced a scheme to compensate business tenants who quit when their tenancies end for certain improvements which they have made. Some modifications to the scheme were made by the Landlord and Tenant Act 1954, Part III. To obtain compensation for an improvement, the tenant has to serve on the landlord notice of a proposal to make such improvement.[48] The compensation system itself, as will be explained, is of little practical significance; but the service of a notice of an intention to make an improvement is important

---

46 [1997] 1 EGLR 37.
47 [1989] 2 EGLR 42.
48 LTA 1927, s 3(5).

because in some instances it can operate to authorise improvements that the lease itself prohibits.[49] The procedure is therefore sometimes used by tenants as an alternative to an application to the landlord for consent to alterations.

Qualifying tenancies

A tenant is entitled to serve a notice of an intention to make an improvement, and to claim compensation for a proper improvement, only if he is the tenant of a holding of premises held under a lease (which includes an under-lease and an agreement for a lease or an under-lease[50]) and used wholly or partly for carrying on thereat any trade, profession[51] or business.[52] Mining leases[53], agricultural holdings[54], and holdings of farm business tenancies[55], are excluded,[56] as are lettings to a tenant during a period that he is holder of an office, appointment or employment of the landlord, but only if the contract[57] is in writing and expresses the purpose for which the tenancy is created.[58] If the premises are used only partly for the purposes of a trade, profession or business, Part I applies only so far as the improvement relates to the part so used.[59]

Compensation for improvements

The underlying objective of the Landlord and Tenant Act 1927, Part I, is to allow a tenant, at the termination of the tenancy on quitting his holding, to recover compensation for any improvement (including the erection of any building) which has been made by him or his predecessor in title, and which adds to the letting value of the holding.[60] The parties cannot contract out of Part I.[61]

The rationale for compensation is that the landlord will benefit from the improvements. The provisions do not therefore cover trade or tenant's

---

49 *Ibid*, s 3(4).
50 *Ibid*, s 25(1).
51 See proviso to LTA 1927, s 17(3).
52 *Ibid*, s 17(1).
53 *Ibid*, s 17(1); see definition of "mining lease" in LTA 1927, s 25(1).
54 Within the meaning of Agricultural Holdings Act 1986: LTA 1927, s 17(1)(a).
55 Within the meaning of Agricultural Tenancies Act 1995: LTA 1927, s 17(1)(b).
56 LTA 1927, s 17(1).
57 The "contract" would appear to mean the contract under which the office is held, or the contract of employment or appointment; but some commentators take it to refer to the tenancy itself: see Aldridge, *Letting Business Premises*, 7th ed (1996) FT Law & Tax, 57; Crabb, *Leases: Covenants and Consents* (1991) Sweet & Maxwell, 159–160.
58 LTA 1927, s 17(2).
59 *Ibid*, s 17(4).
60 *Ibid*, s 1(1).
61 *Ibid*, s 9.

fixtures, which are removable by the tenant.[62] The landlord will not benefit from the improvements at the end of a lease protected by the Landlord and Tenant Act 1954, Part II, unless the tenant quits. Since there is a good chance that a tenant under a Part II protected tenancy will be able to obtain a new lease, the compensation provisions are of reduced significance to such tenancies. No claim to compensation can be made in respect of any improvement made less than three years before the termination of a tenancy.[63]

Improvements made under an obligation

A tenant does not lose the right to compensation under Part I of the Act in respect of any improvement merely because it is made in pursuance of a statutory obligation[64], provided the improvement was begun after 1 October 1954.[65] A tenant is not, however, entitled to compensation in respect of any improvement which the tenant or his predecessors in title were under an obligation to make in pursuance of a contract entered into for valuable consideration, including a building lease.[66] The obligation can be to someone other than the landlord. In *Owen Owen Estate Ltd* v *Livett*[67], a head-lessee's covenanting with a third party (a sub-lessee) to install a lavatory sufficed to disentitle him to compensation for the improvement from the head-lessor.

One way in which a landlord may avoid the compensation provisions, therefore, is to insert some consideration for consent to the alterations in the licence, and to put the tenant under an obligation to carry them out. Waiver of an absolute covenant against alterations may be sufficient consideration, but waiver of a qualified covenant is probably not. Obligations imposed merely as part of the consent, such as obtaining the landlord's approval of the plans, are unlikely to be regarded as consideration, provided they are basically permissive in nature.[68]

Conditions for claim

The tenant must serve on the landlord a written notice, together with plans and specifications.[69] If the landlord is not the freeholder, the tenant should also serve notice on the superior landlord.[70] A mesne landlord who is served

62 *Ibid*, s 1(1). See Chap 3.
63 LTA 1954, s 2(1)(c).
64 *Supra*, pp. 156–158.
65 LTA 1954, s 48(1), disapplying part of LTA 1927, s 2(1)(b).
66 LTA 1927, s 2(1)(b).
67 [1956] Ch 1.
68 *Godbold v Martins The Newsagents Ltd* [1983] 2 EGLR 128 (Ch).
69 LTA 1927, s 3(1).
70 *Ibid*, s 3(1).

with a written notice should himself serve a copy on his immediate superior landlord, as a mesne landlord who has paid or is liable to pay compensation under Part I is entitled to reclaim it from his immediate superior landlord at the end of his term, but only if he has served on such superior landlord copies of all documents sent to him relating to proposed improvements and claims.[71]

The landlord may object to the improvements within three months.[72] If the landlord fails to serve a notice of objection within this time, the improvements are treated as authorised, notwithstanding anything to the contrary in the lease.[73]

If the landlord does object within three months, the tenant must ask the court[74] to certify the improvements. The court must do this if it is satisfied that the improvements will add to the letting value at the end of the tenancy, that they are reasonable and suitable to the character of the premises, and that they will not diminish the value of any other property belonging to the landlord or a superior landlord. The landlord and any superior landlord have a right to be heard by the court, which may impose conditions or require modifications of the plans. If the court certifies the improvements to be proper improvements, they are treated as authorised notwithstanding anything in the lease to the contrary.[75] The landlord may resist the claim by offering to effect the alterations personally, and an increased rent (to be fixed by the court in default of agreement) may be charged to cover the cost.[76]

To qualify for compensation, the tenant must (where the landlord has served notice of objection to the improvement) obtain the court's certification of the improvements before they are completed:[77] it is not enough for the tenant merely to have made an application to the court. Therefore, by objecting to a proposed improvement, the landlord can hold it up until the county court can provide a hearing, with no penalty other than costs.[78] The court's certificate may therefore have two effects: it may render an improvement lawful which would otherwise have been in breach of a term of the lease; and it may establish in part the tenant's right to compensation at the end of the lease.[79]

---

71 *Ibid*, s 8(1).
72 *Ibid*, s 3(1).
73 *Ibid*, s 3(4).
74 Either the High Court or (more usually) a county court: LTA 1927, s 21; LTA 1954, s 63.
75 LTA 1927, s 3(4).
76 *Ibid*, s 3(1).
77 *Hogarth Health Club Ltd* v *Westbourne Investments Ltd* [1990] 1 EGLR 89 (CA); where, however, the court left open the possibility that the tenant might become disabled *pro tanto* as each piece of work is carried out: *ibid*, at 90 (Staughton LJ).
78 *Ibid*, at 91 (Staughton LJ).
79 *Ibid*, at 89 (Staughton LJ).

If the tenant executes improvements (either where the landlord has served no notice of objection in response to the tenant's improvement notice, or where the certificate of the court that it is a proper improvement has been obtained), he may require the landlord to furnish him with a certificate that the improvements have been duly executed; and the tenant is liable to pay the landlord's reasonable expenses in furnishing the certificate. If the landlord fails to provide a certificate within one month of being so required, the tenant may apply to the court for a certificate.[80]

To claim compensation at the end of the tenancy, the tenant must have completed the improvement within the time agreed with the landlord or fixed by the court.[81] It is therefore important that the tenant has obtained a certificate from the landlord that the improvements have been properly executed.[82] The tenant must also claim in the prescribed form and within the time-limits prescribed by the Landlord and Tenant Act 1954, Part III. If the tenancy is terminated by notice to quit (whether given by the landlord or by the tenant) the tenant must claim within three months from the date such notice is given.[83] Where the tenancy terminates by the tenant's request for a new tenancy[84], the tenant must claim[85] within three months of the landlord's giving notice opposing the application.[86] If the tenancy comes to an end by effluxion of time, the tenant must claim not earlier than six nor later than three months before the tenancy comes to an end.[87] If the tenancy is terminated by forfeiture or by re-entry, the tenant must claim within three months of the court order or, where re-entry is effected without court order, within three months of the date of re-entry.[88]

The tenant must give details of the cost of the improvements and the date when they were carried out. The amount of compensation is limited to the "net addition" to the value of the holding (thus allowing for the fact that not all the improvements may add to the letting value) or the reasonable cost of carrying out the improvement at the termination of the tenancy.[89]

Where the landlord is liable to pay rates (including water rates) or premiums on a fire-insurance policy in respect of the demised premises, and the tenant has executed an improvement under the 1927 Act which results in an increase in such rates or premiums, the tenant is liable to reimburse

---

80 LTA 1927, s 3(6).
81 *Ibid*, s 3(5).
82 *Ibid*, s 3(6).
83 LTA 1954, s 47(1).
84 *i.e.* under *ibid*, s 26.
85 LTA 1954, s 47(1).
86 *i.e.* under *ibid*, s 26(6).
87 LTA 1954, s 47(2).
88 *Ibid*, s 47(3).
89 LTA 1927, s 1(1)(a), (b).

the landlord for such increases. For this purpose, such increased sums are deemed to be in the nature of rent and recoverable as rent from the tenant.[90] This provision is of limited application, since in practice the payment of such sums is usually a liability of the tenant.

Practical limitations of the compensation system

Although the parties cannot contract out of the compensation provisions in the Landlord and Tenant Act 1927, Part I, it appears that they are virtually a dead letter. The Law Commission has suggested that their neglect is the cumulative result of a number of causes.[91] The security of tenure provisions introduced by the 1954 Act mean that a tenant who has made improvements will not necessarily lose the benefit of them at the end of the term. The machinery for claiming compensation is inherently wasteful and cumbersome, and it is impractical to retain the necessary records over the long periods of time involved. There is evidence that the compensation scheme is not in practice suitable for retail properties. There is widespread use of contractual arrangements designed to exclude the payment of compensation – imposing an obligation on the tenant either to do the work initially or to reinstate at the end of the lease. Another reason is the relatively short life-span of improvements, whereby tenants make their decision whether or not to carry out improvements in the light of the period remaining of the lease, and frequently write off the expenditure over that period. Finally, many tenants are apparently unaware of the compensation scheme, and may therefore negotiate an improvement with their landlord on an informal basis without realising the need to set the preliminary procedures in motion.

THE EFFECT OF ALTERATIONS ON RENT

Improvements may increase the market rental value of the property, and this could obviously operate unfairly on a tenant who has paid for the alterations in the first place. The tenant could effectively be paying for the alterations again in the increased rent. The Landlord and Tenant Act 1954, section 34, therefore provides for the disregard of improvements made by a tenant on fixing the rent under a new lease under Part II of the Act. It is common for a rent-review clause also to provide that improvements effected by the tenant are to be disregarded in assessing a new rent.

---

90 *Ibid*, s 16.
91 *Landlord and Tenant Law: Compensation for Tenants' Improvements*, Law Com No 178 (1989), paras 3.5–3.14.

Disregard under the Landlord and Tenant Act 1954, Part II

The Landlord and Tenant Act 1954, section 34(1)(c), provides that in fixing rent under a new tenancy under the Act there shall be disregarded "any effect on rent of any improvement carried out by the tenant or a predecessor in title of his otherwise than in pursuance of an obligation to his immediate landlord."

In *East Coast Amusement Co Ltd v British Transport Board*[92], the House of Lords held that this provision applied only to improvements carried out during the currency of the lease to be renewed. Section 34 was therefore amended[93], by the addition of sub-section (2), which provides that an improvement qualifies to be disregarded if it was effected within 21 years before the application for a new tenancy, if the holding has been subject to a business tenancy ever since then, and if the tenant did not quit at the end of any of the tenancies. This effectively abrogates the decision in *East Coast Amusement Co Ltd v British Transport Board*.[94]

Because alterations may therefore need to be disregarded in assessing rent for up to 21 years after completion, a careful record should be kept of any alterations carried out.

The section applies to alterations made by a tenant or a predecessor in title. It was held in *Euston Centre Properties Ltd v H & J Wilson Ltd*[95] that this did not include improvements carried out by the tenant when he was a licensee only, and such improvements should be ignored.

The obligation to the landlord will probably have to be more than requirements imposed upon the tenant in the licence as to the way in which the alterations are effected.[96]

Many leases contain a covenant by the tenant to comply with requirements as to the state of premises laid down in any statute.[97] Such a covenant would put the tenant under an obligation to the landlord to carry out the alterations in addition to any statutory obligation, and such alterations would therefore fall outside the disregard provision of section 34(1)(c).[98]

Disregard under a rent-review clause

A rent-review clause will often include a provision that improvements made

---

92 [1965] AC 58.
93 By LPA 1969, s 1(1).
94 [1965] AC 58.
95 [1982] 1 EGLR 57 (QB).
96 *Godbold v Martins The Newsagents Ltd* [1983] 2 EGLR 128 (Ch).
97 See the clause on pp. 156–157.
98 *Forte & Co Ltd v General Accident Life Assurance Ltd* [1986] 2 EGLR 115.

by the tenant are to be disregarded when fixing a new rent. Sometimes this will incorporate the wording of the Landlord and Tenant Act 1954, section 34(1)(c), either specifically or by reference to the section; for example:

> "There shall be disregarded such matters as would by virtue of section 34(1)(a) to (c) inclusive and section 34(2) of the Landlord and Tenant Act 1954 be disregarded were the tenant applying for a new tenancy under that Act on the review date."

From the tenant's point of view, it may be important to ensure that the reference to the section is to its amended form, including sub-section (2). In *Brett v Brett Essex Golf Club Ltd*[99], a reference only to section 34(1)(c) in a lease made in 1978 was construed (when looked at in the light of other provisions in the lease where the draftsman had expressly mentioned amended legislation) as being a reference to the unamended section, and this discounted earlier improvements. In that case, a nine-hole golf-course made by the tenant on adjoining land, not held by him under the same lease, had been added to the holding by the 1978 lease. It was held that this could not constitute an improvement to the demised premises as it was not part of the premises as originally demised.

If the rent-review clause does not provide for improvements to be disregarded, they will be taken into account.[1]

Improvements in Short Leases Taxable as Premiums

In a lease not exceeding 50 years where the tenant covenants to carry out any work on the premises, the amount by which the value of the landlord's estate is thereby increased is liable to income or corporation tax as if it had been a premium payable by the tenant.[2] For this purpose, work on the premises does not include work of repairs or maintenance, or other work the payment for which would, if the landlord and not the tenant were obliged to carry it out, be deductible from the rent in computing the profits liable to tax.[3] The premium so calculated is reduced by $\frac{1}{50}$ for every complete year of the lease after the first year.[4]

If the tenant pays to the landlord a sum demanded by the landlord as a condition of his giving consent to make improvements, such sum is taxable

99 [1986] 1 EGLR 154.
1 *Ponsford v HMS Aerosols Ltd* [1979] AC 63.
2 Income and Corporation Taxes Act 1988, s 34(1), (2).
3 *Ibid*, s 34(3), referring to the deductions in ICTA 1988, ss 25–30.
4 *Ibid*, s 34(1).

in the landlord's hands as a premium.[5] If, however, the landlord requires the tenant to reinstate the premises as consideration for the variation or waiver of any terms of the lease, the work of reinstatement is not taxable as a premium, since it is not "a sum ... payable" within the statute.[6]

---

5 *Ibid*, s 34(5).
6 *Ibid*, s 34(5).

Chapter 8

USER

INTRODUCTION

A landlord will invariably want to take a covenant from a lessee as to the user of the demised premises. He may have various reasons for this, such as to preserve the letting value of the premises and of the reversion, to avoid complaints as to user from any neighbouring tenants, or to comply with any restrictions as to user which affect him, such as restrictive covenants on the freehold title and planning requirements. Both the landlord and the tenant will be greatly concerned with matters entirely extraneous to the lease which affect the user of the demised premises, and the first part of this chapter considers these matters and their bearing on the drafting of user clauses in leases.

The form of user covenants in leases is important not only as regards the use to which the demised premises may be put, but also because of the effect of user covenants on the interpretation of other covenants, such as covenants against disposition and rent review. It is necessary, therefore, to consider the nature and effect of user covenants on these matters.

It is possible too that there may be other covenants in a lease which affect user, and the scope and effect of these covenants will be considered.

EXTRANEOUS MATTERS WHICH MAY AFFECT USER

Restrictive covenants on the freehold title

A restrictive covenant on the freehold title will be binding on all purchasers of a legal estate in the land, including sub-tenants,[1] provided it is registered (if created post-1925) as a Class D(ii) land charge in land with unregistered title, or (whenever created) as a minor interest in the charges register of the freehold title at HM Land Registry in land with registered title. If it is not

---

1 *Mander* v *Falcke* [1891] 2 Ch 554.

so protected by registration, the restrictive covenant will be void against a purchaser[2] for money or money's worth[3] (in unregistered land) or against a registered disposition for valuable consideration[4] (in registered land). Non-registration therefore never avails a squatter.[4a]

A tenant who takes a lease under an open contract has no right to call for the freeholder's title in either registered or unregistered land.[5] It is quite possible that there will be restrictive covenants on the freehold title which affect its use, and a tenant should therefore always ensure that the contract includes a clause for deduction of the freehold title. In unregistered land, a prospective tenant will not be able to search the land charges register without the names of estate owners against whom to search. In registered land, the covenants will appear in the charges register of the freehold title; but without sight of the office copy entries, the tenant will not know about them.

Procedures for dealing with restrictive covenants affecting land

Application for declaration

Because the law relating to the passing of the benefit and burden of restrictive covenants to subsequent landowners is complicated, and many such covenants are old ones (sometimes even imposed in the 19th century!) it is possible to make an application to the court for a declaration as to whether any particular land is in fact affected by a covenant and by whom such a covenant would be enforceable.[6]

Waiver

If there have been continuous breaches of a restrictive covenant over a long period in which the person entitled to the benefit of the covenant has acquiesced, or if there is any other conduct from which an inference of waiver of the covenant can be drawn, then it will no longer be enforceable. Even though the court may not be prepared to enforce it by granting an injunction however, damages may be obtainable.[7]

---

2 As defined in LCA 1972, s 17(1).
3 LCA 1972, s 4(6).
4 LRA 1925, ss 20, 23.
4a cf *Re Nisbett and Potts' Contract* [1906] 1 Ch 386.
5 See Chap 2.
6 LPA 1925, s 87(4).
7 *Shaw* v *Applegate* [1978] 1 All ER 123.

Discharge or modification

Under the Law of Property Act 1925, section 84[8], "any person interested" may apply to the Lands Tribunal for the discharge or modification of a restrictive covenant affecting freehold land or leasehold land held under a lease of more than 40 years of which 25 years have expired. The grounds for an application are:

> (a) that the restriction should be deemed obsolete because of changes in the character of the property or the neighbourhood, or for other circumstances;

> (aa)[9] that the continued existence of the covenant would impede the reasonable user of the land;

The Lands Tribunal here must be satisfied that the covenant does not secure practical benefits of substantial value or advantage to those entitled to the benefit, or is contrary to the public interest. It should have regard to the development plan under the Town and Country Planning legislation and to any planning applications granted or refused.

> (b) that the persons entitled to the benefit agree, expressly or impliedly, to the discharge or modification of the covenant;

> (c) that the proposed discharge or modification will not injure those entitled to the benefit of the covenant

Indemnity policy

A purchaser can take out an indemnity policy against the possibility of incurring liability for breach of a restrictive covenant. For a fairly recent covenant, the cost of this may be prohibitive; but for an older covenant it may be more reasonable, and this course of action may save the time and costs which a hearing by the Lands Tribunal would necessarily involve.

Restrictive covenants contained in another lease

If the landlord who leases more than one property to different tenants enters into a restrictive covenant with one tenant relating to the user of the other properties, such tenant will be able to enforce the restrictive covenant, under the doctrine of *Tulk v Moxhay*[10], against the tenant of any of the other properties, except one who can establish the defence of a bona fide purchaser for value of the legal estate without notice.[11]

---

8 As amended by LPA 1969.
9 Widened by LPA 1969.
10 (1848) 2 Ph 774.
11 *Holloway Bros Ltd v Hill* [1902] 2 Ch 612; *Walker v Arkay Caterers Ltd* [1997] EGCS 107.

Restrictive covenants in a head-lease

Unless the contract for the sub-lease stipulates otherwise, the only title for which a sub-tenant may call is the immediate head-lease from which his sub-lease is to be created.[12] He is, however, bound by restrictive covenants in the head-lease and in any other superior lease. In unregistered title, the restrictive covenants are not registrable under the Land Charges Act 1972. In registered title, they will be referred to in office copy entries by reference to the lease. Ideally, therefore, in the case of a sub-lease, the sub-lessee will want to see all superior leases. A sub-lessee, or an assignee from him, should therefore always seek to include a clause in the contract under which he purchases for inspection of any head-lease.

A tenant should ensure that covenants in a head-lease are repeated in any sub-lease, as otherwise he would put himself in the invidious position of being liable to his landlord for breach of a covenant in the head-lease which he has no means of enforcing against his own sub-tenant. An additional safeguard for a tenant is also to take a covenant from his sub-tenant to observe and perform all the covenants in the head-lease (other than the covenant relating to the payment of rent).

From the point of view of the landlord, an exhaustive form of user clause, whereby the tenant covenants "**not to use or permit or suffer the premises to be used...**" is desirable, as this may extend his right of action against the tenant to cover the acts of any sub-tenant. There are conflicting judicial opinions, however, as to whether the granting of a sub-lease under which the sub-tenant is not expressly bound by the covenants in the head-lease amounts to "permitting" a breach of a user covenant in the head-lease. The scope of a covenant against "permitting" a certain user of premises was considered by Swanwick J in *Norton v Charles Dean Productions Ltd*.[13] He adopted a definition by Atkin LJ in *Berton v Alliance Economic Investment Co Ltd*[14] that "to permit" was synonymous with "to suffer", and that both meant allowing an act to happen which someone could have prevented (but did not prevent) if it was an act which he could reasonably foresee might have occurred.

A head-lessor may apply to restrain by injunction a sub-tenant whose use of the premises breaches a negative user covenant in the head-lease.[15] The court is, however, empowered to grant the landlord damages in lieu.[16] Since there is no privity of estate between the head-lessor and a sub-lessee,

---

12 See Chap 2.
13 (1969) 214 EG 559.
14 [1922] 1 KB 742.
15 *i.e.* under the principle of *Tulk v Moxhay* (1848) 2 Ph 774.
16 Supreme Court Act 1981, s 50, re-enacting Chancery Amendment Act 1858 (Lord Cairns' Act).

the former cannot seek to forfeit the sub-lease for the sub-tenant's breach; but the head-lessor may be able to forfeit the head-lease. The precise wording of the covenant in the head-lease is therefore important: the wider the words used, the easier it will be to establish a breach.

If the tenant is unaware of the sub-tenant's breach of covenant but takes action against the sub-tenant as soon as he is aware of the breach, this may well be good grounds upon which he could apply for relief against forfeiture[17].

Restrictions under the Town and Country Planning Acts

A prospective tenant will need to ensure that the premises can be used for his business purposes. He should therefore require to see any valid planning permissions and any conditions attached. A condition restricting user to a named use may prevent a change even within a Use Class.[18] A tenant should be aware, however, that a covenant restricting user to a particular Use Class is not a warranty by the landlord that such user is legal.[19] The landlord will often cover the point with an express declaration however, such as:

> "Nothing contained in this lease or in any consent granted by the landlord under this lease shall imply or warrant that the demised premises may be used under the Planning Acts for the purpose herein authorised or any purpose subsequently authorised and the tenant hereby acknowledges and admits that the landlord has not given or made at any time any representation or warranty that any such use is or will be or will remain a permitted use under the Planning Acts."

If there is no planning permission but an established use, it may be possible to apply for a certificate of lawfulness of an existing use.[20]

Any "material change" of user requires planning permission; but this will not always be necessary if the user is another use within the same Use Class under the Town and Country Planning (Use Classes) Order 1987.[21]

The intention of the Order is to allow for some flexibility in use within the different Classes. Also, a change of use of a subsidiary part of the premises, where the use is ancillary to the main use of the premises, will not constitute a material change requiring permission. Abandonment of a permitted use may, however, constitute a change and result in a planning permission no longer being valid.

---

17 *Glass* v *Kencakes Ltd* [1966] 1 QB 611.
18 *City of London* v *Secretary of State for the Environment* (1971) 23 P & CR 108.
19 *Hill* v *Harris* [1965] 2 QB 601.
20 See Chap 2.
21 See Chap 2.

Planning controls are enforceable against the occupier of premises, but the Town and Country Planning Act 1990 provides that an enforcement notice may also be served upon the landlord of premises. The landlord therefore has an interest to ensure that there is no breach of any planning requirements. To this end, he may require a covenant from a tenant to comply with any planning conditions and not to carry out any development without consent. An example of such a covenant would be:

> "To comply at the tenant's expense in all respects with the Planning Acts and to indemnify the landlord against any breaches thereof and not to apply for any consents whatsoever under the Planning Acts without the prior approval of the landlord."

The covenant may be more specific in requiring the tenant to maintain the established use, or to use the premises only for purposes within a particular Use Class. An example of such a covenant would be:

> "Not to use the demised premises or any part thereof nor permit or suffer the same to be used otherwise than as offices within Class B1 of the Town & Country Planning (Use Classes) Order 1987."

Such covenants would maintain the letting value of the premises and the value of the reversion for the landlord. In addition to any planning enforcement against the tenant, the landlord would then also have a right of forfeiture for a breach of such a covenant.

In *Brewers' Co v Viewplan plc*[22] a reference to the 1972 Use Classes Order was not construed as a reference to the 1987 Order which replaced it.[23]

Many advertisements are also subject to planning controls under the Town and Country Planning (Control of Advertisements) Regulations 1992,[23a] and it is therefore advisable for the landlord to extend the covenant to comply also with any Regulations made under the Town and Country Planning Acts. Provided that any advertisement does not infringe the Regulations, user for a particular business would usually include advertisements usual to that type of business.

Licensing or registration of certain uses

Certain use of premises requires either a licence or registration under the relevant statutes. For example, a licence is necessary under the Firearms Act 1968 to sell firearms; and a justices' licence is necessary to sell alcohol.

22   [1989] 2 EGLR 133 (Ch).
23   For a fuller discussion, see Chap 2.
23a SI 1992 No 666, as amended by Town and Country Planning (Control of
     Advertisements) (Amendment) Regulations 1994, SI 1994 No 2351.

Nursing homes are required to be registered under the Registered Homes Act 1984, section 1, and premises used for the purposes of a food business under the Food Safety Act 1990, section 19.

A landlord of such premises will usually require a covenant in the lease that the tenant will obtain any necessary licence or registration, and will do nothing to prejudice any such licence once granted. An example of such a covenant would be:

> "At all times to observe and comply with the provisions of or imposed under any statute licence or registration regulating or permitting the use of the demised premises for the purpose for which they are for the time being used and the requirements of any competent authority in that connection and at the expense of the tenant to do all that is necessary to obtain maintain and renew all licences and registrations required by law for the use of the demised premises for that purpose."

Covenants in restraint of trade

A covenant which imposes an excessive restraint of trade may be illegal under the general law of contract. Such covenants are sometimes taken by a vendor on the sale of freehold business premises, or by a mortgagee on the grant of a mortgage on freehold or leasehold business premises. Although in theory they might be included by a landlord in a lease, in practice a tenant is unlikely to accept a lease of premises which unduly restricts the user as such a covenant would make it more difficult to assign the lease. Such a covenant might not be to the landlord's advantage either as it will necessarily have a depressing effect on any rent review.

Generally, such covenants are unenforceable insofar as they exceed what is necessary to protect the business interests of the covenantee. In *Amoco Australian Property Ltd* v *Rocca Bros*[24], the Privy Council held that covenants by a sub-lessee that a service station would buy only the products of its landlord (a petroleum company) were void as being in restraint of trade. In *Alec Lobb (Garages) Ltd* v *Total Oil GB Ltd*[25], however, it was held that only clauses in a lease which were void as being against public policy should be struck out, and that all the other clauses in a lease should stand. It seems unlikely, therefore, that normal user clauses in a lease would be affected by excessive clauses in restraint of trade.

Such "tied trade" covenants are covenants having reference to the subject-matter of the lease within the Law of Property Act 1925, section 141, and so are enforceable by an assignee of the reversion of a pre-1996 lease. They will be "landlord and tenant covenants" for the purposes of

24 [1975] AC 561.
25 [1983] 1 WLR 87.

the Landlord and Tenant (Covenants) Act, 1995, the burden and benefit of which will pass under a post-1995 lease.

User as between neighbouring tenants of the same lessor

Similar user by two or more tenants

If the landlord lets out nearby premises to different business tenants, he will often wish to ensure that the respective tenants' businesses are not directly in competition with each other, as this might reduce the value of each letting and could drive a tenant into bankruptcy, which could result in the landlord's suffering a loss of rent and a void period before a new tenant can be found. In *Premier Confectionery (London) Co Ltd* v *London Commercial Sale Rooms Ltd*[26] a tenant sought consent to assign the lease of a kiosk separately from the lease of a tobacconist's shop of which he was the tenant, and the landlord's refusal of consent on the ground that the two would be in business competition with each other was held to be reasonable.

A tenant could seek to protect itself against the landlord's letting other premises to a competing business by taking a covenant in the lease to this effect; the area or properties to be subject to such covenant must be clear. Breach of such a covenant gives rise to an action for damages[27], and the tenant can obtain an injunction to restrain a letting in breach.[28] If no express covenant has been entered into, however, the court will not readily imply a covenant on the landlord's part not to allow the use of nearby premises for a competing purpose.[29] It was held in *Port* v *Griffith*[30] that the implied covenant not to derogate from his grant does not preclude the landlord from letting nearby premises for the same or a similar use, as this does not impede the actual user of the demised premises for the purpose for which they were let, and since it cannot be within the reasonable contemplation of the parties that the landlord should be so fettered, given the difficulty of determining which business activities would comprise a breach and how physically close they would need to be.

This principle was affirmed recently in *Romulus Trading Co Ltd* v *Comet Properties Ltd*[31] where Garland J rejected the argument that the doctrine can now be used to protect the tenant's purely economic interest. In that case the landlord had, by a deed of variation and licence some years earlier, permitted the first tenant to use the premises demised to it

---

26 [1933] Ch 904.
27 *Stanley* v *Kenneth Properties Ltd* (1957) 170 EG 133.
28 *Brigg* v *Thornton* [1904] 1 Ch 386.
29 *Romulus Trading Co Ltd* v *Comet Properties Ltd* [1996] 2 EGLR 70.
30 [1938] 1 All ER 295.
31 [1996] 2 EGLR 70.

(which were situated in central London) as a bank and security deposit, there then being only six retail security deposits in that area. Subsequently the landlord leased almost adjoining premises to another tenant for the same purpose. The plaintiff's claim against the landlord for damages for breach of a covenant for good estate management and for non-derogation from grant was struck out as disclosing no reasonable cause of action.

Letting scheme

Even if the tenant has taken an express covenant by the landlord not to let nearby premises for similar uses, the tenant generally has no direct cause of action against any other tenant to whom the landlord has granted a lease in breach of such covenant.[32] The tenant will have a direct right of action against such other tenants only if a letting scheme has been created in which all the tenants are subject to mutually enforceable rights and obligations.[33] This is the leasehold equivalent to a building scheme or scheme of development in freehold land[34], which enables negative or restrictive covenants to be enforced by and against purchasers of plots from a common vendor.

The same requirements which pertain to a building scheme apply *mutatis mutandis* to a letting scheme. It must be proved[35] (1) that the plaintiff and defendant derive their leasehold titles from a common lessor; (2) that before letting the premises to which the plaintiff and defendant are respectively entitled the lessor had laid out his estate or a defined portion thereof (including those parts demised to the plaintiff and the defendant) to be let as units subject to restrictions intended to be imposed on all the units, and which, though varying in details as to particular units, are consistent and consistent only with some general letting scheme; (3) that these restrictions were intended by the common lessor to be and were for the benefit of all the units intended to be let, whether or not they were also intended to be and were for the benefit of the lessor's reversion or of any other land retained by the lessor; (4) that both the plaintiff and the defendant, or their predecessors in title, took a lease of their units from the common lessor upon the footing that the restrictions subject to which the leases were granted were to enure for the benefit of the other units included in the general scheme whether or not they were also to enure for the benefit of the lessor's reversion or of other land retained by the lessor;

---

32 *Brigg v Thornton* [1904] 1 Ch 386.
33 *Newman v Real Estate Debenture Corporation Ltd* [1940] 1 All ER 131.
34 *Ellison v Reacher* [1908] 2 Ch 665, affirming the principles relating to such schemes laid down at first instance by Parker J: [1908] 2 Ch 374.
35 The first four requirements were laid down in *Ellison v Reacher* [1908] 2 Ch 374, 384–5. The fifth was added by *Reid v Bickerstaff* [1909] 2 Ch 305.

and (5) that the area subject to the scheme is clearly defined.[36] No scheme could therefore arise in respect of a block of flats where each tenant had a lease of a floor, rather than a separate self-contained flat.[37] Any reservation in a lease by the landlord of a right to consent to a change of user would be inconsistent with a letting scheme.

The intention to create a letting scheme must be clearly shown. It is not enough that all the tenants are subject to similar obligations, since these may have been imposed by the landlord merely in the interest of good estate management,[38] or (where the landlord is himself a tenant) to ensure compliance with the terms of the head-lease.[39] For this reason, a letting scheme is more difficult to establish than a scheme of development in freehold land, and the existence of a letting scheme appears to be rarely argued in the modern cases.

Even if a letting scheme were established, it remains unclear whether the implied covenants would need to be protected by registration as a land charge or as a minor interest. Restrictive covenants between landlord and tenant are not so registrable[40], but it is doubtful whether such exemption could be relied upon by a tenant seeking to enforce the covenants of a letting scheme against another tenant.[41]

Non-derogation from grant

If the landlord has leased out various units in a shopping centre to different tenants, he may be liable to tenant A for breach of the implied covenant of non-derogation from grant if he does not take steps to stop a nuisance committed by tenant B which makes tenant A's premises materially less fit for the purpose for which they were let. The landlord was held to be in breach of such a covenant in *Chartered Trust plc v Davies*.[42] The Court of Appeal in that case placed importance upon the fact that the purpose for which the premises had been leased was that of user not merely as "a separate and independent retail unit", but as "such a shop in its place in a shopping arcade."[43]

---

36 *Reid v Bickerstaff* [1909] 2 Ch 305 (building scheme).
37 *Kelly v Battershell* [1949] 2 All ER 830 (CA).
38 *Levene v Clapham Super Market Ltd* (1958) 171 EG 719.
39 *Kelly v Battershell* [1949] 2 All ER 830 (CA), where the presence of similar covenants in the sub-leases could be explained on this ground.
40 LCA 1972, s. 2(5)(ii); LRA 1925, s. 50(1).
41 In *Newman v Real Estate Debenture Corporation* [1940] 1 All ER 131, Atkinson J was able to side-step this issue because the defendant, who was a sub-tenant, was also the owner of the leasehold reversion, and his Lordship said that it was in the latter capacity that the defendant was being sued.
42 [1997] 49 EG 135 (CA), discussed in Chap 3.
43 *Ibid*, at 137–8, per Henry LJ.

USER COVENANTS IN A LEASE

Types of user covenant

A covenant as to user may be **"wide"**, *i.e.* one which prohibits only certain types of use; or **"narrow"**, *i.e.* one which prohibits all uses except for certain specified ones. A user covenant may be **absolute**, *i.e.* one which does not provide for any change in use; **qualified**, *i.e.* one which allows a change of use with the landlord's consent; or **fully qualified**, *i.e.* one which allows a change of use with the landlord's consent, such consent not to be unreasonably refused.

An example of an absolute user clause would be:

> **"Not to use or permit or suffer to be used the demised premises or any part thereof other than as an office in connection with the tenant's business."**

An example of a qualified user clause would be:

> **"Not to use the demised premises or suffer the same to be used except as an office in connection with the tenant's business without the landlord's consent in writing."**

A fully qualified user covenant is one which adds the words implied into covenants against assignment and alterations by the Landlord and Tenant Act 1927, section 19, that such consent shall not be unreasonably refused. An example of this would be:

> **"Not without the landlord's consent which shall not be unreasonably refused to use or permit or suffer the demised premises or any part thereof to be used other than as solicitors' offices or for any other use within Class A2 of the Town and Country Planning (Use Classes) Order 1987."**

Unless these words are expressly added to the covenant, there is no requirement that the landlord's refusal to consent to a change of user be reasonable. Furthermore, no such term will be implied[44], unless perhaps the covenant is a negative and specific one of a regulatory nature – such as the approval of plans.[45]

A tenant with merely a qualified (as distinct from a fully qualified) covenant against a change of user is therefore in much the same position as a tenant with an absolute covenant as regards obtaining the landlord's consent; although, in the case of a qualified covenant not involving structural alterations, section 19(3) applies, and the landlord may require the payment of a reasonable sum in respect of any damage or diminution in value.[45a] If the change of use involves structural alterations, then section

---

44 *Guardian Assurance Co Ltd v Gants Hill Holdings Ltd* [1983] 2 EGLR 36 (Ch).
45 *Cryer v Scott Bros (Sunbury) Ltd* (1988) 55 P & CR 183.
45a See p. 189 *infra*.

19(3) will not apply, but section 19(2) will apply (with similar payment provisions for the landlord) if the lease contains a qualified covenant against alterations provided the alterations can be construed as "improvements."

In the case of a fully qualified covenant, the tenant is obviously in a much stronger position to contest the landlord's grounds for refusal of consent. In *Anglia Building Society* v *Sheffield City Council*[46], where there was a fully qualified covenant against change of use, the user covenant was for use as a travel and employment agency and theatre ticket bureau. The Council refused consent to an assignment to a building society on the ground that service use would depress the rents in a nearby shopping area. Such refusal was held unreasonable: for the landlord to require user as a retail shop would in fact have given it an advantage not reserved to it in the original lease. This was the same ground upon which the court found refusal to consent to assign to be unreasonable in *Bromley Park Garden Estates Ltd* v *Moss*[47]; and it is thought that much the same criteria of reasonableness would apply to fully qualified covenants against change of use as are applicable in the case law on refusal of consent to assign. The Landlord and Tenant Act 1988, which requires a landlord to give his reasons in writing for a refusal of consent to assign or sub-let, does not, however, apply, and the burden of proof to show that the landlord's refusal of consent was unreasonable is on the tenant.

A further difference is that, because section 19(1) does not apply to user covenants to make them fully qualified, it is open to the parties to stipulate what shall be regarded as a reasonable refusal. If grounds for reasonable refusal are specified, however, the landlord's reasons must then fall within them. In *Berenyi* v *Watford Borough Council*[48], it was expressly provided that the landlord's consent should not be regarded as being unreasonably withheld on certain grounds. The court found that the real reason for withholding consent to a change of user was increased vehicular access to the premises if they were used by more than one occupier. As this was not among the grounds set out, it was not available to the landlord as a ground for objection when the court of first instance had reached a conclusion, on the evidence, that this was not a valid reason.

Qualified user covenants and the Landlord and Tenant Act 1927, section 19(3)

Section 19(3) provides that a covenant condition or agreement against alteration of the user of the demised premises without licence or consent

46 [1983] 1 EGLR 57 (CA).
47 [1982] 1 WLR 1019.
48 [1980] 2 EGLR 38 (CA).

shall, if the change does not involve any structural alteration of the premises, be deemed, notwithstanding any express provision to the contrary, to be subject to a proviso that no fine or sum of money in the nature of a fine, whether by way of increase of rent or otherwise, shall be payable for or in respect of such licence or consent. It does not apply to agricultural or mining leases.[49]

In essence, sub-section (3) means that, provided no structural alteration is involved, a landlord cannot demand a sum of money for giving his consent to a change of use, and there can be no contracting out of this provision. Where a change of use involves structural alteration to the premises, sub-section (3) does not apply[50], and so (unless the lease provides otherwise) does not prevent the landlord from demanding a fine; but if there is a qualified covenant against the making of improvements, sub-section (2) applies, and will restrict the landlord in what sum he may reasonably demand by way of payment.[51]

A "fine" for the purposes of the Law of Property Act 1925, section 144, and of the Landlord and Tenant Act 1927, section 19(1), has been widely construed. A condition for consent to assign the lease of a public house that the tenant should sell only the landlord's beer, so that it became a tied house, was held to be a "fine" within section 144.[52] In *Barclays Bank plc* v *Daejan Investments (Grove Hall) Ltd*[53] the judge observed the similarity in the wording of sections 19(3) and 144, and decided that "fine" should be given the same wide interpretation, so that it would include a demand by the landlord to include a break clause in the lease.[54] If the landlord does demand a fine, the tenant is entitled to effect the change of use without consent and without any obligation to pay the sum demanded. If the tenant does pay the fine, however, he cannot recover it back.[55]

A proviso to section 19(3) states that the landlord is not precluded from requiring the payment of a reasonable sum in respect of any damage to or diminution in the value of the premises or any neighbouring premises belonging to him and of any legal or other expenses incurred in connection with such licence or consent. It further provides that where a dispute as to the reasonableness of any such sum has been determined by a court of

---

49 LTA 1927, s 19(4).
50 *Barclays Bank plc* v *Daejan Investments (Grove Hall) Ltd* [1995] 1 EGLR 68 (Ch).
51 For discussion of LTA 1927, s 19(2), see Chap 7.
52 *Gardner & Co Ltd* v *Cone* [1928] Ch 955. For other cases interpreting the word "fine" in the context of LPA 1925, s 144, see Chap 6.
53 [1995] 1 EGLR 68 (Ch).
54 In the case itself, there were structural alterations in addition to the change in user, so that it was not in fact necessary to apply s 19(3).
55 *Comber* v *Fleet Electronics Ltd* [1955] 1 WLR 566.

competent jurisdiction (which probably means only the High Court and not the county court) and the sum so determined to be reasonable is paid by the tenant, then the landlord is bound to grant the licence or consent.

Interpretation of user covenants

The interpretation of user covenants has given rise to some litigation and careful consideration should therefore be given to their drafting in regard to the user allowed.

From a tenant's point of view, a wide user clause will allow some flexibility in his trading, and may make it easier to assign the lease or to sub-let. A wide clause may, however, have an adverse effect on rent review. It has already been mentioned[56] that a tenant with merely a qualified (as opposed to a fully qualified) covenant as to change of user is not likely to be in any better position than a tenant with a user covenant which is absolute, except in regard to the landlord's ability to require payment for his consent.

From a landlord's point of view, it will be particularly desirable to restrict and maintain control of user if the landlord has leased other units or shops which may be in competition with the tenant. The case of *Basildon Development Corporation* v *Mactro Ltd*[57] concerned an action brought by a landlord to restrain a supermarket from selling goods which would compete with the businesses of other tenants, and possibly cause such tenants financial hardship. The more restrictive the user, however, the more adverse its effect on any rent review.[58]

A landlord will also be concerned to ensure that the tenant's user does not infringe any of the restrictions as to user of the premises binding on the landlord.[59]

Interpretation of exact terms used

Problems may arise in the interpretation of the words used, either because the description of the business is general (*e.g.* supermarket), or because the meaning of certain trades may change with time so as to infringe upon other trades. It would obviously be unwise to use words often found in older leases – such as "draper", "hosier" and "haberdasher" – which have little meaning today. It has been held, however, that user as a hairdresser covered the sale of contraceptives[60] and that user as "a garage with car sales

56 *Supra.*
57 [1986] 1 EGLR 137 (CA).
58 See pp 200–202 *infra.*
59 See pp 177–186 *supra.*
60 *Bier* v *Danser* (1951) 157 EG 552.

and vehicle repairs" included the sale of vehicle accessories, but not sweets and confectionery.[61]

It was held in *Texaco Antilles v Kernochan*[62] that user words should be construed as at the date they are used. In that case, restrictive covenants imposed in 1925 restricted user to a public garage; they were held to include use also as a filling station, which would have been usual in 1925. In *Basildon Development Corporation v Mactro Ltd*[63], which concerned a user covenant in a lease, it was conceded by counsel that the relevant date for determining the meaning of use as a food and drink supermarket and purposes incidental thereto was the date the lease was granted. Doubts were, however, expressed in the Court of Appeal as to whether this should be the sole test, and it was thought that other circumstances might also be relevant.

The courts have been reluctant to find that general descriptions of trade import an exact meaning which should remain unchanged for all time. Thus, in *Stevenage Development Corporation v Baby Carriages & Toys (Stevenage) Ltd*[64], it was held that "nursery goods" did not include baby clothes. In the *Mactro* case, it was said that "supermarket" was a technical word and that the goods sold by a "supermarket" might well change.

Ancillary use of part of the premises

A further cause of litigation has arisen where the tenant has used some part of the premises let for an ancillary use not specifically covered by the user covenant. What proportion of the premises used, or the business carried on, may relate to a purpose ancillary to the main one without constituting a breach of the user covenant?

In *Calabar (Woolwich) Ltd v Tesco Stores Ltd*[65], the use of premises was restricted to a supermarket and the sale of certain ancillary goods. The sale of freezers, which constituted 15% of the business carried on, was held not to be sufficient to constitute a breach. In *Montross Associated Investments SA v Moussaieff*[66], the use of premises as offices in connection with the business of high class retailers of jewellery was held to satisfy a covenant in a lease to use premises for the retail sale of high class jewellery. The Court of Appeal accepted that such a business does not begin and end at the point of sale to the customer, but can include the

---

61 *Atwal v Courts Garages* [1989] 1 EGLR 63 (CA).
62 [1973] AC 609.
63 [1986] 1 EGLR 137 (CA).
64 (1968) 207 EG 531.
65 [1978] 1 EGLR 113 (CA).
66 [1992] 1 EGLR 55 (CA).

storage of stock, office work in connection with the business, and negotiating with suppliers.[67]

Keep-open covenants

A landlord with several units in a shopping centre will be anxious to maintain the shopping attractions of the whole centre, and to this end covenants have been included in the leases of this type of property to keep a business open and to trade during normal shopping hours. An example of such a covenant might be:

> "To keep each level of the demised premises having any frontage to a pedestrian mall open for trade to the general public during normal Shop Hours as defined in the lease and to trade actively and continuously throughout substantially the whole of the demised premises and not to permit the demised premises to remain vacant."

The clause will usually allow for closed periods if the premises are damaged or altered, or where it would be contrary to any local bye-law to open.

The Sunday Trading Act 1994, section 3(1), provides that a requirement to open business premises during "normal" trading hours shall not include Sunday trading in any lease made before the Act came into force on 26 August 1994, unless the lease specifically specifies Sunday trading, or is varied by an agreement made after that date. Sunday trading in a precinct will necessarily increase service charges, however, and most service-charge clauses will allow the landlord to recover a proportion of these from the tenant, even though the tenant does not open its own shop on Sundays.

A "keep open" covenant is an onerous one and will have a depressing effect on rent review.

Keep-open obligation not specifically enforceable

Such covenants have caused problems for tenants where their business has not thrived, and the courts have had to consider to what extent they are enforceable. In *Co-operative Insurance Society Ltd* v *Argyll Stores (Holdings) Ltd*[68], the House of Lords (reversing a majority of the Court of Appeal) recently affirmed the rule established in earlier cases[69] that the courts will not grant a landlord an order for specific performance of, or a mandatory injunction[70] requiring compliance with, any such covenant.

---

67 *Ibid,* at 56 (Nourse LJ).
68 [1997] 3 All ER 297 (HL); noted by Gareth Jones, "Specific performance of a lessee's covenant to keep open a retail store" [1997] CLJ 488.
69 *F W Woolworth plc* v *Charlwood Alliance Properties Ltd* [1987] 1 EGLR 53.
70 *Braddon Towers Ltd* v *International Stores Ltd* [1987] 1 EGLR 209, 213 (Slade J).

In the *Argyll* case, CIS Ltd, which owned the Hillsborough Shopping Centre in Sheffield, had leased premises in the Centre to Argyll for a term of 35 years. Argyll used the premises for one of their chain of Safeway supermarkets. Safeway was the anchor store in the Centre, in that its presence encouraged shoppers to use the Centre, thus enhancing the business of the Centre's 24 smaller shops, which were also leased to traders by CIS Ltd. Because its Safeway store in the Centre was losing money, Argyll decided to close it down. CIS Ltd tried to encourage Safeway to come to some arrangement until an assignee could be found; but Safeway ignored CIS Ltd's letter, closed the store, and stripped out its fittings. CIS Ltd sought an order for specific performance but the House of Lords refused to grant such an order.

The view of the House of Lords is contained in the speech of Lord Hoffmann, who made it clear that there were several reasons besides adequacy of damages why the court's practice was not to order the defendant to carry on a business.[71] The order would require the constant supervision of the court, in that it could be asked to give a whole series of rulings as to whether the order had been breached. Additional litigation could also result from the fact that it was difficult to draw up an order of this sort with precision. In any event, the order could be enforced only by contempt, which was an unsuitable means of deciding disputes of this sort. To have to run a business under the threat of contempt proceedings was not a way to run a business. The tenant's loss through having to comply with the order might be far greater than the landlord's loss from the covenant being breached. Moreover, were an order for specific performance or a mandatory injunction available, the landlord might be able to use the threat of obtaining such order as a means of increasing the damages obtainable from the tenant above the landlord's actual and anticipated losses.[72]

In addition, the particular covenant in Argyll's lease "to keep the demised premises open for retail trade" was not sufficiently precise to be capable of specific performance, saying nothing about the level of trade, the area of the premises within which trade was to be conducted, or even the kind of trade. It could not simply be assumed that, if ordered to keep the business open, Argyll would merely carry on the business as before. An order to compel the defendant to carry on a business could be oppressive to the defendant. Unless it could find an assignee, Argyll would have to continue trading on the premises until the lease expired in 2014, and its losses, which were unquantifiable, might drive it into insolvency. It was

---

71 *Dowty Boulton Paul Ltd v Wolverhampton Corporation* [1971] 1 WLR 204, 211 (Pennycuick V-C).
72 *Isenberg v East India House Estate Co Ltd* (1863) 3 De GJ & S, 263, 273.

doubtful that the court could vary or discharge such an order at a later date on the ground of impending insolvency. Argyll might have been discourteous in failing to reply to its landlord's letter; but its decision to close and to strip out the fixtures would have been based on its understanding of the practice of the courts at that time, which was that a keep-open covenant could not be enforced. Finally, the landlord and the tenant were large sophisticated commercial organisations whose interests were purely financial; no personal breach of faith was involved.

The sheer weight and number of these objections make it very unlikely that keep-covenants in leases will ever be enforced except in the most exceptional circumstances. Drafting the covenant in more detail than that in the *Argyll* case might overcome one objection; and the parties could state explicitly in the lease that they intend that the covenant should be specifically enforceable.[73] But it is difficult to see how drafting could overcome some of Lord Hoffmann's other objections. A landlord might try an alternative strategy of providing that the rent is to be considerably increased in the event of the tenant's ceasing to carry on trade in breach of a keep-open covenant[74]; the increased rent will be a factor which the tenant will take into account when deciding whether it is economically worthwhile continuing to trade, and may therefore act as a disincentive to closure.

If the tenant does close down in breach of covenant, the landlord may be left with a papered-over or empty display window, which may further deter customers to any neighbouring shops which the landlord has also leased out. If the landlord re-enters to dress the windows himself, the tenant might claim that the re-entry has effected a forfeiture or surrender by operation of law[75], or that the landlord is in breach of its covenant for quiet enjoyment. It is therefore desirable for the lease expressly to reserve a right of re-entry for the landlord to dress the display windows.

Damages

Save in exceptional cases, it is now clear that the landlord's remedy for breach of a keep-open covenant will be damages only.[76] An action for damages for breach of covenant can be brought only for existing breaches; but the plaintiff can bring further actions in respect future breaches.[77]

---

73 See P H Kenny, "Keep-open covenants," [1997] Conv 325.

74 As in *Transworld Land Co Ltd v J Sainsbury plc* [1990] 2 EGLR 255, 256.

75 But in *Charville Estates Ltd v Unipart Group* [1997] EGCS 36 re-entry for this purpose was held not to comprise an unequivocal act of forfeiture or surrender by operation of law.

76 *Co-operative Insurance Society Ltd v Argyll Stores (Holdings) Ltd* [1997] 3 All ER 297 (HL).

77 cf *Ryan v Mutual Tontine Westminster Chambers Association* [1893] 1 Ch 116, 125–126 (Lord Esher MR), 128 (Kay LJ).

Damages might alternatively be awarded in lieu of specific performance[78]; such equitable damages can take account of the loss that the plaintiff might suffer from anticipated future breaches, but no further claims for damages can be made.[79]

The measure of damages for breach of covenant is usually the diminution in the value of the landlord's reversion; and this might be an appropriate measure if the landlord is disposing of its reversion.[80] If the landlord forfeits the lease, it cannot obtain damages for future losses resulting from the breach, since the future breaches have not yet occurred, and forfeiture of the lease also terminates the right to sue on the covenants which it contains. Subject to this, the landlord can recover damages for breach of covenant to put it into the position it would have been in had the contract been performed.[81] Its damages might therefore include an element for the rent lost under other leases, perhaps from rent concessions which the landlord is effectively forced to make to its other tenants[82]; but causation may be difficult to establish, as the losses may be attributable to other causes, such as competition from other traders or a decline in the area generally. The landlord would also be under a general duty to mitigate his loss.[83] If the tenant has made a profit from the breach (for example, from trading elsewhere), the landlord might be able to recover some part of it as restitutionary damages; but the point has been left open.[84] Damages will be awarded as at the date of the hearing or (depending upon the circumstances) at an earlier date.[85]

From the foregoing it is evident that the calculation of damages is in many instances likely to prove both difficult and speculative. The problem of computing damages for breach of a keep-open covenant can be overcome by the inclusion in the lease of an agreed damages clause.

---

78 Supreme Court Act 1981, s 50.
79 See *Jaggard v Sawyer* [1995] 1 WLR 713.
80 As in *Costain Property Developments Ltd v Finlay & Co Ltd* [1989] 1 EGLR 237.
81 *Johnson v Agnew* [1980] AC 367, 400 (Lord Wilberforce), quoted in *Transworld Land Co Ltd v J Sainsbury plc* [1990] 2 EGLR 255, 263.
82 As in *Transworld Land Co Ltd vJ Sainsbury plc* [1990] 2 EGLR 255, 260-261.
83 *Transworld Land Co Ltd v J Sainsbury plc* [1990] 2 EGLR 255, 264.
84 See comments of Millett LJ in the Court of Appeal in *Co-operative Insurance Society Ltd v Argyll Stores (Holdings) Ltd* [1996] 3 All ER 934, 950.
85 *Transworld Land Co Ltd v J Sainsbury plc* [1990] 2 EGLR 255.

Covenants in a Lease, other than User Covenants, that may Affect User

In addition to user covenants, a lease may include other covenants which affect the use of the premises. Examples of these would be a covenant: not to cause a nuisance or annoyance to the landlord or to the owners or occupiers of neighbouring premises; not to carry on a noxious or offensive trade; or not to use the premises for illegal or immoral purposes. Where several such restrictions are to be imposed, they could each be contained in a separate covenant. Alternatively, they could all be comprised in a single covenant such as the following:

> "Not to use or permit or suffer the demised premises or any part thereof to be used for any dangerous offensive noxious noisome illegal or immoral activity or in any manner that may become a nuisance or annoyance to the landlord or to the owner or occupier of any neighbouring premises."

A very usual covenant as to user is one by the tenant not to use the premises in such a way as to vitiate, or increase the premiums on, any insurance policy. Such a covenant might be:

> "Not to do or permit to be done anything that will or may render void or voidable any policy of insurance covering the demised premises [or any neighbouring premises] or increase the premium payable thereon."

Covenants against nuisance or annoyance

The landlord may be sued by nearby owners or occupiers for any acts of his tenant which amount to a nuisance. It is desirable, therefore, to safeguard the landlord's position by including in the lease a covenant by the tenant not to cause a nuisance or annoyance to the landlord or to any neighbouring owners or occupiers. The wording of such covenants may differ quite widely. For example, the tenant may additionally covenant not to cause grievance or inconvenience, and the covenant may extend expressly to noise.

It is doubtful whether "nuisance" should be restricted to a tortious act; but, in any event, the word "annoyance" has been held to be wider than "nuisance". In *Tod-Heatly* v *Benham*[86], it was held that a hospital for ear, nose and throat, skin and eye infections, was likely to cause a reasonable apprehension of the risk of infection, and was therefore an infringement of a covenant against causing an annoyance or grievance to neighbours

---

86 (1888) 40 Ch D 80.

without any proof of damage. From a landlord's point of view, therefore, the covenant should be worded as widely as possible.

Covenants against noxious trades

Such covenants may again vary as to the actual words used, and may also specify, for example, "noisome" or "dangerous" trades. Covenants in some older leases often add a list of prohibited trades to the end of a general covenant. Each covenant will, of course, fall to be interpreted according to its exact wording.

It is possible that a trade which is not in itself offensive may nevertheless be so in a residential locality. Thus in *Duke of Devonshire* v *Brookshaw*[87], a fried fish shop emitting smells was held to be a breach of a covenant against carrying on an offensive trade.

Statutes may define certain trades as being offensive or dangerous. For example, certain offensive trades were listed in the Public Health Act 1936. The statutory definition will not be binding upon the court, but is likely to have some persuasive value. Many of these trades now require authorisation under the Environmental Protection (Prescribed Processes and Substances) Regulations 1991.[87a]

Covenants against immoral or illegal user

Such covenants may be of assistance to a landlord where shop premises are used to sell pornographic films or literature, or club premises for prostitution or illegal gambling. In such cases, the continuing "stigma" attaching to premises may be grounds for refusing an application by a tenant for relief against forfeiture.[88] If, however, the immoral user is by a sub-tenant without the tenant's knowledge, and the tenant takes steps to stop it as soon as he is aware of it, then relief is likely to be granted.[89]

THE EFFECT OF USER COVENANTS ON OTHER PROVISIONS IN THE LEASE

When drafting a user covenant, it is important to consider its effect on the operation of other provisions in the lease, and in particular on covenants against assignment and under-letting and on rent review. The landlord may

---

87 (1899) 81 LT 83.
87a SI 1991, No 472, as amended by SI 1991, No 836 and SI 1992, No 614.
88 *British Petroleum Pension Trust Ltd* v *Behrendt* (1986) 52 P & CR 117.
89 *Glass* v *Kencakes Ltd* [1966] 1 QB 611.

have to weigh the increased control which he could obtain from a strict user covenant, possibly preserving the value of the reversion, against the depreciating effect which such a covenant might have on rent review. Similarly, any benefit to the tenant of a wider user covenant may be offset by a possible increase in rent on review. It is proposed to consider the possible effects in the light of the cases.

Effect of user covenants on covenants against assignment or under-letting

A qualified covenant against assignment or under-letting (which in practice will usually also be against "parting with possession of the whole or any part of the demised premises" and may therefore include a licence) is governed by the Landlord and Tenant Act 1927, section 19(1). This implies into the covenant that the landlord's consent may not be unreasonably withheld. This section was given more muscle to coerce reluctant landlords by the Landlord and Tenant Act 1988, which requires the landlord to give, within a reasonable time, written reasons for any refusal of consent, and exposes him to the risk of an action for damages in tort if he fails to do so.

As has already been mentioned, section 19(1) does not apply to user covenants, so that the only cases where there will be grounds to consider reasonableness of a refusal to grant consent to a change of user will be where the user covenant is fully qualified – that is, where it is expressly stated in the lease that the landlord's consent to a change of user will not be unreasonably refused.

A covenant against assignment or under-letting is taken to protect the landlord from having either an undesirable tenant or an undesirable user of the premises. It is inevitable, therefore, that the courts have also had to consider user clauses in cases dealing with an unreasonable refusal of consent to assign.

Where a proposed assignment will necessarily involve breach of a user covenant, it will be reasonable for the landlord to refuse consent.[90] Where, however, the proposed assignment may or may not result in a breach of the user covenant, refusal to consent will be unreasonable, as it was said in *Killick v Second Covent Garden Property Co Ltd*[91] that the landlord would still have a remedy against an assignee for a breach of the user covenant, if it occurred.

The narrower the user clause, the more difficult the tenant may find it to assign or to sub-let. At the extreme end of the spectrum, a covenant restricting user of the premises to the tenant's business only makes the

---

90 *Wilson v Flynn* [1948] 2 All ER 40.
91 [1973] 1 WLR 658.

lease virtually unassignable.[92] Even where there is a very narrow user clause restricting user to a few specified purposes, it may still be reasonable for the landlord to refuse, on grounds of user, consent to assign to an assignee who proposes to comply with the user covenant.[93]

In *International Drilling Fluids Ltd v Louisville Investments (Uxbridge) Ltd*[94], Balcombe LJ formulated certain propositions from the cases on refusal of consent to assign. He came to the conclusion that the general principle – that a landlord need consider only his own interests in deciding whether or not to grant consent – should be qualified to require also a consideration of the tenant's interests where the detriment to the tenant of a refusal far outweighs the benefit to the landlord. In that case, the tenant had vacated the premises and, after a year of marketing the property, had found only one interested assignee. The permitted user of the premises was for offices with ancillary showrooms, and the proposed assignee wanted to use the premises for serviced office accommodation. Although this was within the user clause, evidence was given that it could adversely affect the value of the landlord's reversion. There was no evidence, however, that the landlord intended to sell or mortgage the reversion, and he was fully covered for rent by a covenant from the assigning tenant, which was financially sound. Although a refusal of consent might have been reasonable on the ground of some slight benefit to the landlord, this was outweighed by the hardship to the tenant, which was paying rent on vacant premises for which it was difficult to find an assignee. Balcombe LJ therefore concluded: "it is not reasonable for the landlord to refuse consent on the grounds of the proposed use (being within the only specified type of use) where the result will be that the property is left vacant and where (as here) the landlord is fully secured for payment of the rent."

In the *International Drilling Fluids* case, the Court of Appeal considered *Premier Confectionery (London) Co Ltd v London Commercial Sale Rooms Ltd*[95], a decision at first instance. In that case, a tenant of two separate leases, granted consecutively, of a shop and an adjoining kiosk, sought consent to assign the leases separately. User of both was restricted to the sale of tobacco. Despite the very narrow user restriction which there was no question of the proposed assignee breaking, the landlord's refusal of consent to assign was held to be reasonable. Commenting in *International Drilling*, Balcombe LJ said that, insofar as this case might be authority for the proposition that it must always be reasonable for a

92 *Granada TV Network Ltd v Great Universal Stores Ltd* (1963) 187 EG 391.
93 *Bates v Donaldson* [1896] 2 QB 241.
94 [1986] Ch 513.
95 [1933] Ch 904.

landlord to refuse consent to assign for the purpose of a single permitted
user, he would not be prepared to follow it. It is possible, however, to
distinguish *Premier Confectionery*, as the landlord's concern there was
that, if the leases were assigned separately, the two businesses would be in
competition with each other, which could affect the tenant's ability to pay
the rent. It was therefore for the benefit of both the landlord and his
tenant to refuse consent to assignment.

Potential harm to the landlord's own business interest can also justify a
refusal on grounds of proposed user. In *Whiteminster Estates* v *Hodges
Menswear Ltd*[96], the landlords refused consent to an assignment of 8 Elgin
Gate on the ground that the proposed assignee (Dunn's) intended to use
the premises as a men's outfitters, which would compete with the similar
business which the landlords themselves carried on from number 10, Elgin
Gate. It does not appear that the lease contained any restriction upon user
for such a purpose, but the landlords' refusal was held to be reasonable.

A moral objection to a proposed user may also comprise a reasonable
refusal of consent to assign. In *Rodney* v *Austerfield*[97], the landlord's
refusal to consent to an assignment because the proposed assignee
intended to use the premises as a bookmaker's, to which business the
landlord had a moral objection, was held to be reasonable.

It has already been mentioned that a landlord cannot, by refusing
consent to assign on grounds of user, seek to obtain an advantage not
reserved in the original lease.[98]

The Landlord and Tenant (Covenants) Act 1995, which applies to all
leases made after 1995, inserts a new section 19(1A) into the Landlord and
Tenant Act 1927, which allows a landlord to prescribe what shall amount
to a reasonable ground for his refusal to consent to an assignment of a
commercial lease. A likely condition for consent is that the tenant enters
into an authorised guarantee agreement[99]; but there is no reason why a
landlord should not include some requirement as to user as a reasonable
condition for granting his consent to an assignment.

Effect of a user covenant on rent

A user covenant will be a relevant consideration when fixing a new rent
under a rent-review clause or on the granting of a new lease under the
Landlord and Tenant Act 1954. It was held in *Plinth Property Investments
Ltd* v *Mott, Hay & Anderson*[1] that an arbitrator was right to take such a

---

96 (1974) 232 EG 715.
97 [1979] CLY 1572.
98 *Anglia Building Society* v *Sheffield City Council* [1983] 1 EGLR 57 (CA).
99 See Chap 5.
1 (1978) 38 P & CR 361.

covenant into account, as the landlord could demand a considerable sum to waive it.

In *Bovis Group Pension Fund Ltd* v *G C Flooring & Furnishing Ltd*[2], the rent-review clause directed the arbitrator to fix a rent on the basis of office user for which planning permission had not been obtained. It was held that this, rather than the actual user, was the user which the arbitrator should consider. Nor will an actual user which is in contravention of planning permission be taken into account: *e.g.* residential property being used partly for offices. In *C & A Pensions Trustees Ltd* v *British Vita Investments Ltd*[3], the landlord sought to widen the user covenant by unilaterally authorising further uses of the premises. It was held that, for the purposes of rent review, this too should be disregarded.

It has been pointed out that a tenant with a qualified user covenant is in no better position as regards obtaining the landlord's consent to its relaxation than a tenant whose covenant is absolute. However, the fully qualified form of covenant (where the landlord's consent to change of user is not to be unreasonably withheld) should have a less depreciatory effect on rent.

In seeking to obtain the best of both worlds, landlords have tried to avoid the depressing effects on rent of strict user covenants by inserting a provision in the rent-review clause that rent shall be assessed on the basis of some hypothetical user. The fact that planning permission has not been obtained for such hypothetical user will presumably not invalidate such a basis of review.[4] However, from a landlord's point of view, the clause could be made more watertight by providing that the premises are assumed to be suitable for the hypothetical use and that the use is assumed to be lawful. It will be recalled that *Hill* v *Harris*[5] decided that there was no such assumption of lawful use with regard to a tenant's actual proposed use. It is, of course, quite conceivable that a tenant would argue strongly against the inclusion of such provisions.

A landlord should, nevertheless, be wary of extracting from a tenant covenants which are very extreme. A hypothetical use which is too far removed from the real use runs the risk of being totally disregarded. This occurred in *Basingstoke & Deane BC* v *Host Group Ltd*[6], where the rent-review clause provided for a new rent to be fixed on the basis of a vacant

2 [1984] 1 EGLR 123 (CA).
3 [1984] 2 EGLR 75 (Ch).
4 *Bovis Group Pension Fund Ltd* v *G C Flooring & Furnishing Ltd* [1984] 1 EGLR 123 (CA).
5 [1965] 2 QB 601.
6 [1988] 1 WLR 348.

site. The original lease of the site was in consideration of the tenant building a public house, and this had been done, so that user was in fact limited to this. The landlord contended that rent review should be on the basis that it was still a vacant site available for development in any way and not limited to that of a public house. The Court of Appeal ignored the hypothetical user and decided that rent review should be on the basis of a vacant site with user as it actually was, namely, a public house. Similarly, a restriction to use by one tenant only (making the premises unassignable) may be opened up on rent review to include all user of the same type as the tenant's.[7] The curious result is that this form of extreme restriction may have a less depreciatory effect on rent than a restriction to certain specified trades or businesses! The courts have, however, been even-handed about this, and in *Jefferies* v *O'Neill*[8], where the realities of the situation were that the demised premises could be used only by the particular tenants, it was held that rent review should be on the basis prescribed in the lease of "a willing tenant". The tenants in that case were a firm of solicitors who had taken a lease of adjoining premises at first floor level, and had extended their offices by breaking through from their own existing offices. The sole access was from their offices, and they were, therefore, the only possible tenants.

In *SI Pension Trustees Ltd* v *Ministerio de Marina de la Republica Peruana*[9], the user covenant which was to be taken into account on the hypothetical letting, for the purposes of rent review, covered office use for mortgage finance and insurance consultancy. The licence to assign to a diplomatic mission restricted use to this. It was held, however, that the reference in the rent-review clause to the provisions of the lease meant the original provisions as to user and not the more restricted variation in the licence to assign.

---

7 *Law Land Co Ltd* v *Consumers' Association Ltd* [1980] 2 EGLR 109 (CA).
8 [1984] 1 EGLR 106 (Ch).
9 [1988] 1 EGLR 119 (Ch).

Chapter 9

RENT AND RENT REVIEW

INTRODUCTION

The nature of rent

Rent was at one time an incident of tenure and represented consideration for the leasehold estate in the land. For this reason, rent was originally known as rent service. In recent years, however, there has been an increasing tendency to emphasise the contractual nature of a lease, rather than the estate which the contract creates. The payment of rent is an important part of that contract.

Nevertheless, the notion that the rent is payable for an estate in the land is still to be found in certain areas of the law relating to leases, and it is for this reason, for instance, that a tenant is still liable for rent even if the premises on the land are destroyed. The lease should therefore contain a provision that rent will be suspended (wholly or partially) for any time during which the premises are unusable as a result of damage, and the landlord may want to include loss of rent as one of the insurable risks. A clause providing for the suspension of rent is as follows:

> "Provided that if the demised premises or any part thereof shall be destroyed or damaged by fire or any other risk for which the landlord has insured so as to be unfit for occupation and use the rents hereby reserved or a fair proportion thereof according to the nature and extent of the destruction or damage shall be suspended until the demised premises or the destroyed or damaged portion shall be rendered fit for occupation and use."

A clause providing for insurance covering three years' loss of rent is included in Chapter 11.

It is only fairly recently too that the House of Lords accepted in *National Carriers Ltd v Panalpina (Northern) Ltd*[1] that the doctrine of frustration, which applies to terminate a contract, might also apply to terminate a lease.[2]

---

1 [1981] AC 675.
2 See Chap 12.

Certainty as to rent

Rent in money, services, or kind

Although rent is almost invariably a money payment nowadays, it may be in kind, and the most common example of rent in kind is a service tenancy.[3] Whatever form the rent takes, however, it must be certain or capable of being rendered certain, even if it is work.[4]

Formula for determining rent

A formula for arriving at a figure for rent is sufficiently certain, even if there is no actual machinery for determining it, as it was held by Megarry J in *Brown* v *Gould*[5] that the court then has jurisdiction to make the determination. A common method of fixing a rent is for the lease to provide that, failing agreement between the parties, it is to be such rent as shall be fixed by an independent third person.

In the absence of such a formula, and on a failure of the parties to agree, it is possible that the lease will be void for uncertainty. Thus in *King's Motors (Oxford) Ltd* v *Lax*[6], the lease contained an option to renew at a rent to be agreed between the parties, but with no indication as to the criteria. The option was held to be void.

If there is an existing lease, however, the courts are more reluctant to hold it void for uncertainty on this ground. In *Beer* v *Bowden*[7] there was a complete hiatus as to rent on an extended lease when the parties failed to agree; but the tenant had remained in possession for some two years. The judge took a robust approach, deriving some support from a provision that the tenant's improvements should not be taken into account in deciding a new rent. He held that it must have been intended that the tenant should pay some rent, and ordered that the rent be fixed by the Master after hearing expert evidence.

Terminology relating to different kinds of rents

Rent service. The correct name for rent payable to the landlord under a lease is rent service. It can be distinguished from a rentcharge, this being a rent issuing out of and payable on freehold land.

Different terms are used to distinguish different types of rent.

---

3 See Chap 1.
4 *Barnes* v *Barratt* [1970] 2 QB 657.
5 [1972] Ch 53.
6 [1970] 1 WLR 426.
7 [1981] 1 WLR 522.

Best rent. The highest rent which can reasonably be expected to be obtained for the premises.

Rack rent. A rent of the full annual value of the property. If the rent is fixed during a period of rent restriction, it will be the highest rent that it is possible to reserve at that time and not the full market rent.[8]

Ground rent. A small annual rent which arises where the landlord has in effect capitalised part of the rack rent otherwise obtainable by taking a premium (*i.e.* a capital sum) when the lease is granted. A ground rent is therefore less than the rack rent.

Peppercorn rent. A nominal rent which it was often considered wise to reserve to ensure that the transaction was a lease.

Dead rent. The basic minimum rent payable on a mining lease, whether the mine is worked or not. There will usually be an additional rent fluctuating according to the amount of mineral mined.

Geared rent. The rent payable under a head-lease which is to be determined by reference to the rent payable on a sub-lease or sub-leases.

Headline rent. The increased rent payable to compensate the landlord after the tenant has been allowed a rent-free period.

Hard-core rent. If the open market rent that premises would command if let is lower than that currently payable under an existing lease, that lower open-market rent is called the "hard-core rent." If, for instance, T, is presently paying £100,000 per annum in rent under a lease of premises the open-market rent of which has since fallen to £75,000 per annum, the latter sum is the hard-core rent.

Froth rent. This is the difference between the hard-core rent and the higher rent presently being paid.[9] In the foregoing example, the froth rent is therefore £25,000.

Fluctuating rents

Sometimes rent will be fixed by reference to other fluctuating factors. It is common practice in mining leases for rent to vary according to the amount of mineral mined.

Turnover rent

A turnover rent is a rent based on a proportion (usually a percentage) of the trade turnover for a business. It is a rent sometimes used in leases of supermarkets. The basis for calculation of the proportion must be carefully

---

8 *Newman* v *Dorrington Developments Ltd* [1975] 1 WLR 1642.
9 *Blockbuster Entertainment Ltd* v *Leakcliff Properties Ltd* [1997] 1 EGLR 28, 32 (Neuberger J).

stated in the lease, although there should be provision for varying this if there is a material change of use, as the calculation suitable for a low turnover/high profit business may be very different from that suitable for one with a high turnover/low profit.

A tenant should ensure that any turnover elements in the rent are linked to net turnover and not gross turnover. This is to avoid the type of problem which arose in *Tucker* v *Granada Motorway Services Ltd*[10], where an increased tax on tobacco showed an increased gross turnover on sales but did not affect net turnover.

There should also be a provision for production of accounts and a certificate of turnover.

Such a lease may provide for a minimum rent, being a proportion of the open market rent, to be payable in any event, and the landlord may wish to include a provision that the open market rent shall be payable if the tenant ceases trading.

The following clause is a rudimentary example of a reservation of a basic rent, and additionally a turnover rent, being a percentage of net profits over a certain figure, (although the full clause would contain definitions of turnover and provision for certification by an accountant):

> "YIELDING AND PAYING therefor by equal quarterly payments in advance a basic rent of [sum] per annum and in addition [x%] of the net turnover for the year preceding the rental year exceeding [£X,000]."

Geared rent

Another form of fluctuating rent is one which is variable according to the rent received from sub-leases. This type of rent is sometimes used in building leases where the lessee will be unable to afford much rent initially, but will eventually benefit when there is an income from the property. In such an arrangement, it is important to synchronise the rent review in the head-lease with rent reviews in the sub-leases. The rent-review dates for the sub-leases may vary, so that it may be preferable simply to provide that the rent on the head-lease is to be a percentage of the rent on the sub-leases as they vary from time to time.[11]

The fact that the market may improve so that the tenant may be able to sub-let at a higher rent in the future is not a reasonable ground for the landlord's refusal of consent to sub-let.[12]

---

10 [1979] 2 All ER 801.
11 See p 150 *supra* for a precedent for synchronisation of rent reviews.
12 *Blockbuster Entertainment Ltd* v *Leakcliff Properties Ltd* [1997] 1 EGLR 28 (Ch).

THE RESERVATION OF RENT

Express reservation

Rent must be reserved in the lease expressly. A reservation of rent will not be implied, although it may be possible to seek rectification of a lease if it is clear that there was an enforceable agreement to include a rent reservation which has been omitted from the lease itself. In addition to the reservation of rent, if the landlord had taken a covenant from the tenant to pay the rent, privity of contract between the original landlord and the original tenant allowed the landlord to sue the tenant on the covenant throughout the duration of the term.[13] This right has now been severely curtailed, in respect of post-1995 leases, by the Landlord and Tenant (Covenants) Act 1995.

The definition of a "term of years" in the Law of Property Act 1925[14], expressly includes a term of years "whether or not at a rent"; and in *Ashburn Anstalt v WJ Arnold & Co Ltd*[15], the Court of Appeal confirmed that rent is not essential for a lease. In practice, there will be very few leases which do not reserve a rent, and any arrangement which does not involve the reservation of a rent is more likely to indicate a licence.[16]

If the lease makes no provision for interest on late payments, the landlord may ask the court for interest in an action for rent arrears; but the award of interest lies within the court's discretion.[17] From the landlord's point of view, it is therefore advantageous for the lease to provide expressly for interest to be payable on rent in arrears, as it can then be demanded as of right. The rate of such interest should, however, be related to the landlord's anticipated loss, otherwise it may be void as a penalty. The interest is often expressed to be a specified number of points above the base lending-rate for the time-being of one of the major clearing banks, with provision being made for the substitution of the base lending-rate of another bank of the landlord's choosing should the first specified bank fail to publish a base lending-rate. Although the landlord may be tempted to lay down a minimum rate of interest, this runs the risk of comprising a penalty if in the future interest rates fall considerably below the specified percentage.[18]

The lease will usually confer upon the landlord the right to forfeit if the

---

13 See Chap 5.
14 LPA 1925, s 205(1).
15 [1989] Ch 1.
16 See Chap 1.
17 Supreme Court Act 1981, s 35A; County Courts Act 1984, s 89(1).
18 See Sweet, *Commercial Leases: Tenants' Amendments,* 2nd ed (1995) FT Law & Tax, 44–45.

rent is unpaid for more than a specified number of days (often 14 or 21) after falling due. The lease will often concede an equivalent period of grace to the tenant in relation to interest on unpaid rent, so that interest becomes payable only if the rent is more than a specified number of days in arrear.

If the lease expressly provides for interest on late rent, it should also provide for the interest to be recoverable as rent, otherwise the landlord would need to serve a section 146 notice under the Law of Property Act 1925, in order to recover the interest.

When payable

Rent will be payable in arrear unless the lease specifically states (as do most modern leases) that it is payable in advance. A lease for a term of years will usually specify an annual rent payable quarterly in advance. For centuries, leases have required such instalments to be paid on the usual quarter days, *viz* 25 March, 24 June, 29 September and 25 December.[19] This practice remains common today, as it is clearly in the interests of good estate management for a landlord of several properties to have all the rents under different leases falling due on the same dates. A reference in the lease to "the usual quarter days" is an unequivocal reference to these dates.

Deductions

The tenant's covenant to pay rent usually provides that he will pay the rent reserved "without any deductions", so that the rent reserved is a net rent. Even where the lease contains such a proviso, however, the tenant may make certain deductions authorised by statute. Such deductions include: landlord's tax recovered from the tenant; rent paid by a sub-tenant directly to the landlord to avoid distress on the tenant's default; charges on the premises payable by the landlord; compensation for improvements due from the landlord under the Landlord and Tenant Act 1927; and the cost of repairs on which the landlord has defaulted and which the tenant has carried out.[20]

Excluding tenant's right to set-off

A covenant by the tenant to pay rent "without any deductions" will not be sufficient to exclude the tenant's equitable right to set off damages for

---

19 In old leases, but (alas) more rarely in the prosaic world of the modern commercial lease, these days were often referred to respectively as Lady-day, Midsummer-day, Michaelmas, and Christmas-day.

20 See Chap 10.

breach of the landlord's repairing covenant. Thus in *Connaught Restaurants Ltd* v *Indoor Leisure Ltd*[21], the tenant's covenant was:

> "to pay the rents at the times and in manner aforesaid without any deductions ... and if so required by banker's standing order."

In that case, Waite LJ said:

> "The term "deduction" is one of those words for which the convenience of flexibility has been achieved at the price of some inherent ambiguity. Draftsmen who are concerned to exclude the tenant's equitable right of set-off would therefore be well advised to do so explicitly."

It was held in *Electricity Supply Nominees Ltd* v *IAF Group plc*[22] that an exclusion of the right to set off such damages against rent did not fall within the Unfair Contract Terms Act 1977. The reason is that rent is an integral part of the creation of a lease, which is an interest in land, and the Act does not apply to "any contract so far as it relates to the creation or transfer of an interest in land or to the termination of such an interest...".[23] The relevant wording in the *Electricity Supply* case was more specific than that in *Connaught Restaurants*, as the tenant covenanted:

> "to pay rent and all other sums payable under this lease at the time and in the manner hereinbefore provided without any deductions or set-off whatsoever."

This was held to cover the equitable right to set off damages for a landlord's breach of repairing covenant, so that the tenant was not entitled to deduct these damages from the rent.

Apportionment

Rent is apportionable, and should therefore be apportioned at the commencement and termination of the tenancy. To avoid any dispute, the lease should expressly provide (and most leases do) for a proportion of the rent to be payable as from the date of the lease, or the date when the tenant takes occupation of the premises. This would be effected by the following clause:

> "YIELDING AND PAYING therefor the rent of [£X,000] or such other rent as may from time to time be agreed or determined payable by equal quarterly instalments in advance on the usual quarter days the first of such payments or a proportionate part thereof to be made on the date hereof and the last payment being (if appropriate) of a proportionate sum."

---

21 [1993] 2 EGLR 108 (CA).
22 [1993] 3 All ER 372.
23 UCTA 1977, Sched 1, para 1(b).

Other monetary payments

It is also usual for the lease to provide that any premiums for insurance payable by the tenant, or any service charge similarly apportioned, shall be paid as rent, and therefore recoverable as rent[24] without the necessity of first serving a section 146 notice. A clause providing for this would follow the rent clause and might read as follows:

> "AND ALSO YIELDING AND PAYING as additional rent (i) a fair proportion of the amount paid by the landlord for insuring the Building and the loss of rent and other risks hereunder in accordance with the landlord's covenant and (ii) the service charge payable hereunder."

Interest on any overdue rent and any VAT payable may similarly be made payable as rent.

THE PAYMENT OF RENT

Rent should be tendered in cash unless the parties agree otherwise; in practice the parties will usually agree to payment by another method, such as by cheque or by standing order.[25] Even then, rent tendered by cheque is not regarded as paid until the cheque is cleared. In *Official Solicitor* v *Thomas*[26] it was said that tender of a cheque does not discharge a debt even where the parties have agreed that this is the way in which rent should be paid. In *Stoneman* v *Brown*[27], Lord Denning MR was prepared to regard payment as made when the letter containing the cheque was posted, but this was not material to the decision in that case.

Rent is payable to the landlord or his agent and any service charge should be made similarly payable if it is to be paid as rent.

RECOVERY OF RENT ARREARS

Action to recover rent arrears

An action to recover arrears of rent must be brought within six years from the date the rent becomes due.[28] Any action against the tenant's guarantor is

---

24 See Chap 11.
25 For discussion of the waiver implications when rent is paid by cheque or standing order, see pp 338–339 *infra*.
26 [1986] 2 EGLR 1.
27 [1973] 1 WLR 459.
28 Limitation Act 1980, s 19.

subject to the same time-limit, even if (as is usual) the guarantee is by deed.[29] Even if the liability of the guarantor is not for rent, the action on a guarantee is one for "damages in respect of arrears of rent" and so falls within the six-year period specified in the Limitation Act 1980.[30]

Distress

Distress is a common law remedy available to a landlord where the rent is unpaid. It entitles the landlord to enter the premises leased, to seize the goods which he finds there, and to hold them until the arrears are paid.

The right to distrain is an incident of the relationship of landlord and tenant, and (unlike the right of re-entry for breach of covenant) does not need to be expressly reserved to the landlord in the lease. At common law, distress is available only in respect of arrears of rent. It would appear, however, that the landlord may distrain for other sums unpaid (*e.g.* payments of a service charge, or of insurance) if these other sums are expressed in the lease to be recoverable as rent.[31] The landlord's right to distrain in such cases is not an incident of the landlord and tenant relationship, but a contractual right.[32]

In drafting the lease, therefore, the landlord should consider carefully the respective merits of expressing such other payments to be recoverable as rent or not.[33] A form of wording making a service charge recoverable as rent was set out earlier in this chapter.[34]

When distress is available

Distress is, for the most part, available only during the subsistence of the tenancy in respect of which the arrears are owed. A landlord has a right to distrain against a tenant only if the relationship of landlord and tenant exists between them both at the time that the rent accrues due and at the time that the distress is levied. Thus, an assignee of the landlord's reversion may distrain for arrears of rent which accrue due during his own time as landlord, but not for arrears which accrued due before the reversion was assigned to him. Similarly, a landlord may not distrain against an assignee of the lease in respect of rent arrears accrued by the assignor.[35] Where,

---

29 *Romain v Scuba TV* [1996] 2 All ER 377 (CA).
30 Limitation Act 1980. s 19.
31 *Concorde Graphics Ltd v Andromeda Investments SA* [1983] 1 EGLR 53 (Ch.).
32 *Yorkshire Metropolitan Properties Ltd v Co-operative Retail Services Ltd* [1997] EGCS 57.
33 This is discussed further in Chap 11.
34 See p. 210 *supra.*
35 *Wharfland Ltd v South London Co-operative Building Co Ltd* [1995] 2 EGLR 21 (QB).

however, the tenant has assigned only a part of the premises subject to the lease, the landlord may distrain for rent arrears against either part.[36]

If a tenant of business premises protected by the Landlord and Tenant Act 1954, Part II, is holding over after the expiry of the contractual term, the landlord is entitled to distrain, during the continuation tenancy, in respect of rent due before, as well as during, the period of holding over.

By statute, a landlord is entitled to distrain for arrears within six months of the termination of the tenancy (other than by forfeiture) so long as the tenant remains in possession.[37] This right could be useful to a landlord of business premises if the tenant remains in possession after the termination date where a new lease has not been granted. The landlord cannot, however, distrain for arrears under the old tenancy after a new one has been granted.

The landlord has a right to distrain for rent even if there is no legal lease, provided (under the principle of *Walsh* v *Lonsdale*[38]) the tenant is in occupation under a valid contract to grant a lease.

At common law, a sum can comprise rent only if its amount can be calculated precisely on the day that it falls due. This means that the landlord cannot distrain at common law for back-dated rent, simply because it is not strictly speaking rent. Thus if, on review, rent is increased retrospectively to the review date, the increased amount cannot be subject to common law distress.[39] It is possible, however, that the landlord can rely on a contractual right to distrain for such additional "rent," if this is provided for expressly in the lease.

The limits on distress where the tenant is bankrupt or insolvent are discussed in chapter 14.

Levying distress

The landlord may levy distress in person or through a certificated bailiff, *i.e.* one certificated by the county court.[40] The former method is not, of course, available if the landlord is not an individual but a corporation. A certificated bailiff is the agent of the landlord, who may therefore be liable for the bailiff's wrongful acts.

Only goods, *i.e.* choses in possession, may be distrained. The landlord cannot distrain against choses in action: he may not, for instance, distrain on share certificates.

---

36 *Whitham* v *Bullock* [1939] 2 KB 81.
37 Landlord and Tenant Act 1709, s 6.
38 (1882) 21 Ch D 9.
39 *C H Bailey* v *Memorial Enterprises Ltd* [1974] 1 WLR 728.
40 Law of Distress Amendment Act 1888, s 7.

The landlord has a right to distrain upon all goods found on the premises, whether they belong to the tenant or to a third party. A third party may, however, avoid distress by removing its goods before the commencement of the distress. Even after distress has begun, a third party may be able to avoid the distress by serving a notice upon the landlord.

Certain types of goods can never be distrained. These include tenant's fixtures; items in use at the time of the distress; and items on the premises for a temporary purpose of trade, such as goods left for repair. Certain types of goods can be distrained only if the distress cannot be satisfied by distraining upon other goods on the premises. These include tools of trade (including the books of a professional person) not exceeding a value of £150.[41]

Goods of third parties

Subject to the exceptions relating to privileged goods, the goods of a third party which are on the tenant's premises may be subject to distress at common law. The third party can avoid distress on his own goods by paying the landlord the rent due and then claiming an indemnity from the tenant.[42] Furthermore, if some of the tenant's goods are charged to a third party, the landlord should levy distress first against goods not so charged.

Under the Law of Distress Amendment Act 1908, a third party may protect its goods by serving upon the landlord or the landlord's bailiff a written notice specifying the goods and stating that they are the property of the third party and that the tenant has no property or beneficial interest in the goods. If the person serving the notice is a sub-tenant, its relief from distress is conditional upon its paying the rent under the sub-lease direct to the head-landlord. The effect of the service of a notice by a sub-tenant is to create the relationship of landlord and tenant between it and the head-landlord until the rent arrears are paid. Until such time, the tenant's right to the rent from the sub-lease passes to the head-landlord.

Some goods of third parties are, however, excluded from the protection of the Act. These include: goods within the reputed ownership[43] of the tenant; goods which belong to the tenant's spouse or business partner; and goods which are in a company's offices and which belong to the company, where the premises themselves are leased to a tenant who is a director, officer or employee, of that company.

---

41 Law of Distress Amendment Act 1888, s 4.
42 *Exall v Partridge* (1799) 8 Term Rep 308.
43 See *Salford Van Hire (Contracts) Ltd v Bocholt Developments Ltd* [1995] 2 EGLR 50 (CA), where hired vans on the tenant's premises were held not to be in the reputed ownership of the tenant because it should have been known to the landlord that such vans were probably the subject of hire agreements.

Distress and set-off

In *Eller* v *Grovecrest Investments Ltd*[44], it was held that set-off is available to a tenant against a landlord's claim to distress in the same way as against an action for arrears of rent. If the set-off is in respect of an unliquidated sum, such as damages for breach of a landlord's repairing covenant, it is dangerous for the landlord to distrain, since there will be doubt as to the amount in respect of which he may distrain. If the landlord levies excessive distress, he may be liable in damages to the tenant for the inconvenience thereby caused.

Distress as waiver of right to forfeit

Since distress is available only during the subsistence of the relationship of landlord and tenant, a landlord who distrains for rent is affirming the continued existence of the lease and will therefore waive a right to forfeit the lease for the non-payment of the rent. If, however, the lease provides that the landlord's right to forfeit arises only if there is insufficient distress on the premises, the levying of distress will not itself effect a waiver of the right to forfeit. Similarly, if the landlord is proceeding for forfeiture and arrears of rent under the Common Law Procedure Act 1852, he will first need to levy distress in order to meet the requirement of section 210 that "no sufficient Distress was to be found on the demised Premises."

RENT REVIEW

Introduction

Rising property values and inflation mean that a landlord who wants the investment advantage of a fairly long term has to include in the lease a rent-review clause in order to maintain the real value of the rent received. During the 1980's leases would often provide for a rent review every three years, and three- or five-yearly reviews are now quite common, although older leases may have reviews every seven years.

Upwards and downwards review

Many rent-review clauses provide for an upwards-only review. In *Blythewood Hire Ltd* v *Spiers Ltd*[45], an upwards-only rent-review clause was included in a new lease under the 1954 Act, as it was said that the

---

44 [1995] QB 272 (CA); noted [1994] 26 EG 139.
45 [1992] 2 EGLR 98.

landlord's interest would otherwise be adversely affected.

In *Boots the Chemists Ltd v Pinkland Ltd*[46], the parties agreed that a new lease under the 1954 Act should include provision for rent reviews notwithstanding that the original 21-year lease, granted in 1965, had not done so. The judge refused to make the rent-review clause an "upwards only" review clause. He took account of the fact that rents obtainable had fallen and felt that the future was unpredictable, and held that it would not operate unfairly to the landlord if the rent-review clause in the new lease were one allowing for adjustment of the rent either way.

An example of an upwards-only rent-review clause would be one which provides for the rent on review to be:

> "a rent equal to the rent payable hereunder immediately prior to the review date or such revised rent as may be determined as herein provided whichever is the greater."[47]

The Joint Committee of the Law Society and the Royal Institution of Chartered Surveyors have produced model forms of rent-review clauses which provide a choice of upwards and/or downwards review. In the absence of an "upwards only" rent-review clause, a new rent may be higher or lower than the existing one.

Drafting rent-review clauses

Rent-review clauses are a constant source of litigation between landlord and tenant and should therefore be drafted as carefully and precisely as possible. A rent-review clause needs to provide for the following matters: the period of rent reviews; how the rent-review procedure is to be commenced and its mechanism; the formula by which a new rent is to be fixed; a procedure for determining any dispute; and an interim rent pending agreement on a new rent. Each of these may be considered in turn.

The period of rent reviews

The period of rent reviews will tend to depend upon the rate of inflation

---

46 [1992] 2 EGLR 103.

47 In New Zealand, a clause such as this is known as a "ratchet clause": *Melanesian Mission Trust Board v Australian Mutual Provident Society* [1997] 41 EG 153, 154 (Lord Hope of Craighead, giving the advice of the Privy Council). If the lease does not state expressly whether the review is to be upwards only, the court will construe the lease to ascertain the parties' intentions. In *Standard Life Assurance v Unipath Ltd* [1997] 38 EG 152 (CA) (Peter Gibson LJ dissenting), the fact that rent review could be triggered only by the landlord was an indication that the parties intended the review to be upwards only. In *Great Bear Investments Ltd v Solon Co-operative Housing Services Ltd* [1997] EGCS 177, either party could initiate rent review, but it was clear from the context that the words "whichever is the higher" had been omitted from the rent-review clause by mistake; the court was able to achieve rectification by construction.

and other prevailing market conditions when the lease is granted. Nowadays, five-year or three-year rent reviews are usual.

If the lease bears a different date from the commencement of the term, it may be preferable to state specifically the date of the first rent review to avoid any ambiguity as to whether time is to run from the date of the lease or the commencement of the term.

It could be dangerous to state specified dates for the rent review throughout the term of the lease. If dates are so specified, they may be imported into the hypothetical lease itself, which will progressively lose its reviews at each successive review date. An illustration of this would be a 20-year lease commencing in 1998 with review dates specified as being 2003, 2008 and 2013, and with a direction that the rent is to be assessed at each review date by reference to a hypothetical lease of the same length and upon the same terms (except as to rent) but commencing at the review date. At the date of the first review, in 2003, the hypothetical lease commencing on that date would be treated as making provision for only two reviews (in 2008 and 2013), with the (no doubt unintended) consequence that such hypothetical lease would have no review for the last ten years of its term. By the date of the second review, in 2008, the hypothetical lease would make provision for only one review date (in 2013); and by the third review, in 2013, the hypothetical lease would effectively have no provision for rent review at all. It is generally better therefore to state when the reviews are to occur by reference to the period of time that has elapsed since the commencement of the term. In the foregoing example, this could be accomplished by stating that the rent is to be reviewed on the fifth, tenth, and 15th anniversaries of the commencement of the term.

End-of-term review

From a landlord's point of view, a rent review at the end of the term is desirable because this should enable the landlord to secure a market rent, which might be expected to be higher than an interim rent determined by the court under Part II.[48] If the rent-review clause makes its own provision for an interim rent to be payable until the rent is determined in accordance with the review machinery, the landlord will also be able to obtain any additional rent immediately, rather than having to wait for an interim rent to be determined by the court. An end-of-term review also saves the landlord from having to apply to the court, which he would have to do to obtain an interim rent under Part II.

The rent-review clause could specify the last date of the term as a

---

48 LTA 1954, s 34(1); see Chap 15.

review date. If a lease for a term of 12 years provides for review at the completion of every third year of the term, and at the expiration of the contractual term the tenant remains in occupation under a Part II continuation tenancy, the landlord may wish to argue that the first day of holding over is a review date. This will be so only if, at least for the purposes of rent review, the lease defines "the term" to include any period of holding over under the 1954 Act.[49] If the lease does not extend the definition in this way, there can be no rent review on that date, since "the term" will be taken to mean the contractual term, which will have expired at the end of the previous day.

If the lease is to contain a landlord's break clause, the landlord might also find it desirable to have a rent review at the expiration of the notice to break. Care in drafting is again required. If the lease does not extend the definition of "the term" in the way suggested, the landlord is likely to lose the benefit of any review date specified in the lease which falls after the earlier determination of the contractual term by notice.[50]

Initiating review

A lease will usually provide that a rent-review procedure is to be started by the landlord giving notice of the review to the tenant. The lease might express it thus:

> "The landlord may call for a review of the rent payable hereunder from the end of the review year by serving notice to that effect on the tenant not earlier than six months prior to the review date."

Sometimes this will be a "trigger" notice stating what the landlord proposes that the new rent shall be. The basic form of such notice might be as follows:

> "The open market rental value [to be ascertained by the rent review] shall be such annual sum as shall be specified in writing signed by or on behalf of the lessor and posted by recorded delivery to the tenant at the demised premises."

Where rent review is started by a landlord's trigger notice, the lease will often provide that the rent stated in the landlord's trigger notice will be the new rent unless the parties agree a different sum within a specified period (often three months) after the service of the notice, or unless the tenant serves within such period a counter-notice on the landlord, in which event the rent is to be determined by a third party (either an independent expert

---

49 This has become common practice since *City of London Corporation v Fell* [1994] AC 458.
50 *Willison v Cheverell Estates Ltd* [1996] 1 EGLR 116 (CA); noted [1996] 33 EG 87.

or a surveyor) to be appointed for the purpose.[51] The landlord is under no implied obligation to propose in the trigger notice a rent which is a bona fide and genuine pre-estimate of the open-market rental value.[52] Templeman LJ has explained it thus:[53]

> "If a landlord puts forward a preposterous figure for rent, the tenant can always serve a counter-notice ... The court does not exist to punish a landlord for being greedy, especially as the definition of 'greed' varies from Shylock to Portia and from landlord to tenant."

If the lease provides that only the landlord may initiate rent review, it should make it clear whether the landlord is under an obligation to do so. The omission of an upwards-only rent-review clause (with the result that the rent could go down as well as up at review) is not itself sufficient evidence that the landlord is obliged to initiate review.[54]

If the landlord has a discretion whether or not to initiate review, there is little practical benefit for the tenant in having provision for downwards as well as upwards review: a landlord who is sure that a review would result in a lower rent will simply refrain from initiating the review process. The landlord would then have a difficult decision to make only if prevailing market conditions were such that it was unclear whether a review would produce a higher or a lower rent: the landlord might risk serving a notice in the hope of achieving a slightly increased rent only to find that the arbitrator decides that the rent should be reduced. For this reason, even if the landlord has a discretion whether or not to initiate review, a provision in the lease for reviews to be upwards only affords him some insulation against the gamble of initiating the review machinery in uncertain market conditions.[55]

Although in a rising commercial-property market it is usually in the landlord's interest to initiate the procedure for rent review, it may also be in the tenant's interest if he is considering assigning the lease or wishes to have some idea of his future financial liabilities. The tenant should therefore consider a provision which allows him to serve notice initiating the procedure, either as an alternative to the landlord's notice, or if the landlord fails to do so within a certain time.

---

51 A trigger notice of this type was contained in the lease considered in *Glofield Properties Ltd v Morley (No 2)* [1989] 2 EGLR 118 (CA), and part of the relevant clause is set out in the judgment of Nourse LJ (*ibid*, at 119). The decision itself, however, was on a different point.

52 *Amalgamated Estates Ltd v Joystretch Manufacturing Ltd* [1981] 1 EGLR 96, 98, where Lawton LJ pointed out that to imply such a term would lead to disputes and there would be no certainty. See also *Davstone Holdings Ltd v Al Rifai* (1976) 32 P & CR 18 (Goulding J); *Fox & Widley v Guram* [1998] 3 EG 142 (QB) (Clarke J).

53 *Amalgamated Estates Ltd v Joystretch Manufacturing Ltd* [1981] 1 EGLR 96, 99.

54 *Board of Trustees of the National Provident Fund v Brierley Investments Ltd*, 24 June 1996 (PC) (unreported; Lexis Transcript).

55 See *Sunflower Services Ltd v Unisys New Zealand Ltd* (1997) 74 P & CR 112 (PC).

It may also be in the tenant's interest, but not in the landlord's, to initiate a review during a period of recession if the rent-review clause is an "upwards or downwards" one. In *Royal Bank of Scotland plc v Jennings*[56] the Court of Appeal took the view that the reddendum of the lease and the rent-review clause clearly contemplated five-year reviews, and that the appointment of an expert by agreement between the parties or (in default) by the President of the Royal Institution of Chartered Surveyors upon the application of the landlord was merely the machinery by which the review was to be achieved. It therefore followed the House of Lords' decision in *Sudbrook Trading Estate Ltd v Eggleton*[57] and held that, in a position of impasse due to the landlord's unwillingness to apply to the President, the court could implement the necessary machinery itself. These cases were applied by Jacob J in *Addin v Secretary of State for the Environment*[58] where rent review was to be initiated by the landlord's trigger notice; but Jacob J distinguished this from *Harben Style Ltd v Rhodes Trust*[59] where the lease clearly provided that in the event of there being no review the rent was to be that which had been payable for the preceding year.

Time not presumed to be of the essence

It used to be thought that time was of the essence for such a notice, but the House of Lords in *United Scientific Holdings v Burnley Borough Council*[60] established that there is a presumption that time is not of the essence in such clauses, so that a failure to give notice within a specified time will not be fatal for the landlord.

The presumption that time is not of the essence may however be rebutted.

Making time of the essence

Counter-indication in review clause

First, the review clause may itself make time of the essence. This can be done expressly[61], and it may be either of general application or selective, *i.e.* applicable to only parts of the review procedure. Thus a rent-review clause may provide that time shall be of the essence only as regards one particular step in the procedure, such as a tenant's counter-notice. A provision that the rent is to be conclusively presumed as stated in the landlord's notice unless the tenant serves a counter-notice within a certain time could have

56 [1997] 1 EGLR 101.
57 [1983] 1 EGLR 47.
58 [1997] 1 EGLR 99.
59 [1995] 1 EGLR 118.
60 [1978] AC 904.
61 See clause on p 223.

this effect.[62] The *Joystretch* case also demonstrates clearly that the requirements for a counter-notice must be carefully complied with, and a mere letter inquiring as to the landlord's method of calculation of a proposed rent will not suffice as a counter-notice.

If it is intended that time is to be of the essence as regards one particular step only, this must be made clear. In the absence of a clear statement to this effect, time may, by association, become of the essence for other parts of the procedure too. Thus in *Art & Sound Ltd v West London Litho Ltd*[63] a clear statement that time was to be of the essence with regard to an agreement between the parties was construed as applying also to an arbitrator's determination.

That time is to be of the essence may also be inferred. An inference to this effect may be made if the rent-review clause sets out a very specific time-schedule stating the times within which each step should be taken, as in *Henry Smith's Charity Trustees v AWADA Trading & Promotion Services Ltd.*[64] Even a specific time-schedule, however, may be held to be merely elastic and not mandatory, and so may fail to make time of the essence. If a particular consequence is stated to occur in the event of failure to act within a given time limit, this is an indication that the wording was intended to be mandatory rather than elastic. Such a consequence might, for instance, be a deeming provision as to rent. Even such a default clause must, however, be read in the light of all the terms of the lease.[65]

In *Mecca Leisure Ltd v Renown Investments (Holdings) Ltd*[66] a similar procedure to that in *Henry Smith's Charity* was set out, but Eveleigh LJ said in that case that each rent-review clause should be construed on its own merits and that "deeming" provisions as to time in other cases are therefore not likely to assist in construing such clauses in other leases.

It is obvious from this that even a very slight variation in wording may result in a different construction of such clauses, and if it is intended that time should be of the essence, it is desirable to state this unequivocally.

Tenant's break clause linked to review

Secondly, the presumption that time is not of the essence is likely to be rebutted if the tenant has a right to terminate the lease under a break clause which is linked to the rent review.[67] In such circumstances, it may be

---

62 *Amalgamated Estates Ltd v Joystretch Manufacturing Ltd* [1981] 1 EGLR 96 (CA).
63 [1992] 1 EGLR 138 (Ch.).
64 [1984] 1 EGLR 116.
65 See *dicta* of Millett J in *Power Securities (Manchester) Ltd v Prudential Assurance Co. Ltd* [1987] 1 EGLR 121.
66 [1984] 2 EGLR 137 (CA).
67 *C Richards & Son Ltd v Karenita Ltd* (1972) 221 EG 25; *Coventry City Council v J Hepworth & Son* [1982] 1 EGLR 119.

inferred that it was the intention of the parties that the tenant should be able to exercise the break clause (in respect of which time is of the essence) in the light of its knowledge of what the new rent will be.[68] Since this advantage would be lost to the tenant if the landlord were to be permitted to initiate rent review out of time, it may be presumed that time was intended to be of the essence for the rent-review procedure also.[69]

The courts have, however, gone further, and have treated time as being of the essence for the service of a review notice even when the last date for serving such a notice by the landlord alone is also the last date by which the tenant may serve a notice to break.[70] The landlord's serving the review notice late will result in the tenant's having to decide whether or not to break without knowing what the new rent might be; but in practice the tenant might reasonably expect that notice will be served in sufficient time to enable him to make an informed decision whether to break or not.

Time has also been treated as being of the essence where, although the break notice may be served by the tenant alone, the review notice may be served by either party.[71] There is, indeed, only one reported case in which it was held that time was not of the essence for rent review despite the presence of a tenant's break clause. This was the decision of the Court of Appeal in *Metrolands Investments Ltd* v *JH Dewhurst Ltd*[72], which did not concern a rent-review notice, where the lease provided for the reviewed rent to be determined by arbitration. The first basis upon which the court reached its decision was that, as the arbitration could take longer than the time specified in the lease, compliance with the timetable for rent review was out of the landlord's hands. The court alternatively based its decision on the fact that the rent-review procedure could be initiated by the tenant as well as by the landlord.

This latter distinction, which had not been drawn in earlier cases, was not made in the most recent pronouncement by the Court of Appeal in *Central Estates Ltd* v *Secretary of State for the Environment*[73], which has sought to restrict its earlier decision in *Metrolands* to the first and narrower ground. In the *Central Estates* case, the rent review could be upwards or downwards and could be activated by either the landlord or

68 *United Scientific Holdings Ltd* v *Burnley Borough Council* [1978] AC 904, 946 (Lord Simon of Glaisdale), 962 (Lord Fraser of Tullybelton).

69 *Legal & General Assurance (Pension Management) Ltd* v *Cheshire County Council* [1984] 1 EGLR 102, 103 (Dillon LJ).

70 *Al Saloom* v *Shirley James Travel Service Ltd* (1981) 42 P & CR 181 (CA); *Legal & General Assurance (Pension Management) Ltd* v *Cheshire County Council* [1984] 1 EGLR 102 (CA).

71 *Stephenson & Son* v *Orca Properties Ltd* [1989] 2 EGLR 129 (Scott J).

72 [1986] 3 All ER 659 (CA).

73 [1997] 1 EGLR 239.

the tenant, and either party was entitled to break. The court did not, however, consider these to be features justifying a departure from the presumption that time is of the essence of a review notice where it is interrelated to a notice to break.

In drafting any break-clause procedure, the parties should therefore be mindful of the potential effect that it might have upon rent review, so that they can ensure that the former does not inadvertently make time of the essence in the latter. This is best dealt with by an express statement whether or not time is of the essence, and in respect of which parts of the review procedure.

A further aspect of the *Central Estates* case was that the lease, which was for a term of 42 years, made provision for four rent reviews, but only one right to break, which coincided with the second review, this being the review considered by the court. The court was not called upon to determine what the effect of the interrelationship of a break clause with one rent review might be on the other three; but only Glidewell LJ expressed no opinion on it. Morritt LJ considered that time would be of the essence only for the second review; whereas Sir John May thought that time would be of the essence for all three. In view of this uncertainty, it is especially important where not all review dates are linked to break clauses that the lease state expressly whether time is of the essence for all or any of the rent reviews, specifying which.

Service of notice

Thirdly, it is always open to one party or the other to serve a notice making time of the essence. Any such notice should state very clearly that this is the party's intention, so that the notice will not merely be regarded as another stage in the procedure.

Where "time of essence" provision cannot be relied on

Waiver or estoppel (whether promissory or proprietary) will preclude the landlord from relying on a provision making time of the essence, but only if there is clear supporting evidence. Mere non-exercise by the landlord of his contractual right is not itself sufficient to cause that right to be lost: in this context "abandonment" is neither a term of art nor a separate basis of claim, and no analogy can be drawn with the abandonment of chattels.[74] Even an undue delay in giving notice will not be fatal to the landlord in the absence of an agreement to abandon the review, or a promise made by the landlord to do so on which the tenant has acted to his detriment, so raising an estoppel.[75] In practice, it will be difficult to show that a delay in

---

74 *Amhurst v James Walker (Goldsmith & Silversmith) Ltd* [1983] Ch 305 (CA).
75 *Ibid.*

increasing a rent can operate detrimentally to a tenant, so that the circumstances where an estoppel might be pleaded must be rare.

In *Patel v Peel Investments (South) Ltd*[76] there was provision for the tenant to elect for arbitration "by notice in writing to the lessor not later than three months after the lessor's notification [of the new rent] in writing (time in this respect to be of the essence hereof)." The landlord inadvertently served two notices, and there was correspondence for over a year; but the tenant's claims based on waiver and estoppel both failed. The tenant had alleged that the landlord had represented that he would not rely on the time-limits for the tenant's notice; but the court found that no clear and unambiguous representation had been made. The claim based on promissory estoppel failed additionally because the tenant could not show any requisite act of reliance.

The rent-review clause may confer on the tenant a right to apply for arbitration, but only if the tenant complies with a deadline (of which time is made of the essence) specified in the rent-review clause. The lease could confer on the tenant the right to apply for arbitration within a specified period; but many leases simply require a tenant who objects to the rent proposed by the landlord in its trigger notice, to serve a counter-notice on the landlord within a certain time thereafter – often three months after receipt of the landlord's notice. Whatever the step the tenant has to take to set in motion the procedures which might lead to arbitration, the court may by order, under the Arbitration Act 1996, section 12, extend the time for taking that step.[77]

Section 12 has widened the circumstances in which an application can be made, since under the old law an extension could be granted only if the step was the appointment of an arbitrator or "some other step to commence arbitration proceedings."[78] This had been held not to include the landlord's initial notice of rent review, since there was at that time no dispute referable to arbitration.[79] The court would now be able to grant an extension of time in relation to such notice.

In other respects, however, section 12 has considerably narrowed the scope for applications to the courts for time-extensions. Under the old law, the tenant could obtain an extension of time if he could satisfy the court that he would otherwise suffer "undue hardship."[80] The courts had

---

76 [1992] 2 EGLR 116.
77 Arbitration Act 1996, s 12(1).
78 Arbitration Act 1950, s 27.
79 *Richurst Ltd v Pimenta* [1993] 2 All ER 559. Contrast *Pittalis v Sherefettin* [1986] 1 QB 868 (CA), where the tenant's counter-notice was held to fall within Arbitration Act 1950, s 27, as being "effectively the first step in the arbitration proceedings."
80 Arbitration Act 1950, s 27 (repealed).

construed this broadly and would look at all the circumstances of the case, including the amount at stake, the length of the delay and the degree of fault involved. Provided the tenant could establish "undue hardship", he could obtain an extension even if his omission to serve a counter-notice was entirely his own fault.[81] Now, however, under section 12, the court cannot make a time-extension order unless it is satisfied:[82]

> (a) that the circumstances are such as were outside the reasonable contemplation of the parties when they agreed the provision in question, and that it would be just to extend the time, or
> (b) that the conduct of one party makes it unjust to hold the other party to the strict terms of the provision in question.

These new criteria are more stringent than those they replace, and it is clear that they will be interpreted narrowly by the courts. It has already been stated judicially that section 12 is to be interpreted taking account of the underlying purpose of the Act and of that section, which was to restrict the circumstances in which the court would have power to extend the time.[83] However great a hardship the tenant may now face from missing the deadline, that is not itself enough to justify the court's granting an extension of time. The scope for applications to the court is therefore considerably reduced.

The strictness of the new provisions is seen in *Fox & Widley* v *Guram*.[84] The landlord's trigger notice had proposed an annual rent of £14,000, but the tenant failed to serve a counter-notice within the requisite period of three months (time being of the essence). There was evidence that the open market rent, by reference to which the rent was to be determined, was only £3,500 per annum; but Clarke J rejected the tenant's claim for an extension of time under section 12. Dealing with paragraph (a), he considered that it was within the reasonable contemplation of the parties that the rent-review clause would operate by the landlord's putting forward an inflated figure in his trigger notice, and it must have been within their reasonable contemplation that, if no counter-notice was given, the tenant would have to pay whatever was specified in the landlord's notice, however unreasonable. Turning to paragraph (b), he did not think (for the same reasons) that there was anything in the landlord's proposal of a rent of £14,000 which would make it unjust to hold the tenant to the strict terms of the contract.

---

81 *Peel* v *Patel Investments (South) Ltd* [1992] 2 EGLR 116 (where the landlord's notice had proposed a rent 30% above the market rent); *Pittalis* v *Sherefettin* [1986] 1 QB 868.
82 Arbitration Act 1996, s 12(3)(a)(b).
83 *Fox & Widley* v *Guram* [1998] 3 EG 142 (QB), where Clarke J refers to the similar approach suggested by Judge Jack in *Vosnoc Ltd* v *Transglobal Projects Ltd* [1997] 23 July (QB) (unreported) (Lexis Transcript).
84 [1998] 3 EG 142 (QB).

The formula for determining a new rent

It is important that the method for the calculation of the new rent should be stated as precisely as possible, making it clear what matters are to be taken into consideration and what are to be ignored in arriving at a figure. Draftsmen should bear in mind that rent formulae "can often be expressed more simply and unambiguously in algebraic form."[85]

The usual figure which the parties are setting out to ascertain is the rent which the premises are likely to command in an open market at the review date. This will usually be expressed in a clause such as:

> "The market rent of the demised premises means the best yearly rent at which the demised premises might reasonably be expected to be let in the open market by a willing landlord to a willing tenant at the relevant review date with vacant possession for a term of years equal to the residue of that hereby granted on a lease containing the same terms and conditions (save as to the amount of rent) as are contained herein."

A market rent

"open market rent"

The rent itself may be expressed to be an "open market rent" or a "full market rent", and the courts have indicated that whichever expression is used will make little difference to the actual market rent obtainable. This is the rent which a willing tenant would be expected to pay to a willing landlord for the property on the open market.

A tenant should perhaps be wary of the "best" market rent, which could conceivably include a rent obtainable from some particular tenant owing to peculiar circumstances, although in practice most rent-review clauses do refer to the "best" rent.

Also, subject to contra-indications, a "reasonable" rent will be ascertained by objective standards and may take account of circumstances which are not at all reasonable to consider as between the parties. Thus in *Ponsford v HMS Aerosols Ltd*[86] the House of Lords found that it was "reasonable" to take into account improvements to the premises, even though these had been paid for by the tenant. The result was that the tenant was effectively paying for them twice over. In order to avoid such an unfair result, the rent should have been expressed to be **"reasonable as between the parties"**, or **"in all the circumstances"**.

---

85 *London Regional Transport v Wimpey Group Services Ltd* [1986] 2 EGLR 41, 42, per Hoffmann J.
86 [1979] AC 63.

The hypothetical tenant

"a willing tenant"

The rent-review clause will generally provide for the rent to be assessed as the rent which some willing hypothetical tenant would pay for the property on the open market. The tenant himself is not, however, to be assumed to be among the hypothetical bidders.[87] The reality that tenants in a particular trade, for instance, are experiencing financial difficulties, is therefore irrelevant. Nor will a direction that the property is assumed to be let with vacant possession mean that the *actual* tenant is to be included as a bidder for the premises.

The hypothetical lease

"on a lease containing the same terms and conditions"

The problems associated with the valuation of premises for rent review have mainly arisen on the terms of the hypothetical lease under which the willing tenant will hold. Obviously the terms of the hypothetical lease are of prime importance as regards its value.

Presumption of realism

Landlords have shown considerable ingenuity in the invention of terms for hypothetical lettings, which may vary quite substantially from the terms of the real letting. The courts have frequently shown a dislike for pure fantasy, however, and the general tendency is to adopt a realistic approach wherever possible, on the ground that this is more likely to give business efficacy to any agreement. In *Basingstoke & Deane BC v Host Group Ltd*[88] Nicholls LJ said:

> "... the parties are to be taken as having intended that the notional letting postulated by their rent review clause is to be a letting on the same terms (other than as to quantum of rent) as those still subsisting between the parties in the actual existing lease."

The lease in that case provided for rent review, in certain circumstances, on the basis of a vacant site, whereas in fact the lease was of a public house erected on the site by the tenant. The Court of Appeal held that the notional letting should be one with the same user as the actual letting.

Similarly, in *Dukeminster (Ebbgate House One) Ltd v Somerfield Property Co Ltd*[89] the rent-review clause in a lease of a warehouse at Ross-on-Wye, provided that the rent was to be reviewed by reference to "notional premises", which were defined as "a warehouse unit within a

---

87 *F R Evans (Leeds) Ltd v English Electric Co Ltd* (1977) 36 P & CR 184.
88 [1988] 1 WLR 348.
89 [1997] 40 EG 157.

thirty-five mile radius of Ross-on-Wye." The definition did not, however, specify where within that radius the notional premises were to be located; and the circle described by that radius included areas with a wide variety in rental levels. The judge at first instance had held that the landlord was entitled to select a particular location within that radius; but his judgment was reversed on appeal. Applying the principle that all rent-review provisions "operate in a real world and not in one of fantasy"[90], the Court of Appeal held that the parties could only reasonably have intended that the notional premises be situated in a location comparable to the site of the actual premises in Ross-on-Wye.

If the hypothetical lease directs that assumptions shall be made as to user which are not entirely fictional and removed from reality however, the hypothetical lease may be taken as being a lease with the hypothetical user. In *Sheerness Steel Co plc v Medway Ports Authority*[91] rent review was to be on the basis that the premises were let for industrial purposes whereas in fact the sole industrial use for which they were suitable was steel rolling. It was held that for the purposes of rent review the hypothetical lease should assume user for any industrial purposes. Similarly, where the hypothetical lease required an assumption of user for retail purposes generally, this was held to prevail over the user clause in the actual lease which limited shop premises to the sale of high class china.[92]

In *Laura Investment Co Ltd v Havering LBC (No 2)*[93] the lessee of five acres of undeveloped land was required to under-let various plots with the lessor's consent. Hoffmann J, had decided at a previous hearing[94] that rent review was to be on the basis that buildings erected on the land were to be included in the hypothetical lease, as there was no requirement to disregard improvements. In the present proceedings, he held that the rent review should take into account the under-leases which the tenant had granted. The tenant was obliged to under-let the various plots; and the landlord, whose consent to under-letting was required, could ensure that the under-lettings were at market rents and not at premiums. This decision was consistent with that of Peter Gibson J in *Forte & Co Ltd v General Accident Life Assurance Ltd*[95] who decided that a rent review should not be on the basis of vacant possession but should take into account a sub-lease of part of the premises, made before the review and which would continue for some time after it.

90 *Ibid*, per Nourse LJ, at 158.
91 [1992] 1 EGLR 133 (CA).
92 *PosTel Properties Ltd v Greenwell* [1992] 2 EGLR 130 (Ch).
93 [1993] 1 EGLR 124 (Ch).
94 *Laura Investment Co Ltd v Havering LBC* [1992] 1 EGLR 155 (Ch).
95 [1986] 2 EGLR 115.

In *Law Land Co Ltd* v *Consumers' Association Ltd*[96] the terms of the lease restricted user to that of the tenant's undertaking but directed rent review to be on an open-market basis. The Court of Appeal held that the only feasible basis for a hypothetical tenant was to assume a lease which did not restrict the user of the premises at all. In *Plinth Property Investments Ltd* v *Mott, May & Anderson*[97] it was held that a restriction in the lease to use the premises as offices in connection with the tenant's business of consulting engineers could be taken into account. The curious paradox of these two cases is therefore that a virtually total restriction on user may have to be completely disregarded for the purposes of a hypothetical lease and so have a less depreciating effect on rent review than a more moderate one.

Length of hypothetical term
"for a term of years equal to the residue of the term hereby granted"
Another matter which requires consideration is the length of the hypothetical term which is to be applied for the purposes of rent review. If the hypothetical lease is to be for the unexpired remainder of the actual term, this could depress the rent towards the end. Conversely, if it is to be taken as the full term of the lease at every rent review, this could inflate the rent.

Given ambiguity of meaning, it would seem from *Lynnthorpe Enterprises Ltd* v *Sidney Smith (Chelsea) Ltd*[98] that the court will again construe the hypothetical lease as closely as possible to the actual lease. In that case, a hypothetical tenancy for "a term of years equivalent to the said term" was held to be one which commenced at the time of the actual lease and was commensurate with it, and not one which commenced at the date of the rent review.

Tromans has suggested that a compromise on the length of the hypothetical term might be the remainder of the actual term with a minimum of ten or 15 years.[99]

Assumptions and disregards
All rent-review clauses are likely to include certain matters to be assumed as between the landlord and the tenant, and others which are to be disregarded, in arriving at the market rent. The possible effect of these on the particular property should be carefully considered from the point of

---

96 [1980] 2 EGLR 109 (CA).
97 (1978) 38 P & CR 361.
98 [1990] 2 EGLR 131 (CA).
99 Tromans, *Commercial Leases*, 2nd ed (1996) Sweet & Maxwell, 92.

view of both landlord and tenant.

Sometimes a lease will use a form of shorthand for disregards by referring to the disregards in the Landlord and Tenant Act 1954, section 34. This section was subsequently amended[1], and in its amended form limits the disregard to improvements during the last 21 years. The case of *Brett* v *Brett Essex Golf Club*[2], mentioned more fully below[3], illustrates the difficulties which may arise from such a practice.

(i) Disregard of rent
"save as to the amount of rent"

Sometimes a rent-review clause will provide for a new rent to be fixed having regard to all the terms of the letting **"other than as to rent"**. Taken literally, such a clause could mean that the hypothetical lease had no provisions for rent at all, and that even a forfeiture clause for non-payment of rent did not exist. Such a construction is obviously absurd and the phrase requires further definition, such as "other than as to rent currently payable."

If such wording is to be regarded as excluding from the hypothetical lease all future rent reviews, the landlord will clearly be entitled to a much larger rent than if he were merely receiving a rent that was being determined for a period of three or five years until the next review date. In *British Gas Corporation* v *Universities Superannuation Scheme Ltd*[4] Sir Nicholas Browne-Wilkinson V-C stated what he considered to be the correct approach:[5]

> "(a) words in a rent exclusion provision which require all provisions as to rent to be disregarded produce a result so manifestly contrary to commercial common sense that they cannot be given literal effect; (b) other clear words which require the rent-review provisions (as opposed to all provisions as to rent) to be disregarded ... must be given effect to however wayward the result; (c) subject to (b), in the absence of special circumstances it is proper to give effect to the underlying commercial purpose of a rent-review clause and to construe the words so as to give effect to that purpose by requiring future rent reviews to be taken into account in fixing the open market rental under the hypothetical letting."

In the later case of *Equity & Law Life Assurance plc* v *Bodfield Ltd*[6], the Court of Appeal, whilst approving these guidelines, cautioned that they

---

1 By LPA 1969.
2 [1986] 1 EGLR 154.
3 See p 233 *infra*.
4 [1986] 1 WLR 398.
5 *Ibid*, at 403.
6 [1987] 1 EGLR 124, 125 (Dillon LJ, with whose judgment the other two members of the Court of Appeal agreed).

cannot entitle the court to construe and apply, not the clause which parties
have entered into, but the different clause which they might have, or
probably would have, entered into if their lawyers had thought rather more
deeply about how the intricate scheme they were setting up would work in
practice. It also emphasised the importance of construing the precise words
of the particular rent-review clause in question, and condemned the
approach of trying to ascertain the meaning of a given clause by reference
to authorities which had interpreted broadly similar (but not absolutely
identical) clauses in other leases.[7] Bearing these considerations in mind, the
Court of Appeal concluded that, on the proper construction of the lease
before it, the expressed disregard as to rent was a sufficiently clear
indication of the parties' intention to exclude rent review from the
hypothetical lease.

(ii) Assumption of vacant possession and letting as a whole

*"disregarding any effect on rent of the fact that the tenant has been in
occupation of the demised premises...."*

An assumption of vacant possession, and that the property is to be let as a
whole, could adversely affect the landlord of a large office block, which
might only be readily occupied in smaller units. It might well be to the
landlord's advantage to take into account existing sub-leases on a rent
review of this type of property. On the other hand, an assumption of
vacant possession of a smaller single unit would be reasonable. "Vacant
possession" implies that the tenant's fixtures are to be excluded, which is
fair to the tenant, but it may also imply a free fitting-out period, as it was
held to do in *99 Bishopsgate Ltd* v *Prudential Assurance Co Ltd.*[8] Any
such assumption of vacant possession should therefore expressly exclude
this possibility.

If the premises, or part of them, are sub-let, or the tenant is under an
obligation to sub-let, the court may deem it inappropriate to assume
vacant possession.[9]

(iii) Disregard of rent-free periods

*"disregarding any rent-free period or concession or inducement which
would or might be given to an incoming tenant on the grant of a new lease
of the demised premises"*

A landlord may be prepared to assist a tenant's cash-flow problem by

---

7 *Ibid*, at 125 (Dillon LJ), approving *dicta* of Jessel MR in *Aspden* v *Seddon* (1875) 10 Ch
   App 394, 397.
8 [1985] 1 EGLR 72.
9 See *Laura Investment Co Ltd* v *Havering LBC (No 2)* [1993] 1 EGLR 124 (Ch); and *Forte
   & Co Ltd* v *General Accident Life Assurance Ltd* [1986] 2 EGLR 115.

allowing him to have a rent-free period at the beginning of a lease, during which time the tenant is fitting out the premises to make them suitable for his business and is not actually receiving any profits. The subsequent rent for the remainder of the term may then reflect this, however, by adding this allowance to the market rent, and this increased rent is known as a headline rent. A rent-review clause may well require a disregard of any rent-free period, as a fitting out of the premises will not arise. Such clauses may, however, cause a problem for a tenant if they can be construed to mean that the rent review shall have regard to the headline rent and not the market rent.

In *City Offices plc v Bryanston Insurance Co Ltd*[10] the rent-review clause provided for the market rent to be ascertained by reference to a hypothetical lease which assumed that the premises were suitable for immediate occupation but disregarded any rent-free periods which the hypothetical landlord might offer to the hypothetical tenant. It was held that this should be construed as meaning that the rent should be payable immediately from the rent-review date and that there should be no such period in the hypothetical lease which would inflate the rent for the remainder of the rent-review period, thereby giving the landlord a higher than market rent.

During the recession, a landlord would sometimes offer a tenant a rent-free period at the commencement of the term as an inducement to let the premises; the landlord might well regard this as preferable to letting at a lower rent, thereby reducing the value of his reversion. This type of rent-free period also fell to be considered in the context of rent-review clauses requiring them to be disregarded. There were four conjoined appeals to the Court of Appeal on such clauses.[11] Hoffmann LJ followed the guidance given by Lord Browne-Wilkinson V-C in *British Gas Corporation v Universities Superannuation Scheme Ltd*[12] that wherever possible a commercially realistic interpretation of a rent-review clause should be applied. A disregard of such a period for fitting out, which did not apply on rent review, was clearly common sense, but a rent-free period as an inducement to take the lease could be regarded more as part of an overall financial package. Nevertheless, applying the commercial reality approach, Hoffmann LJ was able to find that rent review was intended to be by reference to the market rent and not to the headline rent in three of the

---

10 [1993] 1 EGLR 126 (Ch).

11 *Co-operative Wholesale Society Ltd v National Westminster Bank plc; Scottish Amicable Life Assurance Society v Middleton Potts & Co; Broadgate Square plc v Lehman Brothers Ltd;* and *Prudential Nominees Ltd v Greenham Trading Ltd;* all reported at [1995] 1 EGLR 97 (CA).

12 [1986] 1 WLR 398.

cases. The rent-review clause in the fourth case, *Broadgate Square plc v Lehman Brothers Ltd*[12a], required the reviewed rent to be that which became payable "after the expiry of any rent-free period", and his Lordship held that this could be construed only as the headline rent.

(iv) Assumption that planning consent for use obtained

"upon the assumption that the demised premises may be lawfully used as [hypothetical use for which planning consent is assumed to have been obtained]"

A direction that rent is to be determined on the assumption that planning consent for the particular use has been obtained for the property, which has not in fact been obtained, will require a rent to be ascertained on that basis rather than on the basis of the actual user.[13] Such an assumption will not, however, require any feat of imagination as regards the physical layout of the premises, however unsuitable it is for the supposed use.[14]

(v) Assumption of tenant's compliance with covenants in the lease

"disregarding any failure by the tenant to comply fully with the obligations on its part herein contained"

A common assumption in rent-review clauses is that the tenant has complied with the covenants in the lease. This is desirable as regards repairing covenants, as otherwise the tenant will obtain an advantage on rent review from breach of any repairing covenants. Any assumption that the premises are reinstated if damaged or destroyed should, however, be carefully considered in conjunction with clauses for reinstatement and suspension of rent. If the tenant is to accept such an assumption, it is desirable that the landlord should not have sole control over the reinstatement.

(vi) Disregard of tenant's improvements

"disregarding any effect on rent of any improvement carried out by the tenant otherwise than in pursuance of an obligation to the landlord...."

Although the assumption of repairs will be made to deny the tenant the advantage of a reduced rent for disrepair, the rent-review procedure will usually require a disregard of any improvements made by the tenant. This is to avoid his effectively paying twice over for these – initially for the improvements themselves, and subsequently in an increased rent which the premises then command.

12a [1995] 1 EGLR 97.
13 *Bovis Group Pension Fund Ltd v GC Flooring & Furnishing Ltd* [1984] 1 EGLR 123 (CA).
14 *Orchid Lodge (UK) Ltd v Extel Computing Ltd* [1991] 1 EGLR 116.

The tenant should ensure that the disregard covers not only improvements made by him, but also by his predecessors in title and persons deriving title under him, such as sub-tenants, to whom the tenant may in fact have given consideration for the improvements.

The tenant should also ensure that the disregard extends to improvements made by him or a predecessor in title when in occupation of the premises under a previous lease or licence. In *Brett v Brett Essex Golf Club*[15] the tenant had constructed a six-hole golf course on adjoining land which was not at the time part of the demised premises, but subsequently became part. The rent-review clause adopted the disregard of improvements under the Landlord and Tenant Act 1954, section 34, and it was held that the improvements to the nearby land which was not part of the demised premises at the time could not be disregarded.

It is usual for the landlord to limit the disregard of improvements to those made with the landlord's prior consent. The purpose of such a provision (which is included in the model clause of the Joint Committee) is to avoid future disputes as to what improvements the tenant has made. The assumption that the tenant has complied with the covenants in the lease will not, however, cover this provision.[16]

There may, however, be an exclusion from the disregard of improvements made pursuant to an obligation (as there is in the Joint Committee's model clause), because the landlord may then have furnished consideration for these. The tenant, for instance, may have been allowed a rent-free period for fitting out the premises, or a reduction in rent for the improvements.

Any such clause requires caution in subsequently drafting a licence to carry out work, which must be drafted in permissive terms and not in an obligatory form if the improvements are still to fall within the disregard.[17] The licence may provide that the works are to be deemed to be carried out in pursuance of an obligation owed to the lessor: this will have the effect of converting a voluntary improvement into an obligation falling outside the disregard.[18]

A further illustration of the caution required in drafting a licence for improvements is *Historic Houses Hotels Ltd v Cadogan Estates*[19], where the rent-review clause in the lease required a disregard of improvements made other than those made pursuant to an obligation to the landlord.

15 [1986] 1 EGLR 154.
16 *Hamish Caithir Travel England Ltd v Insight International Tours Ltd* [1986] 1 EGLR 244.
17 *Godbold v Martins The Newsagents Ltd* [1983] 2 EGLR 128 (Ch).
18 *Daejan Properties Ltd v Holmes* [1996] EGCS 185 (Ch D) (Neuberger J).
19 [1995] 1 EGLR 117 (CA).

Subsequently, the tenant made various improvements to the property at its own expense and with the landlord's licence. The licence contained various covenants (relating to alterations) by the tenant with the landlord, which were not contained in the lease. The licence contained an additional covenant that, on completion of the work, "all ... covenants and provisions contained in the said lease ... shall be applicable to the said premises in their then altered state ... as if the said premises in their then altered state had originally been comprised in the said lease." The landlord argued that the effect of this was that the improvements were not to be disregarded at review; but its argument was rejected. The Court of Appeal affirmed the decision at first instance of Knox J[20], who had followed the decision in the *Godbold*[21] case. Knox J had found that the licence to carry out work was essentially permissive and not obligatory. He had further found that the additional covenant in the licence was applicable only to terms other than rent review. The parties' intention had been to exclude non-obligatory improvements, and this was not changed by the licence to carry out improvements.

The better practice might be nevertheless to limit the exclusion from the disregard to improvements which the tenant is under an obligation *under the terms of the lease* to carry out.

If the tenant has covenanted to comply with statutory requirements, such as fire or Health and Safety at Work regulations, work carried out pursuant to these is work carried out under an obligation imposed on the tenant by the lease.[22] The tenant should therefore also argue for this type of work to be disregarded.

(vii) Disregard of goodwill

"disregarding any goodwill attached to the demised premises by reason of the tenant carrying on thereat the business of the tenant ..."

A rent-review clause should also stipulate a disregard of any goodwill relating to the tenant's business, which would obviously penalise a successful business, and of the tenant's occupation. If the tenant occupies other premises near to the demised premises, such as other units in a shopping precinct, his occupation of those premises should also be disregarded as failure to do so could artificially inflate the rent.

A shorthand for the assumptions and disregards to be made is sometimes used by adopting those set out in the Landlord and Tenant Act 1954, section 34, which apply when fixing the rent for a new lease under the Act. Such adoption may not, however, be entirely suitable. The section

---

20 [1993] 2 EGLR 151 (Ch).

21 See fn 17 *supra.*

22 *Forte & Co Ltd* v *General Accident Life Assurance Ltd* [1986] 2 EGLR 115.

refers to rent for "the holding", which may differ from the premises. It also refers to improvements by the "tenant", which would not cover improvements (for which the tenant may have given consideration) by a sub-tenant or licensee. The section in its original form was limited to repairs carried out during the term of the lease, which may be inappropriate. Although the section was subsequently amended[23] so as to provide for a disregard of improvements made within 21 years of the application, the court may construe any particular lease as incorporating the section in its unamended form.[24]

A procedure for determining any disputes

The rent-review clause may require an arbitrator or an independent expert valuer to determine the rent in the first place, or it may provide for the parties to try first to agree a new rent between themselves with resort to an arbitrator or valuer if they are unable to do so. In any event, the clause should provide some way of resolving disputes.

The clause should provide how the independent valuer or the arbitrator is to be appointed, and a usual provision for this is that he shall be appointed by the President of the Royal Institution of Chartered Surveyors. An example of such a clause would be one providing that:

> "if the landlord and the tenant shall not have agreed the open market rent three months before the relevant review date either party may request the open market rent to be determined by a surveyor to be agreed upon in writing by the landlord and the tenant and in default of such agreement to be nominated by the President for the time being of the Royal Institution of Chartered Surveyors upon the application of the landlord to be made not earlier than two months before the relevant review date."

The Joint Committee's model form of clause provides for resolution of disputes by an arbitrator alone, by an independent expert alone, or by whichever of the two the landlord chooses. There are, however, important differences between an arbitrator and an independent expert.

Differences between arbitrator and independent expert

An arbitrator will essentially be deciding an issue between the parties and his decision should therefore fall between the limits of the parties' differences, whereas an independent expert will be expected to apply his knowledge and skill to a problem, which, although unlikely, he may then decide entirely outside the limits of the dispute between the parties. An

---

23 By LPA 1969.
24 As it did in *Brett v Brett Essex Golf Club Ltd* [1986] 1 EGLR 154.

arbitrator, who is conducting a judicial process, is answerable to the court and must observe the rules of natural justice, whereas an expert valuer will have a discretion as to how he exercises his skills and the court may not have any jurisdiction to intervene.

Unless he can be shown to have acted in bad faith, an arbitrator enjoys judicial immunity in discharging his function.[25] An expert, however, can be sued for negligence, although in practice this may be extremely difficult to prove. An arbitrator has authority to order discovery of documents[26] and to examine a party or witnesses on oath.[27] Although an expert may hear evidence, he does not have the same power as an arbitrator to compel witnesses and his position is not judicial. Arbitration is likely to be a more expensive process than a determination by an expert, and so is more justifiable for large office-blocks and precincts. If the property is a smaller single unit, it may be more appropriate for determination to be made by an expert valuer.

Judicial control of arbitrators

Arbitration is governed by the Arbitration Act 1996. The court has power (provided specified criteria are met) to determine any question as to the arbitrator's substantive jurisdiction.[28] The court[29] may remove an arbitrator if there are justifiable doubts as to his impartiality, if he is not properly qualified, if he is incapable of acting, or if he fails to conduct the proceedings properly or with all reasonable despatch.[30] An application to the court can be made to challenge or to set aside an award if the arbitrator acts outside his terms of reference.[31] An application may also be made to the court to challenge an award if there is a "serious irregularity"[32] of one of the kinds there specified[33] which the court considers "has caused or will cause substantial injustice" to the applicant.[34]

---

25 Arbitration Act 1996, s 74(1).
26 *Ibid*, s 38(4).
27 *Ibid*, s 38(5).
28 *Ibid*, s 32.
29 Either the High Court or a county court: *ibid*, s 105(1).
30 *Ibid*, s 24(1).
31 *Ibid*, s 67.
32 *Ibid*, s 68(1).
33 *Ibid*, as set out in paras (a) to (h) of s 68(2).
34 *Ibid*, s 68(2). *Cf* the court's old power under Arbitration Act 1950, s 23, to set aside an arbitrator's award on the ground of misconduct by the arbitrator. Misconduct covers any prejudicial irregularity or breach of the rules of natural justice in the course of the hearing. For example, in *Henry Sotheran Ltd v Norwich Union Life Insurance Society* [1992] 2 EGLR 9 (QB), it was held to be misconduct sufficient to set aside the award where the arbitrator issued directions for written representations and refused to hear oral evidence as requested by the tenants. This would now appear to rank as a "serious irregularity" within Arbitration Act 1996, s 68(2).

Unless the parties agree otherwise, the court may determine a question of law arising in the course of the arbitral proceedings which the court is satisfied substantially affects the rights of one or more of the parties[35]; but the application will not be considered unless it is either made with the agreement of all parties, or with the permission of the arbitrator and (in the latter case) if the court is satisfied that there are likely to be substantial savings in costs, and that the application was made without delay.[36]

Unless the parties agree otherwise, a party may appeal from the arbitrator to the court on a question of law[37], but (unless the parties agree) only with the court's leave.[38] The court is not to grant leave unless it is satisfied that the determination of the question will "substantially affect" the rights of one or more of the parties[39]; that the question was one which the arbitrator was asked to determine[40]; that the decision of the tribunal is "obviously wrong" or that the question is one of general public importance and the decision of the tribunal is "at least open to serious doubt"[41]; and that it is "just and proper in all the circumstances for the court to determine the question."[42]

Judicial control of independent experts

The basis on which the courts will intervene where there is a provision to refer a dispute to an independent expert is far less clear.[43] The decisions on this matter[44] were reviewed recently by Lightman J in *British Shipbuilders* v *VSEL Consortium plc*[45], who extracted from them five principles:

> (1) The terms of reference to an independent expert are essentially contractual between the parties, so that whether the independent expert has sole jurisdiction, exclusive of the courts, is a matter to be determined from the referral clause.

---

35 *Ibid*, s 45(1).

36 *Ibid*, s 45(2).

37 *Ibid*, s 69(1).

38 *Ibid*, s 69(2).

39 *Ibid*, s 69(3)(a).

40 *Ibid*, s 69(3)(b).

41 *Ibid*, s 69(3)(c)(i)(ii). This appears to be a statutory embodiment of the judicial principles enunciated in *The Nema* [1982] AC 742, which were applied in the context of rent review in *Ipswich BC* v *Fisons plc* [1990] 1 All ER 731 (CA), where Lord Donaldson MR said that there had to be strong *prima facie* evidence for believing that the arbitrator had erred on a point of law.

42 *Ibid*, s 69(3)(d).

43 See Gaunt & Cheffings, "Final and binding?" [1997] 3 EG 128.

44 *Jones* v *Sherwood Computer Services* [1992] 1 WLR 277, *Norwich Union Life Assurance Society* v *P & O Property Holdings Ltd* [1993] 1 EGLR 164 (CA), *Mercury Communications Ltd* v *Director General of Telecommunications* [1996] 1 WLR 48 (HL).

45 [1997] 1 Lloyd's Rep 106.

(2) If the clause states that the independent expert's finding is to be final and exclusive of the courts' jurisdiction, the courts have no ground to intervene (subject to 3 and 4 below) even though there may be strong evidence that the finding is bad.

(3) A finding by an independent expert outside the terms of his remit may be set aside by the court as the parties have never contracted for this.

(4) Where the remit makes the finding of the independent expert final and binding subject only to "manifest error" (wording frequently used in service charges clauses), the courts may intervene if there is evidence of such error.

(5) The courts have jurisdiction to determine in advance the limits and terms of the remit to the independent expert, although in practice they will be reluctant to do so as this is "hypothetical" litigation which anticipates an error by the expert.

Issue estoppel

A judgment of a court on the construction of a rent-review clause on grounds which are subsequently overruled by the Court of Appeal will not preclude an application to the court on a subsequent review under the same clause on the ground that the issue has already been tried.[46] Similarly, in *British Railways Board v Ringbest Ltd*[47], Sir Richard Scott V-C, in refusing leave to a tenant to appeal against an arbitrator's award, nevertheless held that this should not preclude the tenant from appealing to the court for a ruling on an interpretation of the clause on a subsequent rent review. The Vice-Chancellor said that it would be unsatisfactory if the arbitrator's ruling on the first rent review were to govern all future rent reviews during the 125-year lease.

Interim rent pending determination of a new rent

Commencement of revised rent

The rent-review clause should provide for the revised rent to be made payable from the review date, even though no final determination of it may be made for some time after this. From a tenant's point of view, it may be desirable to argue that any increase in the rent shall be recoverable only for a limit of one year from the rent-review date. In any event, provision should be made for the existing rent to be paid during any interim period.[48]

---

46 *Arnold v National Westminster Bank plc* [1978] AC 904.
47 [1996] 2 EGLR 82.
48 See precedent set out *infra*.

Interest on rent payable from review date

If, as a result of review, the rent is increased, and the increase takes effect retrospectively to the review date, the tenant will have additional rent to pay in respect of the intervening period. The rent-review clause often provides for interest to be payable on such additional rent. It is advisable to make this calculable according to the base rate of a bank. If the rent-review clause provides for downward, as well as upward, rent review, the tenant should be able to recover any over-payment of rent, together with interest, as from the review date.

A clause dealing with back-payment of the revised rent and interest might be as follows:

> "If on the relevant rent review date the open market rent shall not have been agreed or determined as aforesaid the yearly rent reserved hereunder immediately before the relevant rent review date shall continue to be payable until the determination of the open market rent pursuant to [reference to clause containing rent review procedure] but so that immediately on demand after such determination the excess difference (if any) over the amount actually so reserved and the amount which would have been payable had the determination been made before the relevant rent review date shall be paid by the tenant to the landlord together with interest thereon at the rate specified herein and if not so paid shall be recoverable as rent in arrear."

Endorsement of review result on lease

The result of any rent review should be endorsed on the lease and signed by the landlord, the tenant and any surety. There will usually be a clause providing for this as follows:

> "Upon the determination of the rent payable after any rent review date a memorandum in the form required by the landlord recording the amount of such rent shall be endorsed on this lease and counterpart thereof and signed by or on behalf of the parties hereto."

Chapter 10

REPAIRS

INTRODUCTION

It is important to consider whether a landlord or a tenant should undertake the liability for repairs; in the absence of any covenants to repair, the obligations implied into a commercial lease are very few.[1]

The obligation to repair will be a matter for negotiation if the premises to be let are a single unit, although in practice it is usual for the landlord to require the tenant to repair and to redecorate. The covenant for redecoration usually requires outside painting to be carried out every three years and interior painting every five or seven years and in any event during the last year of the term. Such a covenant by the tenant would read:

> "To paint the outside wood iron and other work of the demised premises with two coats at least of good quality paint in a proper and workmanlike manner once in every third year of the term and also during the last year thereof;
> To paint all the inside wood iron and other work and the walls and ceilings inside the demised premises with at least two coats of a good quality paint in a proper and workmanlike manner once in every five years of the term and also during the last year thereof."

If the premises are a unit in a larger building (or estate) then it is usual to provide for the tenant to undertake repairs to the unit which is exclusively demised to him and for the landlord to undertake repairs to the structure and common parts. The unit will usually be referred to as "the demised premises" and it then becomes important to know the extent of the demise.[2] The landlord's expenditure in this respect will be recoverable from the tenant as part of the service charges.[3]

An example of a short form of repairing covenant relating to the interior of the unit by the tenant would be:

---

1 On repairs generally, see Dowding and Reynolds, *Dilapidations,* 1st ed (1995) Sweet & Maxwell.
2 See Chap 3 (the parcels).
3 See Chap 11.

"At all times during the said term to keep in good repair and condition the interior of the premises (including all windows and window frames doors and door frames) and the interior surfaces of all ceilings walls and floors and the conduits exclusively serving the premises in good and substantial repair (damage by the insured risks excepted) and in a clean and tidy condition and to renew or replace such parts thereof as may be necessary and to decorate in a good and workmanlike manner with good quality materials the interior at least once in every five years during the term and in any event during the last year of the term."

A landlord's covenant relating to the main structure and exterior of the building might be:

"To keep in repair the structure of the Building including the roof and all external and load bearing walls the outer faces of all walls enclosing the Building and the outer walls separating [the unit] from any access corridor the foundations and main beams of the Building and common parts and all pipes wires drains party walls sewers channels sanitary apparatus passages stairways entrance ways and other things used or capable of being used in common."

It is important that a realistic estimate of the cost of repairs over the period of the lease be made and a proportionate annual charge included in the service charge, as any sudden increase in service charges may not be permitted in a new lease under the 1954 Act.[4]

It is proposed to consider in this chapter the effect of different wording found in repairing covenants, the scope of repairing covenants, and the remedies available to both the landlord and the tenant for breach of a repairing covenant by the other. Before doing so, however, it is pertinent to mention such implied obligations on the landlord and the tenant as there are under common law or statute.

Landlord's implied repairing obligations

Although statute law implies many repairing obligations on the part of a landlord of a dwellinghouse, there is no corresponding legislation with regard to commercial premises. However, it is probable that certain repairing obligations imposed in case law relating to dwellinghouses would also be held to apply to business premises.

In *Liverpool City Council* v *Irwin*[5] the House of Lords held that the Council, which was the landlord of a block of flats, was under a duty to take reasonable care to maintain the stairs, lifts, lighting and rubbish chutes, all of which were essential to the enjoyment of the flats. Without

_____
4 See Chaps 11 and 15.
5 [1977] AC 239.

the implication of these duties, the leases lacked business efficacy. It should be noticed, however, that the obligation was not an absolute one to maintain in any event, but merely to take reasonable care to do so. In that case, it was found as a fact that the disrepair was caused by vandals and the landlord had discharged its duty of care.

This obligation appears to have been extended beyond purely necessary rights of access in *King* v *South Northamptonshire District Council*[6]. There the Court of Appeal held that there was an implied obligation on the part of the landlord to maintain an access way to the rear of a terrace of houses which was important to their enjoyment and intended to be used by their occupants. The court indicated however that the layout of the terraces on the estate was a significant factor in this case.

In *Barrett* v *Lounova (1982) Ltd*[7], the tenant had covenanted to repair the interior of the demised premises but there was no provision in the lease for external repairs. The exterior was in such a bad state of repair, however, that the roof leaked so that it was impossible for the tenant to comply with her covenant. The court held that the tenant's covenant implied an obligation on the part of the landlord to repair the exterior, such an implication being necessary to give business efficacy to the tenant's covenant.

In *Gordon* v *Selico Co Ltd*[8] damage to a tenant's flat (including dry rot) resulted from water escaping from the common parts of a building which the landlord was liable to repair. But for an exclusion clause in the lease, the judge at first instance would have been prepared to hold the landlord liable for breach of an implied obligation to keep the retained parts in proper repair for the protection of the demised premises, and also in nuisance.

The Defective Premises Act 1972[9], makes a landlord liable for injury to a person, or their property, due to the defective state of premises, if he has a right to enter and repair the premises, or is under an obligation to repair them, and knows of the want of repair. The liability is to the tenant as well as to visitors to the premises[10]. This liability would always seem to apply in the case of a weekly tenancy[11]. Although these cases and the statute apply principally to dwellinghouses, it is conceivable that they could also apply to certain business premises. Statutory liability for business premises is more likely to arise under the Health and Safety at Work Act 1974, which imposes obligations on a person in control of business premises to take

---

6 [1992] 1 EGLR 53 (CA).
7 [1990] 1 QB 348.
8 [1985] 2 EGLR 79 (CA), affirming, with variations, [1985] 2 EGLR 79 (Goulding J).
9 Defective Premises Act 1972, s 4(1).
10 *Smith* v *Bradford Metropolitan Council* (1982) 44 P & CR 171.
11 *McCauley* v *Bristol City Council* [1991] 2 EGLR 64.

reasonable care to ensure that there are adequate and safe means of access to and egress from the premises and that any plant and machinery on the premises are safe.

It is an actionable nuisance under the Environmental Protection Act 1990 (which applies to residential and commercial premises) where premises constitute a statutory nuisance or are prejudicial to health by reason of any matters set out in section 79, or constitute a statutory nuisance under any other statutory enactment. The matters referred to in the section include the state of the premises (such as defective wiring), emissions from the premises or accumulations on them, and smells or noises from them. A local authority must investigate a complaint about premises made by anyone and serve an abatement notice under section 80 requiring work to be carried out to remedy any statutory nuisance.[12] Non-compliance with this is punishable by a fine.

Tenant's implied repairing obligations

There are no obligations to repair as such implied on the part of the tenant but he is liable for waste. Different types of waste apply to different kinds of tenants. The most heinous kind of waste is voluntary waste, which consists of acts of wanton destruction, and all tenants, whatever their term, are liable for this. Permissive waste is damage caused by neglect or a failure to act, and tenants for a fixed term and most periodic tenants are liable for this, although not weekly tenants. All tenants, including weekly tenants, are liable however to use the demised premises in a tenant-like manner. This liability was described by Denning LJ in *Warren v Keen*[13] by reference to a number of homely illustrations such as cleaning the chimneys and the windows, mending fused lights and unblocking the sink. It is, in short, the old fashioned requirement of "good husbandry".

A case where there was liability for waste with regard to holes in a wall owing to fixtures having been removed is *Mancetter Developments Ltd v Garmanson Ltd*.[14] The damage was caused by a company which was not an assignee of the lease, so that it was not liable on the covenants in the lease. The company was also insolvent, but the court was able to find its sole active director personally liable in the tort of waste.

The effect of different repairing covenants

Like any other covenant, a repairing covenant will fall to be interpreted on

---

12 The notice will not be valid unless it specifies the want of repair and the work necessary to remedy it: *Kirklees Metropolitan BC v Field* [1997] EGCS 151.

13 [1954] 1 QB 15.

14 [1986] QB 1212. The case is discussed at length in Chap 7.

its own particular wording. The court will, as a general principle of construction, try to give a meaning to each word in a repairing covenant according to the context in which it appears. Many repairing covenants are, however, drafted in a style which has been called 'torrential'[15], in that they contain many different words to describe what is essentially the same thing. Where torrential drafting has been used, some judges adopt a broad brush approach to the covenant as a whole, and treat some of the words as merely repetitive or synonymous.[16]

The most usual form of covenant will be **"to maintain and repair."** There may be variations on this, however, such as **"to yield up the premises in good repair."** This latter form merely requires that the premises should be in good repair at the termination of the tenancy, and imposes no duty to repair during the term itself; unless the scope of the covenant is widened by other words, the landlord will have no right to serve a notice of dilapidations in respect of such a covenant until the end of the tenancy. If the covenant is to yield up in good repair **"at the expiration of the term"**, it may not apply to a yielding up of a tenancy which has been statutorily continued under the Landlord and Tenant Act 1954.[17] To overcome this potential lacuna, the draftsman should add **"or of any statutory continuation thereof."**

The wording **"to put into repair"** may import something more than mere maintenance; it may impose a liability to put into repair something which is in a state of disrepair at the time of the lease. It is possible that this may be implied in any event from a straight repairing covenant if the property is in a bad state of repair at the commencement of the lease.[18] An obligation to put premises in repair that is to be performed upon the tenant taking possession of the premises or within a reasonable time thereafter is not subject to the Leasehold Property (Repairs) Act 1938.[19]

In the context of a repairing covenant, an obligation **"to replace"** will be presumed to be limited to a duty to carry out works of replacement which can in totality be properly described as repairs. Nevertheless, a repairing covenant which contains an express covenant to replace may suggest that "repair" is to import a wider obligation than would be imposed by a covenant merely **"to maintain and repair."** In *Elite Investments Ltd* v *TI Bainbridge Silencers Ltd*[20], the tenant had

---

15 *Norwich Union Life Assurance Society Ltd* v *British Railways Board* [1987] 2 EGLR 137 (Hoffmann J).

16 See *Crédit Suisse* v *Beegas Nominees Ltd* (1995) 69 P & CR 177.

17 *i.e.* on the principle of *City of London Corporation* v *Fell* [1994] 1 AC 458 (HL); see Dowding and Reynolds, *Dilapidations*, 1st ed (1995) Sweet & Maxwell, at para 11-05(b).

18 *Proudfoot* v *Hart* (1890) 25 QBD 42.

19 LP(R)A 1938, s 3.

20 [1986] 2 EGLR 43.

covenanted to "repair [and] replace ... the roof" of the demised premises, which comprised a unit in a large industrial building. The roof had been deteriorating and was in a bad state of repair when the premises were leased. Whilst the court accepted that a renewal or replacement of substantially the whole subject-matter of the demise could not properly be described as repairs[21], the court found that, although the new roof would be very different, being made of the better materials that were then on the market, it would not really alter the basic structure of what was quite a simple building. The replacement of the roof was therefore held to fall within the scope of the repairing covenant.

In *Crédit Suisse* v *Beegas Nominees Ltd*[22] a repairing covenant by the landlord which included the words **"amend"** and **"renew"** and referred to making good any **"defect"** or want of repair was held to be wider than a mere repairing covenant, so that the landlord was liable to replace defective cladding on the walls of a building which had let in water.

Similarly in *New England Properties* v *Portsmouth New Shops*[23], a covenant to **"renew and replace"** required the replacement of a badly designed roof with a 22.5 degree pitch which had let in water with a 30 degree pitched roof, the cost of this being not substantially more than the cost of repairing the existing roof. The judge in this case felt that the work was nevertheless very near to being an "improvement" outside the scope of the repairing covenant, and in *Holding & Management Ltd* v *Property Holding & Investment Trust plc*[24] the Court of Appeal held that a replacement cladding on the exterior walls of a building, which was much more expensive than an inferior repairing scheme, would have been an improvement and not within the scope of a repairing covenant.

A fault caused by a bad design will not necessarily fall within the scope of a repairing covenant. In *Post Office* v *Aquarius Properties*[25] a design fault caused flooding to the basement area of a building, but the flooding had not caused any actual damage to the building. The Court of Appeal applied *Quick* v *Taff-Ely BC*[26] and held that as there was no deterioration to the building itself, there was no breach of any repairing covenant.

A comprehensive form of a tenant's repairing covenant from a landlord's point of view would be:

21 *Elite Investments Ltd* v *T I Bainbridge Silencers Ltd* [1986] 2 EGLR 43, 47, applying *Brew Bros Ltd* v *Snax (Ross) Ltd* [1970] 1 QB 612 (CA).
22 (1995) 69 P & CR 177.
23 (1993) 67 P & CR 141.
24 [1990] 1 EGLR 65.
25 [1987] 1 All ER 1055.
26 [1986] QB 809. This was a case on Landlord and Tenant Act 1985, s 11(1), where it was held that the landlord was not liable under the repairing covenant implied by the statute to repair metal window frames which were causing condensation, as the frames themselves were not in disrepair.

"To put and keep the whole of the demised premises in good and substantial repair and condition (damage by any insured risk excepted unless and to the extent that any act or omission of the tenant renders the insurance money irrecoverable) and to yield up the same (and all fixtures annexed thereto) in such good and substantial repair and condition to the landlord on the termination of the term hereby granted however determined."

In *British Telecom plc v Sun Life Assurance Society plc*[27], Nourse LJ, with whose judgment the other two members of the Court of Appeal agreed, said that the general rule is that a covenant "to keep in repair" obliges the covenantor to keep the demised premises in repair at all times[28], so that there is a breach of the obligation immediately a defect occurs. Nourse LJ said that there is an exception where the obligation is the landlord's and the defect occurs in the demised premises themselves, in which case the landlord is in breach of his obligation only when he has information about the existence of the defect such as would put a reasonable landlord on inquiry as to whether works of repair are needed and he has failed to carry out the necessary works with reasonable expedition thereafter.[29]

Nourse LJ declined to express a view as to whether the position might be different if the covenant were merely one "to repair."[30] There would appear to be good grounds for drawing such a distinction. A covenant "to repair" means "to put into repair"[31]; such a covenant imposes merely an obligation to carry out the work of repair. It is therefore not breached until a reasonable time has elapsed for the repairs to be carried out. In contrast to that, a covenant "to keep in repair" imposes an obligation in relation to the state in which the premises are to be kept; so that, unless it is a landlord's covenant to keep the demised premises themselves in repair[32], it is breached as soon as the premises fall into disrepair.

Standard of repair under a repairing covenant

The standard of repair depends upon the construction of the particular covenant, but the general standard of an unqualified covenant merely "to repair" is to keep the premises in substantial repair; a perfect state of repair

---

27 [1995] 4 All ER 44, 51–52.
28 See *Bishop v Consolidated London Property Ltd* (1933) LJKB 257 (where a dead pigeon lodged in a pipe caused water to overflow in the tenant's flat).
29 *British Telecom plc v Sun Life Assurance Society plc* [1995] 4 All ER 44, 52. The rule which Nourse LJ describes as being in fact an exception to the general rule, was laid down in *O'Brien v Robinson* [1973] AC 912 (HL) (discussed later in this chapter).
30 *British Telecom plc v Sun Life Assurance Society plc* [1995] 4 All ER 44, 52.
31 See Aldous J at first instance in *British Telecom plc v Sun Life Assurance Society plc* [1994] 2 EGLR 66, 67.
32 *i.e.* within the exception contained in *O'Brien v Robinson* [1973] AC 912 (HL).

is not required. A minute crack in a pane of glass[33] or a nail knocked into a wall[34] may not prevent the premises being in substantial repair. The standard of repair may be modified by qualifying words. It seems, however, that the specification of "excellent repair", "good repair"[35], "sufficient repair"[36], "substantial repair"[37], "habitable repair"[38] or "tenantable repair"[39], or a covenant "well and substantially" to repair, add nothing to the standard of repair required under a repairing covenant.

Sometimes a repairing covenant will add a proviso that "fair wear and tear" is to be excepted from the repairing liability. It was held in *Regis Property Co. Ltd v Dudley*[40] that the exception covers damage caused by natural deterioration from weather and normal usage, assuming that the tenant uses the premises in a tenant-like manner. It will not cover damage caused by the negligence of the tenant or his visitors, and nor will it cover damage resulting from the original want of repair which fell within the exception. So Lord Denning in *Regis Property Co. Ltd* said:

> "If a slate falls off through wear and tear and in consequence the roof is likely to let through the water, the tenant is not responsible for the slate coming off, but he ought to put in another one to prevent further damage."

Lewison advises landlords to resist a "fair wear and tear" qualification, as it tends to lead to disputes over dilapidations at the end of the lease.[41]

The test to be applied to the standard of repair required by a repairing covenant was laid down in *Proudfoot v Hart*.[42] The premises should be in such a state of repair as would be acceptable to a reasonably minded tenant, bearing in mind their age[43] and character and their locality at the date of letting. This was followed in *Anstruther-Gough-Calthorpe v McOscar*[44], where it was held that the standard of repair should be judged according to the neighbourhood at the date of the lease and not some 95 years later. In *Ladbroke Hotels Ltd v Sandhuand Singh*[45] the court applied this principle to a repairing covenant where a tenant argued (unsuccessfully) that it should be liable to repair a badly constructed building only for its "commercial life" and not for its "intended life". Robert Walker J accepted that the

---

33 *Stanley v Towgood* (1836) 3 Bing NC 4.
34 *Perry v Chotzner* (1893) 9 TLR 477.
35 *Payne v Haine* (1847) 16 M & W 541.
36 *Anstruther-Gough-Calthorpe v McOscar* [1924] 1 KB 716.
37 *Clowes v Bentley Pty Ltd* [1970] WAR 24.
38 *Belcher v Mackintosh* (1839) 2 Moo & R 186.
39 *Proudfoot v Hart* (1890) 25 QBD 42.
40 [1959] AC 370 (HL).
41 Lewison, *Drafting Business Leases*, 5th ed (1996) FT Law & Tax, at 193.
42 (1890) 25 QBD 42.
43 *Plough Investments Ltd v Manchester City Council* [1989] 1 EGLR 244.
44 [1924] 1 KB 716.
45 (1996) 72 P & CR 498.

commercial life of some buildings, such as a cinema, a supermarket or (as in this case) a motel, might be shorter than their intended lives as buildings, as they could become outdated. He held, however, that it was the building's intended life which the parties had in mind at the commencement of the lease, and the standard of repair should be judged with this period in mind. The difference in cost in this case was marked: it would cost £500,000 to effect repairs that would last for the building's "intended life" (some 60 years), but only £60,000 to effect repairs that would last for the building's "commercial life" (another 15 years only).

As the date of the lease is the relevant date, it is possible that a sub-lease with an identical repairing covenant to that contained in the head-lease may nevertheless impose a different standard of repair. This might occur if, for example, the sub-lease is granted a number of years after the head-lease, and the nature of the locality has changed in the intervening period.

Scope of a repairing covenant

The wording of the repairing covenant will be primarily relevant in indicating the extent of the liability. If the premises leased are a single unit, then the tenant will probably have covenanted to repair and maintain the whole of it. It would be prudent to consider whether the tenant is also intended to maintain any access to the premises and services, such as drainage, water and electricity supplies. If these supply the premises exclusively, then the landlord will want to make the tenant alone liable for these, but if they are shared with other premises, then the tenant should pay a proportionate part. Covenants should be taken from the tenant to reflect these liabilities. The tenant might covenant:

> "to contribute a fair proportion according to use of the cost of repairing maintaining cleansing and renewing all party walls party structures and yards gardens ways sewers drains pipes conduits and wires used by the occupier of the demised premises in common with the occupier of any other property such fair proportion to be determined by the landlord's surveyor whose decision shall be final and binding on the parties."

If the demised premises are a unit in a larger building, the usual repairing arrangements are that the tenant will repair and maintain the premises which are exclusively demised to him while the landlord will repair and maintain the structure, exterior and common parts, recovering the cost of this from all the tenants proportionately as part of the service charges.[46] If this arrangement is adopted, it is very important to define as clearly as possible the extent of the demised premises for which the tenant is solely

---

46 See pp 273–274 *infra*.

responsible, and what is meant by **"structure"** and **"exterior"** for which the landlord is responsible. The lease should therefore specify whether the walls of the unit are within the demise and to be maintained by the tenant, whether they are party walls with an adjoining unit to be maintained by two tenants jointly, or whether they are part of the structure of the building to be maintained by the landlord. Ordinary windows are not walls or part of the walls; but very large windows may effectively comprise the walls.[47] If the repairing obligations are divided between the parties according to whether they relate to the exterior or the interior, it is important to clarify whether the window panes and frames are internal or external features.[48] In *Brown* v *Liverpool Corporation*[49] (which concerned a residential landlord's implied obligation to repair the structure and exterior of premises[50]), it was held that steps giving essential access to the front of a property were part of the exterior.

The term "structure" does not have any precise legal definition, but in *Irvine* v *Moran*[51] Forbes QC thought that the structure of a dwellinghouse referred to in the Housing Act 1961, section 32, meant "those elements of the overall dwellinghouse which give it its essential appearance, stability and shape", excluding fittings, equipment and decoration, but not confined to outside and load-bearing walls, roof and foundations. In *Boswell* v *Crucible Steel Co of America*[52], large plate-glass windows that could not be opened, and which comprised most of the frontage of the ground floor of premises comprising a warehouse and offices, were held to form a part of the structure.

Repair or renewal

A further problem which has given rise to litigation is the difficulty of deciding whether any particular work is a "repair", or whether it is so extensive as to amount to the construction of something new which is therefore outside the scope of a usual repairing covenant.[53] In *McDougall* v *Easington DC*[54] the Court of Appeal reviewed the decisions on what was within the scope of a "repair" and identified three different criteria which

---

47 See *Holiday Fellowship Ltd* v *Hereford* [1959] 1 WLR 211, where Romer LJ points out that the walls of the old Crystal Palace (destroyed by fire in 1936) were made of glass; the issue is of more general importance given the extensive use of glass in many modern buildings.
48 *Reston Ltd* v *Hudson* [1990] 2 EGLR 51 (Ch D).
49 [1969] 3 All ER 1345.
50 Under what is now Landlord and Tenant Act 1985, s 11, replacing Housing Act 1961, s 32.
51 [1991] 1 EGLR 261.
52 [1925] 1 KB 119 (CA).
53 See Smith, "Repairs: a new set of problems", [1990] Conv 335.
54 [1989] 1 EGLR 93.

the courts have applied. These are:

(i) The extent of the renewal

Although all repair involves renewal, it should only be renewal of subsidiary parts and not of the whole. Thus, in *Torrens v Walker*[55] the rebuilding of the front and back walls of a house which had been demolished was held to be outside the scope of a repairing covenant.

(ii) The character of the work

This concerns whether the work carried out would produce something quite different from the demised premises as originally let. In *Halliard Property Co Ltd v Nicholas Clarke Investments Ltd*[56], a tenant who had covenanted to repair was not liable to rebuild an unstable, jerry-built shed at the rear of the premises, as the new building which would have been erected in its place would have been entirely different from that included in the demise.

Work in correcting an inherent defect or a design fault is not work of repair in itself. In *Post Office v Aquarius Properties Ltd*[57] it was held that a tenant was not liable under a repairing covenant to remedy a structural defect whereby a porous concrete floor in a basement allowed seepage which caused flooding. The presence of water on the floor caused the tenant inconvenience, but no damage had been shown to have been caused (*e.g.* to the plaster on the walls, or to floor, or to electric wiring); but work in repairing any resulting damage (including the correction of the defect itself) can sometimes rank as works of repair. There is, however, no rule of law that work to remedy an inherent defect can never be a repair. If damage does result from the defect, it is a matter of degree whether the remedial work involved (including the correction of the defect) would result in the landlord getting back a wholly different thing from that demised.[58] If it would not, even the work of putting the defect right is repair.[59] Therefore, before entering into a lease which imposes upon him an obligation to repair, a tenant should try to negotiate an exclusion of liability to pay for the cost of repairs so far as they are attributable to an inherent defect.

(iii) The relative cost of the work

The third criterion is the relative cost of the work to the cost of constructing an entirely new building, the value of the building after the

---

55 [1906] 2 Ch 166.
56 [1984] 1 EGLR 45 (QB).
57 [1987] 1 All ER 1055; noted Smith, "Inherent defects again?", [1987] Conv 224.
58 *Ravenseft Properties Ltd v Davstone (Holdings) Ltd* [1980] QB 12.
59 *Ibid*; and see *Minja Properties Ltd v Cussins Property Group plc* [1998] EGCS 23 (Harman J).

work has been carried out, and the effect of the work on its lifespan. In *Ravenseft Properties Ltd v Davstone (Holdings) Ltd*[60] a building in Kensington High Street had been constructed without expansion joints, as a result of which extensive structural work was required to prevent stone cladding from falling away from the facade. The cost of building a structure of this kind on the same site would have been about £3 million; whereas the cost of putting in the expansion joints was less than 2% of that figure (only £55,000). The work was therefore held to be within the scope of the tenants' repairing covenants.

On the other hand, in *Brew Bros v Snax (Ross) Ltd*[61] the cost of extensive work to the foundations of a building, the repair of drains and rebuilding of a wall, would have cost nearly £8,000, which was about the same as the value of the building after the works had been done, and not far short of the cost of a putting up a new building (£9,000–£10,000). It was therefore held that such work was outside the scope of a repairing covenant. In *McDougall v Easington DC*[62] itself, the landlord replaced a flat roof of a house with a pitched one, altering the front and rear elevations, and replaced door and window frames. The work cost £11,000, which was slightly more than the value of the house immediately before the work was carried out, and the effect of the work was to increase the market value of the house by 80% and to prolong its life by some 30%. This work was held to amount to renewal and to be too extensive to fall within the scope of the repairing covenant.

In *Elite Investments Ltd v TI Bainbridge Silencers Ltd*[63] it was held that when there was a sizeable difference between the value of the building after the repair and the cost of a comparable new building, it was the latter figure which should be compared with the cost of the repairs as a guide to whether the landlord would be getting back something different from what he had demised. In that case, the cost of the new roof would be just over £84,000, which was well over half the value that the building would have after the work had been carried out (some £140,000–£150,000). The cost of a new building, however, would be nearly £1 million, which was many times the cost of replacing the roof. The work was therefore held to be within the repairing covenant.

There is no obligation under a repairing covenant to carry out work before there is any disrepair or damage which requires to be made good. In *Secretary of State for the Environment v Euston Centre Investments Ltd (No 2)*[64] the tenant's repairing covenant did not require it to remove

---

60 *Ibid.*
61 [1970] 1 QB 612.
62 [1989] 1 EGLR 93.
63 [1986] 2 EGLR 43.
64 [1994] EGCS 167 (Chadwick J).

asbestos from the building because, the premises not being out of repair, the asbestos had not yet become a danger.

Other maintenance

In addition to repairs, the parties should consider whether other related matters, such as landscaping, the erection and maintenance of signs and advertisements on an estate, the cleaning of windows, brickwork and drains and the replacement of electrical equipment, should be covenanted for. Obviously requirements will vary according to the premises and the user of them. However, a lease of a unit in a shopping precinct, for example, might well include covenants by the landlord to cover all these things. The cost would then be recoverable from the tenants as part of the service charge.

Notice of want of repair

A landlord's liability to repair the premises demised generally arises only when he receives notice of the want of repair. Whether the landlord has received sufficient notice will be a question of fact in each case, but two decisions may be contrasted by way of illustration. In *O'Brien* v *Robinson*[65] the tenants of a flat had complained in the course of court proceedings for rent some three years earlier that the ceiling of their flat shook badly when the tenants above were dancing in the course of riotous parties. This was held not to constitute sufficient notice to the landlord of a latent defect in the ceiling which subsequently caused it to collapse. On the other hand, in *Sheldon* v *West Bromwich Corporation*[66] a plumber employee of the Corporation was sent to investigate noises in the tenant's water system and reported back that there was rust in the water tank. This was held to be sufficient notice of the want of repair to make the landlord liable for the subsequent damage when the water tank burst.

The Defective Premises Act 1972[67], imposes on landlords who are obliged to repair the premises a statutory liability for personal injury or damage to property caused by a defect in the premises arising (*inter alia*) from the landlord's failure to repair, but only if the landlord knows, or ought to have known, of the defect.[68] The landlord should therefore consider taking a covenant from the tenant to inform him of any such defect, which might be in the following form:

"**Forthwith on becoming aware of the same, to give written notice to the**

---

65 [1973] AC 912 (HL).
66 (1973) 25 P&CR 360 (CA).
67 Defective Premises Act 1972, s 4(1); discussed *supra*.
68 *Ibid*, s 4(2).

landlord of any defect in the demised premises which might give rise to an obligation on the landlord to do or refrain from doing any act or thing so as to comply with the duty of care imposed on the landlord pursuant to the Defective Premises Act 1972, and to display and maintain in the demised premises all notices which the landlord may, from time to time, reasonably require to be displayed in relation thereto."

Disrepair in the landlord's retained parts

In *Loria v Hammer*[69] the tenant of one of four flats in a house carried out repairs to a leaking roof which was causing damage and sought to recover the cost from the landlord. The landlord, who had covenanted to keep the roof (*inter alia*) in repair, pleaded that he had not received notice of the defect. The court held, however, that want of notice was irrelevant where the landlord's covenant was to keep in repair (which did not itself require notice to be given) and where the disrepair related to the common parts of a building retained by him. In this case, moreover, the landlord was unable to recover the cost of repairing the ensuing damage to the tenant's flat by an increase in the service charge (which covered repairs to the common parts) as to allow him to do so would have been to allow him to recover the costs resulting from his own wrong-doing. The court did, however, recognise that, if the common parts retained by the landlord could be reached only through the tenant's premises, some time might be needed for the landlord (in order to avoid trespass) to give notice to the tenant and to gain access to inspect and repair the retained part.[70]

The principle in *Loria v Hammer* is that a landlord is in breach of a covenant "to keep in repair" from the moment the disrepair occurs (not from the date that he receives notice of it or from a reasonable time thereafter) if the disrepair is in the landlord's retained part. This principle, which is very harsh on the landlord, was confirmed by the Court of Appeal in *British Telecom plc v Sun Life Assurance Society plc*[71], which treated *O'Brien v Robinson*[72] as applicable only to a landlord's covenant to repair the premises demised. In the light of these cases, a landlord covenanting to "keep premises in repair" should insist that it is expressly qualified so that the duty in respect of the common parts is imposed only upon his receiving written notice from the tenant. From the landlord's point of view, it is also desirable that there should be a covenant by the tenant to notify the landlord of any want of repair to the common parts of which the tenant becomes aware. This might comprise a covenant by the tenant:

---

69 [1989] 2 EGLR 249 (Ch D).
70 *Ibid*, at 258.
71 [1995] 4 All ER 44.
72 [1973] AC 912 (discussed *supra*).

"to give notice in writing to the landlord as soon as possible of any want of repair or defect in any common part of the building retained by the landlord and in any pipes conduits or services which the landlord is liable hereunder to maintain or repair."

A further precaution would be for the landlord or his agent to carry out periodical inspections.

Landlord's right to enter and view the state of repair

Whenever a landlord is responsible for repairs to demised premises, there is a right implied at common law that the tenant will allow him to enter and view the state of repair. This applies whether the obligation to repair arises at common law or by statute. The rationale for this was explained by Somervell LJ in *Mint* v *Good*[73] (in relation to a weekly tenancy) as being a right necessary to give business efficacy to the agreement.

Where the tenant covenants to repair the demised premises, it is usual for him to covenant also to allow the landlord to enter to view the state of repair and to make good any want of repair if the tenant fails to do so. A typical covenant of this type would be:

"To permit the landlord to enter the premises for the purposes of examining the state and condition thereof the tenant forthwith making good any defects in the same which are the responsibility of the tenant hereunder in accordance with a notice to that effect given by the landlord, and in default the landlord shall be entitled to make good any such defects and charge the cost thereof to the tenant."

LANDLORD'S REMEDIES FOR BREACH OF A TENANT'S REPAIRING COVENANT

A landlord may serve a schedule of dilapidations on a tenant specifying the repairs which he alleges are required to comply with a tenant's repairing covenant.[74] The schedule should be drawn up by a surveyor and, if a section 146 notice is to be served, the schedule should be attached to it. A landlord has various remedies for breach of a tenant's repairing covenant, but in most cases they are restricted by statute.

Damages for breach of covenant

The breach of a repairing covenant is in effect a breach of contract for

---

73 [1951] 1 KB 517.
74 See p 257 *infra*.

which the tenant is liable to the landlord in damages. The damages are limited however by the Landlord and Tenant Act 1927, section 18(1), which provides that the damages shall not exceed the diminution in value of the reversion as a consequence of the disrepair. It follows from this that if the property is to be demolished or developed, damages may not be recoverable at all. Where a sub-tenant will be entitled to a new lease under the Landlord and Tenant Act 1954 and the open market rent is to be fixed with disregard to the state of repair, the value of the head-lessor's reversion may not be diminished, and he may not therefore be able to claim damages from his immediate tenant.[75] However, in *Crown Estate Commissioners* v *Town Investments Ltd*[76] the tenant had sub-let parts of the premises to sub-lessees, whose repairing covenants were less onerous than the tenant's in that they were not responsible for external repairs, and other parts of the premises were vacant. The Official Referee ruled that it was open to the landlord to bring evidence of non-correspondence on the repairing covenants in the sub-leases, the less onerous repairing covenants of which could cause a diminution in the value of the reversion.

An ingenious argument on section 18(1) for reducing damages for breach of a repairing covenant was put forward by the tenant in *Shortlands Investments Ltd* v *Cargill plc.*[77] The tenant was a sub-tenant of part of business premises during the recession, and argued that it should not be liable to the landlord for damages for repairs at the end of the sub-lease as the landlord would probably have to pay a reverse premium as an inducement to any new tenant who would, in any event, have to fit out the premises for its own requirements. The court did not accept the argument, however, and held that the bad state of repair would be a bargaining point for any new tenant which would be reflected in the rent obtainable, and so awarded damages.

In the case of a lease of seven years or more with three years or more of the term unexpired, the Leasehold Property (Repairs) Act 1938 applies, and in order to claim damages for breach of a repairing covenant, the landlord must first comply with the procedure laid down in the Act.[78] It is not necessary to comply with the procedure, however, if the landlord has a right to enter and carry out repairs himself and to recover the cost as a contract debt.[79]

---

75 *Family Management* v *Gray* [1980] 1 EGLR 46 (CA).
76 [1992] 1 EGLR 61.
77 [1995] 1 EGLR 51.
78 Discussed p 322 *infra*.
79 See *infra*.

Forfeiture

A landlord may forfeit the lease for breach of a repairing covenant only if there is a proviso for forfeiture in the lease. Before commencing forfeiture proceedings, he must first serve a notice under the Law of Property Act 1925, section 146; and, if the lease is within the 1938 Act, the notice must inform the tenant of his right to serve a counter-notice under that Act.[80]

Because of the court's extensive powers to grant relief to a tenant against forfeiture, a well-drawn lease will include a covenant by the tenant to pay any costs incurred by the landlord in connection with the service of a section 146 notice and schedule of dilapidations, and a claim for such costs will still be good even though there is a requirement to comply with the 1938 Act. A usual covenant of this type would be:

> "To pay all costs (including solicitors' costs and surveyors' fees) incurred by the landlord for and incidental to the preparation and service of
> (a) a notice under S.146 of the Law of Property Act 1925 notwithstanding that forfeiture is avoided otherwise than by order of the court and
> (b) a schedule of dilapidations recording breaches of the tenant's covenant to keep and to yield up the demised premises in repair".

The court is empowered to make an award of relief from forfeiture conditional upon the tenant's having complied with a repairing covenant.[81] For further details of this procedure, see Chapter 13.

Decorative repairs

If the section 146 notice served by the landlord relates to internal decorative repairs, the Law of Property Act 1925, section 147, applies. This provides that the court may grant relief to the tenant if it is satisfied that the notice is unreasonable having regard to all the circumstances of the case, and in particular to the length of the term unexpired. The section does not apply:

(i) where there is a breach of an express covenant to put the premises into a decorative state of repair;

(ii) to any matter necessary or proper to keep the property in a sanitary condition;

(iii) to any matter necessary or proper to maintain or preserve the structure;

(iv) to any statutory liability to keep a house fit for habitation;

(v) to any covenant to yield up the premises in a specific state of repair at the end of the term.

---

80 Discussed further in Chap 13, pp 321–324.
81 *Shiloh Spinners Ltd v Harding* [1973] AC 691 (HL).

The section does not apply to a covenant to carry out exterior decoration.

Relief may be whole or partial, and it is usual for the court to grant relief on conditions.

Landlord's right to enter and carry out the repairs itself

The lease may reserve the right to the landlord to enter and carry out repairs if the tenant fails to do so, or there may be an implied right to do so under the common law or statute.[82] In *Saner v Bilton*[83] it was held that a covenant by a landlord to keep the structure of a warehouse in repair implied a licence by the tenant to permit the landlord entry for a reasonable time to carry out the necessary repairs.

If the demised premises are a unit in a building, then it will be necessary to reserve the right to the owners of neighbouring or adjoining premises also to enter to carry out repairs. The right of entry for the landlord and for the neighbouring owners to carry out repairs can be reserved in the same tenant's covenant as follows:

> "To permit the landlord its agents and workmen and the tenants and occupiers of any other parts of the Building or of any adjoining or neighbouring premises and their agents and workmen at any time during the term at reasonable hours in the daytime and upon prior notice (except in case of emergency when no notice need be given) to enter upon the demised premises for the purpose of inspecting and executing repairs or alterations of or upon such other parts of the Building or such other adjoining or neighbouring premises the persons exercising such rights making good all physical damage to the demised premises thereby occasioned."

The Court of Appeal held in *Jervis v Harris*[84] that if the lease additionally gives the landlord the right to recover the cost of the repairs as a contract debt, an action to recover such debt does not rank as a claim for damages, and the sum is therefore recoverable by the landlord without his having to invoke the procedure under the Leasehold Property (Repairs) Act 1938. From a landlord's point of view, it is therefore important that the lease provides expressly that the costs of any repairs which he has a right to carry out are recoverable as a contract debt.

The problems which can arise if a right to recover the cost of repairs is not reserved as a debt are illustrated by *SEDAC Investments Ltd v Tanner*.[85] The lessors had reserved a right to enter and carry out repairs themselves if the lessees failed to do so. They were informed by the lessees that fragments of stonework from the demised building were falling on to

82 See *supra*.
83 (1878) 7 Ch D 815.
84 [1996] 2 WLR 220.
85 [1982] 1 WLR 1342.

a pavement, and they therefore carried out the necessary repairs to stop the danger as a matter of urgency. Their solicitors subsequently served a section 146 notice on the lessees, who served a counter-notice under section 1(2) of the 1938 Act. It was held that the procedure clearly contemplated the breach of a repairing covenant not yet remedied. As no section 146 notice had been served in advance, the lessees had been deprived of their right to serve a counter-notice, which meant that the court had no jurisdiction to give leave to the lessors to proceed in an action for damages.

The other advantage of a right to enter and carry out repairs and to recover the cost as a contract debt is that the Landlord and Tenant Act 1927, section 18(1), will not apply to limit the sum to the diminution in value of the reversion as it does to a sum claimed as damages. A clause which states that the sum is to be recoverable as a debt rather than as damages is the following covenant by the tenant:

> "Upon failure to comply within one month (or such lesser time as is reasonable if the repairs are urgent) with a written request by the landlord to carry out the repairs specified therein (being repairs which the tenant has covenanted to carry out) to permit the Landlord to enter the demised premises with workmen and others to execute the works required to comply with such request and the cost thereof shall be a debt immediately payable by the tenant to the landlord".

Specific performance or mandatory injunction?

Until recently, it had been generally considered, on the authority of Lord Eldon LC in *Hill* v *Barclay*,[86] that a landlord cannot obtain an order for specific performance of a tenant's repairing covenant; and in *Jeune* v *Queen's Cross Properties Ltd*[87], Pennycuick V-C treated *Hill* v *Barclay* as authority for that proposition. Dowding and Reynolds[88] point out, however, that Lord Eldon's observations in *Hill* v *Barclay* were *obiter*, and were made at a time when equity was still evolving the circumstances in which its remedies might be made available. Those authors consider that in modern times a landlord should be able to obtain specific performance of a tenant's repairing covenant.[89] They opine that there can be no objection in principle to the specific performance of such covenants, since in recent years the courts have been willing to grant specific performance of a landlord's repairing covenant.[90] Furthermore, the landlord is able specifically to

86 (1810) 16 Ves Jun 402.
87 [1974] 1 Ch 97.
88 Dowding and Reynolds, *Dilapidations: the Modern Law* (1995) Sweet & Maxwell.
89 *Ibid*, para 22–03 (pp 556–559).
90 *Posner* v *Scott-Lewis* [1986] 3 All ER 513; contrast *Ryan* v *Mutual Tontine Westminster Chambers Association* [1893] 1 Ch 116.

enforce a tenant's building obligations.[91] A mandatory injunction has been suggested[92], and apparently used[93], as a means of achieving the same result. Thus in *Heard v Stuart*[94], Joyce J granted the landlord an injunction to compel the tenant, who had covenanted to keep the premises in repair, to restore a wall that had become damaged through being used for the display of advertisements. In the recent landmark decision of *Rainbow Estates Ltd v Tokenhold Ltd*[94a] the court considered the supposed objections to an order for specific performance of a tenant's repairing covenant to be outmoded, and that a modern law of remedies required that specific performance of such a covenant should be available in appropriate circumstances.

In *Co-operative Insurance Society Ltd v Argyll (Holdings) Ltd*[95], the House of Lords, whilst holding that a landlord could not obtain specific performance of a keep-open covenant, were careful to distinguish such an order, which would require the defendant to carry on an activity, from an order which requires the defendant to achieve a result. Specific performance of the former type of obligation will not be granted since it might involve the court in constant supervision; but such objection does not apply to the obligations of the latter type, which clearly include a covenant to repair. Specific performance will not be ordered, however, if the order cannot be drafted with sufficient precision. It is therefore important for the landlord to detail the works of repair required by means of a schedule of dilapidations prepared by a professional surveyor.

Specific performance is of course a discretionary remedy, and a tenant against whom such order were sought would be able to rely on the usual defences, including hardship and delay. Since specific performance is an equitable remedy, the court would presumably decline to make such an order to compel a tenant to repair if the landlord is himself in breach of another covenant in the lease:[96] he who comes to equity must come with clean hands. The court would similarly no doubt refuse an order for specific performance of a repairing covenant which would involve the tenant in massive expenditure near the end of the lease if there were evidence that the landlord intended to demolish the premises as soon as the lease expired. In the *Rainbow Estates* case, the judge cautioned that

---

91 *Wolverhampton Corporation v Emmons* [1901] 1 KB 505 (building contract).
92 *SEDAC Investments Ltd v Tanner* [1982] 1 WLR 1342.
93 *Redland Bricks Ltd v Morris* [1970] AC 652 (HL).
94 (1907) 24 TLR 104.
94a [1998] *The Times*, 12 March (Lawrence Collins QC, sitting as a deputy judge of the Chancery Division).
95 [1997] 3 All ER 297 (HL); see the speech of Lord Hoffmann. For further discussion of this case, see Chap 8.
96 *cf Walsh v Lonsdale* (1882) 21 Ch D 9.

the court should be astute to ensure that the landlord was not seeking the order as a means of oppressing the tenant. Although the Leasehold Property (Repairs) Act 1938 does not apply to a decree of specific performance, his Lordship was of the view that, in deciding whether to exercise its discretion to make such a decree, the court might take into account considerations similar to those specified in that statute. He also thought that it would be a rare case in which the remedy of specific performance would be the appropriate one. The case before him was exceptional because the lease contained no forfeiture clause and no term entitling the landlord to enter to carry out the repairs itself.

If the court does indeed now have jurisdiction to award specific performance of a tenant's repairing covenant, but were to refuse to award it in a particular case on discretionary grounds, it would be able to award damages in lieu.[97]

Tenant's Remedies for Breach of the Landlord's Repairing Covenants

Although an account is given here of the remedies which have been recognised as available to tenants for breach of their landlords' repairing covenants, it must be remembered that the suitability of the different remedies will vary with the circumstances, and in particular according to whether the property leased is a separate unit, or a unit in a building or on an estate.

Damages for breach of covenant

A tenant's damages for breach of a repairing covenant, like those for breach of a covenant for quiet enjoyment, are assessed on the normal contractual basis of foreseeability, even though there may be no privity of contract between the parties. In *Mira v Aylmer Square Investments Ltd*[98], the tenant, an assignee of a long lease of a flat, claimed damages for the reduced rent which he obtained on a sub-letting owing to construction works carried out by the landlord which caused noise and dirt and amounted to a breach of the landlord's implied covenant for quiet enjoyment. It was held that damages were recoverable as in contract under the first head of *Hadley v Baxendale*[99] even though there was no privity of contract between the

---

97 Supreme Court Act 1981, s 50, re-enacting the effect of s 2 of Chancery Amendment Act 1858 (Lord Cairns' Act).
98 [1990] 1 EGLR 45.
99 (1854) 9 Exch 341.

parties. The possibility of the rent on a sub-letting being reduced was damage which the landlord ought to have known was likely to occur as a result of the breach of covenant, as the lease was a long lease. If these principles are applied to business leases, where under-letting is extremely common, they suggest that a tenant could claim damages for a reduced rent obtainable on a sub-letting owing to a breach of repairing covenant.

Although the cases on a tenant's damages for breach of a repairing covenant mostly relate to dwellinghouses, some of the heads of damages would seem to be equally applicable to business premises.

In *Calabar Properties Ltd* v *Sticher*[1] the Court of Appeal held that the damages which a tenant of a dwellinghouse could recover for breach of a repairing covenant were for (*inter alia*) discomfort, loss of enjoyment and diminution in the market value. In addition, as regards business premises, if the premises have to be vacated, it might presumably be possible to recover damages for loss of business and goodwill, although it might be difficult to quantify the latter. In *McGreal* v *Wake*[2] damages were awarded for the cost of storage of furniture and the cost of temporary accommodation elsewhere while repairs were being carried out, and for making good decorations afterwards, and both of these heads would seem to be possibly applicable to business premises.

In *Crédit Suisse* v *Beegas Nominees Ltd*[3] the tenant's damages for the landlord's failure to repair covered inconvenience, lost premium and costs on a proposed assignment which fell through, rent (less the landlord's counterclaim), service charges and insurance payable after the abortive assignment, and the tenant's obligations to an under-lessee.

An interesting case of unusual damage resulting from a landlord's breach of his repairing covenant is *Marshall* v *Rubypoint Ltd*[4], where the landlord of a town house converted into flats failed to repair the lock on the main outside door. This resulted in the tenant, who had never been burgled before, being burgled four times in one year, and (on one occasion) to his being assaulted. The landlord argued that the presence of the internal door (which the intruders had forced) rendered the damage too remote; but the Court of Appeal held that the judge had correctly applied the foreseeability test in holding that criminal damage to the tenant's flat was within the reasonable contemplation of the parties as a not unlikely consequence of the landlord's breach. Furthermore, the forcing of the door was a substantial cause of the damage, and the criminal act of a third party did not amount to a *novus actus interveniens*,

---

1 [1983] 3 All ER 759.
2 [1984] 1 EGLR 42 (CA).
3 (1995) 69 P & CR 177.
4 [1997] 1 EGLR 69 (CA).

as it was reasonably foreseeable.[5] The tenant was held entitled to recover damages from the landlord for the burglaries and the assault.

Specific performance

This remedy was first recognised as applicable to a breach of a repairing covenant in the lease of a dwellinghouse in *Jeune* v *Queens Cross Properties Ltd*[6] and was given statutory force in relation to dwellinghouses by the Landlord and Tenant Act 1985, section 17. In *Jeune* the want of repair was to a common part of a building which was divided into flats, and section 17 applies the remedy to the common parts of a building or an estate as well as to the part actually demised. It has been applied also to the supply of services such as the repair of boilers on an estate[7], and to the repair of lifts.[8]

Right to carry out repairs and set off cost against rent

This right was recognised in *Lee-Parker* v *Izzet*[9]. Where the landlord has defaulted on his repairing covenant, the tenant may carry out the repairs himself and set off the cost against future rents. The right should be exercised by the tenant with caution. It would be advisable, for instance, to obtain two or three estimates for the work to be done before proceeding, and to limit the cost as far as possible. The repair must be one which is covered by the landlord's repairing covenant, and the landlord must first have been given the opportunity of carrying it out himself.

Additionally, there may be a right in equity to set off an uncertain estimated sum for repairs against a landlord's claim for arrears of rent if the two claims are closely connected. Thus in *British Anzani (Felixstowe) Ltd* v *International Marine Management (UK) Ltd*[10] the plaintiff, who was a lessee under a building lease, agreed to build two warehouses and to sub-let them to the defendant. The agreement contained an undertaking by the plaintiff to put right any defects in the buildings within two years. There was a defect in the flooring of one of the warehouses, and when the plaintiff sued the defendant for unpaid rent, the defendant counterclaimed for the cost of putting right the defective floor. It was held that although this was a claim for unliquidated damages under the agreement as to

5 *Stansbie* v *Trowman* [1948] 2 KB 528.
6 [1974] Ch 97.
7 *Parker* v *Camden LBC* [1986] Ch 162.
8 *Peninsular Maritime Ltd* v *Padseal Ltd* [1981] 2 EGLR 43, where the Court of Appeal confirmed an interlocutory mandatory injunction for the repair of lifts.
9 [1971] 3 All ER 1099.
10 [1980] QB 137.

building and not in the lease itself, there was such a close connection between the lease and the agreement that the defendant's claim went to the foundation of the plaintiff's claim for arrears of rent and was fair and just.

There will be no right to set off the cost of repairs if the lease specifically excludes it. A general clause that rent is payable "without any deduction" will not however exclude the right of set-off for repairs.[11]

Appointment of a receiver

The Supreme Court Act 1981, section 37(1), allows the court to appoint a receiver to collect rents and service charges and to use them to carry out repairs to premises. The order may be made where it is just and convenient to do so. There is further statutory provision for this as regards dwellinghouses in the Landlord and Tenant Act 1987, Part II.

The difficulties experienced with regard to enforcing a landlord's repairing covenants on the retained parts of a block of flats are unlikely to be experienced with business premises however. The landlord will usually only reserve minimal ground rent on residential blocks of flats where the long leases are sold for a premium, and therefore retains very little interest in the property, whereas business premises are usually let at realistic market rents and the landlord's interest is a real one.

---

11 *Connaught Restaurants Ltd v Indoor Leisure Ltd* [1994] 1 WLR 501

Chapter 11

SERVICE CHARGES
AND INSURANCE

SERVICE CHARGES

Where the premises let are part of a larger building or estate which includes other units, such as an office in an office block, a shop in a shopping precinct or an industrial unit on an industrial estate, the landlord will retain the common parts and provision will need to be made for their repair and maintenance. The landlord may also provide services to be used by all the tenants, such as heating and hot water for offices and cleansing and signs for shopping precincts and industrial estates, and the landlord will want to charge for these. It is to cover the expenditure on such matters that the lease of such a unit will provide for a service charge to be payable by the tenant.

Imposition of a service charge

It should be noted that if the lease does not provide for the payment of a service charge by the tenant, none will be payable; and, in the absence of common mistake, rectification of the lease will not be available.[1] It might be possible to impose one, however, on the renewal of a lease, particularly where the original lease is an old one where the landlord did not originally provide such sophisticated services.[2]

The absence of any services would of course indicate a lower rent, and the misrepresentation of a service charge to an assignee-purchaser has been held to be misrepresentation giving rise to a claim for damages. In *Heinemann v Cooper*[3], an assignee recovered £3,000 damages on a 62-year lease in which the service charges were about £800 per annum instead of £200 per annum as had been indicated by the vendor-assignor.

It was held in *Finch v Rodrigues*[4] that a service charge must be fair and reasonable, and that a covenant by tenants to pay a service charge could not give a landlord an unfettered right to spend whatever he liked on

---

1 *Riverplate Properties Ltd v Paul* [1975] 1 Ch 133. For a discussion of rectification, see Chap 3.
2 See analysis of variation of service charge on renewal under LTA 1954, Part II, *infra*.
3 [1987] 2 EGLR 154 (CA).
4 [1976] 3 All ER 581.

maintenance and then charge the cost to the tenants. This does not, however, require the landlord to accept the lowest quotation for services. In *Bandar Property Holdings Ltd* v *Darwen (Successors) Ltd*[5], a tenant was held liable to pay the slightly larger premium for insurance arranged by the landlord than the quotation for identical insurance which the tenant had obtained.

This principle was followed in *Havenridge Ltd* v *Boston Dyers Ltd*[6], where the landlord covenanted to insure the premises "in some insurance office of repute", and the tenant covenanted to pay such sums as the landlord should "properly expend or pay to any insurance company ... for insuring ... the demised premises." The tenant argued that the word "properly" implied that it was required to indemnify the landlord only in respect of sums which were reasonable in amount. The Court of Appeal, however, held that the word "properly" did not mean "reasonably", and was used merely to qualify the verbs "expend or pay", meaning that the payments had to be made in accordance with the landlord's contractual obligations, *i.e.* in an insurance office of repute. The landlord was not therefore under any obligation to shop around for the cheapest insurance; it was enough that the insurance it obtained was effected at arm's length at a rate representative of the market rate. The court distinguished *Finch* v *Rodrigues*[7], where the managing agents were a trading name for the landlords so that their certificate was not independent.

Matters to be covered by a service charge

In order to minimise the risk of disputes, it is important to define as clearly and exhaustively as possible exactly what matters are to be covered by the service charge. These will obviously vary according to the type of property, but in any event the lease will need to include in the definition section a definition of terms such as "the block", "the centre", "common parts", "the refuse area", and "the parking area". These are all likely to be parts not included in any individual demise and therefore retained by the landlord and for which he undertakes the responsibility for maintenance. In the absence of a covenant by the landlord to maintain these, however, he will not necessarily be liable to do so, even though the tenant covenants to pay a service charge. In *Duke of Westminster* v *Guild*[8], the tenant had covenanted to contribute towards the cost of a drain serving the demised premises, but it was held that although the tenant's easement of drainage

5 [1968] 2 All ER 305.
6 [1994] 2 EGLR 73 (CA).
7 [1976] 3 All ER 581 (*supra*).
8 [1985] 1 QB 688.

gave him the right to enter and repair the drain, it could not impose an obligation on the landlord to do so in the absence of an express covenant. There may be an implied liability to take reasonable care to maintain services, such as safe access and lighting, necessary to give business efficacy to an agreement[9], and to repair a right of access which it might reasonably be expected that the property would enjoy.[10]

In addition to the maintenance of the common parts, the landlord will usually undertake to provide services for the whole block, and it is equally important to state clearly what services will be provided and to define them as precisely as possible. For example, it is advisable to specify the dates and hours between which heating will be provided and the temperature of any hot water supplied. In the lease of a unit in a large block, provision for apportionment and payment of service charges and the services covered by it are usually set out in a schedule to the lease. Services provided by the landlord are likely to include the repair, redecoration and cleansing of the common parts of the building or precinct, heating and lighting and the maintenance of machinery for these, security and emergency services, staffing (such as receptionists and resident caretakers), refuse disposal, the provision of signs, furniture and facilities, landscaping, management, publicity, VAT and possibly a reserve fund.[11] Particularly in shopping precincts, there may also be attractive features such as seats, fountains and Christmas decorations. Depending upon the nature of the property, the landlord may also be under statutory obligations as to the safety of the retained parts, and he might therefore have to make adequate fire arrangements (which might include the provision of sprinklers) and ensure that staircases have handrails. The service charge should cover all the obligations undertaken by the landlord in his covenants or pursuant to his statutory duties.

Qualifying landlord's responsibility for services

From a landlord's point of view, his covenant as to the provision of services should be qualified to exclude a failure which is beyond his control, such as inadequate heating during a severe fuel shortage. A comprehensive form of exemption for the landlord would be as follows:

> "The landlord shall not be liable and the tenant shall have no claim against the landlord for:-
> (a) any interruption in any of the services by reason of necessary repair or maintenance of any installation or apparatus or damage thereto or

9 *Liverpool City Council v Irwin* [1977] AC 239.
10 *King v South Northamptonshire District Council* [1992] 1 EGLR 53 (CA).
11 For discussion of reserve funds, see *infra*.

destruction thereof by fire or other cause beyond the landlord's control or by reason of mechanical or other defect or breakdown or frost or unavoidable shortage of fuel or labour or

(b) any act omission or negligence of any employee of the landlord in the performance of any duty relating to the provision of the services or any of them."

Such an exemption will not however exonerate the landlord from reasonable maintenance, and in *Yorkbrook Investments Ltd v Batten*[12] it was held that such wording would not exempt the landlord from liability if the heating boiler frequently failed because it was antiquated and unserviceable and had exceeded its expected functioning time. However, it would be reasonable for the tenant to require a covenant from the landlord to use his best endeavours to ensure that any interruption of services is as minimal as possible and remedied as soon as possible.

Variation of service charge

It was recommended by the Joint Sub-Committee of the Law Society and the RICS on Model Clauses in Commercial Leases that there should be provision for variation of a percentage or proportionate service charge[13] to allow for additional units to be added or new services to be provided and for services no longer required to be dropped. The definitions of the common parts and any list of services should be subject to some variation to cover this. Any such variation should, however, be reasonable.

A general clause allowing for new services to be added to the service charges would be one entitling the landlord to recover from the tenant:

"any additional costs and expenses which the landlord may incur in providing such other services and in carrying out such other works as the landlord may deem desirable or necessary for the benefit of the [building] or any part of it, or for securing or enhancing any amenity of or within the [building]."

Provision for the variation of the calculation of service charges could be made by a clause in the following form:

"If in the reasonable opinion of the landlord as substantiated by written evidence and calculations it should at any time and for any reason become necessary or equitable to do so by reason of any change in the comparative floor areas of the demised premises and other premises in [the building] the landlord may recalculate the percentage payable in respect of the demised premises and will notify the tenant accordingly and the revised percentage shall have effect from the date of the event giving rise to the need for such recalculation provided always that any such recalculation shall be made on

12 [1985] 2 EGLR 100 (CA).
13 See precedent *infra*.

the same basis of comparative floor areas as has been applied for the current percentage and in no circumstances shall any such calculation result in the landlord being entitled to receive more than the actual cost of the matters which caused the percentage recalculation."

From the landlord's point of view, provision should cover capital expenditure as well as the running cost of any new service or repair, as a clause allowing for additional services may be construed strictly. In *Mullaney* v *Maybourne Grange (Croydon) Management Co Ltd*[14] it was held that the costs of replacing wooden window-frames with double-glazing units was not covered by an allowance for the costs of "additional services or amenities."

A service charge may be varied in a new lease granted under the Landlord and Tenant Act 1954, Part II. In *Hyams* v *Titan Properties Ltd*[15] the court permitted a variation from a fixed service charge to one based upon the proportion of expenditure in a new lease under the 1954 Act. Any variation must be fair and reasonable, however, and in *O'May* v *City of London Real Property Co Ltd*[16] the House of Lords held that the burden of proof of showing that any variation is fair and reasonable is on the party seeking it. In that case the landlord sought to impose, in a new lease under the 1954 Act, a fluctuating service charge of undefined risk and cost to the tenants, offering as compensation a reduction in the rent. The rent reduction was fixed at 50 pence per week, however, and was held not to be an adequate compensation for the comparatively unlimited risk which the landlord sought to impose on the tenants.

Interest

The landlord will not be able to charge interest on money which he has had to borrow to carry out expensive repairs to something covered by the service charge unless this is specifically allowed for in the service charge covenant. In *Boldmark Ltd* v *Cohen*[17] a provision that the landlords could charge "such sums as the landlords may from time to time expend in respect to the general administration and management of the block" was held not to cover interest on money borrowed. The judge indicated that a provision for charging interest might have been sensible, although the Joint Sub-Committee were of the opinion that any such interest charges should be borne by the landlord.

14 [1986] 1 EGLR 70 (Ch).
15 (1972) 24 P & CR 359 (CA).
16 [1983] 2 AC 726.
17 [1986] 1 EGLR 47 (CA).

Management costs

The landlord should ensure that the management costs of any service charges are also covered by the service-charge covenant. This will include the costs of producing accounts and a certificate of expenditure and the fees of a management company or other person who deals with the day-to-day running of the property. A clause allowing for the recovery of accountancy fees could be in the following form:

> "The landlord shall be entitled to include in the service charge the fees of any accountant engaged by the landlord in connection with the provision of services and a certificate of expenditure."

Accounting year

Because of the tax position with regard to service charges[18], it is probably preferable that the accounting year for their calculation should be the same as the landlord's accounting year, and the lease should provide for such calculation to be varied on notice to the tenants to allow for a change if the reversion is sold. This would be covered by the following clause:

> "The financial year for the purposes of the service charge shall be from the first day in January every year to the thirty-first day of December of that year or such other period as the landlord may, in its absolute discretion, from time to time reasonably determine."

Dispute resolution

The lease should contain a provision for resolving any disputes concerning the service charge. It is important that the landlord should comply strictly with any procedure laid down, as he may otherwise find that the costs are irrecoverable. The procedure should give the tenant the right to inspect receipts and so verify the landlord's certificate of costs, and require the tenant to give notice of any objection to the service charge demanded within a specified time.

If the parties are unable to agree, it should be possible to refer the matter to a third party. If the third party is to arbitrate between the landlord and the tenant, it is important that he should be entirely independent. Thus in *Concorde Graphics Ltd* v *Andromeda Investments SA*[19], the lease provided that the proportion of the service charge payable by the tenant should, in case of difference, be settled by the landlord's surveyor. The landlord appointed as his surveyor for this purpose the same firm which acted as his managing agents. Vinelott J said that the reason

---

18 Considered *infra*.
19 [1983] 1 EGLR 53 (Ch).

that the lease specified that the landlord's surveyor was to perform this duty appeared to be that the parties envisaged that the landlord would retain a surveyor with general authority to keep the estate under proper supervision, and they probably considered that such a person, with his familiarity with the property, would be able to reach a decision more cheaply and expeditiously than someone who came to the matter entirely afresh. But that did not mean that the surveyor, although the landlord's agent, was to act in that capacity in deciding the difference as to the amount of contribution payable by the tenant. Such a function was essentially an arbitral one, and it could clearly not be performed by the same firm which, acting as the landlord's agents, had made the very demand which was the subject of the dispute. The landlord was therefore obliged to appoint other surveyors to resolve the dispute.

If the third party appointed is acting in an arbitral capacity, his decision must fall between the two figures claimed to be correct by the landlord and the tenant. If he is acting as an expert, however, then he may settle on a figure outside these boundaries. If the calculation of the service charge is complex and requires some specialised knowledge, then it may be preferable to provide for the determination of a dispute by an expert rather than an arbitrator.

Reserve or sinking fund

The lease may make provision for a reserve or sinking fund to meet either capital expenditure (such as the cost of replacing equipment) or additional expenses (such as those of redecoration) which are incurred only every few years. The establishment of such a fund should avoid the need to borrow monies to cover such items, and should also save the tenants from being subjected to a sudden exceptionally heavy service charge in any one year. The size of contributions to the fund should be based upon a realistic expectation of the useful life of equipment and anticipated repair and redecoration of the property. A clause enabling the creation of a reserve fund would be one that provides for the service charge to include:

> "such annual provision as the landlord may, in its absolute discretion, decide as being proper and reasonable for the establishment and maintenance of a reserve fund for the replacement of any boilers, plant, machinery, apparatus and equipment and for the redecoration of the common parts."

The lease should make it clear whether any part of the fund unexpended at the end of the lease is to be returned to the tenant. If the lease does not provide for this expressly, the court will draw inferences from the purpose of the fund. In *Secretary of State for the Environment* v *Possfund (North West) Ltd*[20], the landlord had covenanted in the lease to maintain an air-conditioning plant which had only just been installed, and which had a life expectancy of some 20 years; and the tenant's service charge included an amount set aside for the replacement of such plant. The air-conditioning system had in fact not been replaced by the time the lease came to an end some 20 years later. The tenant claimed repayment of the sums which it had paid for the replacement, which (with interest) totalled £1 million. Rimer J, however, dismissed the claim. He looked at the commercial realities underlying the provision for the service charge, and found that the tenant's payments were not intended to be merely on account of future expenditure, but were made by way of an indemnity for annual depreciation in the value of the plant which the landlord had actually and irreversibly suffered.

Declaration of trust

If it is intended that any unexpended part of a sinking or reserve fund is to be repaid to the tenant at the end of the lease, it is advisable from the tenant's point of view, particularly bearing in mind the substantial sums of money which it may contain, that such a fund be constituted as a trust in favour of the tenant as beneficiary. The advantage of this is that, in the event of the landlord's insolvency, the monies will not then be available to the landlord's trustee in bankruptcy or liquidator. The following provisions allow for this:

> "So far as it shall be deemed prudent to make reasonable provision for future expenditure the landlord shall hold such reserve sum on trust for the joint benefit of the landlord the tenant and other tenants within [the building] and shall place the same on deposit in a suitably designated account in a building society or invest the same in any other way authorised by law for the investment of trust funds with power to vary and transpose the same;
>
> Within the perpetuity period the landlord shall apply the said sums or the investments for the time being representing the said sums and the income thereof whenever necessary in or towards the purposes of [replacement or renewal or other matters for which the reserve fund is to be established];
>
> The expression 'the perpetuity period' shall mean in relation to each such sum a period of eighty years from the date upon which the same shall have been set aside."

If a trust is set up, then ideally a separate deed should be drawn up to regulate the trust fund. It should specify the purposes for which the fund may be applied, allow for investment and an annual audit, specify the

20 [1997] 39 EG 179.

tenants as the beneficiaries and set out the basis for distribution of the fund on its termination – for example, if the property is destroyed. The Joint Sub-Committee suggests that the distribution should be amongst those who last contributed in the proportions in which they contributed. Provision should also be made for transfer of the fund to the new landlord on assignment of the reversion on his entering into similar covenants to the landlord's.

Even if no trust fund is formally set up, it may be possible to infer a trust if the reserve funds are kept in a separate account which is designated as belonging to the tenants.[21]

Means of apportioning service charges

There are three main methods of calculating the individual tenants' shares of a total service charge. First, there may be an equal apportionment at the outset when units are first let. This type of fixed charge is likely to be found only in older leases, and in *Hyams* v *Titan Properties Ltd*[22] the court permitted a change to a proportionate charge on renewal of a lease. If this type of charge were to be applied today, it would seem to be essential to have some formula for reviewing any such apportionment allowing circumstances to change. Secondly, apportionment may be on the basis of rateable values, but this too is not likely to achieve a fair result as the rateable values may change and will take into account amenity value such as ground floor accommodation as opposed to eleventh floor. Thirdly, apportionment may be on the square footage of space demised to each tenant. If this is the basis then it is advisable for the lease to specify how the area is to be calculated. The following clause specifies one such method:

> "The annual amount of the service charge payable by the tenant shall be such proportion of the total cost thereof to the landlord as the superficial floor area of the demised premises bears to the total lettable floor area of the [building] excluding any common parts or accessways thereof."

None of these methods is entirely fair, as they do not take into account the use of the services made by any particular tenant. It may therefore be advisable to make provision in the service-charge clause to charge for additional services. This is important if insurance premiums are included in the service charge and one tenant is carrying on a high-risk trade which requires an additional premium. For this reason, it is preferable to deal with the payment of insurance premiums separately from service charges.

In some cases, service charges may need to be calculated at two tiers. For example, on an industrial estate, there may be an overall service

---

21 *Re Chelsea Cloisters Ltd* (1981) 41 P & CR 98.
22 (1972) 24 P & CR 359 (CA).

charge for the roads, lighting and signing on the estate to be apportioned between the buildings on the estate, and another service charge to be apportioned between the tenants of individual units in the different buildings. This would obviously lead to a very complicated calculation, and would probably be best avoided if possible.

If the property is mixed, such as shops with offices or residential accommodation over, there may be some merit in merely providing in the lease that the tenant shall pay a "fair proportion" of the total service charge. In this case, it would be prudent to provide for determining any dispute as to a fair proportion by reference to the landlord's surveyor.[23] An example of this would be a covenant by the tenant:

> "to contribute a fair proportion according to use of the cost of [services] used by the occupier of the demised premises in common with the occupiers of any other properties such fair proportion to be determined by the landlord's surveyor whose decision shall be final and binding on the parties hereto."

The lease should provide for the landlord to pay the appropriate percentage of service charge for any period during which any unit is not let. It should also give the landlord access to the demised premises for the purpose of repairing any common parts, or repairing or renewing services for which the landlord undertakes responsibility. An example of this is a covenant by the tenant:

> "To permit the landlord to enter the demised premises to carry out any works or repairs to the [building] or the conduits serving the same as the landlord may require, the landlord making good any damage to the demised premises thereby caused."

The tenant will generally be liable for the service charge costs only during the term of the lease. In *Capital & Counties Freehold Equity Trust Ltd* v *BL plc*[24], the tenant had covenanted to pay expenses which "may ... during the said term be expended or incurred or become payable." The landlord had contracted with a builder to carry out repairs and decorations, but the work was not to be done until after the end of the term. It was held that the tenant was not liable for the cost of such work as it was not covered by the covenant.

If the service charge includes an element of reserve or sinking fund, on assignment of the lease a purchaser should ideally pay the outgoing tenant for his contribution remaining in the fund. This can no doubt be part of

---

23 As to the capacity in which the landlord's surveyor may be called upon to act, however, see *Concorde Graphics Ltd* v *Andromeda Investments SA* [1983] 1 EGLR 53 (Ch). (*supra*).

24 [1987] 2 EGLR 49.

the negotiations on the sale price. A purchaser should in any event enquire as to provision in the service charge for replacement of expensive items. An assignee of the lease is not liable for any arrears of service charge, however; and it is therefore important that a landlord does not give consent to assignment until all arrears of service charge have been paid. It is thought that a refusal of consent on this ground would be reasonable.

Recovery of service charges

Service charges are usually made payable as additional rent[25] in advance, the future year's expenditure being estimated on the previous year's. During the first year it can of course only be enlightened guesswork. At the end of the year, when accounts are rendered, an adjustment can be made by charging the tenants for any shortfall or setting off any surplus against the following year's demand. The following clauses would cover this procedure:

> "The tenant shall on the quarter days fixed for the payment of the rent pay in addition to the said rent such a sum in advance and on account of the service charge as the landlord or its managing agents shall from time to time specify at their discretion to be fair and reasonable;
> As soon as practicable after the end of each landlord's financial year the landlord shall furnish to the tenant a copy of the certificate and account of the service charge payable by the tenant for the year credit being given therein for the advance payments made by the tenant in respect of the said year and upon the furnishing of such account there shall be paid by the tenant to the landlord any balance of the service charge found payable or there shall be allowed by the landlord to the tenant any amount which may have been overpaid by the tenant by way of advance payments as the case may require."

The lease may contain a provision that interest should be payable on an unpaid service charge after a certain time, and if so, then it would seem fair that interest should also be payable to the tenant at the end of the year on any substantial over-payment.

As mentioned above, the tenants should have a right to challenge any expenditure within a certain time limit, and the lease should provide for this. Any provision in the lease that the certificate of costs prepared by a surveyor is to be regarded as "final" cannot displace the court's jurisdiction to hear any dispute should any arbitral procedure prescribed by the lease fail to resolve it.[26]

In *Morgan v Stainer*[27] the tenants had covenanted to pay to the landlord

---

25 See *infra*.
26 *Re Davstone Estates Ltd's Lease* [1969] 2 All ER 849.
27 [1993] 2 EGLR 73 (Ch).

"all legal and other costs that may be incurred in obtaining the payment of maintenance contributions from any tenant in the building." It was held that this did not cover the landlord's costs incurred in earlier legal proceedings brought against him by the tenants who had sought the appointment of independent managing agents and a declaration that the maintenance contributions paid to the landlord were held by him in trust for them.

In *Royton Industries Ltd v Lawrence*[28] the inclusion of the service charges in the reddendum of the lease was sufficient to enable the landlord of a pre-1996 lease to recover from the original tenant unpaid charges which accrued after the lease had been assigned. It was not necessary that the tenant should have specifically covenanted to pay the service charges throughout the term.

In *Electricity Supply Nominees Ltd v Thorn EMI Retail Ltd*[29], which concerned a pre-1996 lease, the Court of Appeal held that a tenant from whom service charges had been recovered by the landlord could recover these from the sub-tenant whose lease had been extended under the 1954 Act, even after the tenant's own lease had expired.[30] The basis of recovery was a restitutionary claim to prevent the landlord's being unjustly enriched.[31] To have retained its contractual right to recover the arrears from the sub-tenant, the tenant would have had to have brought its action before its lease expired; and this could cause difficulties where the exact amount due cannot at that time be calculated precisely. The difficulty does not arise in the case of post-1995 leases, since the right to sue for the arrears of service charge under the sub-lease is now retained by the tenant, upon the expiry of its own lease, as a separate chose in action.[32]

Reserving service charge as rent

Service charges are nowadays almost always made payable as additional rent. This has the advantage, from the landlord's point of view, that he can distrain for non-payment of the service charge, as he can for rent. It was held in *Concorde Graphics Ltd v Andromeda Investments SA*[33] that a landlord cannot distrain for a service charge if any part of it is in dispute. It was also held that if the tenant makes an overpayment of a service charge because it wrongly includes items of expenditure which cannot be properly

---

28 [1994] 1 EGLR 110 (Ch).
29 [1991] 2 EGLR 46. See further discussion in Chap 12.
30 The former tenant's contractual right in the sub-lease to recover the service charges from the sub-tenant was held to pass to the landlord (by virtue of LPA 1925, s 141) when the tenant's lease expired.
31 *Moule v Garrett* (1870) LR 5 Exch 132.
32 See discussion on p 286 *infra*.
33 [1983] 1 EGLR 53 (Ch).

charged, the excess is irrecoverable. This is because the payment is made under a mistake of law and not a mistake of fact.[34] It is therefore advisable for a tenant who is in dispute with his landlord to pay any disputed sum, pending settlement, into an account in the name of an independent third party.

A further possible advantage to the landlord of making a service charge payable as rent is that it is not necessary to serve a section 146 notice before commencing forfeiture proceedings for non-payment. JE Adams has pointed out, however, that the procedure for forfeiture for non-payment of rent is subject to so many statutory and equitable rights of relief for the tenant that ultimately the forfeiture route under the section 146 procedure might be preferable.[35] He suggests that the clause making the service charge recoverable as rent might therefore be modified to apply only to the right of distraint. The clause might therefore provide that such charge "may, so far as a right of distraint is concerned, be recovered as if rent in arrear."

The tax implications of service charges

VAT is chargeable on services provided to the tenants. A tenant will be able to set off service charges payable by him, along with rent, as expenditure against profits. If a trust is established in respect of a reserve fund, there is the possibility that the fund might some day revert to the tenants, who cannot therefore be regarded as having parted with all interest in payments which they have made into it. This may mean that the tenants cannot deduct as expenses from income any part of a service charge which is paid into a trust ultimately for them. VAT is not, however, chargeable until such time as the fund is spent on the provision of services.

A landlord is liable to tax under Schedule A on both rent and service charges. This means that any reserve or sinking fund can be set up by the landlord only out of net sums after deductions of tax. The landlord must also pay tax on any interest from such a fund. It is not possible, moreover, to set off interest against expenditure until there is a year where expenditure is actually incurred, and this may not be for several years.

These matters need careful consideration in the drafting of the lease at

---

34 *cf Woolwich Equitable Building Society* v *IRC (No 2)* [1993] AC 70 (HL), which suggests that the law may soon come to recognise that money paid under a mistake of law is recoverable under principles of unjust enrichment. If the overpayment is into a reserve fund that is held on trust, the fiduciary relationship thereby created gives the tenant a right to recover in equity: *Re Diplock* [1948] Ch 465; *Ministry of Health* v *Simpson* [1981] AC 251.
35 JEA, ". . . and Otherwise Recoverable as if Rent in Arrear" (Precedents Editor's Notes) [1993] Conv 11.

the outset and may well become negotiating factors on a subsequent assignment of the lease or the reversion.

INSURANCE

Insurance is an important consideration which should be specifically dealt with in the lease. Apart from the actual covenant to insure, there are other matters which should be considered and for which provision should be made.

Different ways of effecting insurance

Insurance arrangements will vary according to the type of property, and in particular according to whether it comprises self-contained premises or merely one of several units, such as a floor in an office block, or a unit in an industrial estate or shopping centre. In each case, the landlord will want to arrange insurance cover himself; but, where the premises demised comprise merely one of several units, the landlord will arrange insurance cover for the whole block and he will make provision in the lease to recover the premiums from the tenants either as part of the service charges or separately. It is probably preferable to charge for insurance cover separately, as some tenants may be carrying on businesses with higher risk factors than others, and their share of the premium will be correspondingly larger. Separate charging also facilitates an adjustment to the share of the premium in the event of there being a change of user of the premises and a consequent increase or reduction in the level of risk.

The tenant will wish to be sure that the landlord has in fact paid the insurance premiums, and the landlord's covenant to insure usually requires the landlord to provide evidence of this. An example is a covenant by the landlord:

> "To keep the building insured against loss or damage by fire and such other risks as the landlord thinks fit and (upon payment by the tenant of any increased premium caused thereby) against such risks as the tenant may from time to time reasonably request for an amount equal to its full reinstatement cost (including all professional fees and the cost of any work which might be required by any statute) and three years' loss of rent in respect of the demised premises (the interest of the tenant if required being noted on the insurance policy) ... and to produce to the tenant on demand (but not more than twice in any one year) the policy of insurance (or a copy thereof) maintained by the landlord and the receipt for the last premium payable in respect of it."

It is just possible that, in the case of individual self-contained premises, the landlord might be prepared to allow the tenant to insure; but the landlord will of course then himself require proof that the premiums have been paid, and will probably specify which insurance company the policy should be with. The landlord will therefore require a covenant from the tenant in the lease to this effect. This way of insuring could be of financial advantage to the tenant, who may be able to take out one policy to cover not only the demised premises, but also his business risks.

A covenant by the landlord to insure will usually state that insurance shall be with a reputable company. This will give the landlord the right to choose the insurance company and will not require him to shop around for the cheapest insurance.[36] Even where insurance is effected by a management company, the landlord has the right to nominate the insurers and is not obliged to choose the cheapest company. In *Berrycroft Management Co Ltd* v *Sinclair Gardens Investments (Kensington) Ltd*[37] the Court of Appeal said that the interests of the tenants were protected by the requirement that insurance must be effected by the landlord with an insurance office of repute.

If the tenant has taken a mortgage to purchase the lease, the mortgagee may also insist on insuring the property, or at least on approving the insurers with whom the property is insured and the policy. This could mean that the property is insured twice over – an expensive practice for the tenant if he cannot persuade either the landlord or the mortgagee to accept the other's insurer. In the event of a claim on the insurance in these circumstances, the insurer against whom a claim is made may claim a contribution from the other insurer.

Matters to be covered on insurance

Insurance should be to the full cost of reinstatement of the premises, to be agreed between the landlord and the tenant, or in default of agreement to be fixed by an independent surveyor. The covenant to insure should require the insurance monies to be spent on reinstatement. There should be a clause therefore that the landlord:

> "shall promptly apply the proceeds of any insurance policy effected by the landlord covering the demised premises and all alterations and fixtures thereto in the rebuilding and reinstatement thereof."

In the absence of any such covenant, the landlord is under no obligation to expend the insurance monies on rebuilding, unless it can be shown that the

---

36 *Havenridge Ltd* v *Boston Dyers Ltd* [1993] 2 EGLR 73.
37 [1997] 1 EGLR 47 (CA).

insurance was effected to cover both the landlord's and the tenant's interests, although this may be implied if the tenant has paid the premiums.[38]

Where insurance has been effected for the benefit of both the landlord and the tenant, the insurers will not be able to recover the insurance moneys paid out to the landlord for a fire caused by the tenant's negligence. It was held in *Mark Rowlands Ltd* v *Berni Inns Ltd*[39] that the insurance for which the tenant had paid was clearly intended to cover this possibility. The landlord had no right of action under the terms of the lease against the tenant in respect of the fire, and the insurers therefore had no right of subrogation.

A covenant by the landlord to reinstate requires him to do so to the same standard where premiums have been paid by the tenant. In *Vural* v *Security Archives*[40] the premises were destroyed by fire, and the landlord was liable for the reinstatement of a wooden parquet floor which was better for the tenant's business than the linoleum one installed by him.

A covenant by the landlord to use insurance moneys to reinstate "forthwith" was held in *S. Turner (Cabinet Works) Ltd* v *Young*[41] to mean within a reasonable time.

It is important also that the insurance should cover rent and service charges during a period when the premises are unusable, as rent is still payable even though the premises have been destroyed.[42] Separate insurance is usually arranged for plate-glass windows, and the tenant may covenant to insure these. A typical clause for this would be a covenant by the tenant:

> "To insure and keep insured for its full replacement value in some insurance office of repute all the plate glass in the demised premises."

The usual property insurance will cover (*inter alia*) damage from risks such as fire, earthquake, flood, subsidence, lightning, explosion, malicious damage and riot. It may also cover third-party risks (injury to third parties and sometimes also third-party property) arising out of accidents in the common parts of the building, precinct or estate. The tenant will effect a separate insurance policy for his own business risks, including third-party cover for accidents or losses on his own premises.

---

38 *Mumford Hotels Ltd* v *Wheler* [1964] Ch 117.
39 [1986] QB 211.
40 (1990) 60 P & CR 258.
41 (1955) 115 EG 632.
42 Unless, very exceptionally, the lease were to be held to be frustrated: see Chap 12.

As well as the buildings, the landlord will want to insure essential machinery and plant, such as lifts and central heating boilers and pipes. In the case of a block insurance, this will be recoverable also from the individual tenants often as part of the service charge or separately. Since the tenant's fixtures become part of the building, they too should be insured by the landlord, and the landlord will require an up-to-date valuation of the fixtures from the tenant for this purpose.

Insurance in name of one or both parties

In the case of a single individual unit, insurance is probably best effected in the joint names of landlord and tenant, and may provide for a third party, such as a mortgagee, to have their interest noted on the policy. A clause providing for this is one which states that:

> "The insurance policy is to be effected in the joint names of the landlord and the tenant with a note to be made on the policy of the names of such other persons interested in the demised premises as either the landlord or the tenant shall from time to time reasonably require."

If there is a clause in this form, both parties will have access to the insurance documents, it will be clear that insurance is to cover the interests of them both, and (should the policy be allowed to lapse) each will receive notice of discontinuance. A clause such as this would avoid the disastrous kind of misunderstanding which occurred in *Argy Trading Development Co Ltd v Lapid Developments Ltd*[43], where, although the tenant had covenanted to insure, he mistakenly believed that the landlord had insured, as he had done previously. In fact the policy had been allowed to lapse, and the tenant was held liable for the premises' destruction by fire.

If insurance is effected in the name of one party only, however (usually the landlord), the other party will require proof that the cover is satisfactory and that the premiums have been paid. The insurance covenant should therefore provide for production on demand of copies of the insurance policy and the last receipt for premiums paid. A purchaser of leasehold premises or a mortgagee will also require to see these to satisfy himself that the policy is extant and that cover is adequate, and the tenant may be required to produce these on a sale. In a block insurance, the tenant's interest should be noted on the insurance policy, and the tenant should ensure that this is done.

---

43 [1977] 1 WLR 444.

User covenants

If the landlord is insuring, he will also require a covenant from the tenant not to do any act or thing, or permit any act or thing to be done, which would either increase the insurance premiums or invalidate the insurance cover. The tenant may therefore covenant:

> "Not to use the demised premises either in such a manner as may render an increased premium to be payable for the insurance of the premises (and to reimburse the landlord in respect of any such increased premium that may become payable as a result) or in such manner as may render the insurance void or voidable."

Such a clause will not give the insurers any right to sue the tenant for damage caused by his negligence, although an insurance risk arising from the tenant's failure to repair might give the insurers a right of subrogation to sue the tenant on his repairing covenant with the landlord.

If the demised premises form part of a block, ideally the tenant will wish to know that a covenant to this effect is included in all other leases of units in the block also. An alternative to this would be for the landlord to covenant to allow to the tenant any increase in premium due to a high-risk user by a neighbouring tenant. An example of such a covenant would be one permitting the tenant:

> "To deduct from the amount of any premium for insuring the demised premises/building any increase therein attributable to the use to which any adjoining or neighbouring property of the landlord is put."

In the event of the landlord's recovering damages for an insured loss from a third party, the insurers will have a lien over the damages, which will give them priority over any other creditors of the landlord.[44]

Entitlement to insurance monies where premises not rebuilt

The lease should make provision for ownership of the insurance monies in the event that the property is destroyed but cannot, for some reason, be rebuilt. It is not unusual to provide that the monies shall belong to the landlord; but it may be fairer to provide that they shall belong to the landlord and the tenant in proportion to the value of their respective interests. A clause to this effect is as follows:

> "In any case in which it is not possible within two years (or such longer period as may be agreed between the landlord and the tenant) to enter into a contract for the rebuilding or reinstatement of the demised premises the insurance monies and all interest earned thereon shall be divided between the

---

44 *Lord Rapier & Ettrick v R F Kershaw Ltd* [1993] 1 Lloyd's Rep 197.

landlord and the tenant in the ratio of the open market value of their respective interests in the demised premises immediately prior to the occurrence giving rise to the insured loss or damage (there being taken into account the likelihood of the tenant being able by virtue of any statutory provision to retain the use and occupation of all or any part of the demised premises after the expiry of the term hereby granted) and any dispute as to the division of such insurance monies shall be determined by arbitration."

The courts have occasionally had to consider the distribution of insurance monies as between landlord and tenant where the lease is silent on this point. In the absence of any specific provision, it now seems that the monies will be divisible between the landlord and the tenant according to the respective values of the reversion and the lease. This was the solution reached in *Beacon Carpets Ltd* v *Kirby*[45], where the sum insured was not sufficient to rebuild the warehouse demised, and the tenant did not wish to take a lease of the smaller warehouse which the landlord proposed to build. The site was therefore left vacant. The landlord had covenanted to insure, but the policy was in joint names. It was held that the lease contemplated that the insurance policy should be for the benefit of both parties, and that they were entitled to the insurance monies in the same proportions as the values of their respective interests.

45 [1984] 2 All ER 726.

Chapter 12

TERMINATION
OF THE LEASE

A commercial lease may come to an end in various ways. One of these, forfeiture, is considered in the next chapter. The present chapter examines other methods of termination. A fixed-term lease may come to an end simply by effluxion of time. Other established methods of termination are: by notice to quit (in the case of a periodic tenancy); by notice under the Landlord and Tenant Act 1954; by the operation of a break clause; by surrender or merger; and by disclaimer. There are, however, indications that two other methods of terminating leases exist: frustration[1], and acceptance of a repudiatory breach.[2] A sub-lease granted in breach of a covenant against sub-letting may also be terminated by the head-lessor's obtaining a mandatory injunction compelling the sub-lessee to surrender the sub-lease to the sub-lessor. These methods will be examined in turn.

Effluxion of time

A periodic tenancy is not subject to termination by effluxion of time, but will continue unless and until one of the parties serves a notice to quit. Termination by effluxion of time can therefore apply only to tenancies for a fixed term. If the tenancy falls outside the protection of the Landlord and Tenant Act 1954, Part II[3], it will terminate upon the expiration of the contractual term. If, however, the tenancy is a business tenancy within Part II, it is statutorily continued after the expiration of its contractual term unless terminated by one of the methods therein specified. For a lease so protected, effluxion of time is therefore not a terminating event.[4] If the tenant wishes to terminate a Part II-protected tenancy at the expiration of the contractual term, it must give the landlord at least three months written notice.[5] It has, however, been held that a lease ceases to be protected by

---

1 *National Carriers Ltd v Panalpina (Northern) Ltd* [1981] AC 675 (HL).
2 See *Chartered Trust plc v Davies* [1997] 49 EG 135 (CA), where the doctrine was accepted, but with no analysis. The doctrine had been accepted in the county court in *Hussein v Mehlman* [1992] 2 EGLR 87, where it is discussed fully.
3 *i.e.* outside LTA 1954, s 23: see further Chap 15 *infra*.
4 See Chap 15 *infra*.
5 LTA 1954, s 27.

Part II as soon as the tenant ceases to occupy the premises for the purposes of its business.[6] If, therefore, a business tenant moves out of occupation at least one day before the expiration of the term, the lease will cease to be a Part II tenancy and so (in the absence of an estoppel) will terminate at the term date without the tenant's needing to serve notice. It is therefore recommended that a landlord who fears that a Part II-protected tenant may be thinking of quitting at the end of the term should initiate the statutory procedure by serving a statutory notice under section 25 of the Landlord and Tenant Act 1954, Part II.

For Part II to apply, the tenant must occupy the premises for the purposes of a business carried on by him or for those and other purposes.[7] The tenancy will therefore fall outside the scope of Part II if the tenant has sub-let the entire premises. If the sub-tenancy itself falls within Part II, its term may be continued under the statute beyond the date at which the head-lease ends by effluxion of time. In this event, in order to prevent the covenants in the sub-lease becoming unenforceable by reason of the destruction of the reversion immediately expectant upon it, the estate which confers the next vested right to the land (*i.e.* the estate of the head-lessor) is treated as the reversion of the sub-tenant's continuation tenancy for the purpose of preserving the same incidents and obligations as would have affected the head-lease had it not expired by effluxion of time.[8] In relation to a pre-1996 lease, the Court of Appeal has expressed the view that the effect of the statutory provisions is to pass to the head-lessor even the sub-lessor's rights against the sub-tenant under any indemnity covenant.[9] In relation to a post-1995 lease, by contrast, it is clear that the sub-lessor would in such circumstances retain the right to sue in respect of breaches which occurred before the expiration of its own term.[10]

---

6 *Esselte AB v Pearl Assurance plc* [1997] 2 All ER 41 (CA).

7 LTA 1954, s 23: see further Chap 15 *infra*.

8 LTA 1954, s 65(2), extending the effect of the Law of Property Act 1925, s 139.

9 *Electricity Supply Nominees Ltd v Thorn EMI Retail Ltd* [1991] 2 EGLR 46, referring to the combined effect of LTA 1954, s 65(2), LPA 1925, s 139 and s 141 of the latter Act as interpreted in *Re King* [1963] Ch 459: see further Chaps 6 and 11 *supra*. The sub-lessor might be advised to bring any action upon the indemnity covenant before its own lease expires, as the issue of the writ would sever the covenant and prevent the right to sue in this action from passing to the freeholder. The institution of proceedings may not, however, be practicable in all cases, *e.g.* where the covenant relates to the payment of a service change which is not calculable before the head-lease expires. In such circumstances, the sub-lessor's right to recover (as in *Electricity Supply Nominees Ltd*) would have to be based upon the rule of restitution exemplified in *Moule v Garrett* (1872) LR 7 Ex 101.

10 Although the effect of the decision in *Re King* [1963] Ch 459 is abrogated by LT(C)A 1995, s 23(1), only in relation to assignments, it is clear that the principle in that case (which depended upon an interpretation of LPA 1925, s 141) has been swept away by the repeal of LPA 1925, s 141, in relation to new (*i.e.* post-1995) tenancies: LT(C)A 1995, s 30(4).

If the tenant has sub-let part of the premises but occupies the remaining parts for the purposes of its business,[11] the tenancy of the whole will not terminate except by one of the methods specified in Part II; the statutory continuation tenancy[12] will therefore apply even to those parts sub-let. The tenant will, however, have a basic right to a new tenancy only of "the holding" – which definition excludes any part not occupied by the tenant or its employee for the purposes of a business.[13]

Notice to quit a periodic tenancy

A periodic tenancy can be terminated at common law by either party's serving notice on the other.[14] Unless the lease specifies otherwise, the relevant period of notice is that laid down at common law. A yearly tenancy can be determined at common law by at least half a year's notice[15], expiring at the end of a year of the tenancy.[16] For tenancies of other periods, unless the lease specifies otherwise, the usual period of notice is one full period of the lease, *i.e.* one month's notice is needed to terminate a monthly tenancy. If the periodic tenancy is within the Landlord and Tenant Act 1954, Part II, a statutory continuation tenancy will arise following the expiry of a common law notice to quit served by the landlord.[17] If the tenant serves a common law notice to quit, however, it loses any rights under Part II unless the notice was given before the tenant had been in occupation in right of the tenancy for one month.[18]

Landlord and Tenant Act 1954, Part II

The LTA 1954 provides specific means by which a tenancy protected within Part II can come to an end.[19] A business tenancy within Part II does not come to an end merely because the contractual term has expired or because the landlord has served a notice to quit (whether to determine a periodic tenancy or to exercise a break clause in a fixed-term tenancy). The Act recognises a tenant's notice to quit or surrender, and a forfeiture by the landlord, as methods of terminating a business tenancy.

11 For the meaning of this, see *Graysim Holdings Ltd v P & O Property Holdings Ltd*
   [1996] 1 AC 329 (HL), noted Bridge [1996] CLJ 197; Ferris [1996] JBL 592.
12 LTA 1954, s 24(1).
13 LTA 1954, s 23(3).
14 The effect of an error in a notice to quit is the same as that in a break notice, and is
   considered in the context of break notices *infra*.
15 Notice is usually served in writing, but at common law writing is not required: *Doe d
   Lord Macartney v Crick* (1805) 5 Esp 196, 197.
16 *Sidebottom v Holland* [1895] 1 QB 378, 383.
17 LTA 1954, s 24(1).
18 *Ibid,* s 24(2)(a).
19 See further Chap 15 *infra*.

Where the landlord and the tenant agree upon the grant to the tenant of a future tenancy of the holding, on terms and from a date specified in the agreement, the current tenancy continues until that date but no longer, and is not a tenancy to which Part II of the Act applies.[20]

Break clause

A lease for a fixed term cannot be determined by notice unless express provision for this is made in the lease in the form of a break clause. Since a lease must be for a term certain, the usual practice is to specify the full term in the lease but to make such term subject to the condition that it is determinable at an earlier date upon notice by either or both of the parties. A break clause therefore operates as a condition subsequent, since (unlike a lease subject to a determinable interest), the earlier termination of the lease is not automatic but at the option of one or either of the parties. A tenant's break clause may be useful to a tenant who fears that it may not be able to continue to pay the rent or perform the other obligations of the lease. The tenant's option to break may, however, be made conditional upon his paying the landlord a monetary sum (perhaps equivalent to a half-year's rent) to compensate the landlord for a void should he be unable to re-let immediately. A landlord's break clause may be useful to a landlord who is contemplating rebuilding or developing the premises before the expiration of the lease.[21] The ability of a party to demand a break clause depends, however, on its relative bargaining strength. Break clauses were less common until the increasing inflation of the 1960s. Since the recession of the early 1990s, tenants have been in a stronger position to demand a right to break, and to break at more frequent intervals.

A fixed-term lease may grant either the landlord or the tenant, or each of them[22], a right to break at any time during the term[23], usually on the occurrence of a condition. The tenant might, for instance, try to obtain an option to break in the event of the premises being destroyed or otherwise becoming unusable for their intended purpose through no fault of the tenant's. A mining lease might contain a tenant's right to break in the event of the mine becoming exhausted. The landlord might seek a right to break in the event of his evincing an intention to develop the premises or

---

20 LTA 1954, s 28.

21 As, in these circumstances, the landlord should be able to make out a ground of opposition to a new tenancy under LTA 1954, s 30(1)(f).

22 A purported option to break which requires the agreement of both parties is, of course, pointless, since neither party could exercise the option unilaterally.

23 As in *Manorlike Ltd* v *Le Vitas Travel and Consultancy Services Ltd* [1986] 1 All ER 573; [1986] 1 EGLR 79, where the lease could be broken by the landlord at any time upon three months' notice.

to occupy them for his own purposes. The condition needs to be drafted with care to avoid uncertainty. If the condition is unambiguously clear, exact compliance with it is necessary. This is illustrated in *Nocton Ltd v Water Hall Group plc*[24], where a lease of a quarry gave the tenant a right to break upon six months' notice when all limestone spar "capable of extraction" had been removed. The court held that this expression unambiguously meant "physically" capable of extraction; so the tenant could not break merely because it was not economically viable to quarry the remaining limestone spar.

In most leases the right to break is restricted to determination at a specified date or dates into the term. Hence a lease for 21 years might contain a tenant's option to break at the end of the seventh and 14th years of the term. Furthermore, the break clause will usually require the service of a notice to break ("a break notice") a minimum period before the lease is determined thereby (the date of determination being "the break date"). A maximum period of notice may also be specified, but this is less common as neither party generally suffers from a longer period of notice.

Time is of the essence for the service of a break notice.[25] In *United Scientific Holdings v Burnley Borough Council*[26], Lord Diplock stated:

> "there is a practical business reason for treating time as of the essence [in a tenant's break clause]; the evident purpose of the stipulation as to notice is to leave [the landlord] free thereafter to enter into a contract with a new tenant for a tenancy commencing at the date ... provided in the break clause."

A right to break is therefore lost if no notice has been served by the end of the last day for service, unless the circumstances give rise to an estoppel.

Error in break notice

Care should be taken to ensure that the break notice complies in all respects with the specifications laid down in the lease, particularly the date upon which such notice is to expire. If, as is common, this is expressed by reference to the term date, this should not be confused with the date of execution of lease, which may be different.[27] If the notice is required to expire "at the end of the third year of the term", this is not the same date as one required to expire "on the third anniversary of the commencement of

---

24 [1997] EGCS 97 (Ch D).
25 *Cadby v Martinez* (1840) 9 LJQB 281. Service of a notice to break even only ten minutes after the deadline would therefore be too late: *cf Union Eagle Ltd v Golden Achievement Ltd* [1997] 2 WLR 341 (PC) (contract for the sale of a flat).
26 [1978] AC 904, 929.
27 *Garston v Scottish Widows' Fund* [1996] 4 All ER 282 (which was heard after the subsequently reversed decision of the Court of Appeal in the *Mannai Investment* case, and which therefore proceeded on the basis of the law as there laid down).

the term." If a term for a specified number of years is stated to commence "from" a particular date[28], then the end of the third year of the term will be a day later than it would have been had the term been stated to commence "on and including" a particular date, or "from" one specified date "to" another.[29] One method of avoiding an erroneous date in the break notice is "by adopting the familiar stratagem of invoking, as an alternative to the specified date, a date identifiable by reference to the terms of the clause itself."[30]

In *Mannai Investment Co Ltd v Eagle Star Life Assurance Co Ltd*[31], however, the House of Lords held that a break notice which contains an error is not necessarily void. Such a notice is not to be construed (as it used to be[32]) as a "technical document"; rather it is to be construed (like a unilateral notice in most commercial agreements) in accordance with business common sense, because this is more likely to give effect to the intention of the parties to a commercial lease.[33] A notice containing an error will be valid if its intended meaning is objectively clear to a reasonable recipient with knowledge of the background (which must be taken to include the terms of the lease).[34] The error might relate to the identity of the premises demised[35]; but a more easily made error is the date of earlier determination.

In *Mannai Investment* case itself[36], the break clause entitled the tenant to terminate the lease by serving not less than six months' notice in writing "such notice to expire on the third anniversary of the term commencement date." The term commenced on 13 January 1992, so that the third anniversary of the commencement date was 13 January 1995. The tenant, however, served a notice, expressed to be pursuant to the break clause, to determine the lease on 12 January 1995. The majority of the House of Lords, overruling an earlier decision of the Court of Appeal[37], held that the notice validly determined the lease on 13 January 1995. A reasonable recipient with knowledge of the terms of the lease and of the third

---

28 *Ackland v Lutley* (1839) 9 Ad & El 879 (Denman J).
29 *Meadfield Properties Ltd v Secretary of State for the Environment* [1995] 1 EGLR 39 (Ch D); see pp 59–60 *supra*.
30 *Mannai Investment Co Ltd v Eagle Star Life Assurance Co Ltd* [1997] 3 All ER 352, 363, per Lord Goff.
31 [1997] 3 All ER 352, reversing [1995] 1 WLR 1508 (CA).
32 *i.e.* as it was in *Hankey v Clavering* [1942] 2 KB 326 (overruled by the *Mannai Investment* case).
33 *Mannai Investment Co Ltd v Eagle Star Life Assurance Co Ltd* [1997] 3 All ER 352, 372, per Lord Steyn; also *Micrografix v Woking 8 Ltd* [1995] 2 EGLR 32.
34 *Mannai Investment Co Ltd v Eagle Star Life Assurance Co Ltd* [1997] 3 All ER 352 (HL); *Carradine Properties Ltd v Aslam* [1976] 1 WLR 442, 444 (Goulding J).
35 *cf Doe d Cox v Roe* (1803) 4 Esp 185.
36 [1997] 3 All ER 352 (HL), reversing [1995] 1 WLR 1508 (CA).
37 *Hankey v Clavering* [1942] 2 KB 326.

anniversary date would have appreciated that the tenant wished to determine the lease on the third anniversary date and had merely misdescribed it as the 12th instead of the 13th.

The decision of Goulding J in *Carradine Properties* v *Aslam*[38], which was approved by the House of Lords in the *Mannai Investment* case, can now be seen to rest on the general principle which their Lordships have laid down. There a lease for a term of 21 years conferred on either party a right to determine upon 12 months' written notice at the expiration of the first seven or 14 years of the term. The expiration of the seventh year of the term was 27 September 1975. Early in September 1974, the tenant served a notice that purported to determine the term on 27 September 1973. As the mistake was obvious, the notice was held valid to determine the lease on 27 September 1975.

The House of Lords also approved the decision in *Micrografix* v *Woking 8 Ltd*[39], where the lease entitled the tenants to determine the lease at the expiration of the fifth year of the term by giving the landlords no less than 12 months' notice. The expiration of the fifth year of the term was 23 June 1995; but the notice which the tenants served stated that they were determining the lease on 23 March 1994 pursuant to the break clause in the lease, and the letter with which it was sent stated that the notice was to determine the lease on 23 March 1995. Jacob J held a reasonable landlord would know that the only date for determination would be 23 June 1995, that the dates specified in the notice and the letter were mere mistakes, and that the tenants plainly wished to leave. He therefore held the notice to be good.

Conditions relating to the exercise of break notices

Although errors in the contents of break notices may no longer invalidate them, it is evident that the House of Lords in the *Mannai Investment* case did not intend to relax the rules requiring strict compliance with any conditions with which they are required to comply. If, therefore, the lease requires the break notice to be on blue paper, it is void if written on pink paper.[40] Errors in relation to formalities are therefore still fatal. If, for example, the lease requires notice in writing, merely oral notice does not suffice.[41]

If the lease does not specify who may exercise the break clause, it will

---

38 [1976] 1 WLR 442.
39 [1995] 2 EGLR 32
40 *Mannai Investment Co Ltd* v *Eagle Star Life Assurance Co Ltd* [1997] 3 All ER 352, 377, per Lord Hoffmann.
41 *Legg d Scot* v *Benion* (1737) Willes 43.

be taken to be exercisable by the tenant alone.[42] If, however, the right to break is stated to be exercisable by "lessees", its exercise requires the authority of all the lessees.[43] If a landlord's break clause requires the notice to be delivered to the tenant, there can be difficulty for the landlord if the tenant has left the premises, as merely sending a notice to the tenant at the demised premises or to the tenant's last known place of residence will not suffice.[44] A landlord's break clause should therefore provide for notice to be left on the demised premises.[45]

A slip that has occurred sufficiently frequently to generate a body of case law is the service of a notice which contains an error as to the identity of the landlord or the tenant (whether as the server or recipient or both). This type of mistake tends to occur where one or both of the parties habitually conducts dealings with the tenancy through an agent. Where one of the parties is a company, this is often a director[46] or an associated company in the same group.[47] For example, instead of serving the break notice "as agent for", or "on behalf of" the tenant, the agent may erroneously serve a notice which does not disclose the agency and which on its face represents that it is itself the tenant. Such a notice will be upheld if the agent has a general authority[48] to deal with the tenancy on the tenant's behalf, provided that the recipient landlord has reason to believe the notice to be binding on the tenant.[49] The same principle applies where the notice is served on the tenant by the landlord's agent.[50] Service upon the agent of either party is valid if the agent has a general authority[51],

42 *Dann v Spurrier* (1803) 3 Bos & Pul 399.
43 *Re Viola's Lease, Humphrey v Stenbury* [1909] 1 Ch 244.
44 *Hogg v Brooks* (1885) 15 QBD 256 (CA).
45 See Woodfall, 1-2043.
46 As in *Harmond Properties Ltd v Gajdzis* [1968] 1 WLR 1858 (CA).
47 As in *Townsends Carriers Ltd v Pfizer Ltd* (1977) 33 P & CR 361; *Lemerbell Ltd v Britannia LAS Direct Ltd* (1997) 22 May (unreported, Lexis Transcript) (Rattee J).
48 But not if it has only a limited authority: *Lemon v Lardeur* [1946] 1 KB 613 (CA); *Divall v Harrison* [1992] 2 EGLR 64 (CA) (both on notices to quit).
49 This could be because the recipient erroneously believes the agent to be the tenant; but the notice can still be valid even if the recipient knows that the person giving the notice is not itself the tenant: *Townsends Carriers Ltd v Pfizer Ltd* (1977) 33 P & CR 361 (Megarry V-C); *Lemerbell Ltd v Britannia LAS Direct Ltd* (1997) 22 May (unreported, Lexis Transcript) (Rattee J), each involving a tenant's notice to break. Contrast *Dun & Bradstreet Software Services (England) Ltd v Provident Mutual Life Assurance Association* [1997] EGCS 89, where the Court of Appeal (surprisingly perhaps) declined on the facts to find a general agency. See JE Adams, "Murkiness in group transactions – some recent examples" [1997] Conv 333.
50 *Jones v Phipps* (1868) LR 3 QB 567; *Harmond Properties Ltd v Gajdzis* [1968] 1 WLR 1858 (CA), each involving a notice to quit where the tenant recipient mistakenly believed the landlord's agent to be the landlord himself. See also *Re Knight & Hubbard's Underlease* [1923] 1 Ch 130 (Sargant J).
51 *Townsends Carriers Ltd v Pfizer Ltd* (1977) 33 P & CR 361 (Megarry V-C), where notice was served on the landlord's agent.

and it has been said that a notice served on a landlord's agent who lacks such authority "might still be good if it could be shown that the agent was likely to pass it on to the landlord."[52] A landlord who receives a notice from an agent lacking general authority to serve it may be estopped from disputing the validity of the notice if, knowing that it contains an error as to the identity of the tenant, he nevertheless indicates that the notice is acceptable, thereby inducing the tenant or its agent not to serve a fresh (corrected) notice in time.[53]

Performance of covenants

Many break clauses end with a proviso that the determination of the lease is to be "without prejudice to any right or remedy by the parties hereto in respect of any antecedent or other obligations hereunder." This is not strictly necessary, however, as the right to sue for breaches of covenant committed during the subsistence of the lease survives its earlier determination.[54] A tenant's power to break may be, and often is, made conditional upon his paying the rent reserved by the lease and observing and performing the covenants therein contained.[55] Such a condition is construed as a condition precedent to the determination of the lease at the break date.[56] Unless the condition expressly states that the tenant must have complied with such obligations "during the whole term of the lease", it can be satisfied even though there have been prior breaches, provided that these have subsequently been made good. To avoid doubt as to the precise date upon which the condition must be complied with, the date should be stated expressly in the break clause. If the condition requires the tenant to perform the covenants "up to the time of service of the notice to break", performance after the service of the notice does not suffice – the notice is invalid.[57] If, however, it requires the tenant to perform the covenants "up to the time of determination of the lease", performance after service of the notice (but before determination) satisfies the condition and the notice is

---

52 *Peel Developments (South) Ltd* v *Siemens plc* [1992] 2 EGLR 85, 87, per Judge Paul Baker QC, sitting as a deputy judge of the Chancery Division.

53 *Dun & Bradstreet Software Services (England) Ltd* v *Provident Mutual Life Assurance Association* [1997] EGCS 89 (CA), where, however, the landlord succeeded on another ground.

54 *Blore* v *Giulini* [1903] 1 KB 356.

55 *Grey* v *Friar* (1854) 4 HL Cas 565; *Trane (UK) Ltd* v *Provident Mutual Life Assurance* [1995] 1 EGLR 33 (ChD).

56 *Stait* v *Fenner* [1912] 2 Ch 504, 515 (Neville J).

57 *Bunch* v *Farrars Bank Ltd* [1917] 1 Ch 616 (where the tenant effected repairs only after serving notice to break).

58 *Simons* v *Associated Furnishers Ltd* [1931] 1 Ch 379.

59 *Trane (UK) Ltd* v *Provident Mutual Life Assurance* [1995] 1 EGLR 33, 36K, per Judge Cooke (sitting as a judge of the Chancery Division); see also *Bass Holdings Ltd* v *Morton Music Ltd* [1988] Ch 493; [1987] 1 EGLR 214(CA) (concerning an option to renew).

valid.[58] A break clause in the latter form is also not invalidated by tenant's breaches which occur after the service of the notice but before its expiration: "what has to be established is that there is no subsisting breach at the break date, *i.e.* that as the clocks chime at midnight there is no obligation left unperformed."[59]

If the condition is in the foregoing form, it must be complied with exactly: even a trivial breach at the relevant date will invalidate the break notice.[60] The tenant may attempt to secure some relaxation of the condition so that it requires only "**reasonable**" compliance. This qualification relieves the tenant of the need to comply with the letter of the covenant: it is sufficient if the object of the covenant is attained in substance. Thus it has been suggested that in some circumstances a covenant to paint with two coats might reasonably be performed with only one; and that a covenant to re-carpet at the end of the lease might not need to be complied with at all if the existing carpet is then in a perfectly good condition.[61] A failure to comply with the substance of the covenant cannot, however, be a reasonable compliance, even if the economic value of non-compliance is not great.[62] From the tenant's point of view, it is important that a condition that can be fulfilled by only reasonable compliance also specifies that such compliance is required only at the date of service of the notice to break or upon its expiration. In the absence of such a restriction, the condition will be satisfied only if the conduct of the tenant has been that of a reasonable tenant throughout the term.[63]

Where the lease imposes obligations upon the tenant at the end of the term, it is a matter of construction whether such obligations are imposed in the event of the earlier determination of the lease through the exercise of a break clause. Thus in *Dickinson v St Aubyn*[64], the lease contained a covenant by the tenant to paint "in the last quarter of the said term." It was held that this imposed an obligation to paint only during the last quarter of the full term, should the lease so long run. The earlier determination of the lease in that case therefore meant that the obligation to repaint never arose. A landlord should therefore require the tenant to redecorate or to replace furnishings, for example, not merely in a specified period before the expiration of the lease, but alternatively in a specified

---

60 *Reed Personnel Services plc v American Express Ltd* [1997] 1 EGLR 229 (Jacob J). See also (in relation to an option to renew) *Bass Holdings Ltd v Morton Music Ltd* [1988] Ch 493 CA); *Bairstow Eves (Securities) Ltd v Ripley* [1992] 2 EGLR 47 (CA).
61 *Reed Personnel Services plc v American Express Ltd* [1997] 1 EGLR 229, 232 (Jacob J).
62 *Ibid*, at 232.
63 *Gardner v Blaxill* [1960] 1 WLR 752 (Paull J); *Bassett v Whiteley* (1983) 45 P & CR 87 (CA); see also Pitchers, "Write to break" [1997] 27 EG 106.
64 [1944] KB 454.

period before its earlier determination through the service of a break notice.

Penalty rents

If a tenant's break clause requires a tenant to pay a penalty rent (such as half a year's rent) by the break date, it is a matter of construction whether the requirement is a condition precedent to the right to break (so that the lease does not terminate if such sum is not paid in time) or whether it is merely an independent obligation (so that the lease will terminate whether or not payment is made in time).[65] If a condition precedent is used, time will be of the essence, so that the right to break is lost if payment is not made by the date specified.[66] The following form of words gives rise to a condition precedent:

> "The Tenant may by serving notice in writing upon the Landlord no less than six months and no more than twelve months expiring on [date] determine this demise on [date] provided that the Tenant shall on or before such date of determination (or on or before the vacation of the property if earlier) pay to the Landlord (in addition to all other payments which may be due and payable to the Landlord under the terms hereof upon the expiration or earlier determination of this Lease or otherwise) a sum equal to...."

The landlord is generally better placed to recover a penalty rent from the tenant if the payment of such rent is a condition precedent to the tenant's right to break. There is, however, a drawback in the use of the condition precedent, in that it does not itself impose on the tenant any obligation to pay. This drawback becomes apparent if the tenant, having served a notice to break, later changes its mind, since it can then prevent the break notice from taking effect simply by failing to pay. The landlord can hold the tenant to the break notice by waiving the condition precedent (which it is entitled to do, as the condition is solely for the landlord's benefit).[67] The lease will then determine at the break date. The waiver of the condition, however, means that the tenant escapes from the lease without having to pay the financial penalty which the break clause prescribes.

Break clauses and rent review

The timetable for service and expiration of notice under a tenant's break clause is frequently linked to the timetable for rent review, with any

65 *Dun & Bradstreet Software Services (England) Ltd* v *Provident Mutual Life Assurance Association* [1997] EGCS 89 (CA), where the words "upon condition that" in the break clause were held to give rise to a condition precedent.
66 *Dun & Bradstreet Software Services (England) Ltd* v *Provident Mutual Life Assurance Association* [1997] EGCS 89 (CA).
67 *Ibid, per* Peter Gibson LJ, delivering the judgment of the Court of Appeal.

increased rent taking effect immediately or soon after the break date is past. The tenant will be better placed to decide whether to break if it is aware (or at least has a good idea) prior to the last date upon which it may serve a break notice of what the new rent will be. The tenant should therefore try to ensure that the timetable for rent review is sufficiently ahead of the timetable to break. Since the process of rent review can take several months, the tenant may need to ensure that the landlord's trigger notice to activate review is served several months before the last date for service of the tenant's break notice – a gap of five or six months is desirable. Although it is normally presumed that time is not of the essence of rent-review clauses[68], the close interlocking of the timetables to review the rent and to break is generally sufficient to raise a presumption the other way[69], at least as regards steps in the review procedure which depend upon compliance by the landlord rather than a third party (such as an arbitrator).[70] For the avoidance of doubt, however, it is better for the tenant to insist that the lease expressly makes time of the essence of every stage in the rent-review procedure. Failing this, the tenant should consider serving a notice when appropriate in order to make time of the essence.

Break clauses and Landlord and Tenant Act 1954, Part II

If the tenancy falls within Part II of the Landlord and Tenant Act 1954, a landlord's break notice, whilst effective to terminate the tenancy at common law, will not preclude its statutory continuation beyond the break date. To terminate the tenancy under the statute, the landlord must additionally serve a statutory notice under section 25 of that Act. It has been held that a single notice by the landlord will suffice both to exercise the break clause and to comply with section 25, provided that the notice is capable of complying (and does in fact comply) with both provisions.[71] In practice, therefore, the landlord can simplify matters by ensuring that the lease specifies a form and length of break notice which enables a single notice to serve doubly as a break notice and a notice under section 25. If the terms of the break clause are such as to make such combined service impossible, two separate notices will have to be served.

With rents generally falling in the early 1990s, a tenant with the benefit of a break clause might consider whether it is possible to break an existing lease (perhaps with a relatively high pre-recessionary rent) and at the same

---

68 *Coventry City Council v J Hepworth & Son Ltd* (1983) 46 P & CR 170 (CA), affirming
   [1982] 1 EGLR 114 (Ch D); *C Richards & Son Ltd v Karenita Ltd* (1971) 221 EG 25.
69 *United Scientific Holdings v Burnley Borough Council* [1978] AC 904 (HL).
70 *Metrolands Investments Ltd v JH Dewhurst Ltd* [1986] 1 EGLR 125 (CA).
71 *Keith Bayley Rogers & Co v Cubes Ltd* (1975) 31 P & CR 412; *Scholl Manufacturing Co
   Ltd v Clifton (Slim-Line) Ltd* [1967] Ch 41 (CA).

time to serve a request for a new tenancy under the Landlord and Tenant Act 1954, section 26, in the hope that the new lease will be at a lower rent and on more favourable terms. An initial problem for the tenant, however, is that it cannot serve a section 26 request after serving a notice to quit[72], which for this purpose includes a break notice.[73] It has, however, sometimes been suggested that the tenant might be able to achieve the desired result if it is able to effect an earlier determination of the lease, not by serving a separate break notice, but by means of a section 26 request alone, since a section 26 notice can request a new tenancy to commence not earlier than the date on which the current tenancy *could* be brought to an end by notice to quit. As a matter of principle, to permit the tenant both to have his cake and to eat it seems to be against the spirit of the 1954 Act.[74] In the event that the device might work, however, it has been suggested[75] that the landlord should require the tenant to give more than 12 months' notice to break, which would therefore preclude the tenant's serving a section 26 request.[76]

The point arose for consideration indirectly in *Garston v Scottish Widows' Fund*.[77] Here the tenants purported to determine the lease by serving a notice to break, and enclosed with the notice a request for a new tenancy under section 26. The notice to break was later accepted to be void because, whereas the break date was 24 June 1995, the tenants wrongly purported to break it on 9 July 1995, and the decision preceded that of the House of Lords in the *Mannai* case. The tenants initially applied to the court for a new tenancy; but on 24 May 1995 they gave notice discontinuing their application. They then argued that the service of the section 26 request was valid because it was a request for a new tenancy to begin not more than 12 and not less than six months after the making of the request; that the request did not infringe the proviso to section 26(2), because the date specified for the commencement of the new tenancy was not earlier than the date on which, at the date of the request, the tenancy could be brought to an end by notice to quit under the break clause; and that they were not disabled from making a request for a new tenancy under section 26(4), because the tenants had not given notice to quit before making their request. The tenants therefore contended that the

---

72 LTA 1954, s 26(4).

73 *Ibid*, s 69(1).

74 See Cheffings and Rickard, [1994] 41 EG 143; Slessenger and Ballaster, [1994] 46 EG 196; also letter by Gillette, [1994] 22 EG 52.

75 Lewison, *Drafting Business Leases,* 5th ed (1996), FT Law and Tax, at 58.

76 Since a tenant's s 26 request cannot be made more than 12 months before "the current tenancy would come to an end by effluxion of time or could be brought to an end by notice to quit served by the tenant": LTA 1954, s 26(2).

77 [1996] 4 All ER 282; discussed by Slessenger, [1996] 18 EG 96.

tenancy came to an end on 24 August 1995, *i.e.* three months after final determination by the court.[78]

Rattee J rejected these submissions. He held that the tenants' section 26 notice was invalid because, as this was a fixed-term tenancy, no new tenancy could commence before the expiration of the term on 23 June 2005. The section 26 notice could not therefore make a request for a new tenancy to begin no more than 12 months after the making of the request. The difficulty with this reasoning is that it restricts the expression "notice to quit" in section 26 to its narrow meaning of a tenant's notice to determine a periodic tenancy; a tenant's notice to break a fixed-term lease is therefore excluded, even though section 69(1) defines "notice to quit" to include a notice to terminate a tenancy for a term of years certain.[79] There might therefore be scope for tenants to challenge this decision in later cases.

Who can break?

A break clause runs with the legal estate of the party entitled to it. It is therefore exercisable only by the person who is the landlord or the tenant (as the case may be) for the time being. Thus, for instance, an original tenant cannot exercise it after assignment of the lease. Similarly, a mere equitable assignee of either party, not having the legal estate vested in him, cannot exercise it.[80]

The benefit of a tenant's break clause may be restricted to the original tenant only.[81] In *Max Factor Ltd* v *Wesleyan Assurance Society*[82], where the right to break was personal to the original tenant[83], it was held that the original tenant, who had previously assigned the lease, could not break upon a re-assignment to it. It therefore seems that a tenant with a personal right to break who assigns the lease thereupon loses the right to break permanently. An "assignment" for this purpose means a legal assignment.[84] If the title to the lease is registered, there is no legal assignment until the transfer is registered at HM Land Registry[85], so that an original tenant with a personal right to break until "the assignment of the lease" retains until registration, as against the landlord, the right to break even after the execution of the assignment,[86] unless the landlord can raise an estoppel

---

78 LTA 1954, s 64(1), (2).

79 There is, moreover, no proviso in LTA 1954, s 69(1), to indicate that the expressions have the defined meaning only where the context does not indicate otherwise.

80 *Stait* v *Fenner* [1912] 2 Ch 504.

81 As in *Olympia & York Canary Wharf Ltd* v *Oil Property Investment Ltd* [1994] 2 EGLR 48 (CA).

82 [1995] 2 EGLR 38 (Ch); affirmed [1996] 2 EGLR 210 (CA).

83 The right to break was conferred on the tenant "(here meaning Max Factor Ltd only)."

84 *Gentle* v *Faulkner* [1900] 2 QB 267, in relation to a restriction on assignment.

85 LRA 1925, s 22(1).

86 *Brown & Root Technology Ltd* v *Sun Alliance & London Assurance Co Ltd* [1997] 1 EGLR 39 (CA).

against its exercise. The mere fact that the landlord grants its consent to an assignment, enters the name of the assignee in its records and accepts rent from what it believes to be the legal assignee, does not, however, suffice to establish a detrimental reliance necessary for such an estoppel.[87]

 A tenant's break clause can be personal to the original tenant and yet binding on assignees of the landlord.[88] There is no reason why these principles should not apply *vice versa* to a landlord's break clause personal to the original landlord.

Effect on sub-lessee of upwards break notice served by sub-lessor

If A leases premises for a fixed term to B, and B sub-leases them for a fixed term to C, it is unclear whether the exercise by B of a break clause in the head-lease affects C's sub-lease. *Dicta* in *Phipos* v *G & B Callegari*[89] suggest that B's act is to be treated as a surrender, so that C's sub-lease continues. This view was, however, doubted by the Court of Appeal in *Pennell* v *Payne*[90] on the ground that, if this were so, and C's sub-lease were to continue, the absence of privity of estate between A and C would preclude A from enforcing the covenants in the sub-lease. These comments were, however, themselves *obiter,* as the Court of Appeal was not concerned with a break notice, but rather with the effect upon an agricultural periodic sub-tenancy of an upwards notice to quit served by the sub-tenant's immediate landlord, who himself held a periodic tenancy. It should in any event be borne in mind that even if C's sub-tenancy is terminated at common law by B's exercise of an upwards break clause, C's sub-tenancy will be statutorily continued if it is within the Landlord and Tenant Act 1954, Part II.

Surrender and offer-to-surrender clauses

Surrender is the yielding up by the tenant of its lease to the person or body with the immediate estate in reversion. The result is to merge the estate surrendered into such reversionary estate. Thus if A, the freeholder owner, leases premises to B, and B sub-leases them to C, A has the immediate estate in reversion on B's head-lease, and B has the immediate estate in

---

87 *Ibid.*

88 *Systems Floors Ltd* v *Ruralpride Ltd* [1995] 1 EGLR 48 (CA), not following *dicta* of Lord Oliver in *P & A Swift Investments* v *Combined English Stores Group plc* [1989] AC 632. The Court of Appeal (which was dealing with a pre-1996 lease) held that the burden of the covenant passed with the reversionary estate by virtue of LPA 1925 s 142(1). With the abolition of the touching and concerning requirement for covenants in post-1995 leases by virtue of LT(C)A 1995, s 3(6)(a), it is clear that the same result would ensue in the case of a post-1995 lease.

89 (1910) 54 SJ 635 (Warrington J).

90 [1995] 1 EGLR 6, criticised by Luxton and Wilkie [1995] Conv 263.

reversion on C's sub-lease. A surrender by C therefore causes C's estate to merge into the estate of B, and thereby cease to exist.

Express surrender

An express surrender must be by deed, unless the lease is for a term of three years or less, in which case it must be in writing.[91] A surrender of even a lease for more than three years, however, may be effective in equity if in writing and for value.[92] The correct form of words for an express surrender is "surrender and yield up."[93]

Implied surrender

An implied surrender (sometimes called a surrender by operation of law) is a surrender which arises where the parties conduct themselves in a way which is inconsistent with the continued existence of the lease. The concept is based upon equitable estoppel.[94] A surrender by operation of law is not required to be by deed.[95] Examples of an implied surrender include the acceptance by the tenant of a new lease to begin during the continuance of the old lease[96], the grant by the landlord of a new lease to a third party with the lessee both consenting and giving up possession to the new lessee at the time it is granted[97], and the landlord's taking possession by some other unequivocal act where the tenant has offered to surrender and has vacated the premises.[98] If the tenant has vacated, steps taken by the landlord merely to protect and secure the premises will not in themselves amount to an

---

91 LPA 1925, ss 52 and 53(1)(a).
92 See *Megarry's Manual of the Law of Real Property,* 7th ed (1993) ed Megarry and Thompson, Sweet and Maxwell, 332.
93 *Precedents in Conveyancing,* Key & Elphinstone, 15th ed, 1246; *Woodfall,* Vol 1, 822.
94 *Lyon* v *Reed* (1844) 13 M & W 285; *Nichells* v *Atherstone* (1847) 10 QB 944; *Wallis* v *Hands* [1893] 2 Ch 75; *Foster* v *Robinson* [1951] 1 KB 149.
95 LPA 1925, s 52(2)(c).
96 *Ive's Case* (1597) 5 Co Rep 11a; *Bush Transport Ltd* v *Nelson* [1987] 1 EGLR 71.
97 See *Re AGB Research plc* [1994] EGCS 73, where the tenant's administrator wished to surrender; he vacated the premises and returned the keys to the landlord. No agreement for surrender or termination had been reached, but the landlord then granted a new lease of the premises to a third party. It was held that the landlord was thereby estopped from denying that the lease had been surrendered.
98 *Phene* v *Popplewell* (1862) 12 CB (NS) 334. In *Griffith* v *Hodges* (1824) 1 Carr & P 419, the landlord had lit a fire in the tenant's kitchen in order to roast a hare; this was held not to amount to a resumption of possession. In *Filering Ltd* v *Taylor* [1996] EGCS 95 (CA), the tenant company having vacated commercial premises, the landlord collected the keys from the son of the guarantor (who was also the tenant company's director). Whilst this would not in itself have been an unequivocal act, the absence of any other viable explanation and the presence of other factors (such as the landlord's failure to demand further rent) were consistent with an intention on the part of both the landlord and the tenant to effect a surrender by operation of law.

unequivocal acceptance that the lease has terminated.[99] A mere oral agreement between the landlord and the tenant that the tenant will surrender before the expiration of the contractual term does not *per se* constitute an implied surrender.[1]

Surrender of head-lease: impact on sub-lease

If A leases freehold property to B, which B then sub-lets to C, the surrender by B of his head-lease during the subsistence of C's sub-lease destroys the estate which comprises the immediate reversion upon C's sub-lease. C's sub-lease, however, survives. The problem at common law was that it left C holding an estate carved out of A's freehold reversion, but with no privity of estate between A and C. This meant that not all the covenants in C's lease were enforceable as between A and C. Statute has remedied this by deeming C to be the immediate lessee of A. This provision (now contained in the Law of Property Act 1925, s 139) means that, upon a surrender by B, A's estate is deemed to be the reversion of C's estate for the purpose of preserving the same incidents and obligations as would have affected the original reversion had there been no surrender. After B's surrender, therefore, covenants in C's sub-lease are enforceable between A and C.

If, however, the surrender by B is effected with a view to B's taking a new lease from A, B can surrender his lease and take a new lease from A without having to surrender C's sub-lease; and B and C can enforce the covenants in C's sub-lease as if B's original lease had not been surrendered.[2] This simplifies the granting of new leases upon a surrender, because it means that sub-tenants do not need to be involved.

Offer-to-surrender clauses

In the past, leases sometimes contained a clause whereby, if the tenant wished to assign the lease, it was first obliged to offer to surrender it to the landlord. The general aim of such clauses was explained by Lord Denning MR in *Greene v Church Commissioners for England*[3] as being to preserve for the landlord the benefit of any rise in the letting value of the property leased. Without such a clause, in the event of a general rise in rents, the tenant could take the benefit by way of a premium upon assignment;

---

99 In *McDougalls Catering Foods Ltd v BSE Trading Ltd* [1997] 42 EG 174, following the tenant's vacating the premises during the term, the site was invaded by gypsies The landlord, under pressure from its insurers to take action, instituted and enforced possession proceedings against the gypsies and constructed an earth mound to prevent re-entry. The Court of Appeal held that such actions, being merely intended to protect the property, did not effect a surrender by operation of law.

1 *Take Harvest Ltd v Liu* [1993] 2 All ER 459 (PC).

2 LPA 1925, s 150.

3 [1974] Ch 467.

whereas, by taking advantage of such a clause, it would be the landlord who would benefit by re-letting at a higher rent.

Such clauses would specify a procedure, including the giving of notice, the time within which any acceptance by the landlord could be effected, and the method of ascertaining any consideration to be paid for the surrender. A typical clause would provide that, in the event of the landlord's not accepting the offer to surrender, the tenant would have a qualified right to assign.

As explained elsewhere[4], a clause in such a form does not infringe the Landlord and Tenant Act 1927, section 19(1)(a) (which deems qualified covenants against assignment to be subject to a proviso that the licence or consent shall not be unreasonably withheld) because the sub-section bites only when the tenant's right to assign (albeit a qualified right) has arisen. Under the clause, however, this right does not arise until after an offer to surrender has been made and has not been accepted by the landlord. The surrender mechanism therefore operates as a condition precedent to the right to assign. Such a clause was accepted as valid in *Adler* v *Upper Grosvenor Street Investments Ltd*[5] (which involved an obligation to offer to surrender the lease voluntarily), and this decision was affirmed in *Bocardo SA* v *S & M Hotels Ltd.*[6]

The usefulness of offer-to-surrender clauses in the context of business leases is, however, curtailed by virtue of the Landlord and Tenant Act 1954, section 38(1). This section is designed to invalidate provisions in the lease which seek to prevent a tenant from invoking the renewal machinery of Part II of that Act. The section provides that any agreement relating to a tenancy within Part II is (subject to specified savings) void in so far as it purports to preclude the tenant from making an application or request under Part II or provides for the termination or the surrender of the tenancy in the event of his making such application or request.

The application of section 38(1) to business tenancies was considered by Megarry V-C in *Allnatt London Properties Ltd* v *Newton.*[7] There the lease contained first an absolute prohibition upon assignment, and then an offer-to-surrender clause. If the landlord rejected the offer (or failed to accept it within 21 days) the tenant could assign subject to the qualified consent of the landlord. The tenant made an offer to surrender in accordance with the clause which the landlord accepted. The tenant then purported to withdraw the offer when he realised that the payment he would receive under the clause would be less than a quarter of what he

4 See Chap 5.
5 [1957] 1 WLR 227.
6 [1980] 1 WLR 17; see further Chap 5.
7 [1981] 2 All ER 290; affirmed [1984] 1 All ER 423.

might expect to obtain by way of premium from an assignee. The landlord claimed specific performance of the agreement and damages.

Megarry V-C found that, although the agreement did not in terms preclude the tenant from applying for a new tenancy, it did have that effect. This was sufficient for him to hold that section 38(1) rendered the agreement to surrender void. Nevertheless, his Lordship held that the section did not strike down the machinery requiring the tenant to offer to surrender: an offer to surrender was not an agreement to surrender, and the section invalidated only the latter. The consequence was that the tenant never acquired a qualified right to assign. Both parties were left stymied.

This decision means that offer-to-surrender clauses are seldom found in new leases of business premises. Furthermore, apart from invalidity under section 38 of the 1954 Act, an agreement pursuant to an offer-to-surrender clause contained in an older lease may well be void for non-compliance with the formalities prescribed by the Law of Property (Miscellaneous Provisions) Act 1989, section 2.[8] If an offer-to-surrender clause is important to the landlord of business premises, the only sure method is for the parties to make a joint application to the court before the lease is granted for authorisation of an agreement for the surrender of the tenancy.[9]

Voluntary surrender (*i.e.* a surrender not pursuant to an offer-to-surrender clause) is a method of terminating a tenancy within Part II of the 1954 Act.[10] Even a voluntary surrender or agreement to surrender is ineffective for this purpose, however, unless the tenant has been in occupation under the tenancy for at least one month before the instrument is executed.[11]

Merger

Merger is the converse of surrender, and occurs where the tenant acquires the reversion immediately expectant upon its lease. In such instance, the general rule is that the lease determines through being merged (or drowned, as it is sometimes expressed) in the reversion.

Merger can occur only where the two estates are both legal or both equitable, and only where they become vested in one person in the same

---

8 See Law Commission Report No 208 (1992), *Business Tenancies: a periodic review of the Landlord and Tenant Act 1954*, at paras 3.16–3.19.
9 LTA 1954, s 38(4)(b); and see Sheldon & Friend (1982) 98 LQR 14.
10 LTA 1954, s 24(2).
11 *Ibid*, s 24(2)(b).

right. Thus merger will not occur if, for example, the lessee takes a conveyance of the freehold in the name of another as trustee for himself.[12]

Equity took a more restrictive view of merger than the common law, and in certain instances would not treat merger as having occurred. Thus, equity looked to the intention of the party acquiring the reversion. In the absence of evidence of intention, equity presumed that merger had not occurred if it was either in that person's interests or if it was consistent with his duty. Furthermore, equity would not treat merger as occurring where, although the same estate became vested in the same person, this was in different capacities: such as a lessee who acquires the immediate reversion of his lease as personal representative. The equitable rules are now of general application: the Law of Property Act 1925, section 185, states that there is no merger by operation of law of any estate the beneficial interest in which would not be deemed merged or extinguished in equity. Thus, if a tenant acquiring the reversion does intend to merge the two estates, its best course is to state this intention in writing.

Where merger does occur, it has the effect of destroying covenants in the lease, even if they affect other land of the covenantor. Thus in *Golden Lion Hotel (Hunstanton) Ltd* v *Carter*[13] the lessor had covenanted in the lease not to build on an adjoining plot. The lessee purchased the reversion, merger occurred, and the covenant was destroyed. The purchaser of the adjoining plot could thereafter not be prevented from building.

Impact of merger on sub-leases

The position is essentially the same as that of surrender. The position at common law was that merger did not destroy a sub-lease created out of the merged leasehold estate, but that the covenants in the sub-lease were thereafter unenforceable. As in the case of surrender, however, the common law has long since been amended by statute. The Law of Property Act 1925, section 139, applies also to merger. Thus if A (a freeholder) leases land to B, B sub-leases it to C, and B then purchases A's reversion, the freehold estate (now vested in B) is deemed to be the reversion of C's sub-lease for the purpose of preserving the same incidents and obligations as would have affected B's reversion had there been no merger.

---

12 *Belaney v Belaney* (1867) LR 2 Ch 138.
13 [1965] 1 WLR 1189.

Disclaimer by liquidator or trustee in bankruptcy

The liquidator of a company in liquidation, or the trustee in bankruptcy of an individual, may disclaim onerous property, which includes a lease. A disclaimer puts an end to the tenant's rights, interests and liabilities under the lease, but not necessarily to those of third parties. The issues are discussed in Chapter 14.

Frustration

The doctrine of frustration has a very limited application in leases. For many centuries, English law adhered firmly to the view that frustration was not an event capable of bringing a lease to an end. Thus a lease of a dwelling house was treated as continuing even though the house had been blown down in a gale or destroyed by fire,[14] or gained upon by the sea,[15] and even though its occupation had been made impracticable by the King's enemies.[16] Similarly, a lease of a wharf which had been swept away by the Thames was, nevertheless, held to continue.[17] For the same reason, a lease of a dwelling house was not frustrated where the premises, without fault of the landlord, became uninhabitable.[18]

In the 20th century, however, resistance to the application of the doctrine to leases weakened. Thus it was held that a licence (as opposed to a lease) for the use of premises could be frustrated.[19] It was also held that an option to purchase a timber yard could be frustrated, even though the option conferred on the grantee an equitable interest in the land.[20] The traditional view was asserted by the Court of Appeal in *Denman* v *Brise*,[21] which held that, because a lease creates an interest in land, a lease of land could not be frustrated. There were, nevertheless, earlier *dicta* of two members of the House of Lords in *Cricklewood Property and Investment Trust Ltd* v *Leighton's Investment Trust Ltd*[22] to the effect that frustration

---

14 *Monk* v *Cooper* (1727) 2 Stra 763; *Balfour* v *Weston* (1786) 1 TR 310, also citing *Ainsley* v *Rutter* (1767) (unreported); *Baker* v *Holtpzaffel* (1811) 4 Taunt 45 (agreement for a lease).

15 *Richard le Taverner's Case* (1544) 1 Dyer 56a.

16 *Paradine* v *Jane* (1647) Alleyn 26.

17 *Carter* v *Cummins* (c 1665) (unreported), cited in *Harrison* v *Lord North* (1667) 1 Ch Cas 83 at 84.

18 *Izon* v *Gorton* (1839) 5 Bing (NC) 502, applied in *Arden* v *Pullen* (1842) 10 M & W 321.

19 See the so-called "Coronation cases", such as *Krell* v *Henry* [1903] 2 KB 740.

20 *Denny, Mott & Dickson* v *James B Fraser & Co Ltd* [1944] AC 265 (HL), where an order made by the Minstry of Supply prevented the import of timber contemplated in the agreement.

21 [1949] 1 KB 22.

22 [1945] AC 221.

might have a limited application, and this has since been supported by *dicta* in *National Carriers Ltd v Panalpina (Northern) Ltd.*[23]

In the *National Carriers* case, the tenants had a ten-year lease of a warehouse which was unusable for a period of up to 20 months because the only means of access to vehicles had been closed by the local authority. On the facts, the doctrine was held inapplicable because the period during which the premises could not be used was only a small proportion of the length of the lease. It might be inferred from this that a much longer interruption might have been sufficed to frustrate the lease. Similarly, several of their Lordships in that case considered that a lease would be frustrated by the total destruction of the land demised. This might occur in coastal areas where land falls into the sea.

The decision of their Lordships' House therefore opens up the possibility that the destruction of the buildings on the land demised might, in some circumstances, cause the lease to be frustrated even though the land itself remains; and similarly that the total destruction of a building of several floors might, in some circumstances, frustrate the leases of the upper floors, even though the tenants theoretically still retain a right to the use of the air space. In practice, of course, a well-drawn lease will provide for destruction through fire or other hazards by means of insurance.

If the doctrine of frustration is held not to apply to the event in question, the lease continues. In such a case, even if the premises are unusable, the tenant remains liable for the payment of rent during the remainder of the term. Nevertheless, the tenant would have an excuse for breaching a covenant (such as a user covenant) compliance with which has been made impossible by the frustrating event.[24]

No argument appears to have been raised in the *National Carriers* case regarding the effect of frustration upon a business tenancy within the Landlord and Tenant Act 1954, Part II. A tenancy within that Part does not come to an end unless terminated by one of the means there specified[25], and (not surprisingly) frustration is not one of those means. Therefore, even if the lease is frustrated at common law, it would seem that, provided it remains within Part II, it would be continued under the statute. The tenant can terminate the continuation tenancy by giving three months' notice to end on a quarter day[26], but if the parties have no prior knowledge of an impending frustration, the statute could have the effect of committing the tenant to paying at least three months' rent for unusable premises. The decision of the Court of Appeal in *Esselte AB v Pearl*

---

23 [1981] AC 675.
24 cf *John Lewis Properties plc v Viscount Chelsea* [1993] 2 EGLR 77.
25 LTA 1954, s 24(1).
26 *Ibid*, s 27(2).

Assurance plc[27], however, suggests that a lease ceases to be protected by Part II in the event of the tenant's ceasing to occupy the premises for the purposes of a business carried on by him[28], which is bound to occur if the premises are totally destroyed or rendered completely unusable for the tenant's business. In view of the uncertainty, prospective commercial tenants might consider seeking to insert a break clause in the lease entitling them to bring the lease to an end upon immediate notice should the premises be destroyed or rendered unusable. Such a clause is in any event desirable for the tenant, since it will enable the tenant to escape from the lease in circumstances which fall short of frustration.

Acceptance of repudiatory breach

Under general principles of contract law, if a breach of contract by one party indicates their intention no longer to be bound by it, the other may accept the repudiation and rescind the contract. In *Total Oil Great Britain Ltd v Thompson Garages (Biggin Hill) Ltd*[29], the Court of Appeal considered that, because a lease creates an interest in land, a lease could not come to an end like an ordinary contract by repudiation and acceptance. Acceptance of repudiatory breach has, however, become an established method of terminating a lease in several Commonwealth jurisdictions[30], and more recent English authorities have accepted the principle into English law.

In *Hussein v Mehlman*[31], the landlord had let residential premises on a three-year assured shorthold tenancy. The premises were in a very bad state of repair – the bedroom ceiling had collapsed, the ceiling in the sitting room was in a dangerous state, the outside toilet was unusable, and there were burst pipes and rising damp. The landlord refused to execute any repairs, and the tenant eventually vacated the premises and returned the keys. The landlord was in breach of the covenant to repair.[32] The assistant recorder of the county court, Stephen Sedley QC[33], relied, by analogy, upon the reasoning expressed in the *National Carriers* case in the context of frustration. He held that the landlord had committed a repudiatory

---

27 [1997] 2 All ER 41.
28 LTA 1954, s 23(1).
29 [1972] 1 QB 318.
30 See, *e.g. Buchanan v Byrnes* (1906) 3 CLR 704, *Progressive Mailing House Pty Ltd v Tabali Pty Ltd* (1984-1985) 157 CLR 17 (both High Court of Australia); *Highway Properties Ltd v Kelly, Douglas & Co Ltd* [1972] 2 WWR 28 (Supreme Court of Canada).
31 [1992] 2 EGLR 87 (county court).
32 This was the covenant which is implied into certain short leases of dwelling houses by the Landlord and Tenant Act 1985, s 11.
33 Now Sedley J, a judge of the Chancery Division.

breach of contract, and this had been accepted by the tenant's giving up possession and returning the keys. From that date, therefore, the lease had come to an end. Thus, although the tenant remained liable for the rent due up to that date, he was not liable for any further payments. He was also awarded damages for the discomfort and inconvenience which the breach had caused.

The Court of Appeal has recently recognised (albeit with little discussion) that the doctrine of repudiatory breach applies also to commercial leases. In *Chartered Trust plc v Davies*[34], the landlord, who leased out units in a shopping mall, consistently failed to take steps to stop the tenant of one unit from causing a nuisance to the defendant, the tenant of the unit adjoining. The landlord was under a duty to the defendant to stop the nuisance by virtue of his implied covenant of non-derogation from grant; and the nuisance was a substantial interference with the defendant's business that was driving her to bankruptcy. Having suffered the nuisance for some 18 months, during which time the landlord consistently ignored her repeated requests to abate the nuisance, the defendant evidently left the premises and wrote to the landlord "disclaiming" the lease. The Court of Appeal affirmed the decision of the trial judge, who had held that the landlord's conduct amounted to a repudiatory breach of the lease, which the defendant had, by her letter, accepted.

Where it is the tenant who has committed a repudiatory breach, there might be several advantages for the landlord in bringing proceedings for repudiatory breach rather than for forfeiture.

First, it might not be necessary for the landlord to serve upon the tenant a notice under the Law of Property Act 1925, section 146, before being permitted to re-enter the premises. At present, the abandonment of the premises by the tenant is characterised as an offer to surrender, which the landlord can accept by re-taking possession: no section 146 notice need therefore be served.[35] Such analysis, however, cannot be applied to acts other than abandonment – such as the serious breach of a repairing covenant, or the failure to pay several instalments of rent. If breaches of the latter types were construed as repudiatory in nature and outside the scope of section 146, the whole statutory machinery for relief would be side-stepped. It seems, therefore, unlikely that English courts would hold

---

34 [1997] 49 EG 135 (CA). For discussion of the non-derogation from grant aspects from this case, see Chap 3.

35 *Preston Borough Council v Fairclough* (1982) 8 HLR 70 (CA); *R v London Borough of Croydon, ex parte Toth* (1986) 18 HLR 493; *Chamberlaine v Scally* [1992] EGCS 90 (CA).

that a repudiatory breach relieves the landlord from having to serve the statutory notice.[36]

Secondly, it might be possible for the landlord to claim damages against the tenant on a contractual basis, thus entitling him to damages for the loss of rent and other covenanted benefits throughout the unexpired residue of the term, subject only to the duty to mitigate. This would be in contrast to the present English position, which holds that the obligations in the lease fall when the lease terminates, so that the plaintiff is not entitled to recover for prospective losses. The possibility of recovery for prospective losses would be particularly attractive to the landlord at a time when average rents are falling. Although some Commonwealth jurisdictions have been prepared to award the plaintiff damages for prospective losses following acceptance of the defendant's repudiatory breach, there is no authority for this as yet in English law. It does not follow that the admission of repudiatory breach into the law of leases necessarily changes the basis for any action for damages. It has been argued that the doctrine of repudiatory breach could be imported in the law of leases by means of an implied condition that neither party will do an act which would deprive the other of substantially the benefit of the bargain entered into.[37] Breach of that condition would give the innocent party the right to terminate the lease. The contractual doctrine would thereby be transmuted into a principle of property law; and the action for damages would remain an action on the leasehold covenants, not an action in contract.

Termination of sub-lease by means of an injunction

A head-lessor may be able to terminate a sub-lease granted in breach of a covenant against sub-letting (whether absolute or qualified) by means of a mandatory injunction compelling the sub-lessee to surrender the sub-lease to the sub-lessor. In *Hemingway Securities Ltd* v *Dunraven Ltd*[38], B granted a sub-lease to C in breach of a covenant against sub-letting without

---

36 An analogy may be drawn with cases where the tenant has denied the landlord's title (a clear case of repudiatory breach), where recent authority holds that the tenant is entitled to apply for relief under LPA 1925, s 146: *W G Clark (Properties) Ltd* v *Dupre Properties Ltd* [1992] Ch 297, doubting *dicta* to the contrary in *Warner* v *Sampson* [1958] 1 QB 404 (reversed on other grounds at [1959] 1 QB 297). Contrast *Nai Pty Ltd* v *Hassoun Nominees Pty Ltd* [1985–86] Aust & NZ Conv Rep 349, where the Supreme Court of South Australia held that a tenant's repudiation of a lease entitled the landlord to terminate it by acceptance without having to serve the South Australian equivalent of a notice under LPA 1925, s 146.

37 Luxton, "Termination of leases: from property to contract", Chap 7, *Termination of Contracts*, Birds, Bradgate and Villiers (eds) (1995), Wiley Chancery, at 181.

38 [1995] 1 EGLR 61; see further pp 124–125, 132 *supra*.

the consent of the head-lessor, A. Jacob J held that A was entitled to a mandatory injunction requiring C to surrender the sub-lease to B. A was entitled to this remedy upon either of two grounds: first, to remedy the tort of inducing a breach of contract[39]; and, secondly, because a covenant restricting disposition was to be treated as a restrictive covenant of which C had notice within the principle of *Tulk v Moxhay*.[40]

This is a novel application of a well-established remedy. The head-lessor may find this remedy preferable to an action for forfeiture against his head-lessee both because of the uncertainty surrounding the scope of relief from forfeiture[41], and because of the apparent willingness of the courts to grant relief from forfeiture even in the face of a deliberate breach where there has been some attempt at concealment and where the lessor has been misled.[42] A mandatory injunction, by contrast, is more likely to be granted where there has been a wilful breach, even if the plaintiff has suffered no serious damage or inconvenience.[43] Although a mandatory injunction may be refused where to grant it would cause hardship to the defendant[44], the hardship factor carries less weight if the defendant has tried to steal a march on the plaintiff, which will usually be the case where there has been a sub-letting in breach, as the defendant will be aware of the restriction upon sub-letting from the lease itself.

An injunction may, however, be granted upon terms. In the *Hemingway* case itself, the consent to sub-let was subject to the condition precedent that the sub-tenant enter into a direct covenant with the head-lessor. The judge granted a mandatory injunction without undertakings; but, in an appropriate case, it would be open to the court to refuse to grant the head-lessor a mandatory injunction upon the sub-lessee's undertaking to enter into such covenant.

---

39 *cf Esso Petroleum Co Ltd v Kingswood Motors (Addlestone) Ltd* [1974] QB 142.

40 (1848) 2 Ph 774.

41 *Hyman v Rose* [1912] AC 623 (HL).

42 As in *Southern Depot Co Ltd v British Railways Board* [1990] 2 EGLR 39 and in *Fuller v Judy Properties Ltd* [1992] 1 EGLR 75 (CA).

43 *Kelson v Imperial Tobacco Co Ltd* [1957] 2 QB 334.

44 *Colls v Home and Colonial Stores Ltd* [1904] AC 179 (HL).

Chapter 13

FORFEITURE

INTRODUCTION

In the event of a breach of covenant by a tenant, the landlord may have a choice of one or more remedies: forfeiture; an action for a monetary sum (*i.e.* arrears of rent or mesne profits, or damages for breach of covenant); distress (for rent arrears)[1]; and an injunction or an order for specific performance.

In recessionary times, forfeiture is often a less than desirable prospect from the landlord's point of view, as it may be some time before the premises can be re-let, and the landlord may not be able to obtain such favourable terms from a new tenant. Indeed, in exceptional circumstances, a tenant who is the only practical occupier of the demised premises may deliberately commit a breach of covenant in the hope that the landlord will forfeit the lease and then have no choice but to re-let to the same tenant on terms more favourable to the latter.[2]

It should be borne in mind from the outset that, even if the landlord seeks to forfeit the lease, the tenant may have a right to seek relief from forfeiture.[3] If a head-lease is forfeited, any sub-lease falls with it. A sub-lessee, however, has a right to claim relief from forfeiture of the head-lease.[4]

The landlord may seek forfeiture only in respect of a breach of covenant in a lease which contains an express proviso for re-entry in that event; or a breach of a condition to which the lease is subject. The condition may be express or implied.

EXPRESS PROVISO FOR RE-ENTRY

There will usually be a proviso whereby the landlord reserves the right to terminate the lease upon the occurrence of specified events, often the breach of any of the tenant's covenants.[5] In the absence of an express proviso for

1 See Chap 9.
2 *cf Grovewood (LE) Ltd v Lundy Properties Ltd* (1995) 69 P & CR 507 (Ch D).
3 Discussed later in this chapter.
4 Also discussed later in this chapter.
5 For examples, see p 313 *infra*.

re-entry, the landlord will be limited to other remedies, such as an action for damages for breach of covenant or for arrears of rent.

Construction

A proviso for re-entry is construed according to the intention of the parties. If the intention is not clear, however, any uncertainty is construed against the lessor.[6] Thus a proviso which entitles the landlord to re-enter for breach of a positive covenant will not entitle it to re-enter for breach of a negative covenant, and *vice versa*.[7]

Effect of occurrence of specified event

A breach of covenant which gives the lessor a right of re-entry does not itself bring the lease to an end. It merely gives the lessor the right to elect whether to forfeit the lease or to affirm (and perhaps to sue only for a monetary sum, perhaps for arrears of rent or damages for breach of covenant). The right to forfeit may however be accidentally waived[8], and the landlord must therefore take all precautions to avoid this.

Where the lease contains a proviso for re-entry for non-payment of rent, the landlord is entitled to forfeit for non-payment of the rent even though the arrears are not owed to him. This novel point was decided only recently in *Kataria v Safeland plc*[9]. In that case, upon an assignment of the reversion of a pre-1996 lease from L1 to L2, L2 assigned to L1 the right to sue for the existing rent arrears[10], and (by means of peaceable re-entry) forfeited the lease for the non-payment of rent two days later. The Court of Appeal held that, despite the assignment of the arrears to its predecessor in title, L2 retained the right to re-enter for non-payment of rent. The decision is of particular importance to assignees of reversions of post-1995 leases, who (unlike the assignees of the reversions of pre-1996 leases) do not acquire, on assignment of the reversion, the right to sue for existing arrears.[11]

Where lease creates term beginning before the date of execution

Even if the term granted by a lease begins at a date earlier than that upon which the lease is executed, the covenants contained in such a lease, and

---

6 *Harman v Ainslie* [1904] 1 KB 698.
7 *Doe d Abdy v Stevens* (1832) 3 B & Ad 299.
8 See pp 335–340 *infra*.
9 [1998] 5 EG 155 (CA).
10 This being a pre-1996 lease, the right to sue for such arrears would have passed to L2 on the assignment to it of the reversion: LPA 1925, s 141(1); *Re King* [1963] Ch 459.
11 LT(C)A 1995, s 23(1).

therefore the right to forfeit for their breach, are not retrospective. This is illustrated in *Bennet* v *Kidd*[12], where the lease contained a covenant against the construction of buildings of less than a specified value. Before execution of the lease, but after the commencement of the term, the tenant constructed a building of a lesser value. The landlord's action to forfeit the lease for breach of covenant failed because the covenant took effect only from the execution of the lease: there had therefore been no breach of covenant. The landlord should therefore ensure that the lease is executed when the tenant's liability is intended to commence.

Forms of proviso for re-entry

For breach of tenant's covenants

Any well-drawn lease will contain an appropriate proviso for re-entry; and the landlord should ensure that the proviso reserves the right of re-entry for breach, not merely of the covenant to pay rent, but of all covenants. A proviso to achieve this might appear in the following form:

> "Provided that if all or any part of the rent hereby reserved shall be unpaid for fourteen days after becoming payable (whether formally demanded or not) or if any of the Tenant's covenants herein contained shall not be observed or performed then in any such case it shall be lawful for the Landlord at any time thereafter to re-enter upon the demised premises or any part thereof in the name of the whole and thereupon the term hereby granted shall absolutely determine but without prejudice to any right of action or remedy by either party against the other in respect of any arrears of rent or any antecedent breach of any of the covenants herein contained."

In regard to antecedent breaches, this proviso is even handed between the landlord and the tenant. The landlord might prefer the following wording:

> "... but without prejudice to any claim by the Landlord against the Tenant for any antecedent breach of any of the Tenants' covenants herein contained."

For insolvency or other events

It is quite common for the lease to provide for re-entry, not merely upon breach of the tenant's covenants, but also in the event of the tenant's insolvency or upon other specified events which would indicate that the tenant is financially insecure (and therefore likely to default on future payments of rent). To include such events, the precedent of a proviso for re-entry set out above would usually be extended by the inclusion of

12 [1926] N Ir 50.

additional words before "then in any such case", on the lines of the following:

> "or if the Tenant for the time being shall become bankrupt or being a company shall enter into liquidation (whether compulsorily or voluntarily) save for the purposes of reconstruction or amalgamation or if the Tenant for the time being shall enter into any arrangement or composition with his or its creditors or shall suffer any process of distress or execution on the Tenant's goods to be levied...".

CONDITION

Unlike a covenant, which defines the parties' rights and obligations under the lease, a condition affects the nature of the estate granted. Thus a lease may be granted subject to a condition precedent or (as is more common) a condition subsequent. The occurrence of the condition subsequent will give the landlord the right to re-enter even if no express proviso for re-entry is contained in the lease. Thus if a lease is stated to be, for instance,

> "subject to the condition that the lessee shall not sub-let",

the lessor may seek to forfeit the lease in the event of its breach even in the absence of any express proviso for re-entry. A section 146 notice must, however, still be served. Since the occurrence of a condition does not itself involve a breach of covenant, it does not give rise to any claim in damages.

Implied conditions

Some conditions need not be express, but will be implied into every lease. One such is a condition that the tenant must not deny the title of its landlord or do acts which are inconsistent with the landlord's title. If the tenant breaches such condition, the landlord has a right to determine the lease by re-entry. Before forfeiting the lease, the landlord must serve a notice under the Law of Property Act 1925, section 146, in the usual way. Even where the tenant has disclaimed the landlord's title, the court is still empowered to grant relief from forfeiture.[13]

---

13 *W G Clark (Properties) Ltd* v *Dupre Properties Ltd* [1991] 3 WLR 579, doubting *dicta* to the contrary in *Warner* v *Sampson* [1959] 1 QB 297 (CA).

EFFECTING RE-ENTRY

In residential tenancies, re-entry by the landlord without a court order is a criminal offence.[14] This is not the case in non-residential tenancies, where actual re-entry can be effected by simply taking physical possession. It is, however, an offence for any person, without lawful authority, to use or threaten violence for the purpose of securing entry into any premises where, to his knowledge, there is someone present on the premises opposed to entry.[15] Therefore physical re-entry by the landlord of business premises is unlawful unless peaceable. It is therefore usually practicable only where the tenant is not on the premises at the relevant time.

The equivalent to re-entry may also be effected by the issue and service of a writ for possession. The lease is forfeited (and notional re-entry occurs), not from the date the writ is issued, but from the date of its service, because only then does the lessee (or assignee[16]) get to know of it and become a trespasser.[17] If the lessee or assignee comprises partners in a firm or joint-tenants, service on one of them is enough.[18]

CLAIMS FOR RENT, MESNE PROFITS AND DAMAGES

Lord Denning MR has explained clearly how, in a writ for possession, the landlord should divide any claim between rent and mesne profits[19]:

> "The rent is payable until the date of service [of the writ for possession]. Mesne profits are payable after the date of service. The writ should be indorsed accordingly. Take an instance where the rent is payable quarterly (*e.g.* on 25th March 1968) and the writ for possession is issued and served during the quarter (*e.g.* on 25th April 1968). If the rent is payable in advance, the writ should claim for the whole quarter's rent due *in advance* on 25th March 1968; see *Ellis v Rowbotham*[20]; and mesne profits from 24th June 1968 to the date of delivery of possession. If the rent is payable *in arrear*, the writ should claim the last quarter's rent due (*e.g.* on 25th March 1968), and then there should be a claim in words for 'rent at the rate of ... from the date of service of the writ till the date of delivery of possession.' The calculation of this sum should not give rise to any extra difficulty; for a

---

14 Protection from Eviction Act 1977, s 2.
15 Criminal Law Act 1977, s 6(1).
16 *Commissioners of Works v Hull* [1922] 1 KB 205.
17 *Canas Property Co Ltd v K L Television Services Ltd* [1970] 2 QB 433 (CA).
18 *Ibid*, approving *Doe d Bennett v Roe* (1849) 7 CB 127.
19 *Canas Property Co Ltd v K L Television Services Ltd* [1970] 2 QB 433, at 442, per Lord Denning MR, with whose judgment the other two members of the Court of Appeal agreed. The decision was applied by a later Court of Appeal in *Capital & City Holdings Ltd v Dean Warburg Ltd* (1988) 58 P & CR 346.
20 [1900] 1 QB 740.

calculation has always to be made in order to insert the proper figure in the judgment. It is not necessary for the plaintiff to bring a second action for the amount due after the writ. He has always been able to claim it down to the date of delivery of possession, see *Southport Tramways Co v Gandy*.[21]"

The landlord is also entitled to sue on the covenants in the lease for damages resulting from breaches of covenant which occur before the date of forfeiture. The landlord cannot, however, recover damages for losses which might arise from the loss of the lease itself (such as the loss of rent during any resulting void, or the incidental costs of re-letting); nor can he recover for losses which might arise from future breaches of covenant, since future rights and liabilities under the leasehold covenants end with the termination of the lease.[22]

FORFEITURE FOR BREACH OF A COVENANT OTHER THAN A COVENANT TO PAY RENT

This is governed by the Law of Property Act 1925, section 146. A statutory notice must be served as specified in section 146(1):

> "A right of re-entry or forfeiture under any proviso or stipulation in a lease for any breach of covenant or condition in the lease shall not be enforceable, by action or otherwise, unless and until the lessor serves on the lessee a notice—
> (a) specifying the particular breach complained of;[22a] and
> (b) if the breach is capable of remedy, requiring the lessee to remedy the breach; and
> (c) in any case, requiring the lessee to make compensation in money for the breach;
> and the lessee fails, within a reasonable time thereafter, to remedy the breach, if it is capable of remedy, and to make reasonable compensation in money, to the satisfaction of the lessor, for the breach."

Any forfeiture made in pursuance of an invalid notice is void. Although paragraph (c) appears to oblige the lessor to ask for compensation, it has been held that a notice is not invalidated by its omission to request compensation.[23] Furthermore, if the breach is irremediable[24], the notice does not need to require it to be remedied.[25]

---

21 [1897] 2 QB 66.
22 See further, Luxton, "Termination of leases: from property to contract?", *Termination of Contracts*, Birds, Bradgate and Villiers (eds) (1995) Wiley Chancery, Chap 7, 170–173.
22a See *Fox Jolly* [1916] 1 AC 1 (HL); *Adagio Properties Ltd v Ansari* [1998] EGCS 9 (CA).
23 *Rugby School (Governors) v Tannahill* [1935] 1 KB 87.
24 Discussed *infra*.
25 *Rugby School (Governors) v Tannahill* [1935] 1 KB 87.

Forfeiture for non-payment of rent is expressly excluded from the procedure specified in section 146(1).[26] Rent for this purpose includes a service charge only if the lease provides that it is recoverable as rent. If the lease does not so provide, an action to forfeit for non-payment of a service charge is subject to the statutory procedure in section 146, so that a statutory notice must first be served.

Condition for forfeiture on bankruptcy or insolvent liquidation of lessee

Specified types of leases

The obligation to serve a statutory notice under section 146(1) does not apply to a condition for forfeiture on the bankruptcy of the lessee or on taking in execution of the lessee's interest if contained in a lease of:[27] (a) agricultural or pastoral land; (b) mines or minerals; (c) a public-house or beershop; (d) a furnished dwelling-house; and (e) "any property with respect to which the personal qualifications of the tenant are of importance for the preservation of the value or character of the property, or on the ground of neighbourhood to the lessor, or to any person holding under him."

In such instances, the landlord may therefore effect a forfeiture (either by an action for possession or peaceable re-entry) without serving the statutory notice. A common thread running through these exceptions is that they all involve circumstances where it could be important for the lessor to be able to regain possession swiftly (in the case of agricultural land, for instance, because there may be seasonable crops; in the case of mines, in the interests of safety).[28]

Although the sub-section refers to bankruptcy, this includes the insolvent liquidation of a corporation.[29] It would nevertheless appear that paragraph (e) can apply only to a tenant who is an individual. It cannot apply to a corporate tenant, since a corporation lacks "personal qualities" and cannot be considered a "neighbour."[30] The "importance" referred to in paragraph (e) is to be assessed objectively.

> "If a lessor wishes to have a person with personal qualities as his lessee in a particular property he can achieve this ... by choosing the tenant carefully

---

26 LPA 1925, s 146(11).
27 *Ibid*, s 146(9).
28 *Hockley Engineering Co Ltd v V & P Midlands Ltd* [1993] 1 EGLR 76 (Ch).
29 LPA 1925, s 205(1)(i); and see *Horsey Estate v Steiger* [1899] 2 QB 79.
30 *Hockley Engineering Co Ltd v V & P Midlands Ltd* [1993] 1 EGLR 76.

and ... by making sure that the tenant has no power whatever to assign or part possession with the property."[31]

From the landlord's point of view, this indicates the importance of an absolute covenant against assignment, under-letting, or parting with possession.

Other leases

In other cases of forfeiture for bankruptcy, the landlord must serve a section 146 notice if he is bringing the forfeiture action against the tenant within one year from the bankruptcy; or, if he is bringing the action against an assignee of the bankrupt tenant, where the lease was sold within one year of the bankruptcy.[32] No notice need therefore be served on the bankrupt tenant for forfeiture more than one year from bankruptcy, nor on an assignee where the lease was sold more than one year from bankruptcy. Bearing in mind the similar wording of this sub-section to section 146(9), it is reasonable to assume that it too applies to forfeiture upon an insolvent liquidation.

The effects of bankruptcy or insolvent liquidation of the tenant under a commercial lease are considered more fully in Chapter 14.

Service of a section 146 notice

The statutory notice under section 146 must be served upon the lessee, and this is defined to include (*inter alia*) an original or derivative under-lessee, and the persons deriving title under a lessee. A mortgagee, whether by sub-demise or by legal charge, is thus included. It has nevertheless been held that service of one notice upon the lessee in possession, or upon a lessee with a subsisting lease, suffices.[33] Therefore, if the lessor serves notice upon such person, it has complied with the section, and the tenant's mortgagee, for instance, has no right to be served.[34] If there are joint lessees, all must be served.[35]

An assignment of the lease validly vests the lessee's estate in the assignee, even if made in breach of a covenant against assignment (whether absolute or qualified).[36] Since the assignee becomes the lessee, it is the assignee upon

---

31 *Ibid*, at 79, per Judge Micklem (sitting as a judge of the High Court).
32 LPA 1925, s 146(10).
33 *Church Commissioners for England v Ve-Ri-Best Manufacturing Co* [1975] 1 QB 332.
34 *Egerton v Jones* [1939] 2 KB 702.
35 *Blewett v Blewett* [1936] 2 All ER 188.
36 *Old Grovebury Manor Farm Ltd v W Seymour Plant Sales & Hire Ltd (No 2)* [1979] 1 WLR 1397.

whom the section 146 notice must be served. Service upon the assignor is invalid.[37]

Except in the case of breach of a repairing covenant[38], service of the section 146 notice may be made by leaving it at or sending it (by registered post or by recorded delivery service) to the last known place of abode or business in the United Kingdom of the person served, or by leaving it or affixing it to land or buildings comprised in the lease.[39]

Once the landlord has re-entered pursuant to a court order, it is too late for the tenant to seek relief from forfeiture. Thus, as stated by Slade LJ in *Expert Clothing Service and Sales Ltd* v *Hillgate House Ltd*,[40] the purpose of the statutory notice is two-fold: first, if the breach is remediable, to give the tenant an opportunity to put it right; and, secondly, to give the tenant an opportunity to apply to the court for relief (provision for which is made in section 146(2)).

These factors are important in regard to the length of the notice which must be given. If the breach is remediable, the notice must be sufficient to give the tenant an opportunity to remedy it. If, however, the breach is irremediable, the notice may be relatively short. Ultimately, therefore, the period of notice depends on the circumstances of each case. In *Scala House & District Property Co Ltd* v *Forbes*[41], the court held fourteen days' notice sufficient in the case of an irremediable breach.

Where the breach of covenant is irremediable (such as the breach of a covenant against assignment), a section 146 notice may still be validly served even after the landlord has peaceably re-entered the premises.[42] The reason is that the tenant still has the opportunity to apply to the court for relief. The result would appear to be otherwise in the case of a remediable breach, such as the breach of a repairing covenant, where the re-entry would prevent the tenant from effecting the necessary repairs. In such a case, the landlord would need to vacate the premises prior to serving the statutory notice and complying with the Leasehold Property (Repairs) Act 1938.

If the landlord does re-enter the demised premises without serving the requisite section 146 notice, the tenant may either bring an action for possession or (where it is possible) effect peaceable re-entry. The tenant may also sue the landlord for damages for trespass and for breach of the implied covenant for quiet enjoyment.[43]

37 See also *Fuller* v *Judy Properties Ltd* [1992] 1 EGLR 75 (CA) (discussed *infra*).
38 See *infra*.
39 LPA 1925, s 196(3), (4); Recorded Delivery Service Act 1962, s 1, Sched.
40 [1986] Ch 340.
41 [1974] QB 575.
42 *Fuller* v *Judy Properties Ltd* [1992] 1 EGLR 75 (CA).
43 See Chap 3.

Remediable and irremediable breaches

At one time, the courts looked to see whether the breach itself was capable of remedy. Thus a breach of a covenant, for example, to build by a certain date, was treated as an irremediable breach.[44] The modern approach, however, is to look, not at the remediability or otherwise of the breach itself, but to the remediability of the harm done to the lessor. This was the view of Slade LJ in *Expert Clothing Service and Sales Ltd v Hillgate House Ltd*[45], who considered that, in the ordinary case, the breach of a promise to do something by a certain time can for practical purposes be remedied by the thing being done even out of time.

This modern approach means that most positive covenants are remediable (*e.g.* by performing the act covenanted to be performed, albeit late). Thus in the *Expert Clothing* case[46], it was held that the breach of a covenant to re-instate premises by a specified date was capable of remedy by the performance of the covenant together with payments of monetary compensation. Exceptionally, the breach of some positive covenants will be irremediable: such as a breach of a covenant to insure where the premises have since been destroyed by fire, since the loss to the lessor cannot be retrieved.[47]

A breach of a negative covenant may be irremediable if it is once-for-all. Thus it was held in *Scala House & District Property Co Ltd v Forbes*[48] that a breach of a covenant against assignment was an irremediable breach. Where the breach is of a continuing nature, such as a breach of a user covenant, or a breach of a covenant to repair, the issue is again whether the harm to the lessor can be retrieved. A breach of a covenant against using the premises for immoral purposes is more likely to be considered to be irremediable, since there may be a lasting taint.[49]

Excusable breach

The landlord is not entitled to forfeit if the tenant has a lawful excuse for non-compliance with its covenants in the lease. The concept of an excusable breach was recognised in *John Lewis Properties plc v Viscount Chelsea*[50],

---

44 *Stephens v Junior Army & Navy Stores Ltd* [1914] 2 Ch 516, where, on the facts, however, the breach was waived.
45 [1986] Ch 340, 355.
46 *Ibid.*
47 *Ibid.*
48 [1974] QB 575.
49 See *Rugby School (Governors) v Tannahill* [1935] 1 KB 87; also *Dunraven Securities Ltd v Holloway* [1982] 2 EGLR 47 (CA) (premises used as a sex shop).
50 [1993] 2 EGLR 77 (Ch).

where the leases in question, which had been granted in 1934, contained covenants by the tenants to redevelop various properties comprised in the leases at specified dates in the future. The tenants were not able to carry out the redevelopment scheduled for completion by 1987, however, because it would entail the demolition of a building which had been listed in 1969. Such statutory controls had not existed when the leases were entered into, and there was no reasonable prospect of listed-building consent being obtained. The court accepted the tenants' argument that they had a lawful excuse for non-performance.

Repairing covenants

Although section 146 provides some protection for tenants in breach of covenant, the onus of bringing proceedings for relief under that section is still on the tenant. In the case of breaches of repairing covenants, this protection was considered inadequate. Thus, where the lessor is seeking to forfeit for breach of a repairing covenant, the tenant is given additional protection by two statutory provisions: the Landlord and Tenant Act 1927, section 18(2), and the Leasehold Property (Repairs) Act 1938.

Landlord and Tenant Act 1927, section 18(2)

The Landlord and Tenant Act 1927, section 18(2), is designed to ensure that the tenant is made aware of the service of a section 146 notice in respect of a breach of a repairing covenant. Merely posting the notice on the premises does not suffice. The sub-section provides that a right of re-entry or forfeiture for breach of such a covenant is not enforceable, by action or otherwise, unless the lessor proves that the fact of service of the section 146 notice was known either to the lessee, or to an under-lessee (holding under an under-lease which reserved to the lessee only a nominal reversion), or to the person who last paid the rent due under the lease, and that a time reasonably sufficient to enable the repairs to be executed has since elapsed. A person is, however, deemed to have knowledge if the notice was sent by registered post or by recorded delivery service[51] to his last known place of abode in the United Kingdom. This can create problems if the lessee is outside the United Kingdom, has sub-let, and receives the rent direct from his sub-tenants.[52]

---

51 Recorded Delivery Service Act 1962, s 1.
52 See *Woodfall*, Vol 1, para 1–1953

Leasehold Property (Repairs) Act 1938

The Leasehold Property (Repairs) Act 1938 was passed in order to put a stop to a common practice of the time which involved

> "speculative builders buying small property in an indifferent state of repair, and then serving a schedule of dilapidations upon the tenants, which the tenants cannot comply with.... [T]his is the general mischief, that the speculator buys at a very low price, turns out the tenants, and gets the reversion which he has never paid for, which is a great hardship to the tenants."[53]

The aim could also be to frighten the tenants into either buying the freehold at a high price, or into submitting to a higher rent.[54] The 1938 Act shifted the onus of bringing proceedings onto the landlord. The statute originally applied only in the case of small houses, since it was tenants of such properties that it was designed to protect. The scope of the Act was, however, subsequently extended.[55] It does not apply to agricultural leases[56], but is otherwise now of general application so that even business tenants are entitled to the protection which it affords.

The Leasehold Property (Repairs) Act 1938, section 1, applies where the lessor serves a section 146 notice relating to breach of a repairing covenant contained in a lease for a term of a least seven years[57], where, at the date of the service of the notice, at least three years of the term remain.[58] In these circumstances, the lessor must inform the lessee in writing of his right to serve a counter-notice within 28 days.[59] The lessor cannot enforce by action any claim for damages for breach of a repairing covenant (where three or more years of the term remain unexpired) unless he has served a section 146 notice on the lessee not less than one month before the commencement of the action.[60]

The lessor's notice[61] is not valid unless it contains a statement, in characters not less conspicuous than those used in any other part of the notice to the effect that the lessee is entitled under the 1938 Act to serve on the lessor a counter-notice claiming the benefit of the Act, and a statement in the like characters specifying the time within which, and the manner in

---

53 *National Real Estate and Finance Co Ltd v Hassan* [1939] 2 KB 61, 78, per Goddard LJ.
54 *Sidnell v Wilson* [1966] 2 QB 67, 76 (Lord Denning MR); *Associated British Ports v C H Bailey plc* [1990] 2 AC 703 (HL) (Lord Templeman). See also note at (1938) 2 MLR 160; and Blundell, (1939) 3 Conv (NS) 10.
55 LTA 1954, s 51.
56 LP(R)A 1938, s 7(1).
57 *Ibid*.
58 *Ibid*, s 1(1).
59 *Ibid*, s 1(4).
60 *Ibid*, s 1(2).
61 Whether a notice served under LPA 1925, s 146(1), or under LP(R)A 1938, s 1(2).

which, under the Act, a counter-notice may be served and specifying the name and address for service of the lessor.[62]

The lessee may within 28 days from the date of the service of the notice serve on the lessor a counter-notice to the effect that he claims the benefit of the Act.[63] Where the tenant serves such a counter-notice, the lessor may not take proceedings, by action or otherwise, to enforce any right of re-entry or forfeiture under any proviso or stipulation in the lease, for breach of the covenant or agreement in question, or for damages for breach thereof, without the leave of the court.[64] The court is, generally, the county court.[65] The lessor's application for leave to the court (unless it relates to a claim for damages only) ranks as a "pending land action" and should therefore be registered as a "pending action."[66]

If the lessee does not serve a counter-notice, the leave of the court is not required. It is important to note that the counter-notice must be served by the lessee itself. A purported counter-notice served by the tenant's mortgagee is ineffective.[67]

The leave of the court is not to be granted "unless the lessor proves" that the requirements of at least one of five specified circumstances are met. The fifth of these is contained in paragraph (e): "special circumstances which, in the opinion of the court, render it just and equitable that leave should be given." Apart from this, however, the other circumstances all in essence require the lessor to prove "that the immediate remedying of a breach of the repairing covenant is required in order to save the landlord from substantial loss or damage which the landlord would otherwise sustain."[68] The normal civil standard of proof applies, *i.e.* the landlord must prove on the balance of evidence.[69] The battle between the landlord and the tenant on this issue is therefore to be fought at this first stage, when the landlord seeks leave, rather than at the trial itself.

---

62 LP(R)A 1938, s 1(4).
63 *Ibid, s* 1(1).
64 *Ibid, s* 1(3).
65 *Ibid, s* 6(1).
66 LCA 1925, ss 5, 17(1); LRA 1925, ss 59(1)(5) (caution against dealing): *Selim Ltd v Bickenhall Engineering Ltd* [1981] 1 WLR 1318 (Megarry V-C). For the consequences of non-registration, see respectively LCA 1972, ss 5(7), 17(1); LRA 1925, s 59(6).
67 *Church Commissioners for England v Ve-Ri-Best Manufacturing Co Ltd* [1975] 1 QB 332.
68 *Associated British Ports v C H Bailey plc* [1990] 2 AC 703 (HL), per Lord Templeman.
69 *Ibid*, approving the earlier decisions of *Re Phillips and Price* [1959] Ch 181, 188-189 (Harman J) and *Metropolitan Film Studio Ltd v Twickenham Film Studios Ltd* [1962] 1 WLR 1315 (Ungoed-Thomas J), and overruling *Sidnell v Wilson* [1966] 2 QB 67 (applied by Megarry V-C in *Land Securities plc v Receiver for the Metropolitan Police District* [1983] 1 WLR 439) which had held that the landlord could discharge the burden of proof merely by bringing evidence to support a *prima facie* case. The practical result of the change is to reduce the number of cases subsequently going for trial.

Urgent repairs

A problem arises if the repairs need to be effected urgently. In such circumstances, the landlord may not be able to afford the delay of having to serve a section 146 notice and to go through the procedure of obtaining leave under the 1938 Act. Even if the landlord can go ahead, effect the repairs himself, and then claim reimbursement from the tenant,[70] there remains the problem that, the repairs having been effected, there is no longer a disrepair in respect of which a section 146 notice can be served. Since the statutory notice is a prerequisite to the landlord's right to forfeit for such a breach, the result is that, even if the landlord were able to recover the cost of the repairs, he could no longer forfeit for the breach.

The landlord might, however, be able to argue that the tenant's breach is of such a serious nature that it comprises a repudiatory breach, and that he, the landlord, elects to accept the repudiation. In these circumstances, it would seem that no section 146 notice need be served, and the lease terminates on the landlord's acceptance of the breach. This line of reasoning has found favour with the courts recently in a slightly different context, but remains undeveloped.[71]

Relief for the tenant

In the case of relief against forfeiture for breach of a covenant other than a covenant to pay rent, relief against forfeiture is provided in the Law of Property Act 1925, section 146(2). This states:

> "Where a lessor is proceeding, by action or otherwise, to enforce ... a right of re-entry or forfeiture, the lessee may ... apply to the court for relief; and the court may grant or refuse relief, as the court, having regard to the proceedings and conduct of the parties ... and all the other circumstances, thinks fit; and in case of relief may grant it on such terms, if any, as to costs, expenses, damages, compensation, penalty, or otherwise, including the granting of an injunction to restrain any like breach in the future, as the court, in the circumstances of each case, thinks fit."

In *High Street Investments Ltd v Bellshore Property Investments Ltd*[72], the definition of "lessee" for the purpose of section 146(2) was held to include an equitable assignee (in that case a purchaser under a contract for sale).

Relief under the sub-section is available only where the lessor "is proceeding, by action or otherwise ...." In *Pakwood Transport Ltd v 15, Beauchamp Place Ltd*[73], the Court of Appeal accepted that the tenant can

---

70 See Chap 10.
71 See Chap 12.
72 [1996] 2 EGLR 40 (CA).
73 (1977) 36 P & CR 112.

apply for relief even before forfeiture proceedings have been instituted. The tenant can therefore apply (in its own action) as soon as a section 146 notice has been served. It has also been held that, where the landlord, after service of the section 146 notice, institutes proceedings and obtains a forfeiture order from the court, the tenant may still apply for relief before the landlord has gone into possession pursuant to that order, *i.e.* until the landlord has taken possession pursuant to such order, it is still "proceeding."[74]

However, where the landlord has (after service of a section 146 notice) instituted proceedings and obtained a forfeiture order from the court, and, pursuant to such order, has re-entered the premises, it is then too late for the tenant to apply for relief under section 146(2).[75] In such circumstances, the landlord is no longer "proceeding by action".

Peaceable re-entry without court order

What, however, is the position if the landlord, instead of entering into possession with an court order, effects a peaceable re-entry without such order, *i.e.* after expiry of the section 146 notice? The words "or otherwise" in the expression "is proceeding by action or otherwise", must refer to taking physical possession without a court order. The sub-section therefore appears to deny the tenant the right to apply for relief from the moment the landlord re-enters, whether pursuant to a court order or not. This was, indeed, the view of the court in the *Pakwood* case[76], where reliance was placed upon *Rogers v Rice*[77], and also of the lower courts in *Billson v Residential Apartments Ltd.*[78] The judgment of the Court of Appeal in *Billson*, not surprisingly, encouraged many landlords to take the route of peaceable re-entry without a court order, on the basis that this was a quicker and cheaper remedy than the obtaining of a court order, which nevertheless still enjoyed the same advantage of barring the tenant's right to relief under the sub-section.

In the House of Lords in *Billson*[79], however, the decision of the lower courts was reversed. Their Lordships held that, where the landlord has not obtained a court order for possession, a tenant is still entitled to apply for relief under section 146(2) even after the landlord has peaceably re-entered. Lord Templeman (with whose speech the other Law Lords agreed) said that

---

74 *Quilter v Mapleson* (1882) 9 QBD 672 (CA).
75 *Rogers v Rice* [1892] 2 Ch 170 (which, like *Quilter v Mapleson,* concerned the statutory predecessor of the LPA 1925, s 146, namely Conveyancing Act 1881, s 14).
76 (1977) 36 P & CR 112.
77 [1892] 2 Ch 170.
78 See [1991] 3 WLR 264 (CA).
79 [1992] 1 AC 494.

"is proceeding" can mean "proceeds". In his view, if the tenant were to lose the right to apply for relief as soon as peaceable re-entry were effected, the tenant would not be safe unless it applied for relief as soon as the section 146 notice were served. He did not think that Parliament could have intended that the tenant's position should be worse if the landlord, rather than effecting forfeiture by "the civilised method" of issuing and serving a writ, embarks on "the dubious and dangerous" method of determining the lease by re-entry.

The effect of the speeches of the House of Lords in the *Billson* case has been to reduce the number of instances in which landlords seek to effect a forfeiture merely by taking physical possession, because it does not bar the tenant's right to apply for relief. Lord Goff, in his speech in *Billson*, nevertheless envisaged that a tenant who delays applying for relief for too long after peaceable re-entry, will find itself debarred from obtaining it. The difficult issue, however, is precisely what length of delay will bar a claim for relief. The tenant will no doubt have a reasonable time; but what this is will ultimately depend upon all the circumstances of the case. In *Khar v Delbounty Ltd*[80], the tenants sought relief more than 11 months after the landlord had peaceably re-entered. The delay was due to their being unable to give joint instructions as they had not been in communication with each other. This was a satisfactory explanation for the delay, and relief was granted.

As a result of *Billson,* a peaceable re-entry by the landlord without a court order validly determines the tenant's legal estate under the lease; but the tenant nevertheless retains a right to seek relief under section 146(2). The right to relief from forfeiture under the sub-section, although statutory in origin, is treated as equitable in nature. If, before the tenant makes such application for relief, the landlord's reversion comes into the hands of a bona fide purchaser of the legal estate without notice of the right to apply for relief, the purchaser takes free of such right.[81] It is therefore in the tenant's interests to prevent this occurring by making an application to the court for relief and registering the pending land action in the register of pending actions.[82]

Relief and third parties

Even where a third party purchaser has in good faith acquired a legal estate without notice, relief may still be granted provided that the third party is not thereby prejudiced. Relief is possible, since section 146(2) enables relief

---

80 [1996] EGCS 183.
81 *Fuller* v *Judy Properties Ltd* [1992] 1 EGLR 75.
82 LCA 1972, ss 5, 17(1): LRA 1925, ss. 59(1)(5).

to be granted "on such terms ... as the court ... thinks fit." The court is therefore able to impose terms which (*inter alia*) prevent the interest of the third party from being harmed. An example of such relief upon terms is provided by *Fuller v Judy Properties Ltd*.[83] The tenant had assigned the lease (which still had eight years to run) to the defendants in breach of a fully qualified covenant against assignment without the consent of the landlord, the plaintiff. The defendants paid the tenant-assignor a premium of £30,000. The plaintiff peaceably re-entered without a court order and shortly after granted a new lease of the same premises to H Ltd for a term of 16 years at a rent, and at a premium of £16,000. H Ltd was a bona fide purchaser of a legal estate without notice of the defendants' right to seek relief. The Court of Appeal considered that, because the defendants had paid a sizeable premium for their assignment, it would be inequitable to deny them relief from forfeiture. Such relief could not, however, lose H Ltd its priority. Relief was therefore granted on the basis that the defendants were retrospectively put into the position of immediate reversioners on H Ltd's lease. They were therefore entitled to the premium that H Ltd had paid to the plaintiff. The defendants would continue to have to pay the plaintiff the rent under their own lease; but they were entitled to receive the rent under H Ltd's lease.

In *Khar v Delbounty Ltd*[84] the landlord had served on the tenants (who had a long lease of a flat) a section 146 notice for non-payment of a maintenance charge (not reserved as rent). The landlord later re-entered the premises peaceably and re-let the premises to a third party on an assured shorthold tenancy. The original tenants later applied for relief, and it was granted on the basis that their original long lease was to be sold on the expiration of the assured shorthold tenancy, and the landlord was to be entitled to take out of the proceeds any arrears of maintenance charge due.

Willingness of court to grant relief

Where the breach is remediable, the court will usually be willing to grant relief to a tenant prepared to remedy the breach and pay damages. Furthermore, some recent decisions indicate a greater willingness than earlier cases to grant relief even where the breach of covenant is irremediable and deliberate, and where there has been an attempt to conceal it from the landlord.[85] By contrast, in *Crown Estates Commissioners v Signet Group plc*[86] relief from forfeiture was refused, the judge asking:[87]

83 [1992] 1 EGLR 75.
84 [1996] EGCS 183.
85 *Southern Depot Co Ltd v BRB* [1990] 2 EGLR 39; *Fuller v Judy Properties Ltd* [1992] 1 EGLR 75.
86 [1996] 2 EGLR 200.
87 *Ibid*, at 210.

"should the message go out from this court that deliberate breaches of covenant against assignment without consent are worthwhile, or may be worthwhile, because at the end of the day relief from forfeiture is likely to be obtained? I think not."

Where the covenant breached is one against user of the premises for immoral purposes, relief will be granted only rarely.[88]

If the breach of covenant comprises non-payment of a sum of money (such as a service charge) which is not reserved as rent, the court will be governed by the same considerations in determining whether to grant relief as if it were non-payment of rent, *i.e.* only in exceptional circumstances will relief be refused.[89]

The court also has jurisdiction to grant relief in respect of a part of the premises only. This was established in *GMS Syndicate Ltd* v *Gary Elliott Ltd*[90], where A leased premises to B, who sub-let part to C. C used that part sub-let to it for immoral purposes in breach of the covenant in the head-lease. A sought to forfeit B's lease, but the court granted B relief in respect of that part of the property which had not been sub-let to C.

The court cannot force a tenant who has applied for relief to accept it. In *Fuller* v *Judy Properties Ltd*[91], the proposed relief was acceptable to the defendants because they had already been refused planning permission to use the premises for their intended purpose.

A residual equitable relief outside the statute?

There is no general equitable jurisdiction to grant relief from forfeiture for breaches of covenant other than a covenant for the payment of rent.[92] However, in *Abbey National Building Society* v *Maybeech Ltd*[93] the court invoked the equitable jurisdiction to grant relief to the tenant's mortgagee after the landlord had re-entered pursuant to a court order for breach of a covenant to pay a contribution to the maintenance of the building in question (such sum not being expressed to be recoverable as rent). There may therefore remain an equitable jurisdiction to relieve after re-entry pursuant to a court order where there has been breach of a covenant to pay a sum of money other than rent (such as a service or maintenance charge, or insurance premiums) where such sums are not expressed to be recoverable as rent. The scope and status of the *Maybeech* decision is, however, uncertain. It has not been overruled; on the other hand it was not

---

88 *British Petroleum Pension Trust Ltd* v *Behrendt* [1985] 2 EGLR 97.
89 *Khar* v *Delbounty Ltd* [1996] EGCS 183.
90 [1982] Ch 1.
91 [1992] 1 EGLR 75.
92 *Hill* v *Barclay* (1810) 16 Ves 402.
93 [1985] Ch 190.

followed in *Smith* v *Metropolitan City Properties Ltd*[94] It may therefore be that any equitable relief was entirely superseded by the statutory relief of section 146.[95]

Relief from forfeiture for bankruptcy or insolvent liquidation

Since relief in this case is based entirely upon section 146, no relief from forfeiture for bankruptcy or insolvent liquidation is available where the service of a section 146 notice is dispensed with by sub-sections (9) and (10).[96] A bankrupt tenant's trustee in bankruptcy must therefore apply for relief or sell the lease within one year of the bankruptcy. The statutory right of sub-lessees and chargees to apply for relief from forfeiture under section 146(4), is, however, preserved.[97]

FORFEITURE FOR BREACH OF A COVENANT TO PAY RENT

As in the case of forfeiture for breach of other covenants, a landlord is not entitled to forfeit the lease for breach of the covenant to pay rent unless the lease reserves to the landlord a right of re-entry for breach, or unless the lease is conditional upon the payment of the rent. Forfeiture for breach of a covenant to pay rent is not subject to the procedure laid down in the Law of Property Act 1925, section 146[98]; rather it is subject to a special statutory regime.

Dispensing with formal demand for rent

At common law, a landlord cannot re-enter unless it has first made a formal demand for rent. The requirements of a formal demand are very exacting: the demand must be made by the landlord or its agent at the place specified by the landlord for payment, or on the demised premises. It must be made before sunset on the last day for payment, and may relate only to the sum due in the last rental period.

However, the lease may (and every well-drawn lease will) dispense with the requirement of a formal demand for rent. The condition or proviso for re-entry will contain a form of words to the effect that the lease is to

---

94 [1986] 1 EGLR 52.
95 *Official Custodian of Charities* v *Parway Estates Developments Ltd* [1985] Ch 151; see also *Barclays Bank plc* v *Prudential Assurance Co Ltd* [1998] 10 EG 159, 163–165.
96 See pp 317–318 *supra*.
97 LP(Am)A 1929, s 1.
98 LPA 1925, s 146(11).

determine even if no formal demand for rent has been made: the expression commonly used[99] is: "**whether formally demanded or not.**" If the lease does not contain these words or other words to this effect, a formal demand may nevertheless be dispensed with if an action for possession is brought at a time when specified circumstances appertain. If the action is brought in the High Court, these requirements are (in essence) that at least a half year's rent is in arrear, and there are insufficient goods on the premises available for distress to satisfy the amount due.[1] If the action is brought in the county court, the requirements are broadly the same.[2]

Relief against forfeiture

The procedure for obtaining relief depends upon whether the landlord brings an action for possession in either the High Court or in the county court, or whether the landlord simply effects a peaceable re-entry without a court order.

Landlord brings action in the High Court

In the High Court, the position is governed by the Common Law Procedure Act 1852, sections 210–212, and by the Supreme Court of Judicature (Consolidation) Act 1981, section 38.

Section 212 of the 1852 Act provides a form of automatic relief. Under it, the forfeiture proceedings are to be discontinued if the tenant or his assignee, before the trial of the action, pays the lessor or into court all the arrears and costs. If the proceedings are so discontinued, the old lease continues. It has been held, however, that the section applies only if the rent is at least one half year in arrear.[3]

Where section 210 of the 1852 Act applies, the tenant, his assignee and all other persons deriving title under him, have six months from the landlord's entry under a court order during which they may pay the rent arrears and costs and apply for relief. At the end of this time, any application for relief is barred. It would appear that relief under this section (like that under section 212) is available only where the rent is at least one half year in arrear. Relief under section 210 essentially circumscribes the original equitable jurisdiction. Equity regards the proviso for re-entry merely as a security for the payment of the rent, and is usually willing to grant relief if the tenant pays off the rent arrears and costs. For this reason, the conduct of the parties is generally irrelevant: thus even a long record of

---

99 See the precedent on p 313 *supra*.
1 Common Law Procedure Act 1852, s 210.
2 CCA 1984, s 139(1).

late payment of rent is insufficient in most cases to deny the tenant relief. The relief, being based upon equitable principles, remains, however, discretionary: thus relief will not be granted if it would damage the interest of a bona fide purchaser of the legal estate without notice. Since forfeiture is complete when the landlord has re-entered pursuant to a court order, relief under section 210 takes the form of a new lease.

Where the circumstances specified under sections 210–212 of the 1952 Act do not apply (as, for instance, where less than one half year's rent is in arrear, or where there are sufficient goods on the premises available for distress to satisfy the amount due), relief remains available under the purely equitable jurisdiction contained in the Supreme Court of Judicature (Consolidation) Act 1981, section 38(1). This section in effect preserves for the High Court the same jurisdiction to grant relief from forfeiture for non-payment of rent as was formerly enjoyed by the Court of Chancery. In practice, this purely equitable jurisdiction has been used most frequently in cases of peaceable re-entry and it is therefore discussed further below.[4]

Landlord brings action in the county court

Where the lessor's action for forfeiture is brought in the county court, the relief is specified in the County Courts Act 1984, section 138. The section provides for both automatic and for discretionary relief.

If the lessee pays into court not less than five clear days before the return day all the rent in arrear with costs, the action ceases, and the lessee holds the land according to the lease without any new lease.[5]

If no such payment is made, and the court considers that the lessor is entitled to forfeit, the statute provides for a deferred order. Thus the court must order possession of the land to be given to the lessor at the expiration of such period, not being less than four weeks from the date of the order, as the court thinks fit, unless within that period the lessee pays into court all the rent in arrear and costs.[6] The period of postponement may be extended at any time before possession is recovered.[7] If within the postponement period the lessee pays into court all the rent in arrear and costs, he holds the land according to the lease without any new lease.[8] The foregoing relief is therefore automatic.

If, however, the lessee does not make such payment within this period, the order is enforceable in the prescribed manner and, so long as it remains

---

3 *Standard Pattern Co Ltd v Ivey* [1962] 1 Ch 432.
4 See pp 332 *infra*.
5 CCA 1984, s 138(2).
6 *Ibid*, s 138(3).
7 *Ibid*, s 138(4).
8 *Ibid*, s 138(5).

unreversed, the lessee is, subject to prescribed qualifications, barred from all relief.[9] The qualifications are two-fold. First, if the lessor has not yet recovered possession in pursuance of the order, the court may extend the period of postponement of possession.[10] Secondly, if the lessor has so recovered possession, the lessee may, within six months thereafter, apply to the court for relief; and the court may, if it thinks fit, grant to the lessee such relief, subject to such terms and conditions, as it thinks fit.[11] A lessee granted such relief holds the land according to the lease without any new lease.[12]

Payment into court by a stranger (*i.e.* by someone other than the lessee, its under-lessee or mortgagee) is not a payment for the purposes of this section.[13]

A lessee who does not apply for relief within the specified period of six months is barred from all relief – not merely in the county court[14], but also in the High Court, under both its statutory[15] and inherent equitable[16] jurisdiction.

Landlord peaceably re-enters without court order

In these circumstances, the tenant may seek relief in the High Court, which in such instance has an inherent equitable jurisdiction to grant relief.[17] It is a condition for the granting of such relief that there is readiness on the part of the person seeking it to pay the arrears within such time as the court thinks fit. There is no statutory time-limit, but the claim must be made with reasonable promptitude. In practice, the court uses the six months period prescribed by the 1852 Act as a guide. The court will also consider whether, in the event of delay, the greater hardship would be suffered by the lessor (were relief to be granted) or by the lessee (were it to be denied). This was stated in *Thatcher v CH Pearce & Sons (Contractors) Ltd*[18], where an application for relief was permitted even though it had been made six months and four days after re-entry.

Alternatively, the lessee may apply for relief to the county court, which may grant such relief as could have been granted by the High Court. The application for relief must be brought within six months of the re-entry.[19]

9 *Ibid*, s 138(7).
10 *i.e.* the period of postponement referred to in CCA 1984, s 138(4): *ibid*, s 138(8).
11 CCA 1984, s 138(9A).
12 *Ibid*, s 138(9B).
13 *Matthews v Dobbins* [1963] 1 WLR 227.
14 *i.e.* under CCA 1984.
15 CLPA 1852, ss 210-212.
16 *Di Palma v Victoria Square Property Ltd* [1986] Ch 150.
17 *Howard v Fanshawe* [1895] 2 Ch 581.
18 [1968] 1 WLR 748, at 756.
19 CCA 1984, s 139(2); *Lovelock v Margo* [1963] 3 QB 786.

Any application for relief after six months can therefore be brought only before the High Court.

PROTECTION FOR HOLDERS OF DERIVATIVE INTERESTS

Where the landlord institutes proceedings for forfeiture, whether for non-payment of rent or for breach of another leasehold covenant, one general safeguard for the holders of derivative interests exists. The landlord must indorse upon the writ for possession the names and addresses of any under-lessees or mortgagees of whom he is aware, and he must send such persons a copy of the writ. This applies whether the action is brought in the High Court[20] or in the county court.[21] A prospective sub-lessee or mortgagee should therefore take what steps it can to ensure that its existence is known to the landlord. It should therefore ensure that the sub-lease or mortgage contains a covenant by the tenant to inform it immediately of any change in the identity of the person to whom the tenant pays its rent (as where there is an assignment of the reversion), and to supply details of the name and address of such person. If the action for possession is in respect of a breach of covenant other than a covenant to pay rent, and the holder of a derivative interest is not served, it may, according to *Abbey National Building Society* v *Maybeech Ltd*[22], apply for relief even after the landlord has re-entered pursuant to a court order; but, as has already been pointed out, it is not clear whether this decision is good law.

The holder of a derivative interest should try to ensure that it is apprised of a breach of covenant at the earlier possible time – preferably well before matters have gone as far as the service of a writ for possession – since it may be able to put pressure on the tenant to remedy the breach. Whilst the tenant's sub-lessee or mortgagee is a person who may be served with a section 146 notice, the landlord can serve a valid notice by serving it on the tenant alone. A prospective holder of a derivative interest should therefore insist upon a covenant in the sub-lease or mortgage which obliges the tenant to notify it immediately of the receipt of such a notice. The value of such a covenant is, however, limited, since it depends upon the tenant's compliance, and the tenant may think that it is in its own interests not to comply.

---

20 RSC, Ord 6.
21 CCR, Ord 6.
22 [1985] Ch 190.

Relief from forfeiture

Relief of general availability

Where the lessor "is proceeding" to forfeit the lease, an under-lessee may apply to the court for relief under the Law of Property Act 1925, section 146(4). Relief under this sub-section is exceptional, since it extends to forfeiture for non-payment of rent as well as for breaches of other covenants. Since the opening words of this sub-section are similar to those used in section 146(2), it is reasonable to infer that the relief under sub-section (4) also remains available after a re-entry without a court order.[23] Under sub-section (4), the court may make an order vesting in the under-lessee all or part of the property comprised in the lease upon such conditions as the court may think fit. The relief takes the form of a new lease granted directly to the party seeking relief, thus creating privity of both contract and estate between such party and the lessor. The applicant cannot, however, obtain a lease for a term longer than it had under its original sub-lease.[24] A sub-tenant or mortgagee can obtain a vesting order under sub-section (4) after the landlord has effected forfeiture by peaceable re-entry; but a vesting order under sub-section (4) cannot be made with retrospective effect.[25]

For the purposes of sub-section (4), an under-lessee includes a mortgagee of the lessee's interest, even if the mortgage is by legal charge.[26] It also includes an equitable chargee.[27] If a mortgagee is granted relief, he must hold the new lease as a substituted security, *i.e.* subject to the mortgagor's (the erstwhile tenant's) equity of redemption.[28] A mortgagee can obtain relief under the sub-section even if the lease has been disclaimed by the mortgagor's trustee in bankruptcy.[29]

Relief specific to breaches of covenant other than a covenant to pay rent

In *Escalus Properties Ltd* v *Robinson*[30] the Court of Appeal held that the

---

23 *cf Billson* v *Residential Apartments Ltd* [1992] 1 AC 494 (HL).

24 LPA 1925, s 146(4).

25 *Official Custodian for Charities* v *Mackey* [1985] Ch 168, 181 (Scott J); *Pellicano* v *MEPC plc* [1994] 1 EGLR 104 (Knox J).

26 LPA 1925, s 87(1), as interpreted by *Grand Junction Co Ltd* v *Bates* [1954] 2 QB 160.

27 *Ladup Ltd* v *Williams & Glyn's Bank plc* [1985] 1 WLR 851.

28 *Chelsea Estates Investment Trust Co Ltd* v *Marche* [1955] Ch 328.

29 *Barclays Bank plc* v *Prudential Assurance Co Ltd* [1998] 10 EG 159 (Hazel Williamson QC, sitting as a deputy judge of the Chancery Division).

30 [1995] 3 WLR 524, (CA), consolidated with the appeal in *Sinclair Garden Investments (Kensington) Ltd* v *Walsh*.

definition of "lessee" for the purpose of section 146(2)[31] was sufficiently wide to embrace a sub-lessee. If the sub-lessee obtains relief under sub-section (2), the head-lease is treated as if it had never been forfeited, and the sub-lease is treated as continuing. If, therefore, the rent payable under the sub-lease is lower than that payable under the head-lease, the sub-lessee might prefer to apply for relief under sub-section (2).

Relief specific to non-payment of rent

Where the circumstances mentioned in the Common Law Procedure Act 1852, section 210, apply, it is specifically provided that the section does not bar the right of a mortgagee of the lease who is not in possession and who, within six months of the re-entry, pays all the arrears of rent and the costs and damages sustained by the lessor, and who performs all the lessee's covenants.

If the landlord's action is in the county court, the right to relief afforded to a lessee by the County Courts Act 1984, section 138, extends to an under-lessee[32], and this includes a mortgagee. It would therefore appear that an under-lessee may make the payments into court.[33] It is furthermore expressly provided that an application for relief within six months of the lessor's recovering possession under the order[34] may be made by a sub-lessee; and on such application the court may make an order to vest the land in such person as lessee of the lessor for the remainder of the term of his sub-lease or for any lesser term.[35] The relief provided by the statute is exclusive; and it has been held that the High Court has no inherent jurisdiction to relieve a mortgagee whose application is made after the statutory period of six months.[36]

WAIVER OF FORFEITURE

If the tenant commits a breach of covenant which entitles the landlord to forfeit the lease, the landlord has a right to elect whether to treat the lease as forfeited or as remaining in force. An election by the landlord to affirm the lease following a breach is often called a waiver, since it deprives the

---

31 LPA 1925, s 146(5)(b): ""Lessee" includes an original or derivative under-lessee, and the persons deriving title under a lessee...".

32 CCA 1984, s 140.

33 *i.e.* the payments specified in s 138(2), (5) and (7): *United Dominions Trust Ltd v Shellpoint Trustees* [1993] 4 All ER 310 (Slade LJ).

34 *i.e.* CCA 1984, s 138(9A).

35 *Ibid*, s 138(9C).

36 *United Dominions Trust Ltd v Shellpoint Trustees* [1993] 4 All ER 310 (CA).

landlord of the right to forfeit for that breach. The onus of proving waiver is on the tenant.[37]

An election is made by the performance of an unequivocal act either of avoidance or of affirmation. The clearest instance of an unequivocal act treating the lease as at an end is the institution of proceedings for possession.[38] An unequivocal act of affirmation is the demand for[39], acceptance of[40], or action to recover[41] rent referable to the period after the breach; but any unequivocal act which indicates that the landlord is treating the lease as still subsisting will suffice, such as a distress for rent[42], or an entry by the landlord to effect repairs pursuant to a right in the lease. The landlord may not blow hot and cold[43] – affirming the lease for some purposes and denying it for others; so that, once the election has been made, the landlord cannot retract it.[44] Therefore, an acceptance of future rent after the breach will not deprive the landlord of the right to forfeit for that breach if the landlord has already instituted proceedings for possession.[45] The landlord needs, however, to exercise caution, because the acceptance of rent after the institution of possession proceedings may evidence the grant of a new tenancy.[46]

"[S]ince a section 146 notice is by statute a necessary prerequisite to forfeiture ... its whole purpose and effect is to operate as a preliminary to forfeiture."[47] Thus the service of a section 146 notice is not itself an act affirming the lease, and the right to elect is in suspense during the period the notice is running. A demand for rent falling due whilst the notice is running will not therefore comprise a waiver, at least if the rent (apportioned if necessary) is referable to a period not after the expiration of

---

37 *Matthews v Smallwood* [1910] 1 Ch 777.

38 *Evans v Wyatt* (1880) 43 LT 176.

39 *Segal Securities Ltd v Thoseby* [1963] 1 QB 887.

40 *Doe d Gatehouse v Rees* (1838) 4 Bing NC 384; *Windmill Investments (London) Ltd v Milano Restaurant Ltd* [1962] 1 QB 373 (CA).

41 *Dendy v Nicholl* (1858) 4 CB (NS) 376 (Willes J).

42 *Doe d David v Williams* (1835) 7 C&P 322.

43 *Birch v Wright* (1786) 1 TR 378, 379 (Ashurst J), 387 (Balcombe J); *Jones v Carter* (1846) 15 M & W 718, 723 (*arguendo*); *Grimwood v Moss* (1872) LR 7 CP 360, 363 (arguendo).

44 *Jones v Carter* (1846) 15 M & W 718, 724 (Parke B); *Toleman v Portbury* (1871) LR 6 QB 245; *Scarf v Jardine* (1882) 7 App Cas 345, 360 (Lord Blackburn); *Civil Service Co-operative Society Ltd v McGrigor's Trustee* [1923] 2 Ch 347.

45 *Evans v Wyatt* (1880) 43 LT 176.

46 *Ibid*, applying *Doe d Cheny v Batten* (1775) 1 Cowp 243, where Lord Mansfield stated (at 245) that the question was "*quo animo* the rent was received, and what the real intention of both parties was." cf *Legal and General Assurance Society Ltd v General Metal Agencies Ltd* (1969) 20 P & CR 953, 959; *Javad v Aqil* [1991] 1 All ER 243. See further Luxton [1991] JBL 342, 347–348.

47 *Church Commissioners for England v Nodjoumi* (1986) 51 P & CR 155, 159, per Hirst J; see also *Old Grovebury Manor Farm Ltd v W Seymour Plant Sales & Hire Ltd (No 2)* [1979] 1 WLR 1397, 1400 (CA) (Lord Russell of Killowen).

the notice.[48] The same principle would presumably apply where the Leasehold Property (Repairs) Act 1938 applies and the tenant has served a counter-notice; in which case a landlord who is taking steps to obtain leave to proceed would be entitled, without effecting a waiver, to continue to demand and to accept rent (referable to the period[49]) until the leave is obtained.

A waiver may arise even through a mere clerical error, such as a demand for rent sent out by the landlord's agents.[50] It is therefore vital that the landlord's managing agents are instructed to put a stop on rent demands. Solicitors acting for landlords should apprise their clients of the importance of this. Only a communication (such as a demand for rent) served on the tenant or its agent can support a waiver.[51] The service of a default notice[52] on a former tenant or his guarantor will not therefore itself cause the landlord to lose the right to forfeit the lease for the breach in question. There is, nevertheless, a risk that knowledge of the service will reach the current tenant, and the right to forfeit be lost.

There can be no waiver, however, unless the landlord or his agents are aware that the breach has occurred. For this purpose, the knowledge of his agents is imputed to the landlord himself. Thus, in *Metropolitan Properties Co Ltd v Cordery*[53], the porter's knowledge of a sub-letting was imputed to the landlord, who was thereby held to have waived a right to forfeit for breach of a covenant against sub-letting. Constructive knowledge, however, will not be sufficient.[54] A clause in a lease which provides that certain acts by the landlord are not to effect a waiver are void.[55] Similarly, expressing a

---

48 *Sed quere:* if a s 146 notice is served on 15 September giving the tenant 28 days in which to remedy the breach, and the landlord demands on 30 September the quarter's rent which fell due the previous day, why should a waiver result if the rent is payable in advance, but not if it is payable in arrear? Even if the rent is payable in advance, the alleged act of waiver occurs during a period when the landlord is obliged to treat the lease as subsisting; and whether there is a waiver should depend upon when the obligation to pay rent falls due, not upon the period to which such payment is referable. This is consistent with *Canas Property Co Ltd v K L Television Services Ltd* [1970] 2 QB 433 (CA) that, where the rent is payable in advance, the landlord is entitled, in a writ for possession, to claim the entire instalment of rent which falls due before the date of service of the writ, even though part of the period to which it is referable falls after the lease is forfeited by such service. No such argument appears however to have been raised on facts similar to those hypothesised in this note (although involving a demand for future insurance rather than rent) in *Yorkshire Metropolitan Properties Ltd v Co-operative Retail Services Ltd* [1997] EGCS 57 (Neuberger J).

49 This is subject to the argument in the preceding note.

50 *Central Estates (Belgravia) Ltd v Woolgar (No 2)* [1972] 1 WLR 1048.

51 See *Trustees of Henry Smith's Charity v Willson* [1983] QB 316 (CA), where the rent demand was served on the tenant's wife.

52 LT(C)A 1995, s 17.

53 (1979) 39 P & CR 10.

54 *Official Custodian for Charities v Parway Estates Developments* [1985] Ch 151.

55 *R v Paulson* [1921] AC 271.

demand for rent to be "without prejudice" is ineffective to prevent a waiver.[56] By contrast, the use of such expression in negotiations between the parties following a breach is effective for this purpose.[57]

It has been pointed out that "the strict rule that acceptance of rent would waive a forfeiture was developed at a time when the power to grant relief from forfeiture was very much more restricted than it is now."[58] This may explain why, in recent years, the courts have, where not bound by authority, adopted a less strict approach to alleged acts of waiver. The modern view, as expressed by Slade LJ[59], is that:

> "where no acceptance of rent (or demand for rent) is involved, the court is ... free to look at all the circumstances of the case to consider whether the act of the [landlord's agent] relied on ... was so unequivocal that, when considered objectively, it could only be regarded as having been done consistently with the continued existence of a tenancy as at [the date of the act in question]."

This dictum was quoted by Neuberger J recently in *Yorkshire Metropolitan Properties Ltd* v *Co-operative Retail Services Ltd*[60], who held that the demand for insurance (not itself reserved as rent) after the alleged breach did not operate as a waiver since it was not in the circumstances an unequivocal act: the demand for payment was sent out by the landlord's agents after the service of a section 146 notice, and after the landlord had told the tenant that it would not accept any more rent and that it intended to bring forfeiture proceedings. The same approach can be discerned in another modern decision in which it was held that a landlord's agreement with a bankrupt tenant's creditors to a voluntary arrangement whereby the lease was to be assigned did not cause a waiver.[61]

The modern approach has, however, made some inroads even where the alleged act of waiver is the acceptance of rent. Thus, if the landlord has made it clear to the tenant that he will not accept more rent, the mere processing of the payment by the landlord's bank will not effect a waiver, provided that the landlord repays the money without delay. In *John Lewis Properties plc* v *Viscount Chelsea*[62], the tenant held properties of the landlord under three separate leases, two of which the landlord sought to forfeit for breach of covenant. The landlord informed the tenant that it would not accept further payments of rent under those two leases, but the

---

56 *Segal Securities Ltd* v *Thoseby* [1963] 1 QB 889.
57 *Re National Jazz Centre Ltd* [1988] 2 EGLR 57.
58 *Yorkshire Metropolitan Properties Ltd* v *Co-operative Retail Services Ltd* [1997] EGCS 57, per Neuberger J. There was no statutory relief from forfeiture for breach of a covenant other than a covenant to pay rent until the Conveyancing Act 1881.
59 *Expert Clothing Service and Sales Ltd* v *Hillgate House Ltd* [1986] Ch 340, 360.
60 [1997] EGCS 57.
61 *Re Mohammed Naeem (a bankrupt) (No 18 of 1988)* [1990] 1 WLR 48.
62 [1993] 2 EGLR 77.

tenant continued to send direct to the landlord's bank a single cheque in respect of all three leases, which was credited to the landlord's account. On each occasion the landlord returned that portion of the rent attributable to the two leases it was seeking to forfeit, and informed the tenant again that it would not accept such rent. Mummery J considered that a bank's processing of cheques was a purely administrative matter not involving business decisions, and that it was not necessary for the landlord to instruct its bank not to accept the cheques. In the circumstances, he was of the opinion that there had been no acceptance so as to constitute a waiver. The facts of *John Lewis Properties plc* v *Viscount Chelsea* are somewhat special; but the decision lends tacit support to the view that, where the tenant pays the rent by standing order, the mere crediting of the landlord's account with such payments is not *per se* an acceptance of them.

The effect of waiver

This depends on the nature of the breach. If the breach is once-for-all, the waiver means that the right to forfeit in respect of that particular breach is for ever lost. Waiver does not, however, cause the covenant itself to be destroyed: waiver of one breach does not prevent the landlord from seeking to forfeit subsequently in respect of a further breach of the same covenant.[63] Acceptance of rent over a long period, however, may evidence a release of the covenant breached.[64]

If the breach is continuing, such as a breach of a repairing covenant, a waiver by the landlord, whilst precluding the landlord from forfeiting for the breach up to the date of the waiver, does not preclude the landlord from forfeiting for the breach thereafter. Furthermore, provided the continuing breaches are substantially the same as those which have been waived, no new statutory notice need be served in order to forfeit for the continuing breaches.[65] The best explanation is that it is not the breach itself which is waived, but merely the right to forfeit in respect of the breach.[66]

Mesne profits

There may often be a considerably delay between the occurrence of the breach and the obtaining by the landlord of an order for possession.

---

63 LPA 1925, s 148.

64 *Wolfe* v *Hogan* [1942] 2 KB 194; *City & Westminster Properties (1934) Ltd* v *Mudd* [1959] Ch 129.

65 *Penton* v *Barnett* [1898] 1 QB 276 (CA), approved and applied in *London Borough of Greenwich* v *Discreet Selling Estates Ltd* [1990] 2 EGLR 65 (CA).

66 This explanation was offered by John Colyer QC *arguendo* in *London Borough of Greenwich* v *Discreet Selling Estates Ltd* [1990] 2 EGLR 65 (CA).

Although, subject as explained above, waiver may be caused by the demand for or acceptance of rent, the landlord is nevertheless entitled to demand and accept mesne profits. Indeed, an additional claim for mesne profits for the relevant period (*i.e.* for the period from the service of the writ for possession until the date of judgment or the date of the order for possession) is usually made in the action for possession. Mesne profits are payments for the mere occupation of the land. A demand for or acceptance of mesne profits does not therefore effect a waiver or evidence a grant of a new tenancy. The rent payable under the lease is good evidence of the value of the mesne profits which may be demanded.

The landlord must take care, before accepting payments tendered by the tenant, that it is not thereby waiving the right to forfeit. Whether the sums in question comprise mesne profits or rents is a matter of evidence. If the tenant offers payment as rent, the landlord cannot accept it as mesne profits.[67]

---

67 *Croft v Lumley* (1858) 5 E & B 672.

Chapter 14

INSOLVENCY

INTRODUCTION

The recession of the late 1980s and early 1990s led to the insolvency of many lessees of commercial premises, and the subject-matter of this chapter is therefore of particular current importance. This chapter does not aim to provide a comprehensive guide to insolvency law; rather it is designed to highlight the practical implications of a tenant's actual or impending insolvency during the running of a commercial lease, and the options which are available to the parties in the variety of situations which can arise.[1]

Lease expressed to be determinable upon insolvency or some other event

An insolvent tenant is hardly a desirable tenant, since default in the payment of the rent is probable and there may be default in the performance of the other obligations in the lease. For this reason, most commercial leases contain an express proviso whereby the lease is determinable upon the appointment of a receiver over the tenant's property; the tenant's entering into a composition or arrangement with its creditors; (in the case of an individual tenant) the tenant's bankruptcy; or (in the case of a company tenant) the appointment of a liquidator or administrator. The occurrence of one of these event would give the landlord the right to take steps to terminate the lease.[2] Such a proviso must, however, be express; it will not be implied.[3] In the absence of an express provision, the landlord has no right to terminate the lease merely because the tenant is insolvent or is facing insolvency.

Breach of a proviso that the lease shall determine upon the appointment of a receiver, a trustee in bankruptcy, or a liquidator, is a once-and-for-all and irremediable breach. If, however, the determining event is the tenant's

---

1 See generally McLoughlin, *Commercial Leases and Insolvency,* 2nd ed (1996) Butterworths.
2 See Chap 13.
3 *cf Hyde* v *Warden* (1877) 3 Ex D 72.

"insolvency", meaning an inability to pay his debts, the breach is a continuing one. Bankruptcy is regarded as an irremediable breach.[4] The landlord may also make the lease determinable upon the insolvency of a third party, such as a guarantor[5] or an original tenant after assignment.

The mere vesting of the lease in a tenant's trustee in bankruptcy does not breach a covenant against assignment (whether absolute or qualified), since such event occurs by operation of law, not by the tenant's own act.[6]

The general rule of construction of forfeiture clauses applies, *i.e.* they are construed against the landlord.[7] Clear words must be used in order for them to be held effective in the particular circumstances.

In certain instances, forfeiture for the bankruptcy or insolvent liquidation of the tenant can proceed without service of a notice under the Law of Property Act 1925, section 146.[8]

LANDLORD'S CHOICES

A tenant which is insolvent or which is facing insolvency may have already defaulted on the rent or other payments (*e.g.* a service charge), or have otherwise breached covenants in the lease, and the tenant's insolvency or other act may (if there is an express proviso to this effect) have made the lease determinable. The landlord has a range of courses of action open to him, depending upon the particular circumstances of the case. The landlord's position where an administrative or Law of Property Act receiver has been appointed is considered below.

Courses of action primarily designed to recover rent or damages

The landlord could threaten to petition for winding up or bankruptcy. A creditor owed at least £750 may petition for a compulsory winding up (where the debtor is a company) or for bankruptcy (where the debtor is an individual) if his claim remains unsatisfied three weeks after making a statutory notice in a prescribed form.[9] In some cases, therefore, the service by a landlord of a statutory demand might be sufficient to encourage the tenant to pay. In practice, however, the landlord, as an unsecured creditor, may not fare so well in an actual bankruptcy or winding up. There is a risk

4 *Civil Service Co-operative Society v McGrigor's Trustee* [1923] 2 Ch 347.
5 *Halliard Property Co Ltd v Jack Segal Ltd* [1978] 1 WLR 377.
6 *Re Riggs, ex p Lovell* [1901] 2 KB 16.
7 See Chap 13.
8 LPA 1925, s 146(9) and (10). See Chap 13.
9 IA 1986, ss 123, 267.

that rent payments made by the tenant at a time when he is unable to pay his debts might be set aside as an unlawful preference. To be so caught, the payments must be made shortly before bankruptcy or insolvency (which can be a period of up to two years).[10] In practice, however, this is unlikely, since the test is whether the tenant had a desire to prefer a creditor, not whether a preference was a natural consequence of the payment. Where, therefore, the tenant pays the rent in order to avoid a forfeiture and so continue in business, the landlord would appear to be safe.[11]

The landlord may also be able to distrain for rent arrears. Provided there are sufficient goods on the premises, distress for rent arrears is generally preferable to an action to recover them. An important advantage is that distress gives the landlord a legal lien, which means that he is in a favoured position, somewhat like that of a secured creditor. Not surprisingly, however, the right to distrain in cases of bankruptcy, liquidation or administration, is hedged with restrictions. The landlord should bear in mind that if he obtains judgment for the rent arrears he can enforce it only by court procedures, not by distress.[12] If he intends to forfeit the lease, he should be wary that a distress (which is an affirmation of the lease) does not cause such right to be waived.[13]

Where the remedy of distress proves inadequate, rent arrears may need to be recovered in an action. In practice, however, an action to recover rent arrears will generally not be advisable. First, where the tenant is already insolvent, permission to bring the action may be required, and will rarely be given: generally the court will authorise an action for a debt only where the debt was incurred after, and for the purpose of, bankruptcy, administration or winding up.[14] Secondly, even where an action can be brought, the costs (and delays) of bringing an action to recover arrears which may never be recoverable from an insolvent tenant will dissuade most landlords from suing. Thirdly, leave of the court may ultimately be required to enforce a judgment.

The landlord may also be able to recover his losses by bringing an action against an earlier tenant or guarantor. This is discussed elsewhere.[15] Disclaimer of the lease does not determine the liability of the tenant's guarantor or (in the case of a pre-1996 lease) any continuing liability of the original tenant.[16]

A head-lessor whose tenant is in arrears with the rent is entitled to serve

10 *Ibid*, ss 239–240, 340–341.
11 cf *Re MC Bacon Ltd* [1990] BCC 78.
12 *Chancellor v Webster* (1893) 9 TLR 508.
13 See pp 335–340 *supra*.
14 *Re Atlantic Computer Systems plc* [1992] Ch 505 (CA).
15 See chapters 4 and 5.
16 See discussion of disclaimer later in this chapter.

a notice on sub-tenants requiring them to pay the rent direct to the head-lessor.[17] Such a notice is effective against the tenant's receiver. In bankruptcy, liquidation or administration, however, the position remains unclear, and the court's leave may be needed before such notice can be served.

If the landlord required the tenant to ensure that its bank provided a guarantee or performance bond for the payment of the rent up to a specified amount, the landlord may look to this for payment. Again, if the landlord obtained a rent deposit from the tenant, the landlord may be able to use this to make good the arrears. Where a tenant is bankrupt or in insolvent liquidation, however, the landlord will not be able to satisfy the arrears out of the deposit if the tenant retains a proprietary interest in it. Furthermore, if the deposit creates a charge, then if legal proceedings are needed to enforce it, the landlord may require the court's leave to do so under the statutory provisions to be examined in this chapter.

A landlord may be able to insure against losses in the event of the tenant's insolvency. The premiums would normally be recouped as a component of a service charge. Such insurance is, however, expensive and somewhat unusual.

Where the tenant is insolvent, the landlord may find he is reduced to proving in the winding up or bankruptcy. In the case of winding up, the landlord can prove for rent up to the date of the liquidation, which means (in the case of a compulsory winding up) the date of presentation of the petition.[18] In the case of bankruptcy, however, the landlord can prove for rent due up to the date of the bankruptcy order.[19] In each case, rent payable in arrear can be apportioned. Rent which accrues subsequently is not proved in the winding up or bankruptcy; but the landlord might be able to claim that it is an expense of such process, and thereby secure payment ahead of the tenant's ordinary creditors. Where the landlord's claim is unliquidated (such as for damages for the tenant's breach of a repairing covenant) its value can be estimated by the trustee in bankruptcy or liquidator.[20] If the landlord, pursuant to a right reserved in the lease, has entered the premises and performed the repairs himself[21], the measure of the claim can be calculated precisely. The landlord's claim may include interest, either where this is provided for in the lease, or under the general law.[22]

If the tenant is in rent arrears, the landlord has a right to be paid out of

17 Law of Distress Amendment Act 1908.
18 IR 4.92.
19 IR 6.112.
20 IA 1986, s 322(3), IR 4.86.
21 See Chap 10.
22 Judgments Act 1838, s 17; IR 4.93 and 6.113.

the proceeds of execution levied against the tenant on behalf of another creditor under a court order in priority to the execution creditor itself. If the execution is pursuant to proceedings in the High Court, the landlord's right is defined and governed by the Landlord and Tenant Act 1709, section 1. The sheriff is under a duty to deal with the landlord's claim (for up to one year's rent arrears) if he receives notice of it, from whatever source, before he has parted with the proceeds of sale. It is therefore in the landlord's interests to notify the sheriff of any arrears due. In the county court, the landlord's rights are to be found in the County Courts Act 1984, section 102; the landlord must claim his right (in signed writing) within five days of the bailiff's seizure or removal of the goods. The only restriction upon the landlord's right to claim priority occurs in the case of the tenant's bankruptcy.[23]

The High Court may appoint a receiver in all cases in which it appears to the court just and convenient to do so.[24] A landlord might seek the appointment of a receiver where the premises need continuous management, which the tenant is not attending to. This is particularly appropriate to premises which are sub-let to numerous separate businesses, each sub-tenant paying a service charge.

Courses of action relating to the premises

The landlord may be willing to accept a surrender from the tenant, particularly if the lease has premium value. If the surrender is for an undervalue, there is the risk that it may be set aside upon the application of the trustee in bankruptcy, liquidator or administrator if at the time the tenant could not pay his debts.[25] As considered further below, dealings by the tenant after bankruptcy or insolvency may be void. Where the tenant is bankrupt or an insolvent company, the surrender may be accepted from the trustee in bankruptcy or the liquidator, who will generally prefer surrender to disclaimer where the lease has premium value, since the consideration for the surrender swells the fund available to creditors. A surrender ends the liability of the surrendering tenant, an original tenant, and any surety in regard to future obligations under the lease. Liability for existing breaches, however, remains. However, a landlord who expressly releases the surrendering tenant from such liability will also be taken to have released earlier tenants and their sureties.[26]

---

23 See *infra*.
24 Supreme Court Act 1981, s 37.
25 IA 1986, ss 238, 339, 436 and 423.
26 *Deanplan Ltd* v *Mahmoud* [1993] Ch 151 (Judge Paul Baker QC sitting as a judge of the High Court). For surrender generally, see Chap 12.

Forfeiture is generally less desirable for the landlord in a recession, since the property may be empty for some time before a new tenant can be found, and the rent payable under the new lease may be less than that payable under the old. If, however, this is not the case (perhaps because the landlord granted the lease at a premium and therefore took a reduced rent), forfeiture may still be advantageous. If, as often occurs in commercial lettings, however, the lease was granted at a rack rent with no premium and subject to periodic reviews, such financial cushion is absent. In such circumstances, forfeiture may be less advantageous. If the landlord seeks to forfeit, the tenant has a right to apply for relief; as does the tenant's mortgagee, sub-lessee or equitable chargee. If the tenant is bankrupt or in liquidation, the trustee in bankruptcy or liquidator has such right, which may be assigned, as a chose in action, to a purchaser. If the forfeiture was for bankruptcy or insolvent liquidation, any application for relief by the trustee or liquidator must be made within one year after the bankruptcy or liquidation.[27] A right to forfeit is not lost if an execution creditor has in the meantime obtained a charging order absolute over the lease under the Charging Orders Act 1979.

A landlord may choose to consent to the lease being assigned, as any capital sum the tenant receives from the assignee may enable it to pay off the arrears. A tenant is more likely to be able to do this if it paid a premium on the grant of the lease and therefore pays less than a rack rent. If the tenant has found a prospective assignee, the landlord (where the right to assign is qualified) may therefore prefer to give its consent to the assignment, rather than forfeiting and being left with a loss of rent before the premises can be re-let.

It is clearly unsatisfactory for a landlord not to know whether the trustee or liquidator will disclaim the lease, since he cannot make definite arrangements to re-let. The landlord can, however, require a trustee or liquidator to disclaim (if at all) within 28 days after the service upon him of a notice.[28]

The court has power, on the application of the other contracting party, to discharge a contract entered into by a bankrupt on such terms as the court considers equitable.[29] Any damages payable by virtue of the order are provable as a bankruptcy debt. A parallel power exists in regard to a company's contracts on a winding up.[30] It might be arguable that this power is applicable to a lease, in which case the landlord could apply to the court for its discharge. There is no authority on the point. Since,

---

27 LPA 1925, s 146(10). See Chap 13.
28 See the discussion of disclaimer later in this chapter.
29 IA 1986, s 345.
30 *Ibid*, s 186.

however, a lease creates an interest in land, it is probably unlikely that such power is available to a landlord.

The landlord may be able to compel the surety to accept a new lease. This is possible if the tenant's surety has covenanted with the landlord to take a new lease of the premises in his own name in the event of disclaimer of the lease by the tenant's trustee in bankruptcy or liquidator. From the landlord's point of view, it is desirable that the surety covenants to take a new lease from the date of the disclaimer.[31]

TENANT'S CHOICES

The tenant's options may, understandably, be somewhat limited. If insolvency is looming, a tenant may be able to fend it off by reorganising its business. Failing this, it may seek to raise funds to pay its creditors through a surrender or an assignment. In a final attempt to stave off disaster, the tenant might seek to enter into a voluntary arrangement with its creditors. If this fails, there may be no alternative to the tenant but to petition for its own liquidation or bankruptcy, or (where it is a corporate body) to petition for an administration order.

Voluntary arrangement

There are separate legal regimes according to whether the tenant is an individual or a corporate entity[32]; but the object of the legislation is in each case the same.[33] The aim of a company voluntary arrangement has been described as being:[34]

> to provide a swift and comparatively informal arrangement whereby the majority of the company's creditors can bind the minority to some arrangement (and there are many) inhibiting the immediate enforcement and/or total enforcement of the debts, thereby avoiding a creditors' free-for-all and giving the company often a period in which it can trade untrammelled by the need for payment of the debts comprised in the arrangement."

The Insolvency Act 1986 enables an individual debtor to obtain a short

---

31 See *infra* and Chap 4.

32 The relevant provisions are IA 1986, Part VIII (ss 252–263) and IR 1986 (SI 1986 No 1925), Part V (r 5) (relating to IVAs); and IA 1986, Part I (ss 1–7) and IR 1986, Part I (r 1) (relating to CVAs).

33 See generally, Milman & Davey, "Debtor rehabilitation: implications for the landlord-tenant relationship" [1996] JBL 541.

34 *Burford Midland Properties Ltd* v *Marley Extrusions Ltd* [1994] BCC 604, 606, per Judge Cook QC, sitting as a deputy judge of the High Court.

moratorium on actions against him, in order to give him time to put proposals to his creditors.[35] The debtor[36] can apply to the court for an interim order (which lasts for 14 days unless extended by the court[37]) nominating a person (the nominee[38]) to act as trustee or supervisor of the arrangement.[39] During the period of the order, no bankruptcy petition may be presented or proceeded with, and no other proceedings, and no execution or legal process may be commenced or continued against the debtor or his property without the leave of the court.[40] If the debtor is a tenant, the effect is that, during this period, the landlord cannot institute or continue proceedings against the tenant, *e.g.* for forfeiture or for arrears of rent.[41] The landlord is, however, entitled to pursue self-help remedies that do not require the assistance of the court, since these do not comprise "other proceedings" or "legal process". During this period, the landlord may therefore recover rent arrears by distress,[42] or may forfeit the lease by peaceable re-entry.[43] This results in anomalies with other aspects of insolvency law, notably with the effect of an administration order[44]; but it has been stated that such anomalies result from the legislature, and must be cured, if at all, by Parliament.[45]

A somewhat similar procedure for voluntary arrangements exists where the debtor is a company[46], but with the important difference that in this case there is no statutory moratorium. For this reason, the procedure is little used on its own; and is really more appropriate in conjunction with an administration order, where there is a statutory moratorium.[47]

Where an interim order has been made, the debtor must submit to the nominee a document setting out the terms of the voluntary arrangement proposed, and a statement of his affairs.[48] The nominee must, before the interim order ceases to have effect, submit a report to the court stating

---

35 IA 1986, s 252.
36 If the debtor is bankrupt, the trustee of his estate or the official receiver may also apply: IA 1986, s 253(3).
37 IA 1986, s 255(6).
38 Who must be qualified to act an insolvency practitioner: IA 1986, s 255(1)(d).
39 IA 1986, s 253(2).
40 *Ibid*, s 252(2).
41 *Re Naeem (a bankrupt) (No 18 of 1988)* [1990] 1 WLR 48.
42 *McMullen & Sons Ltd v Cerrone* [1994] 1 EGLR 99 (Ch).
43 *Re a Debtor (No 13A-IO-1995)* [1995] 1 WLR 1127 (Rattee J).
44 Since, in relation to an administration order, the exercise by a landlord of his right of re-entry on property comprised in a lease to a company does constitute the enforcement of a security over the company's property, and also amounts to "other legal process" (IA 1986,s. 11(3)(c),(d)): *Exchange Travel Agency Ltd v Triton Property Trust plc* [1991] BCLC 396 (Harman J). But see *Razzaq v Pala* [1997] 38 EG 157, 159 (Lightman J).
45 *Re a Debtor (No 13A-IO-1995)* [1995] 1 WLR 1127, 1139.
46 IA 1986, ss 1–7.
47 *Burford Midland Properties Ltd v Marley Extrusions Ltd* [1994] BCC 604, 606.
48 IA 1986, s 256(2).

whether, in his opinion, a creditors' meeting should be summoned to consider the debtor's proposal.[49] If the nominee reports that it should, he must summon a meeting of every creditor of whose claim and address he is aware.[50]

Votes at the creditors' meeting are weighted according to the amount of each creditor's debt as at the date of the meeting (except where a bankruptcy order has been made, when the relevant date is that of the making of the bankruptcy order).[51] A creditor cannot vote in respect of a debt for an unliquidated amount, or any debt whose value is not ascertained, unless the chairman (who will normally be the nominee[52]) agrees to place on the claim an estimated minimum value.[53] A resolution approving any proposal or modification requires a majority of more than three-quarters in value of the creditors voting on it.[54] A vote by a lessor in favour of a voluntary arrangement that involves the assignment of the lease does not waive an existing right of forfeiture.[55] The meeting cannot approve any proposal which affects the rights of a secured creditor to enforce his security[56] except with such creditor's concurrence.[57]

The problem of future rents

Where the debtor is a tenant, the voting power of the debtor's lessor clearly includes the amount of rent then accrued due. There is, however, a serious problem in relation to future rents. Although the obligation to pay rent will have been incurred when the lease was entered into, it would seem difficult to characterise future rent as a debt "at the date of the meeting" since the date for payment of such rent has not yet arrived.[58] If this possibility is discounted, future rent could be the subject of a voluntary arrangement only if it ranks as an unliquidated or unascertained amount on which the chairman agrees to place an estimated minimum value.

In *Burford Midland Properties Ltd* v *Marley Extrusions Ltd*[59], the arrangement provisions were expressed to have effect in full and final settlement of all claims against and obligations of the company "present

---

49 *Ibid*, s 256(1).
50 IR 1986, r 257(1), (2).
51 *Ibid*, r 5.17.
52 *Ibid*, r 5.15(1) (IVA).
53 IR 5.17(3) (IVA); IR 1.17(3) (CVA); the rules are identical.
54 IR 1986, r 5.18(1) (IVA); r 1.19(1) (CVA).
55 This is implicit in *Re Naeem (a bankrupt) (No 18 of 1988)* [1990] 1 WLR 48.
56 This includes the rights of an execution creditor who has the benefit of a walking possession agreement entered into by a sheriff under a fieri facias: *Peck v Craighead* [1995] 1 BCLC 337.
57 IA 1986, s 258(4). The equivalent provision in a CVA is IA 1986, s 4(3).
58 See Wonnacott, "Commercial tenants in individual voluntary arrangements" [1996] 2 EG 104.
59 [1994] BCC 604.

and potential in relation to the liabilities ... whether such claims or obligations are liquidated or unliquidated, their value ascertained or unascertained, future or present, contingent or otherwise." It was held that this form of words was not sufficient to include the liability of a tenant to pay future rent under a lease. Such an obligation was outside the category of prospective debts because one was concerned with:[60]

> "what (time and contingency apart) the company is known to owe at the relevant date as opposed to what the company will owe at a future date when it receives some benefit which at present it does not have – for example, continued possession under a subsisting lease and the continued benefit of the landlord's covenant."

In the judge's view, the obligation to make future rent payments was more akin to an executory contract to pay for goods to be delivered in the future.[61] The judge in the *Burford* case was there considering the effect of the particular arrangement, rather than the legal question whether future rents could ever be the subject of a voluntary arrangement[62]; but his analysis would appear to provide some support for the view that future rents cannot be the subject of such an arrangement.

At first instance in *Doorbar v Alltime Securities Ltd*[63], however, Knox J rejected the submission that future rent was, as a matter of law, incapable of being included in a voluntary arrangement. He took the expression "a scheme of arrangement of his affairs" in the Insolvency Act 1986, section 253(1), as sufficiently wide to comprehend the liability to make such future payments.[64] No such submission was, however, made on the appeal from Knox J's decision to the Court of Appeal, so the point is not beyond argument in a later case. McLoughlin, however, accepts the correctness of Knox J's approach.[65]

If the landlord is permitted some additional votes in respect of future rents, there is then the difficulty of determining the amount of weighting to be allowed, which can obviously be crucial, especially if there is the possibility of its bringing the landlord up to one quarter of the voting power at the meeting. Here also there has been some diversity of judicial opinion relating to the meaning of the word "agrees" in the Insolvency Rules. In *Re Cranley Mansions*[66], Ferris J thought that it indicates that there must be a bilateral concurrence between the chairman and the

---

60 *Ibid*, at 610.
61 *Ibid*, at 610.
62 As pointed out by Knox J in *Doorbar v Alltime Securities Ltd* [1995] 1 BCLC 316, 327.
63 [1995] 1 BCLC 316, 327 (Ch).
64 *Ibid*.
65 McLoughlin, *Commercial Leases and Insolvency*, 2nd ed (1996), Butterworths, 4–5.
66 [1994] 1 WLR 1610, 1628–9.

creditor; although he admitted that this interpretation would result in difficulties where no such agreement could be reached. In *Doorbar v Alltime Securities Ltd*[67], however, Knox J said that, for the purposes of rule 5.17(3), "agrees" refers to the chairman's willingness to put a minimum value on the claim, not to an agreement in relation to the minimum value[68] – a view affirmed on appeal to the Court of Appeal.[69]

On this basis, in the absence of any agreement between the chairman and the landlord, the landlord should attempt to place some realistic minimum value on the claim for future rent. The value may be difficult to ascertain; but the chairman will be acting improperly if he places merely a nominal value (of, say, £1) upon a claim which is clearly worth substantially more.[70] In the *Doorbar* case, the chairman had determined the minimum value of future rent as being that of one year's rent, rather than the total of all future rents during the remainder of the term. Such determination was upheld by Knox J and by the Court of Appeal, which said that the chairman is allowed to take account of what is likely to happen, and to make allowance for the possibility of the landlord's exercising its power of re-entry.[71]

If the rent under the lease is fixed, it will be possible to calculate precisely the sums that will fall due; but such calculation will be impossible if the lease (like most commercial leases) makes provision for rent review. If the tenant has the benefit of a break clause, there can be no certainty that the obligation to pay rent falling due after the break date will ever arise. In every case, there is also the question whether there should be some discounting for the possibility that some future rent may prove irrecoverable, or that the lease may be forfeited or terminated in some other way. Contrary to the approach of the courts in the *Doorbar* case, McLoughlin takes the view that there should be no discounting, since this would be unfair to the landlord unless it were applied also to other debts; and he suggests that the correct approach is "to allow the landlord to vote to the extent that rent is the subject of the arrangement."[72] This would seem to be a convincing argument; but, whatever the true legal position is eventually found to be, the present state of uncertainty in relation to future rents is most unsatisfactory.

---

67 [1995] 1 BCLC 316 (Ch).
68 See also Knox J's decisions on r 5.17(3) to similar effect in *Beverley Group plc v McClue* [1995] BCC 751, 759; and on r 1.17(3) in *Re Cancol Ltd* [1996] 1 All ER 37 (involving a CVA).
69 *Doorbar v Alltime Securities Ltd* [1996] 2 EGLR 33 (CA).
70 As in *Re Cranley Mansions Ltd* [1994] 1 WLR 1610.
71 *Doorbar v Alltime Securities Ltd* [1996] 2 EGLR 33, 37 (CA).
72 McLoughlin, *Commercial Leases and Insolvency*, 2nd ed (1996), Butterworths, 5.

A claim against a surety in respect of future rent is treated as a contingent and unliquidated claim.[73] A creditor of an unliquidated claim who fails to attend the meeting will nevertheless be treated as having been entitled to vote, with the result that the arrangement will be binding on him.[74]

The chairman must notify the court of the result of the meeting.[75] In the case of an individual debtor, if the resolution is rejected, the interim order ceases, so that the moratorium ends. If the meeting accepts the proposals, the chairman must also notify the Secretary of State[76], who will make an entry in the register of voluntary arrangements.[77] In the case of an individual debtor, the interim order ceases to have effect 28 days from the day on which the report is made to the court.[78]

The effect of a voluntary arrangement

The debtor, a person entitled to vote at the meeting, or the nominee, may challenge the decision of the meeting by applying to the court within 28 days from the day on which the report of the creditors' meeting is made to the court.[79] The challenge may be on either or both of the following grounds: that the voluntary arrangement unfairly prejudices the interests of a creditor; or that there has been some material irregularity at or in relation to such a meeting.[80]

In *Re Naeem*[81], the meeting had approved a voluntary arrangement which included the proposed marketing and sale of a leasehold shop of which the bankrupt debtor was the tenant. The landlord of the shop, which was a creditor in respect of arrears of rent under the lease, applied to the court to have the approval revoked on the ground that the sale would be unfairly prejudicial to its interest because it would prevent it from exercising its proprietary right to forfeit and re-enter the demised premises (which right, under the terms of the lease, was exercisable in the event of the tenant's becoming bankrupt or entering into a voluntary arrangement with his creditors). The registrar made an order revoking approval of the arrangement; but Hoffmann J allowed the bankrupt's appeal. He said that the arrangement was only intended to bind the creditors in their character of creditors, and that it did not affect proprietary rights such as those of the landlord to forfeit the lease.[82] The arrangement merely meant that the

---

73 *Doorbar v Alltime Securities Ltd* [1995] 1 BCLC 316 (Ch).
74 *Beverley Group plc v McClue* [1995] BCC 751.
75 IA 1986, s 259(1).
76 IR 5.24.
77 IR 5.23.
78 IA 1986, s 260(4).
79 *Ibid*, s 262(3).
80 *Ibid*, s 262(1)(a), (b).
81 [1990] 1 WLR 48.
82 *Re Naeem (a bankrupt) (No 18 of 1988)* [1990] 1 WLR 48, 50.

premises were to be sold in so far as the bankrupt could obtain relief from forfeiture.[83] Although the effect of the interim order had been to prevent the landlord from commencing forfeiture proceedings, the landlord was now free to do so, as 28 days had passed since the report of the creditors' meeting had been given to the court.

The lease in *Re Naeem* also contained the usual proviso for re-entry for rent arrears. Hoffmann J held that the effect of the arrangement was to modify the landlord's claim for arrears of rent in the same way as the claims of other creditors. He did not think that it was unfair prejudice "that after such modification the right to forfeit should only stand as security for recovery of the modified debt rather than the original one."[84]

In the case of both an IVA and a CVA, if the resolution is accepted, the arrangement binds all creditors who had notice of the meeting and were entitled to vote, whether they did so or not. Such persons are bound by the arrangement, however, only according to its terms. A landlord will not, therefore, be bound in relation to future rents unless the arrangement binds him in relation to such future rents. If, therefore the arrangement is intended to comprehend future rents (assuming them to be legally capable of being included), as opposed merely to arrears, it needs, as the *Burford* case shows, to be clearly worded.

The assignee of the reversion is bound by a voluntary arrangement of the tenant to the same extent as was his assignor. The assignee takes the rights attaching to the reversion[85] as modified by the voluntary arrangement; notice is immaterial.[86]

In *Mytre Investments Ltd v Reynolds*[87], the assignee of a pre-1996 lease had entered into an individual voluntary arrangement with his creditors, including the landlord. The landlord then sought to recover the arrears from the original tenants. The deputy master had struck out the claim on the ground that, were it to be allowed, the original tenants would be entitled (under the implied covenants) to recover from the existing lessee the sum that they had had to pay out to the landlord, thereby driving a coach and horses through the purpose of the individual voluntary arrangement. In an appeal, however, Michael Burton QC, sitting as a deputy judge of the High Court, said that he was not impressed by this argument. The solution would be to give notice of the meeting to such original lessees (and to any intermediate assignees who entered into direct

---

83 *i.e.* under LPA 1925, s 146.

84 *Re Naeem (a bankrupt) (No 18 of 1988)* [1990] 1 WLR 48, 50; but this was considered to be incorrect by Lightman J in *March Estates plc v Gunmark Ltd* [1996] 2 EGLR 38, 40.

85 *i.e.* in the case of a pre-1996 lease, by virtue of LPA 1925, s 141(1).

86 *Burford Midland Properties Ltd v Marley Extrusions Ltd* [1994] BCC 604, 613.

87 [1995] 3 All ER 588 (Michael Burton QC, sitting as a deputy judge of the Queen's Bench Division).

covenants with the landlord), so that the matter could either be sorted out at the meeting or through a challenge in court; or, if necessary, there would be no agreed individual voluntary arrangement.[88] An original or intermediate tenant under a pre-1996 lease whose liability continues through privity of covenant can be said to be contingently liable to pay the rent (*i.e.* in the event of a failure by the current tenant to do so), and so is therefore capable of being bound by a voluntary arrangement.[89]

Alternatively, the arrangement could itself contain a provision prohibiting any claim by any creditor against any other person when the effect of such claim would be likely to increase the aggregate amount becoming payable by the debtor. A clause to this effect (clause 4.2) was included in the individual voluntary arrangement in *Burford Midland Properties Ltd* v *Marley Extrusions Ltd*[90], and was set out in essentially the following terms:

> "except with the prior written consent of the supervision committee, or with the written consent given prior to entry into force of the creditors committee, any claim by any creditor against any person other than [the debtor] or the Deposit Protection Board is hereby for the benefit of [the debtor] prohibited to the maximum extent permitted by law if such claim would or might lead to the recovery by such creditor or such person of moneys equal or corresponding to all or part of the liabilities of such creditor when the direct or indirect effect of such claim would be or was likely to be to increase the aggregate amount from time to time becoming payable by [the debtor] (a) whether pursuant to this voluntary arrangement or howsoever; and (b) whether in consequence of a claim by such person against [the debtor] or for any other reason."

In the *Burford* case, which involved a pre-1996 lease, it was held that, although the original tenant (not being a party to the voluntary arrangement), could not itself enforce the clause, such clause could be enforced against the landlord by the debtor (the assignee of the lease), by means of an injunction. Such debtor would, of course be interested in enforcing such a clause in order to avoid an indemnity claim from the original tenant.

If the voluntary arrangement relates to future rents, it may be treated as a modification of the lease.[91] It is now clear that the continuing contractual

---

88 *Ibid*, at 591; and see the similar remarks of Jacob J in *R A Securities Ltd* v *Mercantile Credit Co Ltd* [1995] 3 All ER 581, 585–586, and of Lightman J in *March Estates plc* v *Gunmark Ltd* [1996] 2 EGLR 38,39.

89 See Knox J in *Re Cancol Ltd* [1996] 1 All ER 37, 43-46, referring to *Re Midland Coal, Coke & Iron Co, Craig's Claim* [1895] 1 Ch 267 (CA), a decision on Joint Stock Companies Arrangement Act 1870, s 2, a direct ancestor of Companies Act 1985, s 425 (which offers a procedure for a company to compromise with its creditors that pre-dates, and survives, Insolvency Act 1986).

90 [1994] BCC 604 (Judge Cooke, sitting as a judge of the High Court).

91 *Re Naeem (a bankrupt) (No 18 of 1988)* [1990] 1 WLR 48.

liability of an original tenant under a pre-1996 lease cannot be varied by any subsequent modification to the estate agreed between his assignee and the landlord.[92] In the case of a post-1995 lease, the liability of a prior tenant can only be that of a guarantor under any authorised guarantee agreement that may have been entered into.[93] Since under general principles relating to sureties, any agreement varying the lease will operate to discharge the surety, a prior tenant's liability as guarantor under a post-1995 lease may be terminated by a voluntary arrangement which relates to future rent.

In the *Burford* case, the judge seemed to accept that a landlord's being a party to an individual voluntary arrangement of an assignee tenant would normally amount to an accord and satisfaction discharging a prior tenant under a pre-1996 lease. This was on the authority of *Deanplan* v *Mahmoud*[94], which held that an original tenant and an assignee fall within the principle that the release of one joint debtor releases the other because their liability is in respect of the same obligation. The judge in the *Burford* case, however, held that clause 4.2 in the arrangement before him operated as a reservation of the right to sue. Ironically, therefore, in his view, the original tenant would have been in a better position had clause 4.2 been omitted.

A different view was, however, taken in *R A Securities Ltd* v *Mercantile Credit Co Ltd*.[95] There, Jacob J said that "[t]he whole scheme [of voluntary arrangements] is not for the benefit of solvent parties who happen to owe debts also owed by the debtor", and that it would "be unfair if a solvent debtor escaped liability as a sidewind of the voluntary arrangement system." The position in relation to a voluntary arrangement is therefore different from the position outside such an arrangement (as where the landlord agrees with an assignee to accept a surrender in consideration for the transfer of goods "in full and final settlement of rent"). In the latter circumstance, the doctrine of accord and satisfaction has been held to discharge a prior tenant.[96] A voluntary arrangement, by contrast, has been described as being not an "accord", but merely "a statutory binding"[97], and does not release a prior tenant even if it provides for surrender.[98]

---

92 *Friends' Provident Life Office* v *British Railways Board* [1996] 1 All ER 336 (CA); LT(C)A 1995, s 18. See Chap 5.

93 LT(C)A 1995, s 16.

94 [1993] Ch 151.

95 [1995] 3 All ER 581, applied in *Mytre Investments Ltd* v *Reynolds* [1995] 3 All ER 588, and in *March Estates plc* v *Gunmark Ltd* [1996] 2 EGLR 38; but see *Johnson* v *Davies* [1998] 2 All ER 649 (CA).

96 *Deanplan Ltd* v *Mahmoud* [1993] Ch 151 (Paul Baker QC, sitting as a judge of the High Court).

97 *R A Securities Ltd* v *Mercantile Credit Co Ltd* [1995] 3 All ER 581, 586.

98 *Ibid.* See, however, *Johnson* v *Davies* [1998] 2 All ER 649 (CA).

An intermediate tenant (T2) of a pre-1996 lease who is a party to an arrangement entered into by his assignee (T3), may be at risk unless either the original tenant, T1 is also a party, or the arrangement prohibits the landlord from recovering from a prior tenant. Unless T2 ensures that it is protected in one of these ways, it may face an indemnity claim from T1 without the right to claim itself in turn from T3.

MORTGAGEE'S CHOICES

Introduction

An institutional lender which has advanced funds to the tenant, whether to assist in the payment of a premium on the grant or assignment of a lease, or for other purposes connected with the tenant's business, will usually have taken steps to secure its own position. Such security could take the form of a mortgage over the lease itself or over other of the tenant's assets. These could, for instance, be plant and machinery or goods used in the tenant's business; or they could be other assets belonging to the tenant, such as his own home. If the tenant-borrower is a company, the lender may require a fixed security over the land, *i.e.* a legal charge of the leasehold title, and a floating charge over other assets used in the business. If the lease has little asset value (*e.g.* because it is granted at a rack rent without a premium), the lender may require the company's directors to mortgage their personal assets, such as their own homes. Security could also take the form of a personal guarantee provided by a third party – such as a director of a company or a parent or grandparent of a person setting up in business.

If the mortgage is of an existing lease, the prospective mortgagee should check the terms of the lease and ascertain whether there are any existing breaches of covenant. The mortgagee should also check to see if the lease contains a covenant by the tenant not to mortgage or charge the property. If the covenant against mortgaging or charging is a qualified one, the landlord's consent is not to be unreasonably refused.[99] A qualified covenant by the tenant against mortgaging or charging the lease might be as follows, namely a covenant:

> "Not to mortgage or charge or permit or suffer to be mortgaged or charged all or any part of the demised premises without the prior written consent of the Landlord."

---

99 See LTA 1927, s 19(1)(a); LPA 1925, s 86(1); and Chap 6, *supra*.

If the lender takes a legal charge over the tenant's lease, the lender (the mortgagee) will need to protect his position so far as possible against breaches by the tenant of the terms of the lease. If the landlord seeks subsequently to forfeit the lease, the mortgagee has a right to apply for relief; but the mortgagee will wish to have as early warning as possible of any default by the tenant. The mortgagee may not itself necessarily receive a copy of the statutory notice that is required to be served under the Law of Property Act 1925, section 146.[1] The mortgage deed should therefore contain a covenant by the mortgagor to inform the mortgagee as soon as it receives service of a section 146 notice. This method is, not, however, necessarily secure; and, although the landlord should inform a mortgagee of whom he is aware, of forfeiture proceedings, the mortgagee cannot be guaranteed to learn of them.[2] In any event, the mortgagee should be advised to notify the landlord in writing of his interest.

Receivership

Appointment of a receiver

The tenant may have mortgaged his lease or his other assets or both. If the lease has been specifically mortgaged, a receiver appointed by the mortgagee to enforce such fixed charge is known as an "LPA receiver", because he is subject, in addition to the provisions of the mortgage deed, to the provisions of the Law of Property Act 1925, section 109. The appointment must be in writing.

If the tenant is a company, it is additionally empowered to issue a debenture creating a floating charge over its assets, including the lease. A receiver appointed to enforce a charge over all or substantially all of a company's assets is known as an "administrative receiver". Such a receiver is subject to the provisions contained both in the debenture creating the charge and in the Insolvency Act 1986.

Where more than one person has been appointed a receiver, it is important for the landlord to know whether the appointment is joint or several. The landlord should check, not merely the document making the appointment, but also the terms of the mortgage or debenture itself. If the mortgage makes provision for a joint appointment only, a purported joint and several appointment is invalid.

Receiver as agent

The mortgage deed or debenture will usually create an express agency, and

---

1 See Chap 13.
2 See further Chap 13.

in practice the receiver will be stated to be the agent of the mortgagor. In the absence of express provision, an LPA receiver is deemed to be the agent of the mortgagor[3]; and a administrative receiver appointed under a debenture is deemed the agent of the company which granted it.[4] The effect of the receiver being the agent of the mortgagor, rather than of the mortgagee, is that it is only the former who is liable for the receiver's defaults.

Although a receiver may be appointed as agent of a mortgagor company, such agency ceases upon a winding-up order or resolution for a voluntary winding up. Similarly, although a receiver may be appointed after the company has gone into liquidation, the receiver will not be agent of the liquidated company. Even after the company's liquidation, however, the receiver retains the powers of disposal conferred upon him by the mortgage deed or debenture. Furthermore, if the receiver has already instituted proceedings in the name of a tenant-company mortgagor, it may continue those proceedings even after the tenant has gone into liquidation. Thus in *Goughs Garages Ltd* v *Pugsley*[5], the receiver was held entitled to continue an application to the court for a new lease (under the renewal provisions contained in the predecessor to the Landlord and Tenant Act 1954, Part II), even though the tenant had been compulsorily wound up since the receiver's action had been commenced.

A receiver in occupation of property as agent of an insolvent tenant would not appear to be itself liable to pay business rates.[6] It may, however, be liable, if the premises occupied are those of a tenant which is a company in liquidation.[7]

Duties of a receiver

The receiver's primary duty is to the chargee who has appointed him. This includes a duty to take reasonable care in managing the property, so that a receiver appointed by a landlord's chargee must, for example, ensure that rent-review notices are served on the tenants.[8] If the receiver is appointed by a tenant's chargee, the receiver owes a limited duty to the tenant, to the tenant's guarantor[9], and to any other chargee in respect of the same property[10]; such persons may complain of fraud or bad faith and of acts

---

3 LPA 1925, s 109(2).
4 IA 1986, s 44.
5 [1930] 1 KB 615.
6 *Ratford* v *Northavon DC* [1986] BCLC 357.
7 *Banister* v *Islington LBC* (1972) 71 LGR 239.
8 *Knight* v *Lawrence* [1991] 1 EGLR 143.
9 *American Express International Banking Corp* v *Hurley* [1985] 3 All ER 564.
10 *Downsview Nominees Ltd* v *First City Corp Ltd* [1993] AC 295 (PC).

outside the terms of the chargee's appointment[11], but the receiver owes them no general duty of care in tort[12] and (if it has powers of management) is not obliged to run the tenant's business at the chargee's expense.[13] In selling the property, the receiver must take reasonable care to obtain market value.[14] No duty at all is owed to other creditors.[15]

A Law of Property Act receiver generally has extensive powers conferred upon him expressly by the mortgage deed; apart from this, a receiver has the statutory powers conferred by the Law of Property Act 1925, section 109. Under the section, the receiver has power to demand and recover all the income of which he is appointed receiver, by action, distress, or otherwise, and to give receipts for the same. An administrative receiver will similarly generally have extensive powers conferred expressly by the debenture, but otherwise he has various statutory powers, including the power to make disposals, to insure, to carry on the company's business, and to grant leases.[16]

The receiver will dispose of or use the charged property in order to pay off the amount owed the chargee. An LPA receiver must apply any income from the property, and the proceeds of sale, in the order specified in the Law of Property Act 1925, section 109(8). Such income might comprise, for instance, rents from sub-lessees. The statutory order for application of payments is: rents, taxes, rates and other outgoings on the property; payments and interest on annual sums of prior mortgages; receiver's commission, insurance premiums payable under the mortgage deed, and proper repairs directed by the mortgagee; interest on principal money due under the mortgage; and the discharge of principal money due under the mortgage, if directed in writing by the mortgagee. Any balance must be paid to the person who would otherwise have been entitled to the income of, or who is otherwise entitled to, the mortgaged property.

If the LPA receiver is given an express power of sale, it would appear that the application of the sale proceeds is governed instead by the Law of Property Act 1925, section 105, so that the order of application is: discharge of prior mortgages; payment of costs of the sale; discharge of the mortgage money, interest and costs; any balance to the person entitled to the mortgaged property.

An administrative receiver appointed under a floating charge must, if the company is not in the course of being wound up, pay preferential debts

---

11 *Re B Johnson & Co (Builders) Ltd* [1955] Ch 634.
12 *Downsview Nominees Ltd v First City Corp Ltd* [1993] AC 295 (PC).
13 *Re B Johnson & Co (Builders) Ltd* [1955] Ch 634.
14 *cf Cuckmere Brick Co Ltd v Mutual Finance Ltd* [1971] Ch 949 (CA).
15 *Hemlata Lathia v Dronsfield Bros Ltd* [1987] BCLC 321.
16 IA 1986, s 42 and Sched 1.

before discharging the principal or interest under the debenture.[17]
Preferential debts include: debts due to the Inland Revenue and to
Customs and Excise, social security and occupational pensions
contributions, and up to four months' salary to employees.

Position of the landlord

The tenant's receivership does not prevent its landlord from pursuing his
remedies of forfeiture or distress, or from bringing an action for rent
arrears, or for damages for breach of any other covenants in the lease. No
leave is required to distrain goods subject to a floating charge or to bring an
action for rent arrears. Furthermore, by serving a notice under the Law of
Distress Amendment Act 1908, a head-landlord is entitled to the sub-rents
even against his immediate tenant's receiver.[18]

Once a receiver has been appointed, however, the receiver has priority
over a judgment debtor, even though the judgment debt was obtained
before the receiver was appointed. Indeed, the receiver has priority even
where the goods have already been seized by the sheriff. In this instance,
therefore, the landlord has an additional reason for preferring to recover
rent by means of distress rather than by action.

Provided its agency is disclosed, the receiver is not personally liable,
even in respect of a new lease which it enters into. In such circumstances,
therefore, a receiver does not incur personal liability if it renews the lease
under the provisions of the Landlord and Tenant Act 1954, Part II.
Similarly, a receiver occupying the demised premises as the tenant's agent
for the purpose of carrying on the tenant's business is not personally liable
for the rent due under the lease.[19]

Although the receiver is generally the agent of the tenant, he is jointly
liable with the tenant for any tort which he commits in the course of his
agency. Thus, if in the course of realising the assets, the receiver damages
the premises demised, the landlord could sue either or both of them for the
tort of waste.[20]

ADMINISTRATION OF A COMPANY

The process of administration, which is in practice quite popular, was
introduced in the 1980s to enable an attempt to be made to rescue a
company in the hope of avoiding liquidation. An administrator is appointed

---

17 *Ibid*, s 40(2).
18 *Rhodes v Allied Dunbar Pension Services Ltd* [1989] 1 WLR 800.
19 *Re Atlantic Computer Systems plc* [1992] Ch 505 (CA).
20 See Chap 7.

by a petition to the court made by the company, by any of its directors or creditors, or by a clerk of the magistrates' court.[21]

If the court considers that the company is unable to pay its debts but that a specified purpose (including the survival of the company or a better realisation of its assets in winding up) will be achieved, it may make an administration order. This appoints an administrator, who has all the powers of management of the company from this date. Conversely, from that time the powers of any administrative receiver cease.

The administrator is the agent of the company and may do all things necessary for the management of the company's affairs.[22] The administrator must prepare proposals to give effect to the purpose of the administration order, and these must be put to a creditors' meeting. If the proposals are approved (which requires an ordinary majority), the court is informed. If they are rejected, the court may discharge the order or make any other order.[23]

From presentation of petition to making of order

During this period, except with leave of the court, no steps may be taken to enforce any security over the company's property, no other proceedings, execution or other legal process may be commenced or continued, and no distress may be levied, against the company or its property.[24]

It is unclear whether this catches the service of a notice under the Law of Distress Amendment Act 1908. As previously mentioned, the court is unlikely to give a landlord the requisite leave, *e.g.* to forfeit the lease, or to sue or to distrain for rent arrears due at the presentation of the petition.

When, at the time of the petition, there is an administrative receiver of the company, no leave is required unless and until the person who appointed such receiver consents to the making of the order.[25]

From the making of the order

As the tenant company's agent, the administrator is not personally liable for the rent or upon the other covenants in the lease. He is, furthermore, under no general obligation as administrator to pay the rent. He does, however, have a discretion to pay it; and, in exercising this discretion, he must act responsibly and take all the circumstances into account. If the aim

21 IA 1986, s 9.
22 *Ibid*, s 14 and Sched 1.
23 *Ibid*, s 24.
24 *Ibid*, s 10(1).
25 *Ibid*, s 10(3).

of the administration order was to preserve the company as a going concern, which entails its being able to pay its outgoings, the administrator ought to pay the rent as it falls due, *i.e.* as an expense in the administration. Even if the order was made with a view to winding up, the administrator ought to pay over to the landlord any rents received from sub-tenants, at least up the value of the rent under the head-lease.[26]

The tenant company itself remains liable for the rent during the period of administration. Therefore, if the administrator declines to pay, the landlord may wish to bring an action to forfeit the lease or for the rent (or both), or to distrain. The landlord however faces two difficulties.

First, the moratorium on actions and distress against the company and its property continues after the order has been made, unless the administrator consents or the court gives leave.[27] Peaceable re-entry by the landlord has been held to require leave within section 11(3), as being either the enforcement of a "security" over the company's property, or a "legal process."[28] If the landlord applies for leave, the court may, as a condition of refusing it, order the administrator to pay the rent. An order for costs can be made in the landlord's favour if the administrator refuses unreasonably.[29] The approach of the court in deciding whether to grant leave (or to refuse it upon terms) under section 11(3) is discussed in *Re Atlantic Computer Systems plc.*[30] Secondly, even if leave is obtained, the landlord may not be able to enforce the terms of the lease against the company.

BANKRUPTCY

Bankruptcy petition

Various persons may present a petition for bankruptcy, including the debtor himself.[31] A creditor with a liquidated debt or debts of at least £750 may petition for bankruptcy if there is no reasonable prospect of the debtor paying.[32] A secured creditor cannot however present a petition for the secured part of the debt without first surrendering the security.[33] Any disposition made by the tenant between the presentation of the petition and

---

26 *Re Atlantic Computer Systems plc* [1992] Ch 505 (CA).
27 IA 1986, s 11(3)(d).
28 *Exchange Travel Agency Ltd v Triton Property Trust plc* [1991] BCLC 396; but in *Razzaq v Pala* [1997] 38 EG 157, 159, Lightman J stated *obiter* that the landlord's right of re-entry could not be a "security" for this purpose.
29 *Re Atlantic Computer Systems plc* [1992] Ch 505 (CA).
30 *Ibid*, at 541–544.
31 IA 1986, s 264.
32 *Ibid*, s 267.
33 *Ibid*, s 269.

the making of the order is void. Following the presentation of the petition, an official receiver may be appointed to manage the property pending the making of a bankruptcy order.[34]

Bankruptcy order

If a bankruptcy order is made, the tenant becomes an undischarged bankrupt. Until a trustee in bankruptcy is appointed, the official receiver manages the property, and will generally seek to preserve it instead of selling it. If a trustee in bankruptcy is to be appointed, the official receiver must call a meeting of creditors within 12 weeks of the bankruptcy order. Upon appointment, the trustee in bankruptcy has all the bankrupt's property automatically vested in him, without the need for any conveyance or assignment. Certain basic personal and business items are, however, excluded. The trustee in bankruptcy's function is to get in, realise and distribute the bankrupt's estate.[35] For this purpose, he is vested with a variety of statutory powers, including the power to carry on the bankrupt's business.[36] A trustee in bankruptcy in occupation of land is the occupier and liable to pay non-domestic rates, even if he disclaims.[37]

Distribution of assets

The trustee in bankruptcy cannot dispose of property free from any specific charge to which it is subject. Thus the mortgagee of a bankrupt tenant has a wide range of choices available, including leaving the charge as it is, valuing or selling the security and suing for the balance, applying to the court for a sale, or putting the trustee to an election whether to exercise his power to redeem at the value placed upon it. In this last instance, the trustee in bankruptcy has six months in which to redeem. The trustee in bankruptcy is, nevertheless, empowered to redeem the charge at the value which the mortgagee has specified, giving him 21 days in which to revalue. Alternatively, and with specified exceptions, the trustee may offer the security for sale.

Subject to the rights of mortgagees, the bankrupt's estate is distributable in the following order: bankruptcy expenses, pre-preferential debts (including, if the bankrupt is deceased, reasonable funeral and testamentary expenses), preferential debts, ordinary debts, interest on debts, and postponed debts. If any surplus remains, it is paid to the bankrupt.

---

34 *Ibid*, s 286.
35 *Ibid*, s 305(2).
36 *Ibid*, s 314 and Sched 5.
37 *Re Lister* [1926] Ch 149.

Before bankruptcy order

The requirement that the debt be liquidated means that, whilst a landlord can bring a petition where sufficient rent is in arrear, he cannot petition for damage caused by a breach of (say) a tenant's repairing covenant, without first obtaining judgment for a sum in damages. If the landlord obtained judgment against the tenant before the presentation of the petition, he may levy execution against the bankrupt's property. The landlord may not retain the benefit of the execution, however, unless it was complete before the making of the bankruptcy order.[38] Even if execution was so completed, the landlord will not be entitled to its benefit if the sum raised by the sale exceeds £500 and, within 14 days of the sale, the sheriff is informed of the presentation of the petition in bankruptcy. The court has an overriding power to permit the landlord to retain the benefit of the execution, but the court will exercise this power only in exceptional circumstances.[39] Where the landlord is not entitled, the benefit of the execution passes to the trustee in bankruptcy.

The landlord may bring an action for forfeiture, rent arrears or breach of covenant or he may levy distress; but the court may stay any action, execution or legal process against the debtor or his property.[40] This does not include distress; but whether it includes the service of a notice under the Law of Distress Amendment Act 1908 is unclear. A landlord who distrains does not thereby lose the right to prove in the bankruptcy[41]; but it would appear that, once a landlord has lodged proof for arrears due before bankruptcy, those arrears (as opposed to arrears which accrue after bankruptcy) cannot later be recovered by distress.

After bankruptcy order

After a bankruptcy order has been made, no creditor may, in respect of a debt provable in the bankruptcy, bring legal proceedings against the property or person of the bankrupt without the leave of the court and upon such terms as the court may impose; or have any remedy against the bankrupt's person or property (which therefore includes levying of execution) except with the leave of the court and on such terms as the court may impose.[42] These restrictions do not, however, apply to an action for forfeiture since, although the occasion for the forfeiture may be the default

---

38 IA 1986, s 346.
39 *Ibid*, s 346(6).
40 *Ibid*, s 285(1).
41 *Ibid*, s 347(10).
42 *Ibid*, s 285(3).

in the payment of rent, forfeiture is not a remedy against the property of the defendant in respect of a debt; rather it is in the nature of an action for trespass.[43] These restrictions do not affect a secured creditor, which remains entitled to enforce its security; but a landlord's right of re-entry is not, for this purpose, a security.[43a]

The landlord has a right to distrain for rent accrued due before the commencement of the bankruptcy, but only for a maximum of six months' such rent.[44] Where a bankruptcy order is made within three months of a distress, the goods distrained are charged with the payment of preferential debts which cannot be met out of the bankrupt's estate.[45]

The trustee in bankruptcy has the bankrupt's lease vested in him. This means that, unless he disclaims the lease[46], he is liable as an assignee for the rent accruing due and in respect of the lessee's other obligations from the date of vesting. The trustee is, however, generally entitled to an indemnity for such payments out of the bankrupt's estate. If the trustee does not disclaim, the landlord has a right (without the leave of the court) to distrain for the rent which accrues due after the commencement of the bankruptcy.[47]

If a tenant against whom execution has been levied is adjudged bankrupt before the landlord has served notice of his claim on the sheriff or bailiff, the landlord's claim is restricted to six months' rent, and does not extend to rent payable in respect of the period after the notice is served.[48] The landlord himself, however, does not need the leave of the court to exercise this right.

COMPANY LIQUIDATION

Voluntary and compulsory winding up

A voluntary liquidation can take place at the behest either of the members (where the company is solvent) or of the creditors (where the company is insolvent). The liquidator can manage the company's business so far as is necessary for the winding up and must pay its debts in the correct order of

43 *Ezekiel v Orakpo* [1977] QB 260 (CA), dealing with similar wording under Bankruptcy Act 1914, s 7(1); *Razzaq v Pala* [1997] 38 EG 157 (Lightman J).
43a *Razzaq v Pala* [1997] 38 EG 157.
44 IA 1986, s 347(1).
45 *Ibid*, ss 347(3).
46 Since the law of disclaimer is broadly the same in the case of bankruptcy and insolvent liquidation, it is given separate treatment later in this chapter.
47 IA 1986, s 347(9).
48 *Ibid*, s 347(6).

priority. A voluntary winding up commences at the time of the passing of the resolution for voluntary winding up.[49]

Compulsory winding up by the court takes place on a number of grounds: one of these is if the company is unable to pay its debts. A company is deemed unable to pay its debts if (*inter alia*) it fails to pay, within three weeks of a written demand from a creditor, a debt of at least £750. A compulsory winding up commences at the time of the presentation of the petition for winding up.[50] Public creditors are responsible for the lion's share of such winding-up orders. Some 55% of these in London are for VAT debt, and another 10% are brought by the Inland Revenue.

Certain dealings by the company with its property before liquidation are liable to be set aside: these comprise dealings at an undervalue or which prefer some creditors over others. The assignment of a lease at an undervalue might therefore be set aside on this ground.

In respect of rent accrued due before the commencement of the winding up, the landlord may put in a claim as an unsecured creditor. If the rent is payable in arrear, the landlord is entitled (under the Apportionment Act 1870) to apportion the rent in respect of the periods before and after the commencement of the winding up. Apart from putting in a claim, the landlord has his usual remedies for rent accrued due before the commencement of the winding up (forfeiture, distress, or action); but these are subject to the following statutory restrictions.

Voluntary winding up

If the landlord has obtained judgment against the tenant company, provided he completes execution before the commencement of the winding up, he can retain the fruits of the execution, unless: (i) the execution is not complete at the time the landlord receives notice of a meeting to propose a resolution for a voluntary winding up[51]; or (ii) a notice of the adoption of the winding-up resolution is served on the sheriff.[52] In these two cases, the sheriff must pay the proceeds of execution to the liquidator. A sheriff who levies execution for a judgment of more than £500 must keep the proceeds for 14 days to allow for notice of winding up to be served.

The commencement of the voluntary winding up does not preclude the landlord from bringing an action for forfeiture, for rent or for breaches of other covenants, or from distraining; but the liquidator or any creditor or

---

49 *Ibid*, s 86.
50 *Ibid*, s 129(2).
51 *Ibid*, s 183.
52 *Ibid*, s 184.

contributory may apply to the court, which has power (*inter alia*) to stay or restrain any action or proceeding.[53] This evidently includes the power to stay a distress.

Compulsory winding up

If the landlord has previously obtained judgment for the arrears and execution is completed before the presentation of the petition, the landlord can retain the benefit of the execution.[54] An exception is where the execution is for a sum exceeding £500 and a notice of the presentation of the petition is served on the sheriff within 14 days. If execution is not complete by the date the petition is presented, the landlord loses the benefit of the execution. The court has an overriding power (exercised only in exceptional cases) to allow the execution creditor to retain the benefit of the execution.

Where distress is effected within three months of a compulsory winding-up order, the goods distrained are charged with the payment of the company's preferential debts which cannot be met out of the company's property.[55]

Between presentation of the petition and the making of a winding-up order, no leave is required to bring an action for forfeiture, for rent or for other breaches of covenant; but the company, a creditor or a contributory, may apply to the court to have any action or proceeding stayed.[56]

Subject to the rights enjoyed by secured creditors (which are broadly similar to those in a bankruptcy), the liquidated company's debts are paid in the following order: liquidation expenses, preferential debts, ordinary debts, interest on debts, and postponed debts. Any surplus is paid to the shareholders. A landlord's debt for rent accrued due before winding up ranks merely as an ordinary debt.

Unless and until the lease is disclaimed or the company itself is dissolved, the company (despite being in liquidation) remains liable under the lease. The liquidator himself, being the company's agent, is not however personally liable under the lease; and this is so, it would seem, even where the liquidator applies to have the lease vested in him.[57]

---

53 *Ibid*, ss 112 and 126.
54 *Ibid*, s 183.
55 *Ibid*, s 176.
56 *Ibid*, s 126.
57 *i.e.* under IA 1986, s 145.

Restrictions on actions

In a compulsory winding up, after a winding-up order has been made or a provisional liquidator appointed, no action may be brought or proceeded with against the company or its property without the leave of the court.[58] This has been held to include a distress.[59] If, however, the distress was begun before the commencement of the winding up, the landlord will generally be allowed to complete it. In the case of an action for rent arrears, leave would not usually be given. (A mortgagee, by contrast, can still enforce its security). It is unclear whether a notice under the Law of Distress Amendment Act 1908 or peaceable re-entry by the landlord falls within the scope of the sub-section.

Rent as liquidation expense

The landlord cannot claim in the liquidation for rent accruing due after the winding up has commenced, but he may have a better chance of recovering it as a liquidation expense under rule 4. 218 of the Insolvency Rules 1986, which lists under 16 paragraphs, the order of priority of payment of such expenses.

Paragraph (a): "the expenses properly chargeable or incurred by the official receiver or liquidator in preserving, realising or getting in any of the assets of the company". The rent will fall within this paragraph if the liquidator retains the lease and actively seeks to sell or surrender it. Similarly, a payment of the rent by the liquidator in order to prevent a forfeiture ranks as an expense in preserving the lease.[60] A payment of a service charge may similarly rank as an expense of the liquidation; but not a claim for breach of other terms of the lease.

Paragraph (m): "necessary disbursement" of the liquidator in the course of his administration. Even if the liquidator does not take active steps to sell or surrender the lease, but merely retains it, the landlord may be able to claim that the rent falls within this paragraph.[61] Such a claim ranks before the liquidator's remuneration (para (o)). This argument might also be used even where the liquidator disclaims the lease, to recover the rent due in the period between the commencement of the winding up and the disclaimer. The statutory order of priority can be varied by order of the court.

---

58 IA 1986, s 130(2).
59 *Re Memco Engineering Ltd* [1986] Ch 86.
60 *Re Linda Marie Ltd* [1989] BCLC 46.
61 *Ibid.*

In both a voluntary and a compulsory winding up, the landlord may distrain for rent which accrues due after liquidation. Although the court has, on application, power to stay such distress[62], it is likely in these circumstances to grant leave.

DISCLAIMER OF LEASES

A trustee in bankruptcy or liquidator may disclaim onerous property.[63] This includes property which may give rise to a liability to pay money or perform any other onerous act[64], and "any unprofitable contract."[65] Both a lease (even during a period of holding over[66]) and a contract for a lease[67] can therefore be disclaimed. In practice, the trustee or liquidator is likely to choose to disclaim where the lease has a negative value, in that it could be disposed of only on the payment of a premium. An assignee tenant's rights and obligations under a licence to assign a pre-1996 lease may be disclaimed; but the licence is treated as ancillary to the lease, so that if there is a purported disclaimer of the licence alone, it will operate as a disclaimer of the lease as well.[68]

A liquidator may disclaim without leave of the court; a trustee requires leave only in exceptional instances.[69] A person dissatisfied or aggrieved by any act or decision of the liquidator or trustee (such as a disclaimer or a decision to disclaim) may challenge it[70]; but in practice the court will not interfere unless there is evidence of fraud or lack of good faith, or unless the decision was so perverse that no reasonable liquidator or trustee could have made it.[71]

Disclaimer is effected by filing notice (and a copy) in court[72]; the liquidator or trustee must within seven days of receiving a copy endorsed by the court serve copies (so far as he is aware of their addresses) on every

---

62 IA 1986, s 112.
63 See *ibid,* ss 315–321 (bankruptcy), and ss 178–182 (liquidation).
64 *Ibid,* s 315(2)(b) (bankruptcy), s 178(3)(b) (liquidation).
65 *Ibid,* s 315(2)(a) (bankruptcy), s 178(3)(a) (liquidation).
66 *i.e.* under LTA 1954, Part II.
67 *Re Maughan, ex p Monkhouse* (1885) 14 QBD 956; *Re Hide, ex p Llynvi Coal & Iron Co* (1871) 7 App Cas 28.
68 *MEPC Ltd v Scottish Amicable Life Assurance Society* [1993] 2 EGLR 93 (CA). There was disclaimer of the licence by an intermediate tenant in *Hindcastle Ltd v Barbara Attenborough Associates Ltd* [1997] AC 70, HL, but the consequences in respect of future liability were not there explored.
69 *e.g.* in respect of after-acquired property: IA 1986, s 307(1). See also ss 308, 308A.
70 *Ibid,* s 303(1) (bankruptcy), s 168(5) (liquidation).
71 See *Re Hans Place Ltd* [1992] 2 EGLR 179, 182.
72 IR 1986, r 6.178 (bankruptcy), r 4.187 (liquidation).

person claiming under the bankrupt or the company as under-lessee or mortgagee.[73] The trustee or liquidator must also send copies of notice to disclaim a lease to every person who (to his knowledge) claims an interest in the property or is under a liability in respect of it.[74]

A disclaimer can be made at any time, unless the landlord puts the liquidator or trustee to his election by applying to him in writing requiring him to decide whether he will disclaim or not[75], in which case disclaimer must be made within 28 days[76] (unless, in the case of a liquidation, the court grants an extension[77]). If no disclaimer is made within that period, the right to disclaim is lost.

Effect of disclaimer

As between the landlord and the insolvent tenant

In a bankruptcy, disclaimer operates so as to determine, as from the date of the disclaimer, the rights, interests and liabilities of the bankrupt and his estate in or in respect of the property disclaimed, and discharges the trustee from all personal liability in respect of that property as from the commencement of his trusteeship. It does not, however, except so far as is necessary for the purpose of releasing the bankrupt, the bankrupt's estate and the trustee from any liability, affect the rights or liabilities of any other person.[78] The equivalent provision in a liquidation is similar in form, the only significant difference being that there is no corresponding release of the liquidator from liability, this being unnecessary as the company's property remains vested in it.[79]

As between the landlord and the insolvent tenant, disclaimer determines, as from the date it is made, the rights, interests and liabilities of the tenant in respect of the lease.[80] The landlord therefore needs to prove in the liquidation or bankruptcy for the loss of future rents. Disclaimer accelerates the landlord's reversion[81]; so the trustee or liquidator should remove any tenant's fixtures before disclaimer, to prevent the landlord's being entitled to them.

---

73 IA 1986, s 317(1), IR 1986, r 6.179(2) (bankruptcy); IA 1986, s 179(1), IR 1986, r 4.188(2) (liquidation).
74 IR 1986, r 6.179(4) (bankruptcy), r 4.188(3) (liquidation).
75 IA 1986, s 316(1)(a) (bankruptcy), s 178(5)(a) (liquidation).
76 *Ibid*, s 316(1)(b) (bankruptcy), s 178(5)(b) (liquidation).
77 *Ibid*, s 178(5)(a).
78 *Ibid*, s 315(3).
79 *Ibid*, s 178(4).
80 *Ibid*, s 315(3) (bankruptcy), s 178(4) (liquidation).
81 *Hindcastle Ltd* v *Barbara Attenborough Associates Ltd* [1997] AC 70 (Lord Nicholls); *Re Finley, ex p Clothworkers' Co* (1888) 21 QBD 475, 485 (Lindley LJ).

Disclaimer retrospectively discharges a trustee in bankruptcy from personal liability from the date of the commencement of the bankruptcy[82]; so that, if he has been in occupation of the premises, he is relieved of liability for business rates to the date of the disclaimer[83], and he cannot (unless he has breached a term of the lease) be required to pay mesne profits for occupation until that date. The landlord might recover the rent accruing due between the appointment of the trustee and the disclaimer as an expense of the bankruptcy.[84]

As between the landlord and an earlier tenant or surety

Disclaimer of a pre-1996 lease by the liquidator or trustee of an assignee tenant does not determine the continuing contractual liability of an original[85] or intermediate[86] tenant, who can therefore be required to pay instalments of rent falling due after (as well as before) the date of disclaimer.[87] Since the contractual liability of a former tenant under a post-1995 lease ends on a lawful assignment of the lease, any liability that it may incur thereafter can arise only under an authorised guarantee agreement (AGA). A tenant who has entered into an AGA is subject to the general rules of law relating to guarantees (and in particular to those relating to the release of sureties)[88], and the position of such a tenant is therefore to be considered in the context of sureties.

Since the disclaimer of a pre-1996 lease vested in an assignee does not end the continuing contractual liability of the original or intermediate tenant, neither does it end the liability of an original or intermediate tenant's guarantor.[89] Nevertheless, it used to be thought[90] that disclaimer did release the surety for the insolvent tenant itself, on the ground that a surety's liability depended upon the liability of his principal. In *Hindcastle Ltd v Barbara Attenborough Associates Ltd*[91], however, the House of Lords made it clear that, whilst a surety's liability does normally end with that of his principal, this general rule has been modified in the case of a

---

82 IA 1986, s 315(3).
83 *Re Lister, ex p Bradford Overseers & Bradford Corporation* [1926] 1 Ch 149.
84 See *supra*.
85 *Hill v East & West Dock Co Ltd* (1884) 9 App Cas 448 (HL), applied in *Hindcastle Ltd v Barbara Attenborough Associates Ltd* [1997] AC 70 (HL).
86 *Hindcastle Ltd v Barbara Attenborough Associates Ltd* [1997] AC 70 (HL).
87 *Ibid*.
88 LT(C)A 1995, s 16(8).
89 *Hindcastle Ltd v Barbara Attenborough Associates Ltd* [1997] AC 70.
90 On the authority of *Stacey v Hill* [1901] 1 KB 660 (CA).
91 [1997] AC 70 (HL).

disclaimer by the special provisions of the insolvency legislation.[92] So far as
the surety is concerned, the lease is deemed to continue. Lord Nicholls said
that if the disclaimer of the lease also discharged the liability of the
insolvent tenant's guarantor, the very object of giving and taking a
guarantee would be defeated.

Although the *Hindcastle* case concerned disclaimer of a pre-1996 lease,
it is also of importance to disclaimers of post-1995 leases, since it means
that the liability of a former tenant under an AGA is not terminated by a
disclaimer effected by the liquidator or trustee of the assignee whose
liability it has so guaranteed.

The liability of a former tenant or surety will determine if the landlord
subsequently terminates the lease, whether by forfeiture or through taking
possession and so ending the lease by implied surrender.[93]

As between landlord and holders of derivative interests

Disclaimer of a head-lease does not destroy a sub-lease.[94] The head-lease is
deemed to continue so far as the sub-lease is concerned, so that the sub-
lessee is entitled to remain in possession during the remainder of the term of
his sub-lease.[95] Although the sub-lessee retains his legal estate, his position is
unsatisfactory, because the disclaimer does not result in privity of estate
between the sub-lessee and the head-lessor. There is therefore no immediate
reversioner of the sub-lease to enforce its covenants, with the result that the
sub-tenant is under no further liability to pay rent or to comply with any
other obligations which the sub-lease contains. On the other hand, the
head-lessor retains a right to distrain for rent under the head-lease, and
(assuming that it contains an appropriate proviso for re-entry) a right to
forfeit the head-lease for non-payment of rent or for other breaches of
covenant. Forfeiture of the head-lease will destroy the sub-lease. The sub-
tenant has a right to seek relief from forfeiture[96], but this will usually be
upon terms that the breaches of covenant in the head-lease are made good.

---

92 IA 1986, s 315(3) (bankruptcy); s 178(4) (liquidation). Strictly, it seems that the House of
   Lords in the *Hindcastle* case could not actually overrule *Stacey v Hill* [1901] 1 KB 660,
   since the action in *Hindcastle* was brought against only the original and intermediate
   tenants and the latter's guarantor, and not (as in *Stacey v Hill*) against the guarantor of
   the insolvent tenant at the end of the line. It is nevertheless clear that the rule in *Stacey v
   Hill* is effectively abolished.
93 *Hindcastle Ltd v Barbara Attenborough Associates Ltd* [1997] AC 70 (Lord Nicholls).
94 For this purpose, a sub-lease includes an equitable mortgage by deposit: *Re Müller, ex p
   Buxton* (1880) 15 Ch D 289 (CA).
95 *Re A E Realisations (1985) Ltd* [1988] 1 WLR 200.
96 See further Chap 13; see also *Barclays Bank plc v Prudential Assurance Co Ltd* [1998] 10
   EG 159 (Ch), where the sub-tenant obtained relief under LPA 1925, s 146(4), it being
   held that no inherent jurisdiction to grant relief in equity could survive the effects of
   bankruptcy and disclaimer.

For practical purposes, therefore, the sub-lessee will usually be able to remain in possession only if it pays the rent reserved by the head-lease and complies with the other covenants which it contains.[97] The head-lessor's position is also unsatisfactory, however, since he will be unable to activate any rent-review provisions contained in either the head-lease or the sub-lease[98], and may find it more difficult to dispose of his reversion.

The position can be resolved by the sub-tenant's applying for a vesting order under the Insolvency Act 1986.[99] An application by a sub-tenant for a vesting order does not, however, preclude the landlord from forfeiting the head-lease (and thereby destroying the sub-lease) in the period before any such order is made. A vesting order, whether made under the Insolvency Act 1986 or under the Law of Property Act 1925, section 146(4), is not retrospective. Therefore, even if the sub-lessee obtains a vesting order, he will be liable to pay mesne profits for his occupation between the service of the writ and his either vacating the premises or his obtaining of the order.[1] It remains to be seen if a sub-lessee could obtain retrospective relief under the Law of Property Act 1925, section 146(2)[2], as this would have the effect of restoring the head-lease to its former disclaimed state. It is unclear whether a sub-tenant who obtains a vesting order under the Insolvency Act 1986 can avoid forfeiture only by making good breaches of the head-lease which occurred before the order was made.[3]

The head-lessor is entitled to put a sub-tenant or a mortgagee to an election whether to accept a vesting order under the Insolvency Act 1986. If the sub-tenant or mortgagee declines to accept, he is excluded from all interest in the property. Ultimately the head-lessor is entitled to a vesting order; but he cannot have the head-lease vested in him subject to the sub-lease, as the latter will necessarily have been already destroyed.[4]

Proof of loss from disclaimer

Any person sustaining any loss or damage as a result of a disclaimer is entitled to prove for such loss or damage as a bankruptcy debt or as a debt in an insolvent liquidation.[5]

---

97 *Re Finley, ex p Clothworkers' Co* (1888) 21 QBD 475, 485–487 (Lindley LJ).
98 See McLoughlin, *Commercial Leases and Insolvency*, 2nd ed (1996) at 184.
99 See further Fife, "Termination of leases" [1995] 41 EG 134, 135.
1 See *Pellicano v MEPC plc* [1994] 1 EGLR 104 (Knox J), where the head-lessor had peaceably re-entered.
2 As in *Escalus Properties Ltd v Robinson, Sinclair Garden Investments (Kensington) Ltd v Walsh* [1995] 4 All ER 852.
3 McLoughlin, *Commercial Leases and Insolvency,* 2nd ed (1996) at 188.
4 *Sterling Estates v Pickard UK Ltd* [1997] 30 EG 124.
5 IA 1986, s 315(5) (bankruptcy); s 178(6) (insolvent liquidation).

The landlord is entitled to prove in principle for all the rent and other payments which he would have been entitled to recover from the tenant for the residue of the term had the lease not been determined, but giving credit for what he might be expected to obtain from a re-letting.[6] No discount is to be made for the risk of default or for the fact that, in a bankruptcy or insolvent winding up, the landlord would not have been able to recover in full.[7] Claims for future rents[8] in an insolvency are discounted by five per cent per annum.[9] No discounting is applied if a liquidator disclaims and the company is solvent.[10] Future rents are discounted to the extent that the landlord might be able to recover them from a surety or from a previous tenant.

An earlier tenant or a surety who remains liable to the landlord after disclaimer also has a right to prove in the insolvent's estate.[11] McLoughlin has expressed the view that the value of the surety's claim should be "the loss representing the liability to make future payments."[12] Presumably the value of the claim should be discounted to take account of the possibility that the landlord might re-enter, that a vesting order might be made, or (if appropriate) that the tenant or surety has a right of indemnity from an intermediate tenant or a surety down the line.

A sub-lessee or mortgagee may also be able to prove in the bankruptcy or liquidation. If the rent payable under the sub-lease is lower than that payable under the disclaimed head-lease, the sub-tenant will be able to prevent the landlord from distraining or from exercising his right of re-entry only by paying the higher rent due under the head-lease. In such circumstances, the sub-tenant is a person who suffers loss or damage as a result of the disclaimer, and is entitled to prove for the amount by which the rent under the head-lease exceeds that under the sub-lease.[13]

Vesting orders

Any person who claims an interest in the disclaimed lease, or who is under

---

6 *Christopher Moran Holdings Ltd* v *Bairstow* [1997] 30 EG 125, 131 (CA) (liquidation); *Re Hide, ex p Llynvi Coal & Iron Co* (1871) 7 Ch App 28 (CA), Mellish LJ at 35.

7 *Christopher Moran Holdings Ltd* v *Bairstow* [1997] 30 EG 125 (CA), reversing Ferris J at [1996] 2 EGLR 49, who had wrongly held that the landlord was entitled to prove only for the capitalised value of the future rent (with a reduction for early payment and the risk of default) less the capitalised value of any actual or estimated re-letting for the residue of the term.

8 *i.e.* rents falling due after the liquidation or order in bankruptcy: IR 1986, r 4.94; r 6.114.

9 IR 1986, r 11.13.

10 As in *Christopher Moran Holdings Ltd* v *Bairstow* [1997] 30 EG 125 (CA).

11 *Hindcastle Ltd* v *Barbara Attenborough Associates Ltd* [1997] AC 70 (HL).

12 McLoughlin, *Commercial Leases and Insolvency*, 2nd ed (1996) at 193.

13 *ex p Walton, re Levy* (1881) 17 Ch D 746.

any liability in respect of it which will not be discharged by the disclaimer may apply to the court for an order that the lease be vested in an appropriate person (which is not necessarily the applicant itself).[14] The application must be made within three months of the applicant's receiving a copy of the notice of disclaimer or (if earlier) of the applicant's otherwise becoming aware of the disclaimer.[15] The court can make an order vesting in a sub-tenant or mortgagee the whole of the premises demised by the head-lease, even though the sub-lease or mortgage related to part only.[16]

The order of priority of applications for a vesting order depends upon the type of interest or liability of the person who is put to election. Priority is accorded to an application by the holder of a derivative interest (*i.e.* a sub-tenancy or a mortgage).[17] Applications from two or more sub-tenants or mortgagees rank according to the order of priority of their respective interests *inter se*.[18] If none of the foregoing is willing to take a vesting order, the application may be made by a surety, an original tenant, and any intermediate tenant who entered into a direct covenant with the lessor. Finally, the landlord may himself apply.[19] If a sub-lessee or mortgagee is before the court, and an application for a vesting order is made by a person in the second or third categories, the sub-lessee or mortgagee is put to his election. No order formally put him to his election is needed if he has made it plain that he does not want to take a vesting order.[20] An application for a vesting order may be valid even if other persons entitled to such an order are not notified; but any interested person not present when the order is made is not precluded from applying for a vesting order in their own favour subsequently.[21]

The court will usually impose a time-limit of 14 days on the period of election; and any person who declines to accept a vesting order is excluded from all interest in the property.[22] In a liquidation it would appear that only a sub-lessee or mortgagee is entitled to decline; with the result that, if it does so, the landlord can compel an earlier tenant or a surety to take a vesting order.

14 IA 1986, ss 181, 320.
15 IR 4.194, r 6.186.
16 See *Re Holmes, ex p Ashworth* [1908] 2 KB 812, where the court treated as a relevant consideration the liability of the sub-tenants (mortgagees by sub-demise) to suffer a distress or to be ejected for non-payment of the rent relating to the whole of the premises.
17 *Re A E Realisations (1985) Ltd* [1988] 1 WLR 200.
18 *Ibid.*
19 *Re Cock, ex p Shilson* (1887) 20 QBD 343.
20 *Ibid.*
21 *Re Morgan, ex p Morgan* (1889) 22 QBD 592, 596 (Bowen LJ); *Re Baker, ex p Lupton* [1901] 2 KB 628.
22 IA 1986, s 182(4) (liquidation), s 321(4) (bankruptcy).

Terms of the order

Subject to important qualifications, the court may make the vesting order on such terms as it thinks fit.[22a] The court may not make an order vesting the disclaimed property in a person who is under a liability in respect of such property, however, unless it considers that it would be just to do so in order to compensate such person.[23]

In a bankruptcy, the court must not make an order vesting leasehold property in any person except on terms making such person subject to the same liabilities and obligations as the bankrupt either (a) was subject to under the lease on the day the bankruptcy petition was presented, or (b) would be subject to if the lease had been assigned to him on such day.[24] In a liquidation, the equivalent statutory provision is narrower because, instead of "any person" it specifies "any person claiming ... as under-lessee or mortgagee."[25]

In a liquidation, therefore, the court can vest the lease in someone who is not a sub-lessee or mortgagee on terms other than those specified in paragraphs (a) and (b), *i.e.* "on such terms as it thinks fit."[26] In *Beegas Nominees Ltd* v *BHP Petroleum Ltd*[27], the lease had been subject to a variation made between the landlord and T3, under which the rent was increased. Upon the disclaimer of the lease by T3's liquidator, T2 applied for a vesting order. In the circumstances, Lindsay J was not bound by paragraphs (a) or (b), and he stated that he was prepared to make such an order so that T2's rent obligation would be equivalent to that of the unamended lease only.

The court is in practice able to achieve an equivalent result in a bankruptcy through the form of the order.[28] In *Re Carter & Ellis, ex p Savill Bros*[29], the Court of Appeal made an order vesting the leasehold property in the mortgagee on the footing that it was liable only as an assignee. It took the view that the landlord's loss of the right to sue the mortgagee for breaches occurring after any assignment it might make was compensated by the fact that it would henceforth have a solvent, rather than an insolvent, tenant.[30]

22a IA 1986 s 181(3) (liquidation), s 320(3) (bankruptcy). See *Re Lee* [1998] *The Times* 24 February (Ferris J), where the vesting order in favour of a mortgagee imposed a condition that any surplus on sale of the lease was to be paid to the trustee in bankruptcy.

23 IA 1986 s 181(4) (liquidation), s 320(4) (bankruptcy).

24 *Ibid*, s 321(1) (bankruptcy).

25 *Ibid*, s 182(1) (liquidation).

26 *Ibid*, s 181(3).

27 [1997] 25 March (unreported), Lexis Transcript; affirmed in part [1998] EGCS 60 (CA).

28 See the order in *Re Walker, ex p Mills* (1895) 64 LJQB 783.

29 [1905] 1 KB 735 (CA).

30 *Ibid,* at 750–751 (Stirling LJ).

In *Re Tasselight 1993 Ltd*[31], Chadwick J upheld the order of the registrar to vest the disclaimed lease in the original tenant subject to the same liabilities as had affected the assignee in liquidation. This resulted in the original tenant becoming liable, as tenant under the revived lease, for rent arrears which had accrued more than six months earlier, and in respect of which no action could have been brought against it in its capacity as former tenant since no statutory default notice had been served upon it in time.[32] The facts were somewhat special, since the original tenant had been in dispute with the landlord over the arrears, and had been granted an extension of time to apply for a vesting order until such dispute were resolved. This delayed matters until after the deadline of 30 June 1996, which was the last date for the service of a default notice in respect of arrears accrued before 1 January 1996. If, however, the decision were later held to be of wider application, the default notice procedure would be seriously undermined where a vesting order is made under the Insolvency Act 1986.

It has been generally assumed (quite reasonably) that if the disclaimed lease is itself a pre-1996 lease, it remains, after a vesting order under the Insolvency Act 1986, a pre-1996 lease for the purposes of the Landlord and Tenant (Covenants) Act 1995, even though the order itself is made after 1995.[33] In this respect, the effect of a vesting order differs from an overriding lease obtained by an earlier tenant or surety who has been required to pay the rent arrears or other fixed charge of the existing tenant[34], since an overriding lease is always a new lease within the meaning of the 1995 Act. In *Beegas Nominees Ltd v BHP Petroleum Ltd*[35], however, Lindsay J expressed the view (but without having to decide) that where the court intends to vest the disclaimed lease in the recipient under the Insolvency Act 1986 upon terms different from those contained in the disclaimed lease itself, the least cumbersome method might be to make an order compelling the landlord to grant a fresh lease on different terms. An order in these terms would create a new lease for the purposes of the 1995 Act. It is therefore submitted that the alternative method suggested by Lindsay J as a means by which vesting on different terms can be effected is preferable. This involves vesting in the recipient the disclaimed lease in the form in which it existed at the date of disclaimer, but either upon the footing that the landlord is not to be able to enforce its terms save as

31 [1997] 19 January (Ch) (unreported); Lexis Transcript.
32 *i.e.* under LT(C)A 1995, s 17.
33 See Fogel and Slessenger, "The Landlord and Tenant (Covenants) Act 1995: where does it fall short of its presumed intent? Part 2", *Blundell Memorial Lectures 1996, Current Problems in Property Law*, 1996, RICS, at 43.
34 LT(C)A 1995, ss 19–20.
35 [1997] 25 March (unreported), Lexis Transcript, affirmed in part [1998] EGCS 60 (CA).

consistent with those which the court thinks it just to add or to substitute, or with a provision that the terms of the lease at the date of disclaimer are to be waived, leaving enforceable only those new intended provisions which the court thinks it just to put in their place.

Disclaimer by the Crown

If a company is dissolved without a winding up, or if the liquidator of a company does not disclaim the lease, the lease vests upon dissolution in the Crown as *bona vacantia*.[36] The Crown has a right to disclaim within a statutory period[37]; and, if it does so, the effect is as if the lease had been disclaimed by the liquidator immediately before dissolution.[38] If a successful application to restore the company's name[39] is made after the Crown has disclaimed, the disclaimer is deemed never to have occurred.[40]

---

36 Companies Act 1985, s 654.
37 *Ibid*, s 656.
38 *Ibid*, s 657(2).
39 *Ibid*, s 653.
40 *Allied Dunbar Assurance plc* v *Fowle* [1994] 1 EGLR 122, 126 (Garland J).

Chapter 15

SECURITY OF TENURE: THE LANDLORD AND TENANT ACT 1954, PART II

THE SCOPE OF PART II

Many business tenants enjoy a measure of security of tenure which is conferred upon them by the Landlord and Tenant Act 1954, Part II. Under the Act, tenants occupying premises for business purposes have a basic right to renew the lease at the end of the contractually agreed term. In the absence of agreement between the parties as to the terms of a new lease, the terms can be set by the court. The landlord can, however, oppose a renewal of the lease on specified statutory grounds. If the landlord successfully opposes a renewal, the tenant will be denied a new tenancy, but (depending upon the particular ground or grounds of opposition established) the landlord may be required to pay compensation to the tenant for disturbance. If matters are not settled before the expiry of the contractually agreed term, the tenancy is continued by the statute, and there is a statutory procedure for the settling of an interim rent. Even if the tenant is denied a new tenancy, the court will generally allow him to continue in possession under the continuation tenancy for a few months in order to give him time to make other arrangements.

In order to obtain the protection of Part II, a tenant must satisfy three requirements: there must be a tenancy; the whole or part of the premises must be occupied by the tenant; and the occupation must be for the purposes of his business, or for those and other purposes.[1] Even if the tenancy satisfies these requirements at the outset, the tenancy will cease to be a tenancy to which the Act applies if the tenant at a subsequent date is no longer occupying the premises for the purposes of his business.[2]

---

1 LTA 1954, s 23(1).
2 *Esselte AB v Pearl Assurance plc* [1997] 2 All ER 41 (CA).

Tenancy

Part II applies only to leases, not to licences[3]; it applies to tenancies by estoppel[3a], but not to tenancies at will.[4] A sub-lease can fall within the scope of Part II even if it was granted in breach of a covenant against sub-letting without the landlord's consent.[5] An agreement for a lease is also protected.[6]

Certain types of leases are, however, excluded from the scope of Part II. These are an agricultural holding[7], a mining lease[8], a service tenancy[9], and a short lease. A short lease means a tenancy granted for a term certain not exceeding six months (unless the lease contains provision for extending it beyond six months, or the tenant has been in occupation for a period which, together with any period during which the tenant's predecessor was carrying on the tenant's business, exceeds 12 months).[10]

The exclusion of a short lease is designed to encourage landlords awaiting, for instance, redevelopment, to let the premises on a temporary basis. A short lease could also be used where the parties intend to grant a longer lease, but the tenant requires occupation of the premises for fitting-out or the making of alterations before such main lease can be agreed[11]; in such circumstances, the short lease should be expressed to be subject to earlier determination upon the grant of the main lease. From the landlord's point of view, a short lease may be preferable to a licence or a tenancy at will, as there is the risk that the court may construe the latter types of arrangement as giving rise instead to a periodic tenancy within Part II.[12]

Leases of on-licensed premises were formerly excluded from Part II, unless the sale of food or other non-intoxicating items comprised a substantial proportion of the business. Tenancies of on-licensed premises entered into on or after 11 July 1989 are, however, now within the scope of Part II.[13] Tenancies granted, or contracted to be granted, before that date, also gain the protection of Part II if they were not terminated before 11 July 1992.[14]

---

3 See Chap 1.
3a *Bell* v *General Accident Fire and Life Assurance Corp Ltd* [1998] 17 EG 144.
4 *Hagee (London) Ltd* v *A B Erikson & Larson* [1976] QB 209.
5 *D'Silva* v *Lister House Developments Ltd* [1971] Ch 17.
6 LTA 1954, s 69(1).
7 *Ibid,* s 43(1)(a).
8 *Ibid,* s 43(1)(b).
9 *Ibid,* s 43(2).
10 *Ibid,* s 43(3).
11 See further Smithers & Willis, "Licence to drill" [1997] 41 EG 146.
12 But see *Javad* v *Aqil* [1991] 1 All ER 243 (CA).
13 Landlord and Tenant (Licensed Premises) Act 1990, s 1(1).
14 *Ibid,* s 1(2) and (3).

Occupation

The tenant must occupy the premises. Premises can be occupied even if there is no building: thus a field used as a car park was held to be occupied.[15] But a right of way does not comprise "premises", and it cannot be "occupied."[16]

So long as the occupation is genuine, it can be through a third party in a representative capacity – which is essential where the tenant is a company. Thus occupation could be through the tenant's managing agent or employee. If the employee has to leave the premises for a short time, he may nevertheless remain in occupation if his stock or other property is left on the premises.[17]

User by third party

Difficulties can arise where the tenant permits others to come onto the demised premises and to use them for some purposes of their own. Whether the tenant remains in occupation is a matter of degree, depending on the nature of the premises, the use to which they are being put, and the rights enjoyed or exercised by the persons in question. Lord Nicholls, giving the only speech in the House of Lords in *Graysim Holdings Ltd* v *P & O Property Holdings Ltd*[18], said that at one end of the scale is the tenant whose business is that of hotelier who provides rooms and facilities once a month for an antiques fair. At the other end of the scale is the tenant who permits another to enter and carry on business on the premises to the exclusion of the tenant himself. An example of the latter is a tenant who carries on a business of sub-letting office accommodation; under the sub-lease he has the usual right as landlord to enter the sub-let property for various purposes, and he receives rent from the sub-letting; but he would not occupy the premises. Lord Nicholls recognised, however, that the question is one of degree, and that there is a grey area between these two extremes. Even though a tenant under a lease is entitled to exclusive possession, his Lordship would not rule out the possibility that, exceptionally, the rights reserved by a landlord might be so extensive that he would remain in occupation of the demised property. In the case of a licence, however, it might in the nature of things be easier for the licensor to establish that he still occupies.

---

15 *Bracey* v *Read* [1963] Ch 88.

16 *Land Reclamation Co Ltd* v *Basildon District Council* [1979] 2 All ER 993.

17 *I & H Caplan Ltd* v *Caplan (No 2)* [1963] 2 All ER 930; see also *Esselte AB* v *Pearl Assurance plc* [1997] 2 All ER 41 (CA), discussed pp 391–392 *infra*; *Bacchiocchi* v *Academic Agency Ltd* [1998] 2 All ER 241 (CA) (occupation for the purpose of compensation under LTA 1954, s 37(3)(a)).

18 [1996] 1 AC 329 (HL); see Ferris [1996] JBL 592.

As a matter of law, Lord Nicholls held that, under the scheme of the Landlord and Tenant Act 1954, Part II, it is not possible for a landlord and a tenant both to occupy the same premises at the same time for the purposes of Part II.[18a] If this were possible, then circumstances could arise (as in the *Graysim* case itself) where both the tenant and the sub-tenant could be entitled to compensation if the competent landlord[19] opposed the grant of a new tenancy and sub-tenancy on certain statutory grounds,[20] so that the landlord would have to pay compensation twice without allowance for the fact that more than one person was entitled to it.

In the *Graysim* case, the tenant converted an empty shell of a building into a market hall which it rented out to 35 different stall-holders. The tenant chose the stall-holders, laid down the opening hours, paid for advertising, retained control over the common parts, and (for a service charge) provided lighting, heating and the services of a superintendent. It did, not, however, retain any keys to the stalls, and had no right to enter them. It was common ground in the case that the traders were themselves in occupation of their stalls for the purposes of their own businesses, and therefore had the protection of Part II. This was fatal to the tenant's own claim to a Part II-protected tenancy.

Lord Nicholls left open the possibility, however, that there could be circumstances in which both the tenant and a sub-tenant could be in "shared" occupation of the same premises at the same time for different purposes. Such were the circumstances before the Court of Appeal in *Lee-Verhulst (Investments) Ltd v Harwood Trust*[21], a decision which could therefore be justified on its facts. In that case, the tenant's business comprised the letting of residential flats. Each resident had exclusive residential occupation of his own flat for the purposes of the Rent Acts. The Court of Appeal, however, held that, even if the residents were considered to be sub-tenants rather than licensees, the facts showed that the tenant was the occupier for the purposes of a business under Part II of the 1954 Act. The tenant's employees and agents had access to all parts of the building in order to provide services, and had control over the manner in which the occupancies were conducted (including, for instance, what cooking was permitted and who could stay in each appartment) of a degree far beyond that which is usual when a flat is let to a tenant under a normal lease.

A tenant who has sub-let all the units in a building for business purposes may retain occupation of the common parts. The tenant will not,

18a Applied *Bassari Ltd v Camden LBC* [1998] EGCS 27 (CA).
19 LTA 1954, s 44.
20 *i.e.* LTA 1954, s 30(e)(f) or (g)
21 [1973] QB 204.

however, be able to obtain a new tenancy of the whole premises demised to him under Part II. In the *Graysim* case, Lord Nicholls said that this could be explained on either of two bases. First, as was held in *Bagettes Ltd v GP Estates Ltd*[22], it could be on the ground that the tenancy is no longer a business tenancy within Part II, *i.e.* once the units have been sub-let, the tenant cannot occupy them for the purposes of Part II; and he cannot be occupying the retained parts for the purposes of Part II because, on the expiration of his own tenancy, it will be impossible for the tenant to carry on a business of managing and servicing the sub-let accommodation as he will no longer be the landlord of the sub-tenants and will not be entitled to receive their rents. This would mean that the head-lease is not protected by Part II and so will expire without any notice under the 1954 Act at the end of the contractual term. Secondly, Lord Nicholls in the *Graysim* case said that it could be reasoned that, before his own lease expires, the tenant is occupying the retained parts for the purpose of a business carried on by him, so that his tenancy remains a Part II-protected tenancy (and so will continue after the expiration of the contractual term unless terminated by notice in accordance with the 1954 Act). According to this second line of reasoning, the tenant cannot claim a new tenancy under Part II on the expiration of his contractual term because he is entitled to a renewal only in respect of the "holding", which is to be identifed by reference to the circumstances existing at the date of the order.[23] If, at that date, because of the exclusion of the sub-let parts from the holding, the tenant can no longer carry on any business on the retained parts, it must follow that there has ceased to be a holding for statutory purposes.

Lord Nicholls pointed out that these routes do not always produce the same results, although it was not necessary for the appeal in the *Graysim* case itself to choose between them. If the entire premises are sub-demised, without the retention of common parts, it appears that the head-lease immediately loses the protection of Part II and will expire at the end of its contractual term.[24] But the *Graysim* case leaves unresolved the position of a business tenant who has sub-let all the units on the premises demised but retained the common parts: does his tenancy expire at the end of the contractually agreed term or does it need to be terminated by notice under Part II? In the absence of clear authority, each party should be advised to treat the lease as subject to Part II, and so to serve the statutory notice in order to terminate it.

---

22 [1956] Ch 290 (CA).
23 LTA 1954, s 32(1); see also *Bassari Ltd v Camden LBC* [1998] EGCS 27 (CA).
24 *cf AB Esselte v Pearl Assurance plc* [1997] 2 All ER 41 (CA).

The decision in the *Graysim* case means that lessees whose business involves admitting others into occupation need to take additional care if they are not to lose the protection of Part II. The granting of a sub-lease which is itself a Part II-protected tenancy will always cause the head-lease to lose any protection under Part II that it might previously have enjoyed. If the sub-lessor intends to occupy the premises for the purposes of its own business again on the expiration of the sub-lease, it should ensure that a business sub-tenancy expires at least 14 months before its head-lease, so that it will remain the competent landlord for the purposes of opposing any renewal under the 1954 Act. If the sub-tenancy is residential, the normal inference is that the sub-lessor is not the occupier of the parts sub-let for the purposes of Part II. The mere passive receipt of rents does not establish occupation.[25] The sub-lessor might be able to establish that it is the occupier for the purposes of Part II, however, if it can show that it has reserved and enforces an exceptional degree of control over the premises sub-demised for residential purposes.

Occupation for the purposes of a business

For the tenancy to fall within Part II, the premises must be occupied by the tenant "for the purposes of a business carried on by him or for those and other purposes".[26] It is not necessary that the business itself is carried on in the premises. Even occupation for an ancillary purpose suffices if it is necessary for the business. In *Chapman v Freeman*[27] a hotel owner took a lease of a cottage near the hotel in order to house some of the hotel staff. Although it was conceded that the hotel owner was in occupation of the cottage, it was held that he was not in occupation for the purpose of his business: it may have been convenient for the staff to live in the cottage, but it was not necessary.[28]

Incidental business user (such as that of a self-employed person who takes work home in the evenings) is insufficient to bring the tenancy within Part II. Where there is mixed residential and business user (such as a shop with a flat above, or a dentist's residence part of which is used for his surgery), the tenancy falls within Part II only, not within the legislation

---

25 *William Boyer & Sons Ltd v Adams* (1975) 32 P & CR 89.
26 LTA 1954, s 23(1).
27 [1978] 1 WLR 1298.
28 See also *Methodist Secondary Schools Trust Deed Trustees v O'Leary* [1993] 1 EGLR 105 (CA).

protecting residential tenants.[29] If the lease contains a user clause restricting the use of the premises to business purposes, a tenant who ceases his business user loses thereby the protection afforded by Part II; and even if such tenant thereafter occupies the premises as his residence, he will not gain the protection afforded to a residential tenant. Conversely, even if the landlord has not consented to the change of use, a residential tenant who begins substantial business user may gain the protection of Part II.[30]

Business purposes

For the purposes of Part II, "business" includes a trade, profession or employment, and any activity carried out by a body of persons whether corporate or unincorporate.[31] Thus for this purpose the activities of managing a hospital have been held to comprise a business.[32] A members' tennis club has also been held to be a business within Part II.[33] The dumping of waste, however, has been held not to comprise a business for the purposes of the Act on the ground that the activity in question must be in the nature of a trade, profession or employment.[34]

Contracting out

Any agreement relating to a tenancy to which Part II applies is void so far as it precludes the tenant from making an application or request for a new tenancy.[35] An agreement to surrender made pursuant to an offer-to-

29 A lawful sub-tenant of the residential part may, however, enjoy security of tenure (and so have a right to remain in occupation after the termination of the Part II-protected head-lease) under either Rent Act 1977, s 137(3) (where the sub-lease was granted before 15 January 1989) or Housing Act 1988, s 18(1) (where it was granted on or after 15 January 1989). In *Pittalis v Grant* [1989] QB 605 (noted Rodgers [1990] Conv 204) the Court of Appeal had held that such protection was not available under Rent Act 1977 to a residential sub-tenancy of part of premises where the head-lease was for mixed business and residential user within LTA 1954, Part II. A differently constituted Court of Appeal recently declined to follow such earlier decision, however, on the ground that it had been reached *per incuriam* as having overlooked Rent Act 1977, s 24(3): see the consolidated appeals in *Wellcome Trust Ltd v Hammad, Ebied v Hopkins, Church Commissioners for England v Baines* [1998] 1 All ER 657 (CA). The sub-tenant will not enjoy the statutory protection under either regime unless he has a lawful sub-tenancy; and the lessor can prevent such a sub-tenancy from being created by ensuring that the lease contains a restriction on sub-letting without the lessor's consent, and then refusing consent to a sub-letting which would enjoy the statutory protection.
30 *Cheryl Investments Ltd v Saldhana* [1978] 1 WLR 1329 (CA).
31 LTA 1954, s 23(2).
32 *Hills (Patents) Ltd v University College Hospital Board of Governors* [1956] 1 QB 90.
33 *Addiscombe Garden Estates Ltd v Crabbe* [1958] 1 QB 513.
34 *Hillil Property & Investment Co Ltd v Naraine Pharmacy Ltd* (1979) 39 P & CR 67 (CA).
35 LTA 1954, s 38(1).

surrender clause is therefore void.[36] Such an agreement is valid, however, if the approval of the court (usually the county court) is obtained pursuant to an application made by the landlord and the tenant jointly.[37] In *Hagee (London) Ltd v A B Erikson & Larson*[38], Lord Denning MR said that the county court always approves such applications where the agreement is made by business people properly advised by their lawyers.

The court is empowered to approve the exclusion only of a tenancy for a term of years certain; and it has been held in the county court that a periodic tenancy is not for this purpose a term of years certain.[39] This conclusion was not challenged on appeal to the Court of Appeal in the same case[40], where it was held that a tenant of a periodic business tenancy retained the protection of Part II despite the purported approval of the county court of an application to exclude it.[41]

If proceedings are commenced in the wrong county court, the judge or district judge may transfer them to the appropriate court, order them to continue in the court in which they have been commenced, or order them to be struck out.[42] An order made in the wrong county court is not a nullity, but merely an irregularity.[43] Millett LJ has recently stated[44]:

> "Where no objection to the jurisdiction of the court is made at the time and the court not noticing the defect proceeds to make an order, that order is not only valid as made within the jurisdiction, but also should not be taken as irregular since the court ought to be treated as having implicitly ordered the proceedings to continue in the court in which they were commenced."

The application to the court may be made before the lease has been granted, or before any contract for a lease has been entered into, in which case the application should append a draft contract or lease. If a contract is made or a lease is granted before the court's approval has been obtained, the contract must be made, or the lease granted, conditionally upon the court's leave being obtained. The condition should be expressed; but, if it is not, the court may be able to infer that the agreement or the lease is conditional upon such consent.[45] If the contract or grant is unconditional,

36 *Allnatt London Properties Ltd v Newton* [1984] 1 All ER 423 (CA): see Chap 12.
37 LTA 1954, s 38(4).
38 [1976] 1 QB 209.
39 *Nicholls v Kinsey* 26 July 1993 (unreported, county court).
40 *Ibid*, [1994] 1 EGLR 131 (CA).
41 See comment at [1994] 17 EG 155.
42 County Court Rules, Ord 16, r 2.
43 *Faulkner v Love* [1977] QB 937 (CA); *Giles v Williams* (unreported) 8 December 1995 (CA).
44 *St Giles Hotel Ltd v Microworld Technology Ltd* [1997] 27 EG 121, 123, referring to Lord Hanworth MR in *R v Judge Lailey, ex p Koffman* [1932] 1 KB 568, 577.
45 *Cardiothoracic Institute v Shrewdcrest Ltd* [1986] 1 WLR 368, discussed in Chap 1.

the tenant will gain the protection of Part II, even though the contract or lease envisages that an application is to be made.[46]

Even if the court's approval is given, Part II is not excluded unless the contracting-out provision is contained in or endorsed on the lease or other document as the court may specify.[47] In *Tottenham Hotspurs Football & Athletic Co Ltd v Princegrove Publishers Ltd*[48], the tenant went into occupation following an order of the court, but without the lease having been executed. It was nevertheless held that the Act had been effectively excluded because the tenant held under an agreement for a lease, which contained the exclusionary term. Since the Law of Property (Miscellaneous Provisions) Act 1989, section 2, this result may not apply to similar tenancies entered into after 26 September 1989.[49]

It would appear that the recession of the early 1990s resulted (somewhat surprisingly) in an increase in the number of applications to the court to exclude leases from the protection of the 1954 Act. Landlords, being forced to concede better terms to tenants in other areas, were anxious that such terms should not form the basis for further leases under a Part II renewal.[50]

Other devices to discourage tenant from relying on Part II

Several devices have been suggested which, whilst not attempting to deny the tenant the protection of Part II, would have the practical effect of encouraging the tenant not to take advantage of the statutory protection. The basic idea is that if it is intended that the tenant should have a business tenancy for a term of, say, five years, the lease should be for a longer period, say seven, but with a tenant's break clause after five, together with some provision designed to encourage the tenant to break. Aldridge mentions three variations on this basic theme: a provision for a very high rent in the last two years; the grant of a sub-lease back to the landlord for the last two years (thereby denying the tenant occupation) or a covenant in the last two years against business user.[51] In most cases, however, the tenant is likely to consider such devices commercially unacceptable.

Another device is to grant the lease to a person other than the person

46 *Essexcrest Ltd v Evenlex Ltd* (1987) 55 P & CR 279 (where the lease contained blanks to be completed later regarding, *inter alia*, the date of the order).
47 LTA 1954, s 38(4).
48 [1974] 2 QB 17.
49 Evans & Smith, *The Law of Landlord and Tenant*, 5th ed (1997) Butterworths, at 464.
50 See [1994] 17 EG 155 (note) and [1994] 19 EG 124.
51 Aldridge, *Letting Business Premises,* 7th ed (1996) FT Law & Tax, 91.

carrying on the business. Where the business is run by the tenant, the lease could be granted to his company; and *vice versa*.[52]

THE STATUTORY PROTECTION

The continuation tenancy

Section 24(1) of the Landlord and Tenant Act 1954 provides that a tenancy protected by Part II of the Act "shall not come to an end unless terminated in accordance with the provisions of this Part of this Act." Thus, unless brought to an end by one of the methods permitted by Part II, a fixed-term tenancy continues even though the contractually agreed term has expired or has been prematurely determined by, for instance, the landlord's exercise of a break clause.[53] Similarly, unless brought to an end by one of the methods permitted by Part II, a periodic tenancy continues even though terminated at common law by the landlord's notice to quit.[54]

If a fixed-term lease is continuing under section 24 and ceases to be a tenancy within Part II (*e.g.* by the tenant's ceasing to occupy the premises for the purposes of his business), the continuation tenancy does not terminate immediately. It may, however, be terminated by the landlord's giving not less than three nor more than six months' notice in writing to the tenant.[55] The operation of such notice is not affected by reason that the tenancy becomes one to which Part II applies after the notice has been given.[56]

The continuation tenancy under section 24(1) is of uncertain duration, and so would be void at common law. It is, however, validated by the statute. The continuation tenancy does not create any new form of interest in the tenant; but it prolongs the tenant's estate, subject to a statutory variation as to the mode of determination.[57] This means that, during the period of the continuation tenancy (often referred to as the period of holding over) the tenant, because he retains an estate in the land, may assign the tenancy. Similarly, the landlord may seek to forfeit the lease for breach of covenant or condition in the usual way. The "tenancy" continued by section 24(1) is the tenancy only of the person holding over.[58]

---

52 *Cristina v Seear* [1985] 2 EGLR 128 (CA).
53 See Chap 12.
54 See further pp 287 *supra* and 390 *infra*.
55 LTA 1954, s 24(3)(a).
56 *Ibid*, s 24(3)(b).
57 *Bolton (HL) Engineering Co Ltd v TJ Graham & Sons Ltd* [1957] 1 QB 159; GMS *Syndidate v Gary Elliott* (1980) 41 P & CR 124.
58 *City of London Corporation v Fell* [1994] 1 AC 458 (HL).

If that person is an assignee, the original tenant under a pre-1996 lease will not, in the absence of express words in the lease, be liable for breaches committed by the assignee during the period of holding over.[59]

The usual rule is that a tenant who purports to grant a sub-lease for a term which exceeds the duration of his own lease will be taken to have made an assignment. It has been held that this principle does not apply where the tenant is entitled to the protection of section 24[60]; but this decision must now be in doubt.[61]

Termination of a Part II-protected tenancy

There are six methods by which a tenancy protected by Part II may be terminated. The first three of these are methods provided for in the Act itself: a landlord's notice[62], a tenant's request for a new tenancy[63], and a tenant's notice.[64] The last three, by contrast, are methods of termination at common law, but are treated as methods of terminating a Part II protected tenancy: tenant's notice to quit, surrender, and forfeiture.[65] Only the first two methods may lead to a new tenancy.

Landlord's section 25 notice

The landlord may terminate a tenancy within Part II by giving the tenant a notice in the prescribed form, or in a form substantially to the like effect.[66] The notice must be in writing, and it must specify the date at which the tenancy is to come to an end (the date of termination).[67]

---

59 *Ibid; also Herbert Duncan Ltd v Cluttons* [1993] 1 EGLR 93 (CA). See further Chap 5.
60 *William Skelton & Son Ltd v Harrison & Pindar Ltd* [1975] QB 361.
61 See Chap 2.
62 LTA 1954, s 25.
63 *Ibid*, s 26.
64 *Ibid*, s 27.
65 *Ibid*, s 24(2).
66 The prescribed form is set out in the Landlord and Tenant Act 1954 Part II (Notices) Regulations, SI 1983 No 133, as amended. A number of cases have considered whether a notice not in the prescribed form is valid as being in a form "substantially to the like effect." The problem has sometimes arisen from the use of outdated forms, as in *Sun Alliance & London Assurance Co Ltd v Hayman* [1975] 1 WLR 177 (CA). In *Tegerdine v Brooks* (1978) 36 P & CR 26 (CA), a notice which omitted certain notes which were contained in the prescribed form, was nevertheless held valid because such notes were wholly irrelevant to the matter to which the notice related. The current prescribed form contains a large and heavily printed box in which the tenant is informed of the need to act quickly and (if in doubt) to seek legal advice. In *Morris v Patel* [1987] 1 EGLR 75 (CA), Dillon LJ (sitting as a single judge of the Court of Appeal) held a notice valid despite its omitting the boxed warning, since the tenant had in fact consulted solicitors and had taken appropriate steps according to the timetable laid down by the 1954 Act. This decision was, however, doubted in *Sabella Ltd v Montgomery* [1998] 9 EG 153 (CA), which held that a notice omitting the boxed warning is void.
67 LTA 1954, s 25(1); and see *Whelton Sinclair v Hyland* [1992] 2 EGLR 158 (CA).

The notice must be generally given not more than 12 months nor less than six months before the date of termination specified in the notice.[68] This requirement is, however, subject to qualification. If tenancy could (apart from Part II) have been terminated by notice to quit given by the landlord, the date of termination specified in the notice must not be earlier than the earliest date on which, apart from Part II, the tenancy could have been brought to an end by the landlord's notice to quit.[69] Notice to quit means a notice to terminate a tenancy given in accordance with its provisions.[70] Such a tenancy includes, therefore, not merely a periodic tenancy, but also a fixed-term tenancy terminable by the landlord's notice in accordance with a break clause. Furthermore, if the tenancy itself requires more than six months' notice to quit, the maximum period for giving notice is six months longer than the specified period of notice to quit.[71] If therefore the tenancy requires the landlord to give nine months' notice to quit, the landlord must give notice under section 25 not more than 15 months, nor less than nine months, before the termination date. In the case of any other tenancy[72], the date of termination specified in the notice must not be earlier than the date on which, apart from Part II, the tenancy would have come to an end by effluxion of time.[73]

A landlord who wishes to terminate the lease must comply both with any requirements for termination specified in the lease or laid down by common law, and with the procedure laid down by section 25. If the lease requires the landlord to serve a notice to terminate it (*e.g.* by means of a break clause), a single notice will suffice if it is capable of complying (and does in fact comply) both with the lease and with section 25(1).[74] In some circumstances, however, a landlord may prefer to exercise a break clause without serving a section 25 notice, such as where he anticipates being able to establish a ground of opposition in the future.[75]

The landlord's notice under section 25 must also require the tenant, within two months after the giving of the notice, to notify the landlord in writing whether or not he will be willing to give up possession at the date

---

68 *Ibid*, s 25(2).
69 *Ibid*, s 25(3)(a).
70 *Ibid*, s 69(1).
71 *Ibid*, s 25(3)((b).
72 *i.e.* a fixed-term tenancy with no landlord's break clause.
73 LTA 1954, s 25(4).
74 *Scholl Manufacturing Co Ltd v Clifton (Slim-Line) Ltd* [1967] Ch 41 (CA); *Keith Bayley Rogers & Co v Cubes Ltd* (1975) 31 P & CR 412; *Aberdeen Steak Houses plc v Crown Estate Commissioners* [1997] 14 EGCS. See Chap 12.
75 See Lewison, *Drafting Business Leases*, 5th ed (1996) FT Law & Tax, at 58.

of termination.[76] It must also state whether the landlord would oppose an application to the court under Part II for the grant of a new tenancy; and, if so, on which of the grounds mentioned in section 30 he would do so.

Notice under section 25 can be given only by the "competent" landlord. This is not necessarily the tenant's immediate landlord. It will be the tenant's immediate landlord (L) if L either owns the freehold or has a tenancy which will not expire within the next 14 months. If neither of these requirements is met, the competent landlord will be L's landlord if that person himself satisfies either of these requirements. This process is repeated, as necessary, until the competent landlord is identified.[77]

If the tenant wishes to obtain a new tenancy, he must, within two months, serve on the landlord a counter-notice unequivocally expressing his unwillingness to give up possession.[78] If the tenant does serve such a counter-notice, he is entitled to apply for a new tenancy under section 24(1). If the parties can agree swiftly on the terms of the new tenancy, the current tenancy ends on the date that the parties agree that the new tenancy is to commence.[79] Failing agreement, a tenant who wishes to obtain a new tenancy must file an application to the court (either the High Court or the county court) not less than two nor more than four months after the landlord's section 25 notice is given.[80] If, however, the tenant does not serve such a counter-notice, the tenancy will end on the termination date specified in the landlord's notice. The tenant, moreover, loses the right to apply to the court for the grant of a new tenancy.[81]

If the tenant ceases to occupy the premises for the purposes of his business during the contractual term, the lease will cease to be one within Part II, and will simply expire at the term date, without either party having to serve a notice under the Act.[82] This potentially puts the landlord in a vulnerable position if the tenant ceases to occupy just before the expiry of

76 LTA 1954, s 25(5). A notice which requires the tenant to notify the landlord only if the tenant is unwilling to give up possession has nevertheless been upheld (on an application of a purposive construction to the statute) on the ground that the service of a counter-notice indicating that the tenant is willing to give up possession is of benefit solely to the landlord: *Bridgers & Hampshire Residential v Stanford* (1991) 63 P & CR 18; *Baglarbasi v Deedmethod Ltd* [1991] 2 EGLR 71 (Judge Paul Baker QC sitting as a judge of the High Court). On incomplete or erroneous notices, see further Haley, "Section 25 notices: perfecting the imperfect" [1996] JBL 576.

77 LTA 1954, s 44(1).

78 *Ibid*, s 29(2).

79 *Ibid*, s 28.

80 *Ibid*, s 29(3).

81 *Ibid*, s 29(2).

82 *Esselte A B v Pearl Assurance plc* [1997] 2 All ER 41 (CA), following *Morrison Holdings Ltd v Manders Property (Wolverhampton) Ltd* [1976] 2 All ER 205 (CA), and not following *Long Acre Securities Ltd v Electro Acoustic Industries Ltd* (1989) 61 P & CR 177 (CA).

the contractual term, the most extreme instance being where the tenant moves out the day before the expiration of the contractual term. The lease will then terminate at common law without the landlord's necessarily having received any period of notice from the tenant.[83] In order to safeguard its position, a landlord should therefore consider serving a section 25 notice on every business tenant the prescribed period before the contractual term expires.

Tenant's section 26 request for a new tenancy

The tenant may request a new tenancy either in the counter-notice where the landlord has served a notice under section 25, or in his own notice under section 26.

A tenant is entitled to request a new tenancy under section 26 only if he has a fixed-term tenancy exceeding one year, or a term of years certain and thereafter from year to year.[84] Subject to this, a periodic tenant cannot apply for a new tenancy under section 26. A tenant may not request a new tenancy under section 26 if the landlord has previously served a section 25 notice (in which case the tenant's request must be in the counter-notice); or if the tenant has given notice to quit or notice to terminate the tenancy under section 27.[85]

The tenant's notice must be in the prescribed form and must be served on the competent landlord as defined in section 44(1).[86] The notice must suggest the terms of the new tenancy:

the property;
This need not be the entire premises comprised in the existing lease.

the length of the term;
In one case a tenant who held under a seven-year lease did not expressly specify the term of the proposed new lease; but he did specify that the other terms should be the same as those of his existing tenancy. It was held that this implied a request for a new tenancy of seven years, and that the tenant's notice was therefore valid.[87]

---

83 *i.e.* the tenancy terminates without the tenant's having to give the landlord the minimum of three months' notice under s 27 which would be required in the case of a tenancy within Part II.
84 LTA 1954, s 26(1).
85 *Ibid*, s 26(4).
86 See pp 391 *supra*.
87 *Sidney Bolsom Investment Trust Ltd v E Karmios & Co (London) Ltd* [1956] 1 QB 529 (CA).

the date the new tenancy is to commence;

This must be not less than six and not more than twelve months after the making of the request; but it cannot be a date earlier than the current tenancy would come to an end by effluxion of time or could be brought to an end by notice to quit given by the tenant.[88] The date so specified for the commencement of the new tenancy will also be the date upon which the old tenancy comes to an end. Thus a tenant cannot apply for a new tenancy more than twelve months before the termination of the existing tenancy.

If the tenant terminates a tenancy by serving a notice under a break clause, this ranks as a notice to quit and the tenant loses the statutory right to apply for a new tenancy under the Act. The question arises, however, whether a tenant, merely by serving a section 26 request, might be able to request a new tenancy to commence from the date when the lease *could have been* determined by a tenant's break notice. In a falling market, a tenant might be tempted to use such a ploy to obtain a new lease on better terms before the existing one has expired. In *Garston v Scottish Widows' Fund*[89], however, Rattee J held that in such circumstances no valid section 26 request could be served.[90] The decision rests, however, upon the expression "notice to quit" in section 26 being restricted to a notice to determine a periodic tenancy, whereas the Act elsewhere defines it to include a notice to terminate a tenancy for a term of years certain.[91] There is therefore a danger that the decision will be overruled in a later case, so it is still advisable for the landlord to guard against this possibility by ensuring that a tenant's break clause obliges the tenant to give more than 12 months' notice. Since the new tenancy suggested in a section 26 request must commence within 12 months after the making of the request, the tenant cannot then exercise the break clause by requesting a new tenancy.[92]

the rent;
other terms.

These will usually be stated to be the same as those of the current tenancy.

The landlord may oppose the request for a new tenancy by serving a counter-notice within two months of the tenant's request for a new tenancy.[93] (The landlord must be informed of this right in the tenant's

---

88 LTA 1954, s 26(2).
89 [1996] 4 All ER 282; see pp 296–298 *supra*.
90 See Chap 12.
91 LTA 1954, s 69(1).
92 See Lewison, *Drafting Business Leases*, 5th ed (1996) FT Law & Tax, at 58.
93 LTA 1954, s 26(6).

request). The counter-notice must indicate upon which of the statutory grounds of opposition in section 30 the landlord will rely.[94]

The tenant must apply to the court for a new tenancy not less than two nor more than four months after making his request for a new tenancy.[95]

The time-limit imposed on the tenant by section 26 may, however, be waived by the landlord's conduct. This occurred in *Bristol Cars Ltd v RKH Hotels Ltd*[96], where the tenant's section 26 request was defective because it specified too early a date; it was held that the landlord had waived the defect because it had initially indicated that it would not oppose a new tenancy, failed to serve a counter-notice under section 26(6), and applied for an interim rent on the basis that the tenancy was continuing. It did not matter that the landlord had not appreciated that the tenant's request had been bad.

Tenant's section 27 notice

The tenant may terminate a fixed-term tenancy at the end of the term by giving to his immediate landlord notice in writing not less than three months before the expiration of the fixed term. Such notice will not be effective, however, if it is given before the tenant has been in occupation in right of the tenancy for one month.[97]

When a fixed-term tenancy is continuing by virtue of section 24, the tenant may bring it to an end on any quarter day by giving not less than three months' notice in writing to his immediate landlord. The tenant cannot give such notice unless he has been in occupation in right of the tenancy for one month.[98]

Tenant's notice to quit: section 24(2)

A tenant who serves a notice to quit loses any protection afforded by Part II. A notice to quit includes a notice to quit served by a periodic tenant, or a notice to terminate a fixed-term tenancy served by a tenant under a break clause.[99] A tenant's notice to quit is not, however, effective to terminate the tenancy unless the tenant has been in occupation in right of the tenancy for one month.[1] This is designed to ensure that any notice to quit is given willingly.

---

94 *Ibid*, s 26(6).
95 *Ibid*, s 29(3).
96 (1979) 33 P & CR 411.
97 LTA 1954, s 27(1).
98 *Ibid*, s 27(2).
99 See definition of "notice to quit" in *ibid*, s 69(1).
1 LTA 1954, s 24(2)(a).

Surrender: section 24(2)

A tenant who surrenders the tenancy loses the protection of Part II unless the instrument of surrender was executed before, or in pursuance of an agreement made before, the tenant had been in occupation in right of the tenancy for one month.[2]

Forfeiture: section 24(2)

If the tenancy, or a superior tenancy, is forfeited, the tenant loses the protection of Part II. Even if the landlord has obtained judgment for possession, however, the tenant retains the protection of Part II (and may thus apply for a new tenancy) so long as he has a pending application for relief.[3]

Interim rent

Because the continuation tenancy prolongs the tenant's estate, subject to a statutory variation as to the mode of determination, its terms are the same as those of the contractual tenancy which has been terminated. In the case of the rent payable, this could work hardship on the landlord, who would thereby lose (during a period of rising rents) the benefit of a higher rent during the period of holding over. It is therefore provided that the landlord may apply to the court for the determination of an "interim rent."[4] Such application may be made only either if the landlord has given a section 25 notice to terminate the tenancy or if the tenant has made a request for a new tenancy under section 26. At a time of falling rents, the landlord is unlikely to apply for an interim rent. The tenant cannot apply for an interim rent, and cannot therefore take advantage of a general fall in rents. From the landlord's point of view, it is still better for the lease to make provision for rent review immediately before the end of the term, however, since this removes the need to apply to the court for an interim rent.[5]

To apply for an interim rent, the landlord must be the competent landlord within the meaning of section 44. A tenant (T) should bear this in mind before sub-letting. If, for instance, T grants a business sub-tenancy to S for a fixed term which expires 12 months before the expiration of T's own contractual term, the competent landlord for the purposes of applying for an interim rent in respect of S's period of holding over is not T but L; yet, at least for the remaining period of 12 months before T's head-lease

---

2 *Ibid*, s 24(2)(b).
3 *Meadows v Clerical, Medical and General Life Assurance Society* [1981] Ch 70.
4 LTA 1954, s 24A.
5 See Chap 9.

expires, any interim rent would continue to be payable to T. The result is that L, who is entitled to apply, has little incentive to do so; whereas, T, who has every incentive to apply, has no right to do so. In such circumstances, there is an additional reason for T to protect himself by ensuring that the sub-lease provides for rent-review immediately before the end of the term.

The interim rent must be one which it would be reasonable for the tenant to pay while the tenancy continues by virtue of section 24.[6] In determining the interim rent, the court must have regard to the rent payable under the terms of the tenancy.[7] Subject to this, however, the interim rent is to be determined in accordance with the provisions contained in section 34(1) and (2) on the basis that a new tenancy from year to year of the whole of the premises comprised in the tenancy were granted to the tenant by order of the court. This means that the interim rent is essentially to be the open-market rent payable by a yearly tenant holding under the terms of the tenancy (other than those relating to rent) and disregarding the matters specified in section 34.[8]

The fiction of a notional yearly tenancy means that the interim rent is generally lower than the final rent which may ultimately be fixed for a new tenancy. Although the court must have regard to the rent payable under the old lease, it is not clear how this regard operates. In *English Exporters (London) Ltd v Eldonwall Ltd*[9] and *Fawke v Viscount Chelsea*[10], the court said that the method was to assess the market value of an annual tenancy in accordance with section 34 and then to discount the rent by reference to the existing rent level. This approach was adopted in *Ratners (Jewellers) Ltd v Lemnoll Ltd*[11], where it led to a tempering of the market value of an annual tenancy by 20%. In *Regis Property Co Ltd v Lewis & Peat Ltd*[12], however, the judge considered that the old rent was relevant only so far as it was of evidential value in calculating the market value of the notional annual tenancy.

An interim rent determined under section 24A is payable from the date on which the proceedings were commenced or the date specified in the landlord's notice or the tenant's request, whichever is the later.[13]

---

6 LTA 1954, s 24A(1).
7 *Ibid*, s 24A(3).
8 See pp 408–409 *infra*.
9 [1973] Ch 415.
10 [1980] QB 441 (CA).
11 [1980] 2 EGLR 65.
12 [1970] Ch 695.
13 LTA 1954, s 24A(2).

The statutory grounds of opposition

There are seven statutory grounds upon which the landlord (either in his section 25 notice, or in his counter-notice under section 26(6)) may oppose an application under section 24(1) for a new tenancy. These grounds are set out in paragraphs (a) to (g) of section 30(1).

There is an important difference between the grounds set out in paragraphs (a), (b), (c) and (e) on the one hand, and those set out in paragraphs (d), (f) and (g) on the other. Paragraphs (a), (b), (c) and (e) set out grounds upon which the tenant "ought not" to be granted a new tenancy. These words mean that, even if the landlord can make out a ground in one of those paragraphs, the court has a discretion whether to order the grant of a new tenancy. By contrast, if the landlord establishes a ground of opposition under paragraphs (d), (f) or (g), the court has no discretion – it is obliged to refuse an application for a new tenancy.

Paragraph (a): breach by the tenant of a repairing obligation

The landlord must show that there is an existing breach (*i.e.* one which exists at the date of the service of the landlord's notice or counter-notice) and that it is so serious that (in the words of para (a)) "the tenant ought not to be granted a new tenancy". The court will take into account past breaches, as well as any undertaking by the tenant to effect the necessary repairs.[14]

Paragraph (b): persistent delay by the tenant in paying rent

Persistent delay means that there must have been delay over a period. The court will take into account the number of times there has been delay, the length of the delays and the reasons for them, and the steps which the landlord needed to take to recover payment. The court will also consider how the landlord might be protected against future delays in rent payments, *e.g.* by requiring the tenant to pay a security deposit.[15]

Paragraph (c): other substantial breaches of obligations under the tenancy or any other reason connected with the tenant's use or management of the holding

The court will look at the seriousness of the breach, whether it is remediable, and whether it has been waived by the landlord. The second

---

14 *Lyons v Central Commercial Properties London Ltd* [1958] 1 WLR 869 (CA).
15 *Hopcutt v Carver* (1969) 209 EG 1069 (CA); *Rawashdeh v Lane* [1988] 2 EGLR 109 (CA).

part of the paragraph is wider than the first. Thus it could include the case where the tenant merely proposed to breach, for instance, a user clause. It has also been held to include an intended user which, although not in breach of the tenant's covenants in the lease, would contravene a planning enforcement order.[16]

Paragraph (d): availability of suitable alternative accommodation

This ground is that the landlord has offered and is willing to provide or secure alternative accommodation for the tenant. The terms of the alternative accommodation must be reasonable having regard to the terms of the current tenancy and all other relevant circumstances. Furthermore, the accommodation and the time at which it is available must be suitable for the tenant's requirements (including the need to preserve goodwill) having regard to the nature and class of the business and to the situation and extent of, and facilities afforded by, the holding. As mentioned above[17], this ground is not discretionary.[18]

Paragraph (d) does not state whether the judge is to assess the suitability of alternative accommodation solely according to the terms of the landlord's original offer, or whether he may consider any improved offer which the landlord may make during the trial. There is county court authority which holds that the judge may consider an offer made before issue is joined in the proceedings[19]; but the point was recently left open by the Court of Appeal.[20] It seems consistent, however, both with the policy of the 1954 Act of encouraging negotiation, and with other provisions in the Act[21], that the court should be able to take account of any revised offers made during the trial.[22]

If the tenant rejects an offer which the court finds reasonable within the paragraph, so that the tenant's application for a new tenancy is withdrawn, the tenant may still accept the landlord's offer if it remains open. There is no obligation on a landlord, however, to keep such offer open. A tenant who therefore rejects what is found to be a reasonable offer might find that it has been withdrawn, so that he is forced to vacate the premises.[23]

---

16 *Turner and Bell v Searles (Stanford-le-Hope) Ltd* (1977) 33 P & CR 208 (CA).
17 See p 397.
18 *Betty's Cafés Ltd v Phillips Furnishing Stores Ltd* [1957] Ch 67.
19 *M Chaplin Ltd v Regent Capital Holdings Ltd* [1994] 1 EGLR 249.
20 *Mark Stone Car Sales Ltd v Howard De Walden Estates Ltd* [1997] 30 January (CA) (unreported, Lexis Transcript).
21 *e.g.* LTA 1954, s 31(2).
22 See Haley, "Termination of business tenancies: new uncertainties?" [1997] JBL 557, 559–561.
23 See Yates and Hawkins, *Landlord and Tenant Law,* 2nd ed (1986) Sweet & Maxwell, at 695–696.

Paragraph (e): in the case of a sub-tenancy of part, that possession is required for letting or disposing of the property as a whole

Because the circumstances in this paragraph are somewhat special, it is relied upon only rarely. It is relevant only where the "competent landlord" within section 44[24] is not the tenant's immediate landlord. Thus where L, a freehold owner, has leased business premises to T, who has in turn sub-let part to S, if S applies for a new tenancy when T's lease has less than 14 months to run, the person to whom the request must be made is L. L may seek to rely on paragraph (e) on the basis that he needs possession in order to dispose of the premises as a whole, *e.g.* by re-letting or sale. Under the paragraph, L must show that the aggregate of the rents which would be reasonably obtainable on separate lettings of the holding and the remainder of the property would be substantially less than the rent which would be reasonably obtainable on a letting of the property as a whole. The landlord will have difficulty in showing this unless T's lease ends very shortly after S's sub-lease.

Paragraph (f): the landlord intends to demolish or reconstruct

This ground is that, on the termination of the current tenancy, the landlord intends to demolish or reconstruct the whole or a substantial part of the premises comprised in the holding or to carry out substantial work of construction on the holding or part of it, and that he could not reasonably do so without obtaining possession of the holding.

The landlord must therefore establish two things: intention and the need for possession.[25] The landlord is not required to bring evidence of a detailed scheme of development or to have entered into contracts, nor is he obliged to show that every potential obstacle in the way has been removed. It is enough for him to establish that his scheme has a reasonable prospect of fulfilment and that general arrangements in regard to planning permission, finance and building have been dealt with.[26] The intention must be shown at the date of application to the court.[27] If, therefore, the landlord changes his mind subsequently, there is nothing the tenant can do, unless it can prove misrepresentation or concealment of material facts, in which case the court may award the tenant compensation for damage or loss.[28]

The landlord is not required to carry out the proposed works personally: he may hire contractors to do the work for him. He may even

---

24 See pp 391 *supra*.
25 See Dear & Clark, "Into the valley of decision" [1996] 44 EG 176.
26 *Capocci v Goble* [1987] 2 EGLR 102 (CA).
27 *Betty's Cafés Ltd v Phillips Furnishing Stores Ltd* [1959] AC 20.
28 LTA 1954, s 55(1).

grant a building lease for this purpose and show the necessary intention to
do the work through the new lessee as his agent.[29]

The landlord's motive is relevant only in so far as it indicates the
genuineness of his intention. If the landlord shows an intention to carry out
the works within paragraph (f), the fact that his motive is to dispose of the
premises with vacant possession is irrelevant. In *Turner v Wandsworth
London Borough Council*[30], the landlord proposed to grant a four-year lease
to a company that was to demolish the premises. It was accepted that the
landlord's motive (as evidenced by the minutes of a meeting of its property
committee) was to dispose of the site at a future date when the property
market was more favourable. The Court of Appeal, reversing the decision of
the county court, held that such motive was irrelevant, and that in the
circumstances the landlord had shown the requisite intention to oppose a
renewal under paragraph (f). This decision extends the opportunity for
landlords whose real motive is to sell the premises with vacant possession to
achieve this object by the granting of short building leases.

Because a tenant who is refused an order for a new tenancy is generally
given a period of a few months after the hearing before being required to
vacate, the landlord does not need to show an intention to demolish or
reconstruct immediately. It is sufficient if he has an intention to do so some
three or four months after the hearing. Even an intention to start within
one year may suffice; but in no case can the landlord secure possession
before the date upon which he expresses his intention to start work.[31]

Reconstruction means rebuilding, and the words "demolish or
reconstruct" are construed conjunctively. A substantial interference with
the existing premises is required. The mere landscaping of a field without
buildings after removing topsoil and depositing waste was held not to
comprise "reconstruction" for this purpose.[32] Works of re-roofing, re-
wiring, the resiting of a staircase and toilets, and the installation of central
heating, were held not to comprise a "substantial work of construction"
within this paragraph.[33] They were, indeed, not treated as works of
construction at all, but were more properly classified as works of
"installation", "refurbishment" or "improvement."[34] It seems that it is
implicit in the generality of paragraph (f) that the works must directly
involve the structure of the building in some way; wooden partitions,

---

29 *Gilmour Caterers Ltd v Governors of the Royal Hospital of St Bartholomew* [1956] 1 QB
   387 (building lease for 48 years); *Spook Erection Ltd v British Railways Board* [1988] 1
   EGLR 76 (building lease for 99 years).
30 [1994] 1 EGLR 134 (CA).
31 *cf* LTA 1954, s 31(2).
32 *Botterill v Bedfordshire County Council* [1985] 1 EGLR 82 (CA).
33 *Barth v Pritchard* [1990] 1 EGLR 109.
34 *Ibid*, at 111 (Stocker LJ).

however extensive, could not therefore fall within the meaning of "construction."[35]

If the existing lease already entitles the landlord to enter the premises to carry out the works, the landlord is unlikely to be able to rely on paragraph (f) because he would not then need to obtain possession from the court.[36]

Originally a landlord could rely on paragraph (f) even though he needed possession for only a short period, or of only a part of the premises. This was, however, qualified by a later statutory amendment[37], which provides that a landlord cannot rely on paragraph (f) if:

(a) the tenant agrees to the inclusion in the new tenancy of a term giving the landlord access and other facilities for carrying out the work intended, and that, as a result, the landlord could reasonably carry out the work without obtaining possession and without interfering to a substantial extent or for a substantial time with the tenant's business user; or

(b) the tenant is willing to accept a tenancy of an economically separable part (defined in section 31A(2)) of the holding, and either the foregoing paragraph is satisfied with respect to that part or possession of the remainder would be reasonably sufficient to enable the landlord to carry out the intended work.[38]

Whether interference within paragraph (a) is substantial is a matter of fact: it has been held that works which would close the tenant's business for two weeks were not a substantial interference[39]; whereas works which entailed closure for 12 weeks were.[40] Furthermore, although section 31A is clearly intended to be for the benefit of the tenant, the tenant is not entitled to waive the requirement that the works will not substantially interfere with his business user.[41]

Paragraph (g): the landlord intends to occupy the premises himself

The landlord must show that, on the termination of the current tenancy, he intends to occupy the holding for the purposes, or partly for the purposes, of a business to be carried on by him therein, or as his residence. A landlord is not entitled to rely on paragraph (g), however, if his interest, or an

---

35 *Ibid*, at 111 (Stocker LJ).
36 See Yates and Hawkins, *Landlord and Tenant Law*, 2nd ed (1986) Sweet & Maxwell, at 699.
37 LPA 1969, inserting s 31A into LTA 1954.
38 LTA 1954, s 31A(1).
39 *Cerex Jewels Ltd v Peachey Property Corp plc* [1986] 2 EGLR 65 (CA).
40 *Blackburn v Hussain* [1988] 1 EGLR 77.
41 *Redfern v Reeves* (1978) 37 P & CR 364.

interest which has merged into that interest, was purchased or created within five years of the termination of the current tenancy, and all times since such purchase or creation the holding has been comprised in a business tenancy within section 23(1).[42] For the purposes of paragraph (g), any business carried on by a company in which the landlord has a controlling interest (as there defined) is treated as a business to be carried on by him.[43]

Where the landlord's interest is held in trust, the intention of any of the beneficiaries to occupy for the purposes specified in paragraph (g) suffices.[44] Where the landlord's interest is held by a member of a group of companies, the intended occupation of the landlord for the purposes of a business to be carried on by him includes the intended occupation by any member of the group for the purposes of a business to be carried on by that member.[45]

The requisite intention for this paragraph is similar to that required for paragraph (f), *i.e.* in this instance a firm intention to occupy within a reasonable time. Where the occupation will require planning permission, the landlord must have applied for it and show a reasonable prospect that it will be obtained.[46] As under paragraph (f), the relevant date for the existence of that intention is the date of the hearing.

The landlord must intend to occupy the premises; but this does not have to be personal occupation: it may be through an agent.[47] The intention must be to occupy "the holding". This means that if the landlord intends to demolish the buildings which comprise the holding he cannot come within paragraph (g).[48]

Where no new tenancy is ordered

Landlord establishes opposition under any ground

If the landlord establishes a ground of opposition under any ground in section 30, the court may not order a new tenancy.[49] The continuation tenancy does not, however, come to an end immediately. It will continue for a limited period. The date specified for termination in the landlord's section 25 notice or the date specified for the commencement of the new tenancy in the tenant's section 26 request (as the case may be) will not

---

42 LTA 1954, s 30(2).
43 *Ibid*, s 30(3).
44 *Ibid*, s 41(2).
45 *Ibid*, s 42(3)(a).
46 *Gregson v Cyril Lord Ltd* [1963] 1 WLR 41 (CA).
47 *Skeet v Powell-Sheddon* [1988] 2 EGLR 112 (CA).
48 *Nursey v P Currie (Dartford) Ltd* [1959] 1 WLR 273 (CA).
49 LTA 1954, s 31(1).

necessarily be the date upon which the tenancy will end.

If, following the service of such notice or request, an application to the court is made under Part II, then, unless the termination date in the notice or the commencement date of the new tenancy in the request is later, the tenancy will end three months from the date the application is finally disposed of.[50] An application is finally disposed of only after the expiration of any time for appeal.[51] Since the period for appeal from judgment is currently four weeks, this means that, in the absence of an appeal being lodged, the tenancy will end four months after judgment. If, however, the termination date in the notice or the date for the commencement of the new tenancy in the request is later than the period specified in section 64, the tenancy will end on that later date.

By lodging an appeal, even in a hopeless case, the tenant may therefore delay the time when he is required to vacate. If the appeal is quite unmeritorious, the landlord's remedy is to apply either for an order to strike out or for an order for security for costs, or for both.[52] Where, however, the landlord has already established a ground of opposition to the grant of a new tenancy which is not the subject of an appeal, and the tenant's appeal is concerned merely with the issue of compensation, it seems "quite absurd"[53] that the tenancy should be automatically continued under the statute for several more months.[54] It has been suggested that this obvious injustice to the landlord could be avoided by "an imaginative judicial interpretation"[55] of section 64, so that an application could be treated as finally disposed of when a court's unappealed decision puts paid to any question of the grant of a new tenancy.[56]

Special provisions relating to grounds (d), (e) and (f)

If the landlord's opposition is based solely upon, or includes, one or more of grounds (d), (e) or (f), then, even though the landlord fails to establish opposition under one of those three grounds, the tenant may still fail to

---

50 *Ibid*, s 64(1).
51 *Ibid*, s 64(2).
52 *Burgess v Stafford Hotels Ltd* [1990] 3 All ER 222, 228 (Glidewell LJ).
53 *Mark Stone Car Sales Ltd v Howard De Walden Estates Ltd* [1997] 30 January (CA) (unreported, Lexis Transcript), per Brooke LJ
54 Thus in *Mark Stone Car Sales Ltd v Howard De Walden Estates Ltd* [1997] 30 January (CA) (unreported), the landlord had established opposition under paragraph (f), against which the tenant did not appeal; the tenant would therefore in any event be obliged to give up occupation. Its appeal under paragraph (d) was therefore concerned solely with the issue of compensation.
55 *Mark Stone Car Sales Ltd v Howard De Walden Estates Ltd* [1997] 30 January (CA) (unreported, Lexis Transcript), per Brooke LJ.
56 *Ibid*, Brooke LJ. His Lordship added, however, that legislative amendment is needed to put the matter beyond doubt.

obtain a new tenancy. This will occur where the court would nevertheless have been satisfied of any of those three grounds if the date of termination specified in the landlord's notice or the date of the commencement of the new tenancy in the tenant's request had been later (but not more than one year later). In such circumstances, the court must make a declaration to this effect, stating of which of the said grounds it would have been satisfied and specifying such later date, but without making an order for a new tenancy.[57] If the tenant takes no action thereafter, the tenancy will simply terminate as has been indicated.[58] The tenant can, however, postpone the termination of his existing tenancy. Thus, if within 14 days from the declaration the tenant so requires, the court must substitute the later date (specified in its declaration) as the date of termination.[59]

Misrepresentation or concealment

If the court refuses an order for the grant of a new tenancy and it subsequently appears that the court was induced to refuse the grant by misrepresentation or concealment of material facts, the court may order the landlord to pay the tenant compensation for his damage or loss thereby sustained.[60] A landlord who, for instance, successfully opposed a renewal of the tenancy by falsely claiming an intention to occupy the premises for himself under ground (g), could be made to pay compensation. The section will not, however, enable the tenant to claim compensation where the landlord genuinely had such an intention at the date of the hearing and merely changed his mind subsequently.

Compensation for disturbance

A landlord who successfully opposes the grant of a new tenancy on grounds (a), (b), (c) or (d) does not have to pay compensation to the tenant. The rationale is evidently that the first three grounds are based on the tenant's own fault, and the fourth involves the tenant's declining an offer of reasonable alternative accommodation.

Compensation is, however, payable if the landlord successfully opposes a tenant's application to the court for a new tenancy under grounds (e), (f) or (g), and upon no other ground. Similarly, compensation is payable if the landlord relies solely on grounds (e), (f) or (g) in his section 25 notice, or in his counter-notice to a tenant's request for a new tenancy, and the tenant does not apply to the court for a new tenancy.[61] These grounds, it should be

---

57 LTA 1954, s 31(2)(a).
58 See pp. 402–403 *supra*.
59 LTA 1954, s 31(2)(b).
60 *Ibid*, s 55(1).
61 *Ibid*, s 37(1).

noted, involve no fault or unreasonable conduct on the tenant's part.

Any compensation must be paid on the tenant's quitting of the holding.[62] Compensation is calculated as the product of the appropriate multiplier[63] and either the rateable value of the holding or twice the rateable value of the holding.[64] Twice the rateable value of the holding is used in this calculation if during the whole of the 14 years immediately preceding the determination of the current tenancy, the premises have been occupied for the purposes of a business carried on by the occupier (or for those and other purposes); and, if during that period there was a change in the occupier, the occupier immediately after the change was the successor to the business carried on by the immediately preceding occupier.[65] In any other case, the rateable value is used.[66] Therefore, successions to a business apart, a tenant who has occupied the premises for the purposes of a business for the previous 14 years obtains twice the compensation of a tenant who has occupied for, say, only 13 years and six months. Compensation received by a tenant under section 37 is not liable to capital gains tax.[67]

In limited circumstances, it is possible for the parties to contract out of the landlord's obligation to pay compensation under the section or to vary the amount of compensation payable. Such agreement is void, however, if the tenant has been in occupation of the premises for the purposes of a business for five years preceding the date he is to quit; or if the tenant has been in business occupation for a lesser period, but he is the successor to the business of the immediately preceding occupier, and their combined periods of business occupation total at least five years before the date the tenant is to quit.[68] In any other case, the agreement is valid.[69]

In *Bacchiocchi v Academic Agency Ltd*[70], the words "occupation" and "immediately preceding" were given a purposive construction. Ward LJ indicated that a period during which the premises are left unattended, or during which there is no business activity, may still be a period of occupation provided such non-attendance or inactivity can be regarded as reasonably

62 *Ibid*, s 37(1).
63 The appropriate multiplier is specified in Landlord and Tenant Act 1954 (Appropriate Multiplier) Order 1990, SI 1990 No 363.
64 LTA 1954, s 37(2).
65 *Ibid*, s 37(3).
66 *Ibid*, s 37(2)(b).
67 *Drummond v Austin Brown* [1986] Ch 52 (CA), interpreting what is now Taxation of Chargeable Gains Act 1992, s 22(1), and holding that LTA 1954 could not comprise an "asset" from which the "capital sum" (the compensation) could be said to be "derived."
68 LTA 1954, s 38(2).
69 *Ibid*, s 38(3).
70 [1998] 2 All ER 241 (CA), doubting *Department of Environment v Royal Insurance plc* (1986) 54 P & CR 26, where Falconer J held that a tenant of a 14-year term had failed to qualify for double compensation because he had moved into the premises one day after the commencement of the term.

incidental to the running of the business, including its commencement or winding down. Simon Brown LJ considered that a tenant's business interest does not invariably require physical possession throughout the whole term, and that, whenever business premises are empty for only a short period, he would be disinclined to find that business occupancy has ceased (or not started), provided there is no other business occupier during that period, and the premises are not being used for some other, non-business, purpose. The case concerned a tenant who had mistaken the date by which he had to quit, and in fact vacated a fortnight before his tenancy determined. The Court of Appeal considered this period to be incidental to the running down of his business activity, and held that he had been in occupation for the purposes of a business for the five years preceding the date he was obliged to quit. A clause in the lease under which the parties had contracted out of the obligation to pay the statutory compensation was therefore void, and the tenant (who had been in occupation for 14 years) was entitled to double compensation under section 37.

Tenant obtains new tenancy

If the tenant has applied to the court under section 24(1) for a new tenancy, then, unless the landlord establishes a statutory ground of opposition, or the circumstances stated in section 31(2) apply[71], the court must order the grant of a new tenancy on the terms there provided.[72] If a tenant's application for a new tenancy is made following a landlord's section 25 notice, such application is not to be entertained unless the tenant has duly notified the landlord that he will not be willing at the date of termination to give up possession.[73]

The court has power to specify the terms of the new tenancy only insofar as they are not agreed between the parties themselves.

Property to be comprised in the new tenancy: section 32

In the absence of agreement between the parties, the court will order the grant of a new tenancy of the holding.[74] "The holding" means the property comprised in the tenancy, but excluding any part which is occupied neither by the tenant nor by his employee for the purposes of a business.[75] If the tenant has, for instance, sub-let a part of the premises in circumstances such that he remains in occupation for the purposes of a business only of the

---

71 See pp. 403–404 *supra*.
72 *Ibid*, s 29(1).
73 *Ibid*, s 29(2).
74 *Ibid*, s 32(1).
75 *Ibid*, s 23(3).

remaining part, the court will order a new tenancy only of that remaining part. The court will designate the property which constitutes the holding by reference to the circumstances existing at the date of the order.[76]

If the landlord opposed the grant of a new tenancy on ground (f), but the circumstances set out in section 31A apply (including that the tenant is willing to accept a tenancy of an economically separable part), the order under section 29 will be for the grant of a new tenancy of that part only.[77]

If the holding does not include all the property comprised in the current tenancy, the landlord may nevertheless require any new tenancy ordered to be granted to be a tenancy of the whole.[78] If the landlord did not have this power, he might[79] find himself landlord of different tenants (including those who were previously sub-lessees) holding parts of the property comprised in the existing tenancy under different leases. The tenant cannot, however, be compelled to accept his landlord's offer of a lease of only part of the premises.

The order for a grant of a new tenancy under section 29 will include "rights enjoyed in connection with the holding", *i.e.* appurtenant rights such as easements, unless the parties agree otherwise or (in default of such agreement) the court otherwise determines.[80]

Duration: section 33

An agreement between the parties on the duration of the new tenancy will be given effect to in the court order, whatever the length of the term may be. In the absence of such agreement, the court will make an order for a term which it considers to be reasonable in all the circumstances, but in this case the court cannot make an order for the grant of a term certain of more than fourteen years. The term ordered by the court begins on the termination of the current tenancy.[81]

Factors which the court will take into account in deciding upon the term include the term of the current tenancy (a longer term will rarely be ordered), the nature of the business and the comparative hardship between the parties. The court may also include a break clause in the new lease: as, for instance, where the landlord intends to redevelop the premises within a few years, but not within the period required to satisfy ground (f) of section 30.[82] In a case where the redevelopment was likely to occur at the

---

76 *Ibid*, s 32(1).
77 *Ibid*, s 32(1A).
78 *Ibid*, s 32(2).
79 *e.g.* by virtue of LPA 1925, s 139.
80 LTA 1954, s 32(3).
81 *Ibid*, s 33.
82 *National Car Parks Ltd v Paternoster Consortium Ltd* [1990] 1 EGLR 99. See p 400 *supra*.

time of the tenant's retirement, however, the factor of comparative hardship was decisive against the inclusion of a landlord's break clause.[83]

Rent: section 34

In default of agreement between the parties, the court will determine the rent payable under the new tenancy as that at which, having regard to the terms of the tenancy (other than those relating to rent), the holding might reasonably be expected to be let in the open market by a willing lessor, but with specified matters being disregarded: section 34(1). This means that the other terms of the new tenancy will need to be settled (by the court, if the parties cannot agree) before the court is able to determine the rent.[84] The expense and inconvenience to which the tenant would be put if obliged to relocate do not justify a higher rent, as a willing lessor would not hold the tenant to ransom in such a manner.[85] For the purposes of section 34, there may be an open market even where there is only one lessor, provided there is a number of potential lessees.[86] Furthermore, a market can still be an open market even though most of the occupiers of the premises belong to a particular profession or engage in a particular trade. Thus in *Baptist* v *Trustees of the Honourable Society of Gray's Inn*[87], Judge Owen held that there was an open market for lettings within the Inn, even though most of its occupants were barristers and, since 1984, there had been no lettings other than to members of the Bar.

The statutory disregards are:

(a) any effect on rent of the fact that the tenant or his predecessors in title have been in occupation of the holding;

(b) any goodwill attached to the holding by reason of the carrying on there of the tenant's business (whether by him or by a predecessor in that business);

(c) any effect on rent of certain types of improvements[88];

(d) any addition to the value of licensed premises attributable to the tenant's licence.[89]

To be disregarded under paragraph (c), an improvement must be one carried out by the tenant for the time being and not in pursuance of an obligation to his immediate landlord. It must, furthermore, be carried out either: during the current tenancy; or within 21 years of the application for

---

83 *Becker* v *Hill Street Properties Ltd* [1990] 2 EGLR 78 (CA).
84 *O'May* v *City of London Real Property Co Ltd* [1983] 2 AC 726 (HL).
85 *Northern Electric plc* v *Addison* [1997] 39 EG 175 (CA).
86 *Air Canada* v *Heathrow Airport Ltd* (30 March 1993, county court, unreported) where the premises comprised an airport passenger lounge.
87 [1993] 2 EGLR 136 (county court).
88 Defined in LTA 1954, s 34(2).
89 LTA 1954, s 34(1).

a new tenancy, where the premises have since the improvement always been let on a tenancy within section 23, and no tenant since such time has given notice to quit.[90]

To illustrate the operation of paragraph (c), it may be helpful to imagine a business tenant (T) who voluntarily effected improvements in 1975 and 1980 while tenant of L under lease 1, which expired in 1985. In determining the rent payable under the new lease (lease 2) granted in that year, the court will disregard both sets of improvements because they were both effected during the current tenancy. If the term granted by lease 2 expires in 1999, and T obtains a further renewal of the tenancy (lease 3) in that year, the 1980 improvement will again be disregarded under paragraph (c), because it was effected within 21 years of the application for the new tenancy. The 1975 improvement, however, will not be disregarded, because it was carried out more than 21 years earlier.

Each party usually presents the evidence of a surveyor with experience in the valuation of business premises in the particular area. Where appropriate, such evidence will be supported by rental values for comparable properties. If there are no comparable properties, evidence of the profitability of the tenant's business may be taken into account.[91] In assessing the open-market rent, the court is not restricted to considering a letting restricted to the use to which the tenant puts the property. It must also consider the most profitable use to which the premises, consistently with the user clause, could be put.[92] The state of repair of the premises is also a relevant factor in determining the market rent. If the landlord has breached a repairing covenant, this may reduce the market value of the premises for the purposes of the section, at least where the breach is a serious one.[93]

The court is specifically empowered to make provision for varying the rent, *i.e.* to include a rent-review clause. It did not become common practice to insert rent-review clauses into leases until inflation took hold in the 1960s. Where a lease from an earlier period (not containing a rent-review clause) comes up for renewal and the parties, whilst agreeing that a rent-review clause should be inserted into the new lease, do not agree on its content, the court has power to order the insertion of a clause which provides for review to be downwards as well as upwards. This might be appropriate where there is specific evidence that rents in the area are likely to fall in the future.[94] The county court in *Boots the Chemists Ltd* v

---

90 *Ibid*, s 34(2).
91 *Harewood Hotels Ltd* v *Harris* [1958] 1 WLR 108.
92 *W J Barton Ltd* v *Long Acre Securities Ltd* [1982] 1 WLR 398.
93 *Fawke* v *Viscount Chelsea* [1980] QB 441.
94 *Janes (Gowns) Ltd* v *Harlow Development Corporation* [1980] 1 EGLR 52 (Ch).

Pinkland Ltd[95] and in *Forbouys plc v Newport Borough Council*[96], however, made an order providing for downwards as well as upwards rent review even in the absence of such specific evidence. If the current lease already contains a rent-review clause, the court will generally retain its terms in the order for the new tenancy; if, therefore, the current lease provides for upwards-only review, so usually will the new.[97]

If the rent is too small to justify the costs of a rent-review clause, the judge may set the new rent at a level to reflect any increases that might have been obtained on review. This was illustrated in *Northern Electric plc v Addison*[98], where both the old and the proposed leases restricted the use of the premises to that of an electricity sub-station. The rent under the old lease had been fixed at £10 per annum. The judge had accepted that the tenant's proposed figure of £15 per annum under the new lease was correct in principle, but had determined that the rent should be £40 per annum to take account of increases which might have been obtainable had the new lease made provision for rent review. The Court of Appeal held that the judge's determination had been correctly made.

Other terms: section 35

In default of agreement between the parties, the other terms of the tenancy are such as may be determined by the court, which is to have regard to the terms of the current tenancy and to all relevant circumstances.[99] In practice, the terms of the new lease will be the same as those of the existing lease. However, in *Cairnplace Ltd v CBL (Property Investment) Co Ltd*[99a] the old lease required guarantors only of an assignee, whereas the Court of Appeal agreed with the trial judge that the new lease should also require guarantors of the tenant obtaining the renewal. The reason was that the tenant was itself an assignee under the old lease, whose directors had provided guarantees, and the court was satisfied that it was fair and reasonable to require the tenant to continue to provide guarantors for the full term of ten years under the new lease.

A variation in the terms, or the addition of new terms, will not generally be ordered unless the party seeking it can provide a convincing justification. A landlord cannot compel a tenant to accept a relaxation of the user covenant for the sole purpose of obtaining a higher rent under the

---

95 [1992] 2 EGLR 98.
96 [1994] 1 EGLR 138.
97 *Charles Follett Ltd v Cabtell Investments Ltd* [1986] 2 EGLR 76; and (in the county court) *Blythewood Plant Hire Ltd v Spiers Ltd* [1992] 2 EGLR 103.
98 [1997] 39 EG 175 (CA).
99 LTA 1954, s 35.
99a [1984] 1 WLR 696 (CA).

new lease.[1] In *Charles Clements (London) Ltd* v *Rank City Wall Ltd*[2] the original lease restricted the use of the premises to that of a retail cutler, and prohibited their use for any other purpose without the landlord's previous consent in writing. The landlord wished to relax the user restriction by adding the words "such consent not to be unreasonably withheld", and increase the rent by £1,750 per annum. In the absence of any special reason being shown for the change, Goulding J declined to approve it, commenting:[3]

> "If the parties are to be at liberty to insist on changes in the terms of the existing tenancy simply because they consider them beneficial to themselves, a field would be opened which I think the court would find it bewildering to traverse."

Any variation to the benefit of one party must be balanced by compensatory changes elsewhere. In *O'May* v *City of London Real Property Co Ltd*[4], the existing lease imposed an obligation on the landlord to repair. The landlord wished the new lease to contain a service charge (not provided for in the existing lease) to cover services and repairs in return for a small reduction in the rent. The House of Lords refused to insert such new terms. It held that such additional financial obligation could not be adequately compensated for in this way. The variation sought would benefit only the landlord by quantifying a liability which, under the existing lease, was unquantifiable.

Carrying out the court's order

The landlord must execute the lease and can require the tenant to execute a counterpart.[5] The court must revoke the order if the tenant applies for its revocation within 14 days of its being made. In this event, the current tenancy ceases to be one protected by Part II, and it continues for such period as the parties may agree, or the court shall determine is necessary to give the landlord a reasonable opportunity to relet or otherwise dispose of the property.[6]

---

1 *Charles Clements (London) Ltd* v *Rank City Wall Ltd* [1978] 1 EGLR 47 (Ch); *Northern Electric plc* v *Addison* [1997] 39 EG 175 (CA).
2 [1978] 1 EGLR 47 (Goulding J).
3 *Ibid,* at 49.
4 [1983] 2 AC 726 (HL).
5 LTA 1954, s 36(1).
6 *Ibid,* s 36(2).

BIBLIOGRAPHY

Books

Aldridge, *Letting Business Premises*, 7th ed (1996) FT Law & Tax
Birds, Bradgate & Villiers (eds), *Termination of Contracts* (1995) Wiley Chancery
Crabb, *Leases: Covenants and Consents* (1991) Sweet & Maxwell
Dowding & Reynolds, *Dilapidations* (1995) Sweet & Maxwell
Evans & Smith, *The Law of Landlord and Tenant*, 5th ed (1997) Butterworths
Fancourt, *Enforceability of Landlord and Tenant Covenants* (1997) Sweet & Maxwell
Fogel & Slessenger, *Blundell Memorial Lectures 1996: Current Problems in Property Law* (1996) RICS Conferences and Training
Halsbury's Laws, 4th ed, (reissue 1993) Butterworths
Key & Elphinstone, *Precedents in Conveyancing*, (15th ed)
Lewison, *Drafting Business Leases*, 5th ed (1996) FT Law & Tax
McLoughlin, *Commercial Leases and Insolvency*, 2nd ed (1996) Butterworths
Megarry's *Manual of the Law of Real Property*, 7th ed (1993) Sweet & Maxwell
Sweet, *Commercial Leases: Tenants' Amendments*, 2nd ed (1995) FT Law & Tax
Tromans, *Commercial Leases*, 2nd ed (1996) Sweet & Maxwell
Tromans & Turrall-Clarke, *Contaminated Land* (1994) Sweet & Maxwell
Woodfall, *Landlord and Tenant,* looseleaf (Sweet & Maxwell)
Yates & Hawkins, *Landlord and Tenant Law*, 2nd ed (1986) Sweet & Maxwell

Articles

Acheson, "Too little too late" [1997] 3 EG 132
Adams, "...and otherwise recoverable as if rent in arrear" [1993] Conv 11
Adams, "Another view of AGAs" [1996] 32 EG 68
Adams, "Murkiness in group transactions – some recent examples" [1997] Conv 333
Barnsley, "Rectification, trusts and overriding interests" [1983] Conv 361
Blundell (1939) 3 Conv (NS) 10
Bridge, "Former tenants, future liabilities and the privity of contract principle: the Landlord and Tenant (Covenants) Act 1995" (1996) 55 CLJ 313
Cheffings and Rickard [1994] 41 EG 143
Cooke, "Adverse possession – problems of title in registered land" (1994) 14 *Legal Studies* 1
Cooklin, *Cheverell Estates* noted (1997) 11 *The Lawyer* (30 September) 12
Cullen & Potterton, "Must a surety guarantee an AGA?" [1996] 19 EG 118
Davey, "Privity of contract and leases – reform at last" (1996) 59 MLR 78
Dear & Clark, "Into the valley of decision" [1996] 44 EG 176
Farrand, "Misreading Reports" [1983] Conv 169
Farrand, "Rectifying Reports" [1983] Conv 257
Ferris, "The Re-evaluation of 'Joing Occupation' for the Purposes of the Landlord and Tenant Act 1954, Part II" [1996] JBL 592
Fife, "Termination of leases" [1995] 41 EG 134

Gaunt & Cheffings, "Final and binding?" [1997] 3 EG 128

Gillette [1994] 22 EG 52

Haley, "A surety covenant: common sense and construction" [1994] JBL 383

Haley, "Section 25 notices: perfecting the imperfect" [1996] JBL 576

Haley, "Termination of business tenancies: new uncertainties?" [1997] JBL 557

Jones, "Specific performance of a lessee's covenant to keep open a retail
    store" [1997] CLJ 488

Kenny, "Keep-open covenants" [1997] Conv 325

Luxton, "The Landlord and Tenant (Covenants) Act 1995: its impact
    on commercial leases" [1996] JBL 388

Luxton "Waiver of Forfeiture: time to shake away the doctrine of election? [1991]
    JBL 342

Luxton & Wilkie "A Tenant's Upwards to Quit: a Bad Break for Sub-lessees?"
    [1995] Conv 263

McDougall, "Completion: speeding the process" [1994] 37 EG 144

McLoughlin, "The expanding liability of sureties" [1989] Conv 292

Milman & Davey, "Debtor rehabilitation: implications for the landlord–
    tenant relationship" [1996] JBL 541

Pitchers, "Write to break" [1997] 27 EG 106

Rodgers "Shopping Residential Subtenants" [1990] Conv 204

Sands, "Life post-privity" [1996] 7 EG 54

Sheldon & Friend (1982) 98 LQR 14

Slessenger "Tenants' Break Clauses Revisited" [1996] 18 EG 96

Slessenger & Ballaster "Tenants' Break Clauses" [1994] 46 EG 196

Smith, "Inherent defects again?" [1987] Conv 224

Smith, "Repairs: a new set of problems" [1990] Conv 335

Smithers & Willis, "Licence to drill" [1997] 41 EG 146

Wonnacott, "Commercial tenants in individual voluntary arrangements"
    [1996] 2 EG 104

INDEX